'I found this book almost unbearably moving. Besides the controversies and scandals I had remembered, there were descriptions of Chinese Bibles landing on a beach, smuggled into a country where religion was being suppressed, plus innumerable stories of common heroism and quiet faith. From an organ floating down the Amazon to the courage of a gay footballer, this volume offers compelling insight and astute commentary on the politics, the commitment, and the hopes and fears of people of faith and beyond over a fifty-year period.'

Baroness Neuberger DBE, rabbi emerita, West London Synagogue

Amanda Hancox is an award-winning producer who joined the BBC in the 1980s. She has produced a wide range of factual programmes for Radios 2, 3 and 4, and for BBC1 and BBC4. In 1999 she became the executive producer for the Religion and Ethics department at BBC World Service. From 2001–20 she was series producer of Factual and Music for the BBC's Religion and Ethics radio department and had editorial responsibility for a wide range of documentaries and programmes, such as *Good Morning Sunday* (Radio 2) and *Beyond Belief* and *Sunday* (Radio 4).

Edward Stourton has been the main presenter of *Sunday* since 2010. He has worked in broadcasting for more than forty years, during which time he has been a foreign correspondent for the BBC, ITN and Channel 4. He was a newscaster on BBC1 for seven years, and one of the main presenters of Radio 4's *Today* programme for ten. He regularly presents *The World at One*, *The World This Weekend* and *Analysis* (all on Radio 4), and has written and presented numerous documentaries for BBC television and radio. He is the author of twelve other books.

SUNDAY

A history of religious affairs through 50
years of conversations and controversies

Edward Stourton
with Amanda Hancox

First published in Great Britain in 2023

Society for Promoting Christian Knowledge
The Record Hall, 16–16A Baldwins Gardens
London EC1N 7RJ
www.spck.org.uk

British Library Cataloguing-in-Publication Data
A catalogue record for this book is available from the British Library

Hardback ISBN 978–0–281–08773–0
eBook ISBN 978–0–281–08775–4

1 3 5 7 9 10 8 6 4 2

Typeset by Fakenham Prepress Solutions, Fakenham, Norfolk NR21 8NL
First printed in Great Britain by Ashford Colour Press Ltd, Gosport, PO13 0FW
Subsequently digitally printed in Great Britain

eBook by Fakenham Prepress Solutions, Fakenham, Norfolk NR21 8NL

Produced on paper from sustainable forests

Contents

Contents

Part 4
MAKING WAVES IN THE WORLD

Part 5
IN SEARCH OF THE GRANDEUR OF GOD

Acknowledgements

The main source for this book is the *Sunday* programme archive, and we are hugely grateful to the BBC for allowing us to mine this treasure trove. Particular thanks are due to Emma Trevelyan, the BBC's senior commercial, rights and business affairs manager, and to Tim Pemberton, the BBC's head of religion and ethics, who allowed Amanda Hancox access to the religion offices in Salford and to the BBC Sounds archive. Helen Grady, the current editor of *Sunday*, has also offered generous support.

More than 280 people spanning fifty years of *Sunday* appear in the book, and we would like to thank them all for their contributions to the programme. We have tried to contact everyone for permission to use those contributions, but it is possible that, despite our best endeavours, our messages have not reached everyone.

Books consulted for research are recorded in the footnotes, and the London Library and its staff provided invaluable help. The library's Catalyst search system was used to track down many of the quotations from newspapers, and we have provided date references where possible. Quotes from newspapers and individuals in the archive material have been reproduced as broadcast. Our thanks also to the Vatican website (http://www.vatican.va) and Hansard online (https://hansard.parliament.uk), where several quoted passages were taken from.

The book was conceived by Philip Law, our editor at SPCK, who has always been supportive. He showed great determination in bringing the project to fruition. We are also grateful to Joy Tibbs for her rigorous copy-edit and for managing the production process. Edward Stourton's agent at Curtis Brown, Gordon Wise, has provided helpful advice throughout.

Introduction

'In a national service to which nothing that pertains to the life of men is foreign,' declared the 1928 edition of the *BBC Handbook*, 'it was natural that from the beginning religion should find its place in British Broadcasting. It could not be otherwise.'[1] The *Handbook* pieces were unsigned in those early wireless years, but the ex cathedra tone of the section on 'Broadcasting and Religion' in this edition bears all the hallmarks of the BBC's founder, John Reith.

Reith put his stamp on almost every aspect of the BBC – indeed the adjective 'Reithian' is still sometimes used today. The impact he made on religious broadcasting was probably more enduring than anything else in his legacy because his personal convictions were so strong. The BBC's religious output continued to reflect the Reithian view of religion and religious broadcasting right up until the foundation of the *Sunday* programme, decades after his departure from the corporation.

A son of the manse, Reith was fiercely Sabbatarian. In his First World War diaries he recorded that he 'thought badly'[2] of his commanding officer for failing to mark the Lord's Day in the trenches, and in a letter to his mother at around the same time he declared: 'I am very strong in the observance of Sabbath. I would like the old Highland sabbaths to come back again, and perhaps they will.'[3]

Something very like the Highland sabbaths did indeed return in the early BBC schedules. In the 1920s there was no broadcasting at all on Sundays before half past three in the afternoon. In the 1930s, that austerity evolved into what Reith's biographer, Ian McIntyre, described as:

---

1 *The BBC Handbook: 1928* (London: British Broadcasting Corporation, 1928), p. 131.
2 I. McIntyre, *The Expense of Glory: A life of John Reith* (New York, NY: HarperCollins, 1993), p. 32.
3 I. McIntyre, *The Expense of Glory*, p. 39.

A programme schedule that reproduced with almost eerie fidelity the unchanging pattern of the Sabbath in the College Church manse thirty or forty years earlier. It began with a service which lasted from 9:30 to 10:45. There followed a lengthy period of silence, broken at 12:30 by a sequence of talks and serious music (Bach cantatas were much favoured). A second service followed at eight in the evening, and then more music until the Epilogue at eleven.[4]

The character of the Christianity reflected in this high-fibre broadcasting diet is laid out in bold colours in that 1928 *Handbook* essay. It should, we are told, be a 'thorough-going, optimistic and manly religion', which 'does not concern itself with a narrow interpretation of dogma, but with the application of the teaching of Christ in everyday life'. To ensure that the sermons preached during the services would appeal to as wide an audience as possible, 'nothing of a controversial character is ever allowed to pass the microphone', so 'the sermon to be preached is normally submitted to the station director several days in advance'.[5]

This manifesto – and the piece reads very much like one – ends with a call to arms: 'At a time when complaint is sometimes made that religion is losing its hold on the world... the BBC is doing the best of service to prevent any decay of Christianity in a nominally Christian country.' For the BBC's first director general, religious broadcasting was a mission, perhaps even a crusade: 'Each year will see developments in this department of its work', we read, 'but it has already done enough to justify the claim that in broadcasting religion it is not only keeping alive but giving new life and meaning to the traditionally Christian character of the British people.'[6]

Not everyone approved of John Reith's *Sunday* offering. His secular critics complained that the schedule of prayers, ritual and reflection represented 'a disdainful flouting of millions of listeners',[7] who might have preferred to be entertained on their day of escape from the grind of

---

4 I. McIntyre, *The Expense of Glory*, p. 188.

5 All quotes in this paragraph are from *The BBC Handbook: 1928*, p. 131.

6 *The BBC Handbook: 1928*, p 133.

7 A. Briggs, *The Golden Age of Wireless: Vol 2 of the History of Broadcasting in the United Kingdom* (Oxford: OUP, 1965), p. 227.

the working week. The national Churches were also – initially, anyway – nervous about the broadcast of services, fearing it might diminish the congregations who actually made it to church.

In fact, the opposite happened; the broadcasts seemed to encourage more people to attend services. There were, for example, regular Sunday broadcasts from St Martin-in-the-Fields, and the BBC's first official historian, Asa Briggs, noted that: 'At St Martin-in-the-Fields it was found difficult to persuade the 6:30 congregation to leave the church before the eight o'clock broadcast service began, and many people sat through both services.'[8]

The BBC developed a close relationship with the national Churches, especially the Church of England, very early, and it was given institutional form by a system of religious advisory committees, which had the task of judging the 'denominations that can be said to be in the mainstream of the Christian tradition,'[9] and were therefore entitled to airtime. The most powerful, the Central Religious Advisory Committee, met for the first time in 1923, in the infancy of what was then the British Broadcasting Company.

Ten years later it had grown to a membership of fourteen. The Anglican bishop of Southwark took the chair, and he was supported by five other Anglicans, five Free Church members and two Roman Catholics. Revd H. R. L. Sheppard, another Anglican priest, was included as a 'supernumerary' in recognition of his star quality as a broadcaster. The committee included no lay members and no representatives of non-Christian communities.

And of course, almost all those responsible for religious broadcasting were themselves ordained clergymen in the Church of England. Revd F. Iremonger, for example, whom Reith appointed as director of religion in 1933, had, before joining the corporation, served as a priest in the East End of London and the Hampshire countryside, worked as an adviser to the archbishop of York and been appointed chaplain to the king. He left the BBC to become dean of Lichfield, and later wrote a well-regarded biography of William Temple, wartime archbishop of Canterbury. There

---

8 A. Briggs, *The Golden Age of Wireless*, p. 234.
9 A. Briggs, *The Golden Age of Wireless*, p. 237.

was a revolving door between the national broadcaster and the national Church.

Fast forward to the late 1960s and early 1970s, and almost nothing had changed – on the surface at least. Despite the trendy new design and colourful jackets, the BBC handbooks published around the time of the *Sunday* programme's founding treat the subject of religious broadcasting in terms Reith would have recognised very well. 'Most of the BBC's religious broadcasts are devotional programmes, designed both to reflect and support the faith of Christians,'[10] the 1966 edition noted, adding that: 'Overall, religious broadcasting seeks both to affirm the Christian faith in its historic formulation, and to reflect the fresh religious insights of the present day.'[11]

BBC Religion did make a small concession to non-Christians in the 1960s. 'Talks for those of the Jewish faith' were introduced 'on appropriate occasions during the year'.[12] And by the end of the decade there was the first real indication of a changing religious landscape when 'two regular weekly broadcasts in television and one in radio' were included in the schedules 'directed to immigrants of Indian and Pakistani origin'.[13]

But the 'broad aims of religious broadcasting', reaffirmed the 1973 *Handbook*, remained as constant as the creed: 'To present the worship, thought and action of the Churches, to explore the contemporary relevance of Christian faith for listeners and viewers, be they Church members or not, and reflect fresh religious insight.'[14] And while that all-powerful Central Religious Advisory Committee had been expanded to include laymen (there is no mention of women at this stage), its membership remained resolutely Christian, with representatives from 'the Church of England, the Church of Scotland, the Church in Wales, the Baptist, Congregational, Methodist and Presbyterian Churches, and the Roman Catholic Church'.[15]

---

10 *The BBC Handbook: 1966* (London: British Broadcasting Corporation, 1966), p. 56.
11 *The BBC Handbook: 1966*, p. 57.
12 *The BBC Handbook: 1967* (London: British Broadcasting Corporation, 1967), p. 53.
13 *The BBC Handbook: 1969* (London: British Broadcasting Corporation, 1969), p. 67.
14 *The BBC Handbook: 1973* (London: British Broadcasting Corporation, 1973), p. 81.
15 *The BBC Handbook: 1973*, p. 82.

So it is unsurprising that when *Sunday* went on the air for the first time in 1970, its focus should to some extent reflect that strong Christian tradition. In a special edition broadcast to mark the programme's fortieth birthday, the founding producer, Colin Semper, recalled that: 'The editorial brief was always that it should be predominantly, but not exclusively, Christian.'

Committed to good journalism

From its earliest days, however, *Sunday* was a challenge to the Reithian idea of Sabbath broadcasting (the former director general died the year after the programme went on the air, but we have no record of what he thought of it). Journalism, not worship or ritual, was to be at the heart of the enterprise, and Semper's ambition was to create a programme unlike anything the Religion department had previously attempted. 'I felt very strongly that religious broadcasting was in a kind of ghetto,' he remembered, 'and I felt that the one way to get out of it was to try and engage ourselves in current affairs as of right. Not in a protected sort of slot.'

The institutional change behind the programme was elegantly summed up by Gerald Priestland, the veteran foreign reporter who moved to become the BBC's religious affairs correspondent not long after *Sunday* was founded, and who frequently contributed to the programme. The staff in the Religion department had, he wrote, been 'transformed from a team of clergy who were interested in broadcasting to one of broadcasters who were interested in religion'.[16]

And Colin Semper gave a very clear sign of his determination to break with the past by his choice of the programme's first presenter, Paul Barnes. Speaking to that fortieth anniversary edition, Barnes had no doubt that 'they chose me because I was an agnostic'. And Semper judged that he sounded – in stark contrast to the suave BBC announcers of old – like 'a cross between a Coventry butcher, which is what I think his father was, and a hippy'.

---

16 G. Priestland, *Something Understood: An Autobiography* (London: Andre Deutsch Ltd, 1986), p. 259.

The new approach meant that church leaders – especially the bishops of the Established Church – could no longer expect the sort of deference the Reithian BBC had shown them for so many decades. We get a glimpse of the Church of England of the day by peering into the pages of *Crockford's Clerical Directory* ('*Crockford*'), the venerable directory of Anglican clergy. This biennial reference book used to include an unsigned preface in the shape of an essay on the state of the Church, and the 1969–70 edition offers a picture of an institution trembling on the edge of modernity:

'We have recently read an account of ministrations provided by a group of the clergy for those attending one of the mass 'Pop' Festivals which have occurred in various parts of Britain in the last two or three years,' the anonymous essayist observes. 'It is very evident that the disenchantment with the Church felt by many young people is by no means a repudiation of the Christian religion, and that some of the excesses of the young represent a search for that which Christianity offers.'[17]

That touchingly optimistic interpretation of the 1960s counterculture continues with: 'It should be remembered that in the long history of mankind religion and sex have been closely intertwined as forces in human nature, and that the present public preoccupation with sex may also in part be evidence of a search for God.'[18] As we shall see, the subjects of sex and sexuality have inspired challenging and sometimes uncomfortable *Sunday* interviews with priests and bishops ever since.

The interviewing style of the early days was nothing like the confrontational knockabout that is standard fare on radio and television today. *Sunday* is sometimes said to be a religious version of the *Today* programme (like *Today* during the rest of the week, it is the first live show of the regular Radio 4 schedule), but even the *Today* studio was a gentler place in the early 1970s, and the really fierce forensic interview only took off with Brian Redhead's arrival in 1973.

But *Sunday*'s journalistic approach to religious issues did mean that presenters and – very often back then – producers would cross-examine

---

17 *Crockford's Clerical Directory 1969–70* (Oxford: Oxford University Press, 1971), p. xii.
18 *Crockford's Clerical Directory 1969–70*, p. xii.

the programme's guests, often rigorously. To some of those who usually spoke unchallenged from a pulpit it was a shock. Here's Colin Semper's successor as *Sunday*'s producer, David Winter, speaking on the programme's fortieth anniversary edition:

It was the first time such a spotlight had been turned on religion, and of course Christianity, therefore. But... religious people had to get used to the idea that this was a critical appraisal; this was the detached examination. And so therefore it wasn't a matter of us being on their side. It was a matter of examining what they were saying and pressing them on the subject.

Female clergy

Many of the early editions of *Sunday* have been lost, and the judgement of the archivists who decided what should be preserved sometimes seems capricious. But the very first item in the archive was judiciously chosen. It was, as subsequent events show, a turning point in the long history of Christianity.

The first woman to become a priest in the Anglican Communion was one Florence Li Tim-Oi, who was ordained by the bishop of Victoria, Hong Kong, in 1944. It was an emergency measure to deal with the challenges of the wartime Japanese invasion of China, and in a gesture designed to avoid controversy, she voluntarily resigned her licence to preach at the end of the war.

But the Hong Kong Synod came back to the issue around the time the *Sunday* programme went on the air, and two women, Jane Hwang and Joyce Bennett, were ordained in November 1971. Not long afterwards, on 5 December, *Sunday* broadcast this interview with Joyce – now Revd Joyce – Bennett. The line of questioning seems to be based on the assumption that a radical step like this can only have been taken for practical reasons, as indeed it was in the case of Florence Li Tim-Oi. The BBC's interviewer, Ann Cheetham, takes it as read that 'it sprung out of a need', and never admits the possibility that a woman might have a genuine vocation.

Joyce Bennett: I was ordained deacon in 1962, but at that time, of course, I never dreamt that one day I would be ordained as a priest.

Ann Cheetham: It's come very quickly then, or unexpectedly.

Joyce Bennett: Nine years, of course, is a very short time in the whole history of the Church. It has come quickly, but particularly quickly, I think, the last two years. I think we could say the Holy Spirit has worked here in the Church, and they are very eager now for this move to be made.

Ann Cheetham: Yes. Well, I say that it's come quickly because the pressure has been for delay, hasn't it, to wait for the rest of the whole of the Anglican Communion – which might take a very, very long time – to make up the whole mind of the whole Church.

Joyce Bennett: This is what is so amazing. And many of us thought that, after the Synod in January 1970 approved in principle the ordination of women to the priesthood, there would still be many years of delay before the rest of the Anglican Communion would agree to any action. But wonderfully, in this spring, the ACC [Anglican Consultative Council] *in Limuru* [in central Kenya] *did agree that the bishop here could go ahead, with the approval of his Synod.*

Ann Cheetham: Why do you think that women priests are needed here in Hong Kong? I should imagine it has sprung out of a need, hasn't it?

Joyce Bennett: I think here in Hong Kong we need women priests, but I think we need them other places, too. I think the Chinese, as Bishop Baker has said, are more open to this.

The final exchange provided a foretaste of some of the arguments that would later be deployed in the long and sometimes bitter battle over women priests within the Church of England itself.

Ann Cheetham: And of course, you've got so many churches crowded into a very small space here.

Joyce Bennett: We have. One of the things about Hong Kong is this pressure of population.

Ann Cheetham: Yes, but surely that means there are also many men who could do the job.

Joyce Bennett: We're not keeping any man out. There's no decision that women should be ordained and men won't be. And we hope, as a result, there will be more men and more women coming forward.

The postcolonial Church

Hong Kong was still a colony at that time. Across most of the world the process of decolonisation was well advanced, but the Anglican churches planted in the days of empire remained strong, and much of the early *Sunday* material that survived relates to the Church in Africa.

South Africa was entering the most violent phase of the struggle over apartheid (the killings at Soweto took place in 1976) and the Church would of course play a central role in that struggle. The way its representatives were questioned speaks eloquently of the attitudes of the day. Alphaeus Zulu was appointed the first black bishop of Zululand in 1966, and was interviewed for *Sunday* in 1973. It seems he had been asked to step up temporarily as archbishop of Southern Africa and his interviewer, Tony Black, kept pressing him over the perceived problems of a black clergyman holding sway over white people.

Alphaeus Zulu: It does not create any problems at all, and I do not anticipate any.

Tony Black: But presumably you would have white clergy under you. You'd have white people for whom you are responsible.

Alphaeus Zulu: Yes, but this will not be strange, since in fact, as bishop of Zululand, I do already have white people, both clergy and laity, under me. And in my relations with them I'm very happy, and there is no problem.

Tony Black: Yes. With respect, Bishop, you say you are happy, but are they happy? I mean, is there any problem from their side, as it were?

Alphaeus Zulu: None. None at all that has been expressed. In fact, I think they would themselves say they are happy with me.

Tony Black: At the moment, how do things work in the churches of the province where perhaps coloured clergy may minister to white people or vice versa? Are there any racial strains, any tensions inherent in this situation?

Alphaeus Zulu: Not in the church situation. There can be, in some remote areas, friction where some white groups may be conservative and refuse to be ministered to by blacks. But by and large, many of our white congregations receive ministrations from black clergymen.

Tony Black: *Now I realise, of course, you can only speak for your own church, but is this a fairly general picture in the Christian community?*

Alphaeus Zulu: *In South Africa? No, it is not general. There are certain denominations where this kind of thing would not happen readily.*

Tony Black: *Now, it's terribly hard in this country for us to judge, because we get so much publicity against apartheid, so much for it. We just don't know quite where things stand. But are you saying, if I read between the lines... that things are not as bad as perhaps they're painted abroad?*

Alphaeus Zulu: *For the black men they are bad, inasmuch as the legal situation puts the black man in an inferior position forever, since he may not exercise responsibility as a person. Therefore, an intelligent black man is not grateful when he relates socially happily with a white man, because he knows that it is a superficial relationship only, since he cannot enjoy the privileges of life which his white brother enjoys.*

Towards the end of the interview, Black asked the bishop for a 'personal view'.

Tony Black: *How do you think that apartheid could be resolved in the future? What will happen?*

Alphaeus Zulu: *Well, I think there must be very few prophets that can tell you about the future of South Africa on this point. As a leader in the Church, I take my cue from what I find in the Scriptures, where the prophets took it upon themselves to declare what they understood to be the will of God. I hope daily that the people in South Africa would hear God, because I believe myself that the discrimination which the black people suffer is contrary to the will of God.*

That interview was conducted in the aftermath of a crisis in relations between the Anglican Church in South Africa and the country's government. The Cathedral of St Mary the Virgin in Johannesburg had a long record of defying apartheid regulations, with black and white mixing freely at its services. The cathedral dean, the Very Revd Gonville ffrench-Beytagh, was a prominent anti-apartheid activist, and in 1971 he was arrested and held in solitary confinement, accused of supporting the African National Congress (ANC) and the South African Communist Party. His detention led to protests at churches right across South Africa.

In August that year, ffrench-Beytagh was tried under the Terrorism Act, convicted on ten counts of subversive activity and sentenced to five years in jail. He successfully appealed, and when he was released from custody in April 1972, he immediately left South Africa for exile in the United Kingdom.

The Church in Johannesburg remained defiant. In 1975, the diocese took a step which would have an enduring impact on the struggle against apartheid. It led to one of the gems of the *Sunday* archive; a very early outing on the airwaves for someone who would become a global star on radio and television. It was broadcast in March 1975.

Gerald Priestland: To be dean elect of Johannesburg is to be heir to a very hot seat indeed. The last incumbent but one, you may remember, was tried for terrorism and expelled. Now the Anglican Church in South Africa has dared to appoint its first black dean, the Revd Desmond Tutu. Mr Tutu has been working here in Britain for the World Council of Churches. David Winter interviewed him and asked if black clergy didn't face certain difficulties in ministering to white congregations in South Africa.

Desmond Tutu: Well, it depends, I think, very much on the particular area. I would like to say that, as a result of the very good work of my predecessors as dean, the cathedral congregation is very largely, actually, a multiracial congregation, and the staff is also a multiracial staff. And from all reports one has got, there have been no hang-ups at all. Obviously, I think people who might want to object would probably leave the parish. But so far as I can make out, and given the limitations of the political situation, it's gone very well indeed.

David Winter: Now, one has heard in the past of difficulties of this nature with white congregations. Does this mean that the white congregations are getting more willing to accept ministry from blacks?

Desmond Tutu: One should not be sort of over euphoric because, as I say, there are parts of the country where it is exceedingly difficult for the white

*congregations to accept black administration. And yet I believe, too, that
people are beginning to be more sensitive to the fundamental nature of
the Church that – this Jesus Christ whom we worship came specifically
to draw all people to himself and, in so doing, to draw them closer to
one another. And I believe that the predominantly English-speaking
churches, and especially our own church, certainly in its leadership, has
tried to proclaim the essentials of the gospel as a gospel of reconciliation.*

Priestland, the presenter of *Sunday* that day, had come to religious
broadcasting after becoming a committed Quaker, a step he took while
recovering from a nervous breakdown. In his autobiography, he writes
that when he was appointed religious affairs correspondent 'half my
friends backed away',[19] and he complained – as his successors have often
done since – that he found it very difficult to persuade his hard-nosed
former news colleagues that religion should be taken seriously. 'What the
newsroom liked was a good dirty vicar story',[20] he declared.

But the 1970s, especially in southern Africa, threw up plenty of
religious stories that made headline news. In early 1977, Archbishop
Janani Luwum of Uganda publicly protested against the human rights
abuses committed by the country's murderous dictator, Idi Amin. On 16
February the archbishop was arrested, along with two cabinet ministers,
and the following day the Amin regime announced that the three had
died in a car crash, caused by their attempts to escape. When Archbishop
Luwum's body was released to his relatives it was riddled with bullets,
and his statue now stands among the select group of modern martyrs
who are immortalised above the Great West Door of Westminster Abbey.

At the beginning of the following month, the Amin regime turned up
the pressure on the Church another notch, expelling the country's last
white bishop. The presenter here, Clive Jacobs, remained *Sunday*'s main
presenter for no less than seventeen years.

Clive Jacobs: *During the early hours of yesterday morning, a freight
aircraft, which picks up supplies from Britain for President Amin, landed*

---

19 G. Priestland, *Something Understood*, p. 259.
20 G. Priestland, *Something Understood*, p. 274.

at Stansted Airport. On this trip, though, it brought one passenger – the last white Anglican bishop in Uganda, the Right Revd Brian Herd. He'd been summoned to Kampala from his remote diocese in the north of Uganda, apparently to have his passport checked. You know the rest.

Our correspondent in Nairobi reported last night that over a third of the Anglican Church hierarchy in Uganda has now fled the country. But this morning, as you probably heard, a group of American journalists have apparently been invited to visit churches and missions today in an attempt to show that all is well. Shortly after Bishop Brian Herd arrived here yesterday, he talked to our religious affairs correspondent, Gerald Priestland, who asked him about his exile and particularly about the mood in Kampala after the death of Archbishop Luwum.

Brian Herd: *I'd been in Kenya seeing my children, and I presumed there'd be a funeral on the Sunday, but heard on Saturday that the bodies had already been buried, and then the midday service was cancelled. So many of us went to the 10 a.m. service at the cathedral. It was completely packed out to the door, and people were very serious, but they were very strong. And when we came out afterwards, the grave had been dug for the archbishop, but it was empty. And somebody pointed out that when we see the empty tomb, then it reminds us of the angels who came to the empty tomb and said that Jesus was not there, but he had risen and overcome death, and the empty tomb became a sort of visual aid to us of the victory over death and how, although the archbishop had died, we had something stronger than death.*

And then people sang many times over the song that the martyrs sang, which is one of the Uganda hymns. And there was a great, quiet strength among the people. And although there was no actual funeral service, many people were greatly strengthened that day. And we know people were praying for us in Kenya and other places at that time, and a lot of people were strengthened that day.

Gerald Priestland: *How is morale among the Church in Uganda now?*

Brian Herd: *Well, I don't know. The leaders sometimes are not in evidence, but the Church doesn't really depend on the strength of its leaders, but on the individual Christians. And there's a very quiet, strong determination among Christians that we have nowhere else to turn to but Christ for* *our eternal life. And there's no giving up. And even if all the bishops were removed from the Church in any way, still the Church would be strong and would go on.*

Gerald Priestland: *You were the last white Anglican bishop in Uganda. Did you ever feel you were an anachronism?*

Brian Herd: *Well, I certainly felt that I shouldn't have been appointed, and argued and refused about it before the time, but was persuaded to take it on because the area is a missionary area that hasn't a strong Church, and there are no suitable people from the place itself. And there were no other Ugandans who seemed willing and able to move in and take on the job at the time. So I took it on for five years, and I'm rather disappointed that after just over a year... I haven't been able to continue with it.*

At the end of the interview, Clive Jacobs read out one of those complaints that programme-makers rather enjoy – because they demonstrate that their programmes are having a real impact:

Shortly after that interview was recorded, our newsroom got a telephone call from the Saudi Arabian embassy who handled Ugandan diplomatic affairs in Britain. They complained about us using the interview because they said the bishop had become involved in politics in Uganda and there had been protests from people in his own congregation. The embassy was at pains to stress that the bishop's expulsion had nothing to do with the fact that he was a Christian. They claimed that, for many years, Bishop Herd has been passing on information from within Uganda to people outside, who were the country's enemies.

Islam in the West

The first non-Christian item preserved in the archive dates from August 1974, so relatively early in *Sunday's* life, and relates to a theme that would, under different guises, recur on the programme again and again during the decades that followed: the place of Islam in modern, increasingly secular Western societies.

The focus for this interview was the segregation of the sexes at school. Dr Syed Pasha, an early campaigner for Muslim rights and the founder, in the year of *Sunday*'s birth, of the umbrella group the Union of Muslim Organisations, convened a meeting to discuss ways of reconciling Islamic teaching, as he understood it, with British educational practice. Speaking to Ted Harrison, he strikingly insisted that Muslims 'have to claim our rights as British citizens' – a proposition that seems self-evident today, but which may have startled some of *Sunday*'s listeners in the mid-1970s.

Syed Pasha: The Qur'an very definitively does not say the man or woman should go separately. But what it does say, it does bring out a concept of Islamic society which will imply that there should be least contact between the different sexes, because this is the only way to preserve the true moral, I mean, criterion.

Ted Harrison: So in practical terms, it's things like PE and swimming that you object to mostly in the schools.

Syed Pasha: Well, that's very true, because the swimming of the women itself is not forbidden. It is only the swimming of the women, along with the men in the same swimming pool, that is forbidden. So obviously the Muslim children try to avoid it altogether by pretending so many excuses. But actually, if you go to the deep, they are as much anxious to learn PE and physical training, but they want to do it separately for the women.

Ted Harrison: So what's the solution going to be? What ideas have come up from the conference?

Syed Pasha: Well, in the morning, two speakers have suggested so many solutions. On the one hand, they have tried to scan through the Education Act of 1944 and see what short-term measures can be adopted in trying to extract some concessions from the education authorities. But actually, we have to claim our rights as British citizens. We cannot claim any extra privileges. We are just claiming, as ordinary citizens of this country, that we also have the right to bring up our children according to the way we think in a multireligious and a multicultural society.

Ted Harrison: Would you like to see separate Muslim schools, say, rather like the English public schools that are run by Jews or by Quakers or by Catholics?

Syed Pasha: Well, that has been one of the proposals advocated by one of the speakers in the morning. We have yet to see how the delegates from various organisations which have assembled here will respond to this call of establishing our own schools. When we are saying our own schools, it will not be along the lines to segregate ourselves from the local host community. We will open our schools to the British students as well. This will be definitely a long-term proposition.

There were only around a quarter of a million Muslims in the United Kingdom at the time of that interview, while in 2018 the Office for National Statistics put the figure at close to 3.5 million. Those figures reflect a transformation in our religious landscape of historic significance, and Islam now plays a central part in *Sunday*'s agenda.

Hard economic times in the United Kingdom

Politically and economically, the decade of *Sunday*'s birth was an anxious period. Both the Heath government of 1970–74 and the Wilson–Callaghan years that followed were dominated by economic decline, inflation and industrial strife. In 1973, during a miners' pay dispute, the country was reduced to a three-day working week in an effort to conserve fuel. In 1976, Jim Callaghan was forced to borrow heavily from the International Monetary Fund to prop up the pound. And the country's economic travails fed through into a more general sense of national malaise.

In 1975, that climate inspired the archbishop of Canterbury, Donald Coggan, to deliver a 'call to the nation', arguing that moral regeneration was as important as economic recovery, and that 'we cannot leave out the moral factor and succeed in the long run'. The archbishop told the country:

Many are realising that a materialistic answer is no real answer at all. There are moral and spiritual issues at stake. The truth is that we, in Britain, are without anchors. We are drifting. A common enemy in two world wars drew us together in united action – and we defeated him. Another enemy is at the gates today, and we keep silence.

His rhetoric explicitly echoed past moments of national peril: 'Each man and woman is needed if the drift towards chaos is to stop. Your country needs YOU!'

The speech and his subsequent broadcasts prompted an extraordinary public response. Approximately 28,000 people wrote to him – 'housewives, MPs, dockers and shopkeepers' – as *The Guardian* reported at the time. The Lambeth Palace press office proudly released some of the choicest samples: 'I thank you from the bottom of my heart for your clarion call to this once great country,' wrote one correspondent. 'Thousands have been waiting for the Church to speak loud and clear. May your words awaken those who slumber, awaiting the leadership you offer.'[21]

But some of the reaction reflected the view that priests should not meddle in politics. When Donald Coggan appeared on *Sunday* on 19 October 1975, Clive Jacobs, the programme's long-serving presenter, quoted an MP who had declared: 'I do not think the archbishop is helping matters, and we're a long way from hellfire yet.'

Donald Coggan: *I'm not worried about that at all. I think our political leaders have shown us that we're in a mess. That we are in a grievous state in many ways. I believe there is a solid core within Britain which is good and strong and clean. But we are in a mess, and I think I'm only stating the obvious when I draw attention to it...*

Clive Jacobs: *Perhaps the most critical editorial that's been aimed in your direction this week came from the* Daily Telegraph, *and here I quote: 'It is an oversimplification to suggest that the present situation of our country can be explained in moral and spiritual terms.' Are you actually suggesting that?*

Donald Coggan: *No, I'm not. It is an oversimplification. There are, of course economic questions involved here – the problems of inflation and so on. Obviously, these are economic considerations, but I believe that underlying these things are certain deep moral and spiritual questions which need to come out into the open and be looked at.*

Clive Jacobs: *You don't think perhaps it is an oversimplification to suggest that, say, a rejection of materialism would solve our problem?*

---

21 Quotes in the paragraph from '4,000 write to Coggan', *The Guardian*, 21 October 1975, p. 7.

Donald Coggan: *Not solve it, but it is one of the things we've got to work at when we're working towards a solution. That's my view.*

Clive Jacobs: *But if we took that to its extreme, everybody would be out of work, for instance.*

Donald Coggan: *Well, I think, if I may say so, that is an unrealistic remark to make, because it isn't likely that sufficient people are going to do that to lead to a very serious issue.*

Clive Jacobs: *But this is what you're urging us to do.*

Donald Coggan: *But I do see your point. I notice, for example, today that the less ostentatious cars are the cars that are being sold most on the market now, and that's no great loss. But I do take the point that if, for example, we were all to go around on bicycles, then Coventry and adjoining cities would be in a mess...*

I'm no economist at all, but I'm wondering whether, if we had more of a global view, if we took more seriously the needs of the Third World, and if instead of producing certain luxury cars, we could produce tractors for India so that they could get on with reaping crops, which hitherto they don't know how to tackle – whether along those lines we might see some contribution made, at least, to the problem of keeping or increasing employment. And at the same time, thinking a little bit less about our luxurious selves and a little more about the Third World.

The archbishop took flak from the left as well as the right. Despite all those thousands of letters of support, there were, even in the 1970s, plenty of people who challenged the Church's right to speak for the nation.

Clive Jacobs: *Let me go on to something else. Archbishop, The Guardian suggests that the tie-up between religion and national rehabilitation is not as obvious as you claim. They say yours is a churchman's view, not necessarily shared by all serious people. You presumably would accept that. What, though, do you expect or hope of those who don't share your view?*

Donald Coggan: *Yes, well you see my appeal this week has gone out to committed Christians. There's no doubt about that. But it has also gone out to a wider range of people, who perhaps have rejected the Christian* *faith or never seriously considered it, but who are deeply concerned for the welfare of our country, deeply concerned for the family life of our nation. That our youngsters should be able to grow up in a society which is healthy and strong and clean.*

I think, if I could put it this way, that round the very considerable circle of 'Church', people of all denominations, there is a wider penumbra of these people who I've been describing. When my appeal goes to them, I want them to sit down alongside the committed Christians, and with them, to sharpen their minds on one another; to be open to the insights of the Christians, and [for] the Christians to be open to the insights of the other people. It's much wider than just a Church appeal...

Clive Jacobs: The Guardian *also points a finger, in some respect, to the fact that you don't appear to give what they would call answers. In other words, you tend more to ask questions rather than provide the answer.*

Donald Coggan: *That is perfectly true. I have said that I don't think it's my job to provide blueprint, easy pat answers to terribly difficult questions. That would be to mock the situation...*

A patriotic revival

Many of the themes reflected in this interview – the accusation of economic innumeracy, the challenge to the Church to provide answers and not just criticism – would be all too familiar to future Church of England bishops who have appeared on *Sunday*. And towards the end of the interview the conversation turned to another perennially sensitive area: the perceived tension between Christianity and love of country.

Clive Jacobs: *I notice the* Daily Mail *calls it a 'gospel of national revival'. Would you take issue with that?*

Donald Coggan: *It's not a phrase that I've used, I think, this week at all. I see it as a spiritual revival. This is our greatest need. If you called it a 'patriotic revival', I wouldn't mind very much that adjective. I'm not as frightened of the adjective 'patriotic' as a good many people are, because you see, I believe that the old Hebrew prophets were great patriots. And I believe that the greatest, greatest patriot in the Bible was our Lord himself, who cared intensely for his nation.*

I remember a moving passage in the Gospels where Jesus is recorded as having looked out from a height over the city of Jerusalem, and wept as he saw it heading for destruction: 'O Jerusalem, Jerusalem, thou that killest the prophets and stones those that are sent to thee. How often I would have gathered thee as a hen gathers her chicks under her wings, but you wouldn't.' [22]*Now that's real patriotism: not my country, right or wrong, but my country, the best it can be under the guidance of God.*

Clive Jacobs*: Forgive me. I'm smiling inwardly and wondering what he would have made of the EEC* [the European Economic Community].

Donald Coggan*: Actually, ha ha, well, I don't see that the two are antithetical. I think you can be a patriot and an EEC man, as I am myself.*

The Church of England was once famously known as 'the Tory Party at prayer'. As we shall see, the Church would, in the years following that interview, find itself again and again at odds with the government of the day – on everything from unemployment to nuclear weapons. And Donald Coggan's successor, Robert Runcie, faced a very direct accusation of a lack of patriotism after Britain went to war in the Falklands.

A broad view

One of *Sunday*'s strengths – and it probably helps explain why the programme has endured for so long – is that it has always taken a very broad view of what falls under the heading 'religious broadcasting'. An interview with the radical playwright Dennis Potter would certainly not have qualified under a Reithian understanding of the term.

Potter's play *Son of Man*, first broadcast in 1969, is an alternative telling of the Passion story, and was condemned by the campaigner Mary Whitehouse as blasphemy. In April 1976, Potter talked to *Sunday* about the way his thinking had changed since he wrote the play. The identity of his interviewer is not clear.

---

22 A paraphrase of Matthew 23:37.

Introduction

Dennis Potter: *I have changed. But even within what people I suppose would call faith, I have to maintain doubt, and that description 'agnosticism carried into religion' still seems to me to be valid. Whatever faith I have, may have or hope to have, it will be within doubt. It would be walled in by doubt, and that doubt is the necessary response of man at this period of time to such claims, such awesome claims, of religion.*

But yes, I've changed. I mean, it's interesting why I should have wanted to write Son of Man. *I wrote it in a certain, almost belligerent, frame of mind in order to put down, I think, certain childhood images – chapel-given images of my childhood – and at the very wrestle of doing so, [it] inevitably turned me back into the parables, into the metaphor of the New Testament, into the challenge and the beauty and glory and pain, and sometimes shadiness, of the New Testament. And it must have been a preoccupation of mine at that time then, and it has grown in me, and the sense of tension and wonder and gratitude and bewilderment has grown in me at the same time...*

I cannot now live without, I cannot sustain myself without, some idea of a loving God. And therefore, my work is addressed to that. But a religion that doesn't go into the dark side, that isn't concerned with pain, that is something you put on on Sunday – best clothes to bend the knee to – is of no interest to me whatsoever. And I think it's an insult to the central struggle of man to know, or sometimes to reject, but at least to come to terms with religious experience.

And if we banish these things, and if we banish them particularly by calling them nauseating or outrageous (and how much of the Bible is nauseating and outrageous, you know, how much of man's religious experience is painful and anguished and horrible, a pain in the heart and the head?), if we don't come to terms with that anguish of being, of existence... then religion is simply an aspirin. It doesn't interest me.

Interviewer: *Many people, I think many believers, see the Church today as increasingly irrelevant. You know, it's an institution that somehow we don't need, or modern man doesn't need. Do you see it that way?*

Dennis Potter: *No, I say we need it. I can't go to it myself because I'm not at that stage... That's beside the point. I think the Church exists as a* *protective institution, an organ which can carry from one generation to another the hard-won experience of one generation...*

It does offer up shelter, even to those who don't believe it is politically necessary. In certain political states, in certain societies, it helps keep out the cranks; the idiocy of the cheapest form of sentimental religion. It is obviously corroded with all the defects of whatever society it is in at the time, but it nevertheless does carry on and convey from one generation to another enough that makes one want to see it there. No, more than that. It must. You know, I would be unhappy if it wasn't there. I would feel... slightly more uneasy if it wasn't there, than I do now, because it is there.

'Religion is not boring'

If we were to attempt a *Sunday* programme manifesto, Potter's vivid, anguished answers might be a good place to start. Most of us who have worked on the programme would endorse that questioning, restless approach to religion. And his conviction that simply ignoring the subject is 'an insult to the central struggle of man' underpins everything we do.

This book is an exercise in archival archaeology. We have dug deep into *Sunday*'s past, and we have tried to make sense of what we have found. The decades we cover have been marked by relentless change. At home, many of the certainties that drove John Reith's idea of religious broadcasting have been swept away, and at the same time we have had to understand and come to terms with religious forces in the wider world that would have seemed quite alien to many of our listeners in 1970.

Most social history takes the decline of organised religion in Western societies as an established fact, and when religion does force itself on our attention – with events like the attacks of 9/11 in New York and 7/7 in London – it is generally presented as a malign and atavistic interruption to modernity. The interviews in this book offer a different perspective on the past half-century.

As David Winter, one of *Sunday*'s early producers, put it in his contribution to the programme's fortieth birthday edition, religion is 'very much part of life as it's lived now for lots and lots of people and, around the world, most people'. History that fails to take account of this basic truth is bound to be fatally flawed.

Winter also said, and we very much hope our selection underlines this point: 'Religion is not boring; I think that's what *Sunday* keeps reminding us.'

Part 1

POPES AND PRIMATES, SAINTS AND SINNERS

1

Speaking truth to power

The process by which archbishops of Canterbury are chosen is extremely convoluted, and this reflects the complex relationship between the Established Church and other institutions of the British state.

In formal terms, the choice is made in the name of the Church of England's supreme governor, the sovereign, but the real power lies with a body known as the Crown Nominations Commission (formerly the Crown Appointments Commission). It consists of two senior bishops, members of the General Synod's Houses of Clergy and Laity, and representatives of the Canterbury Diocese, and it is chaired by a 'communicant lay member of the Church of England' appointed by the prime minister.

After meeting – in secret – several times, the commission sends a name to the prime minister (originally two names, but Gordon Brown tweaked the process in 2007), who forwards the recommendation on to Buckingham Palace, and the new archbishop is publicly nominated in the name of the sovereign. The commission keeps a second name in reserve in case of unforeseen developments.

There is an additional stage, inherited from history, to give this process a religious gloss. All new diocesan bishops must be 'elected' by their diocese's College of Canons. This final flourish was elegantly satirised by the nineteenth-century American essayist Ralph Waldo Emerson. In his 1856 *English Traits*, he wrote: 'The King sends the Dean and Canons a *congé d'élire*, or leave to elect, but also sends them the name of the person whom they are to elect. They go into the Cathedral, chant and pray; and after these invocations invariably find that the dictates of the Holy Ghost agree with the recommendation of the King.'[1]

---

1 R. W. Emerson, *The Works of Ralph Waldo Emerson, Vol IV* (London: Macmillan, 1884), pp. 183–84.

The commission system was introduced in the 1970s to give the Church of England a greater say in the appointment of its bishops (until then, prime minsters pretty much had a free hand) and it was used for the first time to find a replacement for Donald Coggan when he retired in 1979.

But it seems that the newly elected Conservative prime minister, Mrs Thatcher, may have actively intervened in the process all the same. Margaret Thatcher was the daughter of a Methodist lay preacher, and took her duties in the Church of England's affairs very seriously. One of those who served on that 1979 commission later claimed that, at a very late stage in the process, Downing Street produced a list of objections to the leading candidate, Hugh Montefiore, the bishop of Birmingham, who was considered too left-wing.

Whether or not that is true – and others involved in the process have challenged this version of events – the man who emerged as the next leader of the Church of England, Robert Runcie, had a background that looked reassuring to those who believed that the Church of England should be 'the Tory Party at prayer'.

He had been educated at the independent Merchant Taylors' School in Crosby, and at Brasenose College, Oxford. During the Second World War he was commissioned into the Scots Guards, landing in Normandy as a tank commander not long after D-Day in 1944. In the last weeks of war he was awarded a Military Cross for exceptional bravery. He pulled a soldier from a burning tank and knocked out a critical German artillery position at great risk to himself.

Returning to Oxford to complete his degree, Robert Runcie encountered the future Conservative prime minister – Margaret Roberts, as she then was – for the first time. Runcie served on the committee of the Oxford University Conservative Association, of which she had recently been president. His time as archbishop of Canterbury more than three decades later would coincide almost exactly with her time in power.

Britain at war

As things turned out, the relationship between the Church of England and the Conservative government over that period proved to be anything but comfortable. In fact, the Thatcher–Runcie years marked a decisive break. At the beginning of April 1982, Argentina invaded the Falkland Islands (known to Argentinians as *Islas Malvinas*), and Margaret Thatcher immediately despatched a military task force to retake them, at the same time securing a UN Security Council resolution calling for the withdrawal of Argentinian forces. The Labour leader Michael Foot supported her decision – despite his pacifist instincts – and so too did the archbishop of Canterbury.

A couple of years into the job at this stage, Robert Runcie told the House of Lords on 14 April:

> *We all pray that the use of force will be unnecessary, but let us be clear about what our objective must be. It is that the United Nations resolution must be obeyed so that a way can be found which safeguards the rights of the Falkland islanders to live their lives in conditions of their choosing. Those are just aims, and it is right that we should be united and resolute in pursuing them.*[2]

The press was, for the most part, solidly behind the government – indeed, parts of it seemed positively enthusiastic about going to war. With Church, state and Fourth Estate united, there was very little room for public questioning of the government's determination to retake the islands – by force, if necessary.

Four days after Robert Runcie's speech in the House of Lords, a prominent Church of England bishop and distinguished theologian, John Robinson, broke cover on *Sunday*. He gave two interviews to the programme, the first on 18 April and the second on 2 May. *Sunday*'s presenter, Clive Jacobs, headlined the second of those interviews as follows:

> *Good morning. Why the deafening silence from Church leaders on the Falklands crisis? This morning, the Anglican bishop who says that*

---

2 'The Falkland Islands', UK Parliament: Hansard: https://hansard.parliament.uk/lords/1982-04-14/debates/a0101eb0-e16d-48fd-9668-42b939f392f5/TheFalklandIslands (14 April 1982, accessed 15 June 2023).

5

Church people will look back with shame because leaders of the Churches in Britain have made no serious effort to speak out on the crisis...

And his introduction to the item included some well-aimed barbs:

Of all that's been said or written about the Falklands crisis, little has come from Church leaders. A statement by the Roman Catholic leader Cardinal Hume was published this week, but that was simply about the Christian theory of a 'just war'. The archbishop of Canterbury, who arrived home early on Friday morning after a two-week visit to Nigeria, made a speech in the House of Lords three weeks ago in which he supported the sending of the task force. But of course a good deal has happened since, on which Dr Runcie has said nothing. In short, Church people looking for spiritual advice from the leaders of two of the country's main Churches are still looking. In an attempt to fill that gap, we invited Dr Runcie and Cardinal Hume to take part in this programme. Neither felt able to accept. So we turn to the man who, two weeks ago, criticised the Church for its silence: the Church of England bishop John Robinson.

John Robinson had courted controversy for much of his career. His most popular and important book, *Honest to God* (SCM Press, 1963), argued for a radical reassessment of our understanding of the deity as a supernatural being 'out there', and led his critics to accuse him of atheism. He had also appeared as a witness for the defence in the 1960 obscenity trial of *Lady Chatterley's Lover*.

At the time of the Falklands War, he was dean of Trinity College, Cambridge, a role he had taken up after serving as bishop of Woolwich for ten years. The job put him right at the heart of what is sometimes called 'the Establishment', but that did not stop him expressing views that many of his listeners would have considered subversive, perhaps even unpatriotic. His interviewer on 2 May was Ted Harrison.

John Robinson: *Well, I must say I've been rather dismayed to discover the extent to which I appear to have been, publicly at any rate, an isolated voice. I appeared on this programme a fortnight ago, and I've never had* so much mail. Virtually every letter I've got has been supportive and positive, and said, 'Why aren't we hearing this from someone else?' And I'm bound to admit that I find this very difficult. And I regard this as a considerable sign that there's a great body of support that's finding no voice at the moment in the Church.

Ted Harrison: What would you like to be hearing Church leaders saying?

John Robinson: Well, I feel I would like to hear something distinctive or prophetic on the situation... Cardinal Hume did make the sort of classic statement of the 'just war', which is theoretically all right. But I am bound to admit, in this present situation, I cannot really believe that resorting to fighting can actually be the lesser of two evils or will positively solve anything.

Ted Harrison: What would you like the Churches actually to be saying now? You talk about saying something which would be prophetic, saying something which would be Christian. What exactly should they be saying? Preaching a pacifist gospel?

John Robinson: No, I mean, I'm not a pacifist, and I don't think that they should commit to a pacifist gospel. But I do think that the use of force is absolutely the last line, and that we are drifting into a position when we are using this well before the point at which it seems to me that there's any real necessity for doing so. We haven't even tried the kind of diplomatic and economic sanctions which will now be possible once the Americans are on our side.

Ted Harrison: Do you think Church leaders are afraid to speak out against what seems to be overwhelming public opinion, or substantial public opinion, which is in favour of the task force and in favour of a hard line?

John Robinson: I don't think it's primarily fear. At least, I hope it isn't. I think it is obviously a very difficult and complex situation. I don't want to suggest that it is an easy one, but I do think... that there are a great many people who are profoundly uneasy with the way in which we seem to have drifted and gone along with the current jingoism of the media.

Ted Harrison: What do you think that people outside the Churches are going to think of the Church at this particular stage? Not, as you say, giving the lead that perhaps it could be giving?

John Robinson: Well, I think we shall look back with some shame on this, because I think this has been a crunch issue, in which here are two

Christian nations, so-called, fighting each other. And that neither the leadership of the Roman Catholic Church nor of the Anglican Church, which were the ones most involved, has seemed to me to have made a serious effort to prevent the kind of drift into which the politicians are leading us.

A 'just war'?

That same Sunday, 2 May 1982, saw the most controversial military action of the entire Falklands campaign. Just before 3 p.m. Falkland Islands time, the British nuclear-powered submarine HMS *Conqueror* fired three torpedoes at the ARA *General Belgrano*, an elderly light cruiser that Argentina had bought from the United States in 1951. The ship went down with the loss of more than 320 lives. *The Sun* newspaper famously reported the sinking of the *Belgrano* with the headline 'Gotcha' on its front page.

The subsequent controversy arose because when the *Belgrano* was hit, the ship was outside the 200-mile exclusion zone the British government had imposed around the Falklands. Mrs Thatcher and the war cabinet authorised an attack on the *Belgrano* on the basis that it was due to take part in a general assault on the task force, and so represented a threat. The episode still dominated the news agenda when Clive Jacobs said 'Good morning' to the *Sunday* audience a week later. Jacobs's introduction, much longer than the snappier 'cues' favoured in more recent editions of *Sunday*, had a homily-like quality:

The political issues at stake in the Falkland Islands crisis have been discussed and written about in vast detail during the past month. This morning we want to consider the moral issues at stake. Is it the Church's duty morally to guide the nation at a time of crisis like this? In view of the commandment 'thou shalt not kill', and the gospel message of 'love your enemies' and 'turn the other cheek', is the use of force by a Christian nation ever justified? And if humility is an important Christian virtue, does that mean that national pride is not? Well, the answers to those questions and others will, I hope, come this morning from three senior churchmen sitting opposite me.

But before we hear from them, let me just outline what other senior churchmen have been saying during the past few days. The archbishop of Canterbury yesterday went into print, and I quote, 'We cannot accept the position that no principle is worth the shedding of blood. That theory would lead to a world with even greater injustice and with even less stability.' But the archbishop goes on to say that 'in the case of the Falklands, pride should be sacrificed by both sides and mediation by the United Nations is the least each should pursue'.

Scottish churchmen have sent a telegram to the House of Commons: 'What would have been unthinkable a few weeks ago,' they say, 'the sinking of a ship with the attendant loss of life, has become necessary policy.' And they argue this cannot be right. From the Roman Catholic bishops' point of view, the bishop of Arundel and Brighton believes that, in the present situation, any military success diminishes rather than increases the moral justice of our cause.

Indeed, the majority of Church leaders who have spoken out would seem to be saying that violence now has no place in our confrontation with Argentina.

The first of Jacobs's trio of guests, Graham Leonard, the bishop of London, took a very traditional view of the Church of England's role in times of crisis: that it must offer leadership to the nation, but not meddle in matters outside its natural remit. The bishop kicked off with:

I think the Church has got the responsibility for trying to guide the nation. I think the starting point must be the principles. I don't believe the Church should enter into the realm of making political or military judgements.

Like the archbishop of Canterbury, Bishop Leonard had served as an army officer during the Second World War, and he laid out the classic Christian case against pacifism:

On the question of making use of force... I think that one has to face the fact that... there is evil in the world. Are we, in fact, simply to allow that evil to triumph? Is that... a denial of one of the responsibilities of man? Last week, when I was preaching at the Aircrew Association, I said, 'We must never pretend that war is other than horrible and bloody.' But the very fact of man's fallen nature – the fact that he does act in ways which are wrong – may mean that there are occasions when we have to say, and a government has to say, 'It is better for us to stand for what we believe to be right rather than to accept existence at any price.

It is striking – in the light of the way relations between the Church and the government would subsequently develop – that at this stage of the Falklands crisis Robert Runcie was being attacked by some Christian leaders for being too supportive of Mrs Thatcher's policy. *Sunday's* second guest that morning was socialist and pacifist Donald Soper. Lord Soper became the first Methodist minister to sit in the House of Lords, and he was, as Clive Jacobs noted in his introduction, famous as 'somebody who speaks up every Sunday afternoon at Hyde Park, and is perhaps best known for that'.

Clive Jacobs: *Let's come to the Christian gospel of peace, 'turn the other cheek', as I was saying earlier, [and] 'love your enemies'. How do you react to the archbishop of Canterbury['s view] that we cannot accept the position that 'no principle is worth the shedding of blood'?*

Donald Soper: *I think it's very dangerous to use a general phrase like 'shedding of blood', which of course doctors procure. It isn't the shedding of blood that is the issue. The issue is whether or not it is consonant with the Christian faith to practise the way of violence, mass violence, which is a particular expression of force. And I, for one, am a pacifist, and I believe that it is absolutely inconsistent with the basic teaching of the Christian faith that under any circumstances you can resort to that accumulation of evil which is called mass violence in order to solve a moral issue.*

The final member of the panel, Canon Eric James, was introduced as a 'member of the International Affairs Committee of the Church of England', and would have been familiar to many of *Sunday's* listeners as a regular contributor to *Thought for the Day*. He challenged Graham Leonard's reluctance to get to grips with the political and military dimension of the crisis:

> *I think the Church in a situation like this can too easily get a name for abstract statements about goodness and never earthing itself in the minute particulars of the situation. And often we do have to have the courage to come out and say, maybe reluctantly and sadly, 'That is wrong.'*

Towards the end of the discussion, Clive Jacobs called time on 'abstract statements' and asked his three guests to address the immediate issue facing the nation.

Clive Jacobs: *Let's... talk specifically about the Falklands. And as a final question to each of you: is the Falkland Islands issue such that we could be said to be fighting a 'just war', Bishop?*

Graham Leonard: *In my judgement, yes – provided that we continue to try and observe all the conditions which are laid down for the 'just war', if we've got to use that phrase, and which include, among other things, continuing to make every possible effort to resolve it by non-belligerent means.*

Clive Jacobs: *Canon Eric James?*

Eric James: *I believe some of the goals are just. I think the means that we are promoting to get the goals are not just. I think that to land on the Falklands, for instance, is bound to cause, or almost bound to cause, such bloodshed that would be disproportionate to the goal we have in mind.*

Clive Jacobs: *Lord Soper?*

Donald Soper: *The real hope is when, for the first time, we renounce the use of mass violence – even if it humiliates us in the process – in order that we may take up that alternative policy, which is the way of nonviolent love.*

On 20 May, Robert Runcie made a second speech in the House of Lords. He again supported the use of force as a last resort, although the intervention included hints at the kind of caveats that would later cause so much tension with the government. 'If a greater degree of force now has to be used – and this seems likely – let us remember that its purpose must always be to achieve a just political settlement and not a military victory,' the archbishop of Canterbury declared. 'We need to be very clear that our objective is not to punish or to avenge hurt pride.'

Large-scale amphibious landings on the beaches around San Carlos Water began the following day. After just over three weeks of sometimes fierce fighting, the islands' capital, Port Stanley, was retaken on 14 June. The Argentinian forces surrendered on the same day. Figures show that 255 British personnel and three Falkland Islanders lost their lives in the conflict. The number of dead on the Argentinian side was 649.[3]

Church versus state

The acrimony between Downing Street and Lambeth Palace in the aftermath of the conflict is now very much part of the Falklands story. It centred on the service at St Paul's Cathedral to mark the end of the conflict. Contrary to much of the press coverage at the time, the most serious arguments blew up during the planning for the event.

The prime minister wanted a service of thanksgiving, but that in itself was controversial. The dean of St Paul's, Dr Alan Webster, argued for a service of 'reconciliation' instead, and suggested that the Lord's Prayer should be said in Spanish. One of Mrs Thatcher's officials recalled that her 'eyes widened in absolute horror'[4] at this last proposal. The service was to be ecumenical, and Cardinal Basil Hume objected to combatants reading any lessons. Dr Kenneth Greet, president of the Methodist Conference that year, was a committed pacifist and rejected the very idea that there should be a celebration.

Mrs Thatcher was every bit as determined as the church leaders. Charles Moore, her official biographer, records that 'going through the

3 S. Tudor, 'Sovereignty since the ceasefire: The Falklands 40 years on', House of Lords Library: https://lordslibrary.parliament.uk/sovereignty-since-the-ceasefire-the-falklands-40-years-on (1 August 2022, accessed 16 June 2023).

4 C. Moore, *Margaret Thatcher: The Authorized Biography, Vol 1: Not for Turning* (London: Allen Lane, 2013), pp. 756–57.

proposed text, she put her wiggly line against a prayer which asked God for the will to build defences against poverty, hunger and disease "instead of against each other".

So when the service took place at the end of July 1982, its form reflected compromises hammered out in emotionally charged negotiations. That background helps explain the reaction to the sermon given by the archbishop of Canterbury. Robert Runcie declared:

> *People are mourning on both sides of this conflict. In our prayers we shall quite rightly remember those who are bereaved in our own country and the relations of the young Argentinian soldiers who were killed. Common sorrow could do something to reunite those who were engaged in this struggle. A shared anguish can be a bridge of reconciliation. Our neighbours are indeed like us.*

Towards the end of his life, Runcie recalled that after the sermon Mrs Thatcher 'gripped my hand and said, "Well done".[5] But that was not at all the way the story was subsequently reported.

The Sun, which had led the pack in jingoism during the conflict, headlined its story 'Maggie Fury at Runcie's Sermon'. 'The Prime Minister was last night "spitting blood" over yesterday's Falklands service at St Paul's,' it claimed. 'Mrs Thatcher was said to be furious over the "wet" sermon delivered by the archbishop of Canterbury. And the controversial remembrance service led some Tory MPs to lash out bitterly at "pacifists and cringing clergy".[6]

The story was the same at the other end of the political spectrum, even if the language was more measured. *The Guardian's* political editor, Ian Aitken, suggested the prime minister was more than disappointed by the St Paul's service, and irritated by the apparent refusal of clerical attendees to celebrate Britain's great victory in the Falklands.

Aitken's piece quoted an unnamed cabinet minister who took the view that the service had more closely resembled a meeting of pacifist Quakers than a national thanksgiving service for the South Atlantic victory. He

---

5 C. Moore, *Margaret Thatcher*, p, 757.

6 H. Carpenter, *Robert Runcie: The Reluctant Archbishop* (London: Hodder & Stoughton, 1997), pp. 256–57.

also reported the complaint of the Tory MP for Brighton Pavilion, Julian Amery, that the service had not included hymns like 'Fight the Good Fight' and 'Onward Christian Soldiers'.

There may have been rather more sympathy for Dr Runcie's approach among those who actually fought in the Falklands. In a *Sunday* discussion to mark the fortieth anniversary of the Falklands War, broadcast in April 2022, Revd David Cooper, who was the chaplain attached to the Second Battalion, the Parachute Regiment (2 Para), spoke to William Crawley.

David Cooper: *I knew that there was some disagreement between, I suppose, the government and the archbishop, who, incidentally of course, himself had a Military Cross. I was myself coming to terms with what the war itself had meant for me personally. Throughout the war, I'd been supporting other people. When we got back from the Falkland Islands, I visited the families of all our dead, and it was wearing to see such distress. But on this topic of triumphalism, I didn't detect any triumphalism within the force. What I did witness after the* Belgrano *had been sunk, when The Sun ran the headline 'GOTCHA', was a really unhappy sailor who came to me and said, 'They think we're playing games here.' It is more serious than just this off-the-cuff remark.*

William Crawley: *So all of that was going on. And then you had this sermon from Robert Runcie. How did you hear that sermon? Did you hear it in the way that some within the government did, as insufficiently patriotic, for example, [not] celebrating the victory? Or did you think he nailed it?*

David Cooper: *I certainly didn't feel it was inappropriate in its entirety. I think the dean at St Paul's at one time suggested that the Lord's Prayer might be said in Spanish. I thought that was perhaps insensitive to the families of those who had been killed...*

William Crawley: *With the benefit of hindsight, though, when you look at that sermon, when you look at the words that were used praying for the families of the fallen of both sides, does that seem inappropriate in that context?*

David Cooper: *No. And I don't think many, if any, of my soldiers would have found that it the case. I mean, there's a very curious relationship between soldiers and their enemy. And certainly, it was clear to me and obvious to me in the Falklands that the only other people who knew what* *it was like were the enemy. There was a real dislocation between the majority of the British public and the members of the task force.*

In the same programme, Dr Clifford Williamson, a historian at Bath Spa University, set the row over Archbishop Runcie's sermon in the context of the tension inherent in the institution of the Established Church, which is expected to act as part of the state, while at the same time upholding religious values that may not always coincide with the interests of the state – or at least with the state's interests as they are interpreted by the government of the day.

Clifford Williamson: What we had in the Falklands and in 1982, particularly the service, were differing expectations of what was perceived to be needed by the state, which was a reinforcement – a moral reinforcement of the legitimacy of what they were doing, and what the Church was seeking to do, which is about ensuring that the domination of the conversation should be about compassion. I can't help but keep going back to what Runcie said: that the role of the Church is spiritual, not political.

Dr Williamson also suggested the Falklands episode reflects a broader tension between the Church of England and the Conservative government, which had been growing ever since Mrs Thatcher's election in 1979:

Well, this was, in some respects, a battle which had been building for some time during the early 1980s, where the Church of England had emerged in some respects as a powerful moral voice, especially in the context of the economic conditions of the time: 3 million unemployed, tremendous uncertainty economically. And so, therefore, by the time we get to the Falkland Islands conflict and its aftermath, there are really battle lines being drawn.

The miners' strike

Less than two years after the Falklands conflict, Britain faced the most divisive strike of the late twentieth century – arguably, as the BBC's retrospective account put it, the 'most bitter industrial dispute in British history'.[7] The miners' strike began in March 1984 in an attempt to prevent pit closures. It lasted more than a year, and involved tens of thousands of workers. Dozens of strikers and police were injured in violent clashes on picket lines, and more than 11,000 arrests were made. Division over the miners' action ran through every level of British society, right down to individual villages, where some miners stayed on strike until the bitter end while others returned to work – usually so they could feed their families, but earning the curse of 'scab' nevertheless. The strike also exposed a fault line in the Church of England.

The Church's claim to be truly 'national' rests in part on in its proud tradition of maintaining a presence in every parish. It also accepts a duty of care to everyone in the communities it serves – not just regular Anglican churchgoers. For vicars working in mining parishes in 1984, that meant, almost inevitably, solidarity with the strikers.

In a *Sunday* report marking the twenty-fifth anniversary of the strike, the BBC's Luke Walton visited a former mining community near Sunderland. His report began with an interview with a striker, Bob Heron, who remembered the way the police protected the miners who had decided to return to work.

Bob Heron: *The police lined themselves up across next to that fence... so that when the vans came up the road they went straight in through the gates, which had been removed.*

Luke Walton: *At the rusty gates of the old Eppleton Pit, former miner Bob Heron recalls the daily standoffs here between strikers and police. The site is now a quarry; a colliery wheel on a pedestal – the only reminder of an industry that was once the mainstay of the local village. But memories of the dispute of 1984 remain vivid; not just for Bob, but also for the Revd John Stephenson. At the time he was the local vicar, and had no hesitation in supporting the strike.*

John Stephenson: *The poverty that was here, people were on the bottom.*

---

7 'The Miners' Strike', *The Reunion*, BBC: https://www.bbc.co.uk/programmes/b03zxmyt #:~:text=When%20five%20hundred%20Yorkshire%20miners,industrial%20dispute%20in %20British%20history (11 April 2014, accessed 15 June 2023).

They were struggling. I was going to them in the parish, helping wherever I could and in any practical way I could.

Luke Walton: *The Revd Stephenson raised money and used it to buy groceries for miners' families. He joined demonstrations and sometimes the picket itself.*

John Stephenson: *I saw that as part of my ministry because I was absolutely one hundred per cent on the side of the miners. Their case was just.*

Luke Walton: *As time went on, financial problems forced more strikers back to work. That put their local vicar in a sensitive situation.*

John Stephenson: *Even if they broke the strike by coming into work before the strike was officially ended, they knew... that I would not condemn them. I could understand why it was.*

Luke Walton: *There will be those within the Church who said you shouldn't take sides in such a dispute.*

John Stephenson: *Yes. One or two people who talked with me didn't think I was going along the right lines. They said the miners themselves were being hoodwinked by their leader, Arthur Scargill, and all that kind of thing.*

The stand taken by vicars like John Stephenson was supported by David Jenkins, who became bishop of Durham in the summer of 1984, when the outcome of the struggle between the miners and the government hung in the balance. At his enthronement in Durham Cathedral, the new bishop declared that: 'The miners must not be defeated. They are desperate for their communities and this desperation forces them to action.'

He also proposed a new basis for negotiation, to include the removal of Ian MacGregor, the controversial Scottish-American industrialist whom the Thatcher government had appointed to run the National Coal Board the previous year. In language that was widely criticised as 'un-episcopal', Jenkins made the challenging claim that: 'The withdrawal of an elderly imported American to leave a reconciling opportunity for some local product is surely neither dishonourable nor improper.'[8]

---

8   D. Jenkins, *The Calling of a Cuckoo: Not quite an autobiography* (London: Continuum, 2002), p. 113.

Archbishop of Canterbury Robert Runcie had criticised striking miners at the beginning of the dispute, expressing dismay that some had 'taken [the] law into their own hands and unleashed violence'.[9] But as the year of industrial action ground on, he became more sympathetic to the bishop of Durham's position, which meant that in addition to the division between the Church and the government, there was another fault line between the Church leadership and its active members. The veteran political commentator Anthony Howard told *Sunday*'s anniversary programme:

> *My guess would be that, at the time of the miners' strike, the vast majority of those people who filled Anglican pews, particularly probably in southern England, were in support of the government, were foursquare behind the police and thought that the miners should lose this strike.*

Bishop David Jenkins himself, however, was unrepentant when he spoke to Luke Walton for the same programme. And he saw no contradiction between his opposition to the government and his role as a bishop in the Established Church. Quite the reverse, in fact.

David Jenkins: *I was called on in my first few days in office – I hadn't [even] been to the cathedral – by a group of miners' wives. And they said, 'Look here, Bishop, what are we going to say to our children? The police are against us. Who's going to help us in the village?'*

Luke Walton: *But you gave more than just pastoral support to individuals. As a bishop, you actually criticised the government. You got involved in the politics of it.*

David Jenkins: *Yes. After all, I was a member of the House of Lords ex officio, being such a senior bishop. And politics is what concerns people. It isn't, as you know, some highfalutin nonsense left to entirely stupid politicians or left to entirely irrelevant theoreticians. It's people.*

Luke Walton: *But there would have been, and there were, many people in the C of E who felt you shouldn't have taken sides in such a divisive dispute.*

---

9   H. Carpenter, *Robert Runcie*, p. 272.

David Jenkins: Oh, yes. Of course there were. In other words, you mustn't get either... your boots muddy or mixed up in the mess. But the point was, I think the crucifixion shows that God mixes himself up in the mess. And if you're not down-to-earth, what's the hope?

Faith in the city

The miners' strike ended in March 1985 – in the near total defeat of the National Union of Mineworkers and its leader, Arthur Scargill. Later that year, the Church of England published a report ('Faith in the City: a call for action by the Church and nation') on inner-city deprivation, drawn up by the archbishop of Canterbury's Commission on Urban Priority Areas. The burden of the commission's conclusion was that, in the words of *The Times*'s political writer David Watt:

> *The values on which Mrs Thatcher is trying to base the revival of the country are at least in danger of becoming un-Christian – in the creation of wealth, the principle of just distribution has been forgotten; in the concept of efficiency, the principles of responsibility and trust; in the notion of a free market, the idea of fellowship.*[10]

'Faith in the City' quoted Karl Marx and paid tribute to liberation theology – the belief, developed especially in the Latin American Catholic Church, that Christianity dictates a 'preferential option for the poor'. It also proposed a raft of measures to meet the needs of the inner city, which would have meant a significant increase in government spending.

'Faith in the City' was denounced by Conservative MPs, and the Conservative party chairman, Norman Tebbit, sought to cast doubt on the neutrality of the commission's chair, Sir Richard O'Brien, on the grounds that he had once been a Labour Party member. There was an irony here, as Sir Richard had also chaired the Crown Appointments Commission and advised Mrs Thatcher on the selection process which led to Robert Runcie's appointment as archbishop of Canterbury.

---

10 'Church report - the real flaw: Faith in the City controversy', *The Times*, 20 December 1985.

It is also an irony that these repeated rows between the Church of England and the government should have blown up during Robert Runcie's time as archbishop of Canterbury. He was not himself a radical; indeed, one of his chaplains described him as 'a bit of a wet Tory'. The fraught relationship was in part the result of the Thatcher government's way of doing business, which was often confrontational. But differences between Church and government persisted even when Margaret Thatcher and Robert Runcie had both left office and, over time, it became more and more evident that the tension was structural and perennial.

Nuclear weapons

There were some issues on which the Church of England seemed destined to disagree with Westminster governments of both colours. In 1982, the year of the Falklands War, for example, the bishop of Salisbury, John Baker, published a report – drawn up by another Church of England working party – on nuclear deterrence. 'The Church and the Bomb: Nuclear weapons and Christian conscience' argued that the United Kingdom should give up its independent nuclear deterrent.

Twenty years later, in July 2002, the bishop of Bath and Wells, Peter Price, took on a Labour government on exactly the same issue. Tony Blair's administration was planning to replace the ageing Polaris system of submarine-based nuclear weapons with the Trident system, and Bishop Price told *Sunday*'s Roger Bolton why he objected.

Peter Price: Because it places in the hands of governments who possess it the capability of destroying the very creation that's been given to humanity by God. And it's the well-being of humanity that is so important. It's anti-human because the effect of nuclear fallout will impact on generations unborn and despoil the land with no regard for borders affecting both friend and foe alike.

Roger Bolton: So it sounds as if you're not just opposed to Trident; you are opposed to all nuclear weapons.

Peter Price: Yes, I am indeed opposed to all nuclear weapons. I believe that they are the very antithesis of a God who creates, and a God who seeks to provide hope for humanity.

Roger Bolton: *Well, many doubtless would share your view about the use of those weapons, but possession does not mean use. And as you know, the West's strategy since the Second World War has largely been to use nuclear weapons as a deterrent, and people would say it has worked.*

Peter Price: *Well, that may be the case. At the same time, the very fact that we have them, the very fact that we are prepared to invest the vast sums of money in them, means that at one point or another we would be prepared to use them – and any use would be to the detriment of humanity, both for friend and foe.*

No moral compass

Not long after that interview, Rowan Williams was chosen as archbishop of Canterbury, and he remained in the post for the remainder of Labour's years in power. Both Tony Blair and Gordon Brown, who succeeded Blair as prime minister in 2007, had a well-developed sense of Christian ethics and the Church of England's place in society. Tony Blair was a communicant Anglican, and later converted to Roman Catholicism, while Gordon Brown's father was a Church of Scotland minister.

But the Labour governments they led did not, in the famous phrase of Alastair Campbell, the Downing Street spin doctor, 'do God'.[11] Instead 'New Labour', as it was known, pursued a progressive social agenda on issues such as same-sex relationships – introducing civil partnerships for same-sex couples in 2004.

In the aftermath of the terrorist attacks of 9/11 and 7/7, the government also – perhaps inevitably – focused on minority faiths, and Islam in particular. That, together with New Labour's very secular agenda, led to a feeling among some in the Church of England hierarchy that the Established Church was being ignored, and in June 2008 the Von Hügel Institute, a research centre based at St Edmund's College, Cambridge, published a report that suggested they were right.

---

11 D. Margolick, 'Blair's Big Gamble', *Vanity Fair*, June 2003.

The report, 'Moral, But No Compass: Government, Church and the future of welfare', was commissioned by Stephen Lowe, the suffragan bishop of Hulme in Manchester and the Church of England's bishop for Urban Life and Faith. Its focus was the Church's role in welfare provision, but its conclusions – based on interviews with politicians, civil servants, voluntary sector workers and faith leaders – were much broader. This is how Roger Bolton introduced the report on *Sunday*:

> *This Labour government is moral, but it doesn't have a moral compass. That is the conclusion of a new report commissioned by the Church of England. The report, released tomorrow, also says that the government discriminates against the Christian churches in favour of other faiths and is guilty of deep religious illiteracy.*

The report 'uncovered huge gaps in government evidence about faith communities in general and the churches in particular', and the authors stated: 'We encountered on the part of Government a significant lack of understanding of, or interest in, the Church of England's current or potential contribution in the public sphere. Indeed, we were told that Government had consciously decided to focus its evidence-gathering almost exclusively on minority religions. We were unsurprised to hear that some of these consequently felt "victimised".'[12]

Roger Bolton picked up on some of those ideas with Francis Davis, the report's lead author.

Roger Bolton: *You seem to suggest there's a particular, as you call it, 'illiteracy' in government about the Church of England. Why is that?*
Francis Davis: *Well, people of other faiths have said to us that they feel picked upon a little bit because government has not made the effort to research the Christian communities in the way that it's expended huge amounts of effort in trying to understand minority faiths.*
Roger Bolton: *Muslims, for example.*
Francis Davis: *Muslims and Sikhs have said this to us. And what this*

---

12 Quotes in this paragraph are from F. Davis, E. Paulhus and A. Bradstock, *Moral, But No Compass: Government, Church and the future of welfare* (Cambridge: Von Hügel Institute, 2008), p. 15.

means in practice is that if you go to cathedrals, where for example one cathedral educates 35,000 schoolchildren a year, another one has engaged in relaunching the government's academies programme and rolling out excellent examples of wonderful musical practice in inner-city areas, none of this is captured by government. So government keeps focusing in on tiny little community projects run by faiths, having major concerns about their ability to work together. And the wider picture of the thousands of volunteers that get involved in the community motivated by faith is missed.

That interview was followed by a discussion between Bishop Stephen Lowe and Hazel Blears, the secretary of state for Communities and Local Government. The bishop clearly felt the report confirmed the suspicions that had led him to commission it.

Stephen Lowe: *In terms of the work the researchers did, they went in and talked to Hazel's department, the staff there, and said, 'What information do you have about the Muslim community in this country?' There was a massive amount of mapping and information available about Islam in this country; quite rightly, in many ways, because there are major issues facing extreme radical elements of Islam, which the government needs to know about. When asked about what they know about the Church of England, nothing. Absolutely nothing.*

Hazel Blears's response was instructive, because it implicitly cast doubt on the Church of England's traditional claim to occupy a special place in the nation's life.

Hazel Blears: *Well, I think that we can always do better. But equally, you know, we live in a secular democracy. And actually, I think that's a precious thing in this country that we don't live in a theocracy. People want us to live in a secular democracy. But I have always accepted – and in fact, I think it's a matter for celebration – that hundreds of thousands of people in this country do fantastic things motivated by faith. And I think that the right balance is having a secular democracy, but then saying faith is really important to people.*

The Equality Bill

In 2010, the Brown government introduced its Equality Bill, designed to extend protections against discrimination for, among other groups, gay people, and to replace a raft of earlier legislation – including the Sex Discrimination Act, the Race Relations Act and the Disability Discrimination Act. Both the Roman Catholic and the Anglican Churches objected to the new bill on the grounds that it could be used to force them to appoint people whose beliefs and choices ran counter to traditional Christian teaching.

As the bill entered its final stages, Roger Bolton reported on *Sunday* that: 'The Equality Bill is due to be debated in the House of Lords tomorrow, and Anglican bishops have written to peers asking them to vote against what they see as a weakening of the Church's special status.' The BBC's religion correspondent Robert Pigott explained the extent of the bishops' concerns:

They don't want to be forced to go against their doctrine, or at least their Church's position, on homosexuality by being forced to employ people as clergy, but also in leadership positions in the Church, who are gay or transgendered. For example, the Church has long had an exemption from the law, which does let it discriminate, in a way that other employers couldn't, in choosing clergy. So it could refuse a clergy post to actively homosexual or transgendered people. They can discriminate on the grounds of marriage, too. For instance, the Roman Catholic Church could discriminate against women in selecting them for training for the priesthood. So that's where the law is at the moment. The Equality Bill, as it stands, could end that exemption.

The bishops won the day, and the bill was amended to include the exemptions they wanted. The relevant clause (790) reads:

This specific exception applies to employment for the purposes of an organised religion, which is intended to cover a very narrow range of employment: ministers of religion and a small number of lay posts, including those that exist to promote and represent religion. Where

*employment is for the purposes of an organised religion, this paragraph
allows the employer to apply a requirement to be of a particular sex or
not to be a transsexual person, or to make a requirement related to the
employee's marriage or civil partnership status or sexual orientation.*[13]

That meant the Churches could safely continue to discriminate when
they ordained priests, and the reference to 'a small number of lay posts'
also allowed them to discriminate when, for example, they appointed the
head of a Church school.

This victory put the Church of England in a very peculiar position for
an Established Church. Its bishops are part of a legislative process, and
they had used their political power to put themselves beyond the reach
of the law, as it applied to almost everyone else. They had also taken a
position that ran contrary to the tide of public opinion in the nation
they served. A YouGov survey in 2007 suggested that ninety per cent of
British people supported the outlawing of discrimination on the basis of
sexual orientation.[14]

The pursuit of equality was continued by the Conservative–Liberal
Democrat coalition that took over from Labour in 2010. David Cameron's
government followed through on Labour's civil partnership legislation
by introducing same-sex (or equal) marriage in 2014. The Church of
England continued to insist that marriage can only be valid between
a man and a woman, and at the time of writing, Church of England
priests are forbidden to marry same-sex couples (for a full account of the
position, see chapter 7). This stance appeared to be at odds not just with
the government, but with society more generally.

Immigration and Partygate

More recent clashes between the Church of England and the government
have given rise to the sort of bishop-bashing in the popular press

---

13 'Equality Act 2010 Explanatory Notes', Legislation.gov.uk: https://www.legislation.gov.uk/
ukpga/2010/15/notes/division/3/16/26/1 (accessed 15 June 2023).

14 H. Muir, 'Majority support gay equality rights, poll finds', *The Guardian*: https://www.
theguardian.com/society/2007/may/23/equality.gayrights (23 May 2007, accessed 15 June
2023).

that marked the Runcie–Thatcher years. Justin Welby, who became archbishop of Canterbury in 2013, used unusually robust language when he condemned the border policy introduced by the Conservative government in 2022. In an attempt to discourage the traffic of small boats arriving from France, Boris Johnson's administration proposed to deport immigrants who reached Britain illegally to Rwanda. In his Easter sermon – broadcast on Radio 4 – Archbishop Welby declared:

> *The details are for politics. The principle must stand the judgement of God, and it cannot. It cannot carry the weight of resurrection justice, of life conquering death. It cannot carry the weight of the resurrection that was first to the least valued, for it privileges the rich and strong. And it cannot carry the weight of our national responsibility as a country formed by Christian values, because sub-contracting out our responsibilities, even to a country that seeks to do well like Rwanda, is the opposite of the nature of God who himself took responsibility for our failures, on the cross.*[15]

Even the most radical bishops of the Thatcher years never accused the government quite so directly of departing from Christian teaching. The country's second-most-senior Church leader, Stephen Cottrell, the archbishop of York, was equally direct when he was interviewed live by William Crawley on *Sunday* that same Easter morning. Stephen Cottrell declared that he was 'appalled at what is being proposed', and when the presenter suggested that some Christians might support the policy, he responded: 'Well, if there are any, I haven't met them.'

The row over immigration policy took place against the backdrop of mounting public concern about the so-called 'Partygate scandal' – the evidence that staff in Downing Street, including the prime minister himself, had participated in sometimes riotous social assemblies while the rest of the country was under the yoke of lockdown regulations introduced as a result of the Covid pandemic. William Crawley asked

---

15 J. Lee, 'UK's Rwanda asylum plan the "opposite of nature of God" - Welby', BBC News: www. bbc.co.uk/news/uk-61130841 (17 April 2022, accessed 15 June 2023).

the archbishop of York whether he wanted to join the many voices then calling for Mr Johnson's resignation.

Stephen Cottrell: Well, what I do think is that Boris Johnson and our government need to look really long and hard at themselves, because what has happened in recent months – the revelations of what has gone on in Downing Street – has really tested the trust of British people to breaking point. I know here I speak more as a priest than as a bishop. I only actually took one funeral during the lockdown, but it was the saddest, hardest funeral I've ever taken in nearly forty years of ministry, to see people unable to hold and touch their loved ones. So people have sacrificed a lot, and therefore we expect from those who lead us much better than this. So what I do think must happen is that work must be done to rebuild trust in public life. And it's up to the individuals themselves and the Conservative Party to decide how they're going to respond to that.

Sly revenge

During Mrs Thatcher's years in power, she worried about relations with the Church of England and its bishops. In November 1987, she invited Robert Runcie and a group of senior bishops to lunch at Chequers (the prime minister's country house) in the hope of patching things up. The Johnson government, by contrast, simply ignored the protests about its immigration policy from the archbishop of Canterbury – and later most of his bishops.

There is some evidence of a sly revenge by the Church. At the thanksgiving service during the Queen's Platinum Jubilee weekend, which took place in St Paul's Cathedral on Friday 3 June 2022, the prime minister was asked to read a famous passage from Paul's letter to the Philippians: 'Whatever is true, whatever is honourable, whatever is just, whatever is pure, whatever is pleasing, whatever is commendable, if there is any excellence, and if there is anything worthy of praise, think about these things' (Philippians 4:8, NRSVA).

Since the prime minister's commitment to truth and honour were being widely questioned at the time as a result of the Partygate scandal, there was a certain amount of mischievous speculation in the press about how the passage had come to be chosen. Revd George Pitcher, an East Sussex vicar who had previously served on the staff of Lambeth Palace, confirmed to *Sunday* that for big national occasions like that, the form of service would normally be carefully planned and closely scrutinised by all concerned – and the example of the Falklands service in 1982 bears that out.

George Pitcher expressed surprise that no one on the prime minister's staff had noticed the danger of giving Mr Johnson a passage that blew up in his face like a rhetorical bomb, and he speculated that it may have happened because it was 'in the nature of this prime minister not to read it until he got there'.

2

Relations with Rome

It seems to have taken a while for *Sunday,* with its deep Anglican roots, to meet Vatican stories head on. The early Catholic items in the archive are about the way Rome was seen from an Anglican or British perspective, not about the Catholic Church in its own right. The first, from May 1977, is a Gerald Priestland report on a meeting between the archbishop of Canterbury, Donald Coggan, and Pope Paul VI.

Archbishop Coggan was building on the ecumenical efforts of his predecessor, Michael Ramsey, whose Anglo-Catholic sympathies had taken him to Rome just over a decade earlier. During that visit, Pope Paul presented the archbishop of Canterbury with the episcopal ring he had worn as archbishop of Milan, and the two leaders issued a common declaration, claiming their encounter as a landmark in 'sincere efforts to remove the causes of conflict and to re-establish unity'.[1]

Shared Communion

The meeting generated high hopes of reconciliation between the Anglican and Catholic Churches, and Archbishop Coggan began his own Roman adventure with a dramatic sermon at the Anglican church in the Eternal City on the eve of his meeting with the pope. 'Has not the time now arrived when we have reached such a measure of agreement on so many fundamentals of the gospel', he challenged, 'that a relationship of shared Communion can be encouraged by the leadership of both our Churches?'

---

1 'The Common Declaration by Pope Paul VI and Archbishop of Canterbury Michael Ramsey', Anglican Communion News Service: https://www.anglicannews.org/news/2016/10/1966-the-common-declaration-by-pope-paul-vi-and-archbishop-of-canterbury-michael-ramsey (5 October 2016, accessed 15 June 2023).

It was, as Priestland remarked in his *Sunday* commentary, 'a bold statement to make on the Vatican's front doorstep'. And there was more:

The day must come when together we kneel and receive from one another's hand the tokens of God's redeeming love, and then go directly again together to the world which Christ came to redeem. I said the day must come. In many places around the world, as those of us who travel know perfectly well, the day has already come without waiting for official sanction, and indeed, sometimes, with local official sanction. Has not the time, God's time, for such official sanction arrived? I think it has.

Unfortunately, the archbishop had not bothered to inform his hosts of what he was planning to say. Non-Catholics are still forbidden Holy Communion in Catholic churches today (although in practice individual priests often choose to be flexible about the way this discipline is enforced), and in the 1970s most theologians on both sides accepted that full intercommunion could not be achieved without dealing with all the weighty baggage of the Reformation.

Donald Coggan had, furthermore, failed to take account of the change in Pope Paul's standing, which had taken place during the decade since Michael Ramsey's visit. Paul was nearing the end of a long but troubled reign on the throne of St Peter. He had been elected in the summer of 1963 on a wave of optimism and renewal engendered by the Second Vatican Council, the great liberalising meeting that opened up the Catholic Church to the changes of the twentieth century. But in 1968 he issued his famous (or infamous, depending where you stand on these matters) encyclical *Humanae Vitae*, which confirmed the Vatican's ban on artificial means of contraception.

In Western Europe and North America, it was widely seen as a brutal gear change that reversed the Church's progressive direction, and it created a crisis of confidence in papal authority. The reaction hit Pope Paul so hard that it paralysed the last decade of his reign. He never issued another encyclical, and in 1977, with little more than a year to live, he was in no mood to take the kind of radical step Archbishop Coggan was proposing.

Priestland's *Sunday* commentary on the visit was decidedly sceptical:

The pope himself, in a statement welcoming the archbishop, had remarked somewhat obscurely that full Communion between the two Churches must represent spiritual reality rather than mere nostalgia. The consensus of divines here seems to be that this means, 'Let's not rush this thing.' Dr Coggan himself expects the pope to take some time to think his remarks over. But an important member of the Vatican Secretariat for Christian Unity told me, 'I can understand the archbishop being able to say something like this, because his word is not law. However, it rings strangely in Roman ears. It would seem very odd for the pope to use a personal opinion like that to justify a major change of course.'

The report was followed on the programme by an interview with a relatively new and, as time would prove, highly influential figure on Britain's national religious scene. Dom Basil Hume, abbot of the Benedictine monastery of Ampleforth in North Yorkshire, was chosen to be the archbishop of Westminster in 1976, and would remain the leader of Catholics in England and Wales until his death in 1999.

Although his Catholic faith was inherited from his French mother (his father, a cardiologist from Scotland, was a Protestant), Hume's public persona was quintessentially English – his passions included fly-fishing and Newcastle United – and one of his most significant achievements was to make Catholicism more acceptable to British society.

His response to Dr Coggan's suggestion was characteristic. It was a straight-bat restatement of the formal Catholic position, couched in the kind of thoughtful language likely to sound well in English, rather than – in the vivid turn of phrase of Priestland's report – 'Roman ears':

My own view on this is fairly certain, and it is that there is a very close link between the Body of Christ, which is the Eucharist and the Body of Christ, which is the Church. And we've always argued that intercommunion is the goal towards which we work in our ecumenical activities, but it isn't part of the steps which we take to go towards it. And my fear is that if intercommunion becomes part of the order of the day, there's a great danger of it being done without a sufficient understanding of what the Church is, and without a sufficient understanding of what the Eucharist is. There is no point in ducking the issues. It's most important to face up to the divisions and then, together, go in a relentless pursuit of the truth.

The pope with the rockstar reputation

Hume was to play a central role in the way the United Kingdom saw the pope who dominated the Catholic Church for most of *Sunday's* first half-century, John Paul II. Elected in October 1978 (after the very brief reign of John Paul I), John Paul II immediately caught the world's imagination with a burning energy that stood in marked contrast to the quietude of Paul VI's final years.

His visit to Poland during the summer after his election was a world-changing moment that set in train the events that led to the founding of Solidarity, the first free trade union in the Soviet bloc. He was to make more than a hundred foreign tours (more than all his predecessors combined), and in the course of them he was probably seen by more people than any other leader in history. By the time he announced his intention to visit the United Kingdom in 1982, he already had a rock-star-like reputation.

This first visit here by a reigning pope very nearly came to grief over the Falklands War (which, as we noted in the previous chapter, also provoked great tension between Downing Street and Lambeth Palace). When, at the beginning of May 1982, a British submarine struck the *General Belgrano* – which sank with the loss of more than 320 lives – Cardinal Hume and his Scottish counterpart, Cardinal Gray, wrote to the prime minister questioning whether 'there is any longer a due proportion between ends and means in the Falklands conflict'.[2] They received a characteristically tart response from Mrs Thatcher: 'It was Argentina who first used force in this dispute, and we cannot allow them to profit from their invasion.'[3]

---

2 C. Moore, *Margaret Thatcher*, p. 722.

3 C. Pepinster, 'Pope John Paul II, the Falklands war and a crisis of sovereignty', *The Tablet*: https://www.thetablet.co.uk/features/2/21762/pope-john-paul-ii-the-falklands-war-and-a-crisis-of-sovereignty (14 April 2022, accessed 15 June 2023).

Three weeks before the papal visit was due to begin, Cardinals Hume and Gray flew to Rome and found Pope John Paul's advisers deadlocked over whether it should go ahead. It took a second trip, by Archbishop of Liverpool Derek Worlock, Archbishop of Glasgow Thomas Winning and the Church historian Professor Henry Chadwick (representing the Church of England), to hammer out a compromise. Pope John Paul would come, but he would also visit Argentina, and he would meet no representative of the British government during his six-day journey around England, Scotland and Wales.

One consequence was that, on his arrival at Gatwick Airport, the pope was greeted not by the foreign secretary (Francis Pym at the time), but by the local bishop. Cormac Murphy-O'Connor, then bishop of Arundel and Brighton, would himself become leader of the Catholic Church in England and Wales, and much later he recalled the day of the pope's arrival for *Sunday*:

> *About five o'clock, the sun came out and the plane landed, and I was privileged to be the first on the plane to greet him with the papal nuncio* [the Vatican's ambassador in Britain]. *And there he was, sitting rather nervous[ly] on the plane, wondering what was going to happen. It was the Falklands War, remember, at the time. So anyway, he came down and kissed the ground, and from then on it just went from event to event. And it was really an extraordinary week, very happy. Obviously, it was of enormous significance to the Catholics of the country. But I think for the pope, too. He enjoyed it.*

The idea of the supremely confident Polish pope being nervous is difficult to come to terms with. He certainly gave every indication of enjoying the week that followed.

Anti-Catholic sentiment

Strikingly – and this must be a quirk of the way the early archive was curated, but it is a telling one – the only surviving *Sunday* coverage contemporary to the visit is an interview with two of its opponents.

Anti-Catholic sentiment was much stronger then than it is today, and a small minority of Protestant clergy campaigned vigorously against the pope's presence on this historically Protestant island.

Trevor Barnes, a regular reporter and sometimes presenter for *Sunday* over many years, covered a protest rally in Trafalgar Square. 'About 800 Protestants assembled to listen to speeches, prayers and hymns amid banners, Union Jacks and slogans,' he reported.

His despatch included interviews with two prominent campaigners against the visit, Pastor Jack Glass, a Scottish Protestant minister closely associated with Northern Ireland's anti-Catholic firebrand Ian Paisley, and Revd David Samuel, another vociferous opponent of ecumenism, who later formed his own breakaway Anglican Church.

Trevor Barnes: *Like it or not, and clearly no one present did, the pope had arrived. Did the Revd David Samuel, general secretary of the Protestant Reformation Society, feel that the warm welcome extended to the pope in Canterbury would affect relationships within the Anglican Church?*

David Samuel: *Well, the mere welcoming of the pope doesn't affect the position of the Church of England or the other Churches. But if it is followed by formal moves towards union and the acceptance of this proposal that the pope become universal primate, that would change things radically. And then I think every reformed minister in the Churches would have to reconsider his position in relation to them. There's got to be some sort of registration of our opposition to the doctrines of the Church of Rome. And also, we must register the fact that we do not want to see unity between the Church of England and the Church of Rome. And that is the purpose of this, and also to point people to the differences that do exist – because these are very profound and real, and have far-reaching implications. The fact of the matter is that these differences are not faced in all this talk about love and unity and reconciliation...*

Trevor Barnes: *There were attacks from the platform on the ecumenical movement and on Church leaders. There were denunciations of the political significance of the papal visit. Pastor Jack Glass, Glasgow leader of the Twentieth Century Reformation Movement, remained impassive during the speeches and the anthem, but revealed keener feelings when* *asked for his own view of the state of Church leadership* [specifically the leaders of the Free Church and the Church of England, both of which welcomed the pope].

Jack Glass: *Both of them are traitors and dishonest men. For example, the moderator of the Free Church, when he takes his ordination vows, claims to uphold the Westminster Confession of Faith* [drawn up on parliament's instruction during the English Civil War]. *Now, that confession of faith says that the pope is the man of sin, and the antichrist. Now, he* [the moderator] *was a dishonest man to enter the Church on those grounds and yet accept the pope as a brother in Christ.*

Dr Runcie, on the other hand, at his ordination claims to uphold the Thirty-nine Articles, which states the Mass is a blasphemous fable and a dangerous deceit. So you can see from these words we're dealing with two dishonest men who are Romanisers, and would seek to hand over the Protestant Churches to the Roman pontiff. The trouble with the Church is they've departed from Jesus Christ. When this nation gets back to the Bible, they'll recognise the pope for what he is: the man of sin and antichrist. And he won't be passing cheering crowds. He'll be rejected as the villain of the piece he is.

Despite the occasional eruptions of antipapal protests (in Glasgow Jack Glass and Ian Paisley led a march, to chants of 'the Beast is coming', to Bellahouston Park, where the papal helicopter was due to land), the visit was widely judged a success. On the twenty-fifth anniversary, *Sunday* interviewed some of those who had attended Pope John Paul's huge outdoor gatherings about their memories. The interviews are recorded in the archive as 'vox pops', broadcasting shorthand for *vox populi,* the view from ordinary people.

Vox pop: *We were told that if we wanted to go, we'd have to go at midnight because there were going to be so many there that you'd have to get into your place. Because once people started coming in, you wouldn't have been able to get through. It's wonderful. Everybody was so excited for him to be in my country, say a Mass with me there. I just couldn't believe it.*

Vox pop: *I think it was a week that in my lifetime I don't think I could ever repeat. It really gave you a strength, you know, your faith. He was a man that you could relate to with that. You know, he was our hope for the young people, really. It was just so inspiring. So inspiring.*

A step back

In the same programme, the Catholic comedian Frank Skinner described the atmosphere in even more colourful terms: 'It was like a Madonna tour, times a thousand. It's incredibly exciting, and I think it did a lot for people's faith and brought a lot of lapsed Catholics back to the Church because he was a very dynamic, very charismatic figure.'

But *Sunday's* anniversary report also looked at the deeper question of whether the visit had the enduring impact it had promised at the time. As the presenter, Roger Bolton, pointed out: 'One of the most memorable images of the visit was that of the pope and the then archbishop of Canterbury, Robert Runcie, kneeling together at the tomb of St Thomas Becket. There were great hopes of the two Churches moving closer together.' He posed the question 'Has this happened?' to the Catholic writer John Cornwell.

The answer he received was defined by two hugely important developments in the intervening quarter of a century. The first was the Church of England's decision to ordain women as priests (which we explore in chapter 6) and the second was the publication, in 2000, of *Dominus Iesus* ('The Lord Jesus'), a Vatican document that categorised the Anglican Church as an 'ecclesial community' rather than a Church, and declared that such communities 'are not Churches in the proper sense'.[4] The reaction to that document was, as John Cornwell pointed out, in marked contrast to the spirit of optimism in the spring of 1982.

John Cornwell: I remember that time. It was one of enormous hope. And I think, in fact, we had been moving more and more closely together. But of course it was [the] women priests issue that I think started to divide again. And I think that as many Anglican priests who were against

---

4 'Declaration "Dominus Iesus" on the Unicity and Salvific Universality of Jesus Christ and the Church', Vatican: https://www.vatican.va/roman_curia/congregations/cfaith/documents/rc_con_cfaith_doc_20000806_dominus-iesus_en.html (6 August, 2000, accessed 15 June 2023).

women priests came over to the Catholic Church and they were greeted with considerable enthusiasm by some bishops... I think that that was another wedge.

Roger Bolton: *So are Rome and Canterbury then further apart than they were twenty-five years ago?*

John Cornwell: *Oh, I think very much so. And seven years ago, the Vatican document called* Dominus Iesus, *'The Lord Jesus', in which, first of all, Cardinal Ratzinger* [then prefect of the Congregation for the Doctrine of the Faith (CDF)]... *said that the Anglican faith was not a proper Church. And I remember George Carey* [archbishop of Canterbury at the time] *being absolutely amazed and astonished. Of course, being a papal document, you know, a major Vatican document, it was not something... one could easily go back on.*

Dominus Iesus was part of a wider campaign by Pope John Paul to reassert traditional Church teaching, and he worked closely in this enterprise with the like-minded Cardinal Joseph Ratzinger, the Vatican's theological watchdog. It lost him votes in the pews in Britain, where the Catholic Church had become increasingly liberal. The liberally inclined Cardinal Hume himself became irritated by what he saw as sometimes high-handed Vatican behaviour.

When the popular Catholic writer and broadcaster Sister Lavinia Byrne came under fire from the CDF over a book she wrote on women priests, Hume supported her in her battle with the Vatican. *Sunday* covered the episode in a 1998 edition marking the twentieth anniversary of John Paul's election.

By this stage, the pope had published *Ordinatio Sacerdotalis* ('On Priestly Ordination'), which, as well as repeating the Church's doctrine that women could not be ordained, declared that 'this judgement was to be definitively held by all the faithful'.[5] This meant that Catholic theologians could not even debate or write about the question, and it reinforced the view of those who, in the words of the presenter, Roger

---

5 'Apostolic Letter Ordinatio Sacerdotalis of John Paul II to the Bishops of the Catholic Church on Reserving Priestly Ordination to Men Alone', Vatican: https://www.vatican.va/content/john-paul-ii/en/apost_letters/1994/documents/hf_jp-ii_apl_19940522_ordinatio-sacerdotalis.html (22 May 1994, accessed 15 June 2023).

Bolton, saw John Paul as 'an old man in a hurry, increasingly manipulated by reactionaries in the Vatican'.

Roger Bolton: *In July it was revealed that a Catholic publisher had been told to pulp copies of one of Sister Lavinia's works, in which she had discussed the theological issues surrounding the question of women's ordination. Sister Myra Poole of Catholic Women for Ordination was not impressed.*

Myra Poole: *When I heard this book was being pulped, it reminded me of the burning of women who were called witches in the Middle Ages, and also there was burning of books at the time of the Inquisition. But to burn books at the end of the twentieth century... is an incredibly nasty thing to do.*

Roger Bolton: *The new editor of the [traditionalist] Catholic Herald, William Oddie, was rather impressed.*

William Oddie: *I think that once the pope has defined that something is essential Catholic belief, somebody under obedience has the duty either to remain silent or certainly not to argue against it. All Catholics are under obedience.*

Roger Bolton: *A fellow editor, John Wilkins of* The Tablet *[a progressive publication], took a more relaxed view.*

John Wilkins: *Sister Lavinia Byrne herself, I know, would be the first to say that she couldn't write such a book now, and nor, in her view, could any other theologian write such a book. But it is not heretical to believe in the ordination of women. Even now it's an error. And I think that at a time when the Roman Catholic Church wants to wipe the slate clean before the third millennium – and that is the pope's policy – one of the things they want to wipe it clean of is the Inquisition. You don't want to give any impression that the Inquisition is alive and well and living in Rome.*

By this stage, Pope John Paul's health had become frail. His Parkinson's was not officially admitted by the Vatican until 2003, but his illness had by then been all too apparent for many years. The serious injuries he sustained in the assassination attempt of 1981 had taken their toll, and he also suffered from severe osteoarthritis.

When he celebrated his Silver Jubilee in December 2003, Jane Little, the BBC's religious affairs correspondent, reporting for *Sunday* from St Peter's Square, noted that 'his voice [was] slurred and his words hard to distinguish' during the service. The contrast to the vigorous, charismatic figure who had wowed so many people on his British tour in 1982 – 'like a Madonna tour times a thousand' – could not have been greater.

Continuity with change

John Paul died in April 2005. *Sunday* had become a very different programme during his long reign. It no longer focused on the Church of England in the same way, and its agenda was much broader. John Paul's death fell on a Saturday evening, and the following morning Radio 4 cleared its schedule for a double edition of *Sunday,* presented jointly by Roger Bolton in Manchester and Edward Stourton in Rome. The Catholic commentator Margaret Hebblethwaite reminded the audience of the curious procedure by which the cardinals, the 'princes of the Church', choose a new leader.

Margaret Hebblethwaite: There's an immense secrecy surrounding it. It's called a conclave because they're locked up. It means with a key. And this is the first time that the cardinals will actually be staying in rather more comfortable quarters in the Santa Marta hostel. They'll be transported to the Sistine Chapel. All this won't begin for fifteen days. And then, in that period, all telephone lines are cut. All communication with the outside world is broken. The very few other people – you know, cleaners and so on – are under strict vows of secrecy. And we just really wait, watching the smokes until it goes white [the ballot papers are burned after each vote, and once there is a result a chemical is added to the fire, sending out white smoke as a signal to the outside world], *which could be a day or it could be two weeks.*

Edward Stourton: We're talking about a group of men who, although many of them will be unknown to most of us, probably know each other rather well in many cases. In their conversations – I know you're not supposed to campaign and all that, but of course they'll talk to each other – what sort of a leader do you think they'll be looking for?

Margaret Hebblethwaite: *Well, I think they will want continuity with change, if that doesn't sound too paradoxical. No one is going to say we want to undo what John Paul II has done. They will want to affirm it, but with a different style – because no one can do it quite the way that John Paul has done it. So they may go, for example… for someone who is quiet. I mean, John Paul's been this tremendous communicator, this tremendous traveller. But in the end, I mean, they have to live this fantasy that they are electing a Holy Father. And one of the most important things is that sort of charisma of holiness that's got to set alight the spirits of all the cardinals so that they can live that dream.*

Edward Stourton: *But is there a sense among some of them that, after this very long papacy, there are some things that need to be dealt with quite urgently in the Church, particularly in view of the fact that in his last years, this pope was not very active because he was old and quite sick?*

Margaret Hebblethwaite: *Well, opinions are different on this. I belong to the group that thinks that the witness of this pope in his last years, being old and sick, and very freely exhibiting that on television, is exactly the kind of witness that the pope should give. And that his finest witness in all his rule, all his pontificate, were the moments when he was almost assassinated and broadcast his forgiveness for his would-be assassin from the hospital, and the moments of his dying. So I think it's a mistake – although there are a lot of people who do hold this view – I think it's a mistake to look for a sort of very active executor. Do we want a pope who actually rules everything in the Church? Or do we want decentralisation with a focal figure who portrays different values?*

New pope, new visit

Her prediction that the cardinals would opt for 'continuity with change' proved well-judged. Joseph Ratzinger, who took the name Benedict XVI, had of course been John Paul's closest collaborator. It was not an especially popular choice in the United Kingdom. Liberal British Catholics had hoped for a pope who would give the Church a new direction, not someone who had earned the nickname 'Panzer Cardinal' because of his energetic efforts to crack down on dissent. And the Church of England was still reeling from the blow of *Dominus Iesus* – which had, of course, been drafted by the new pope himself.

Nevertheless, Gordon Brown invited Pope Benedict to come to Britain in 2009, and the visit went ahead in September the following year (by which time Mr Brown had been succeeded by David Cameron as prime minister). There was some opposition of the Pastor Glass variety – Ian Paisley described the visit as a 'mistake'[6] – but secular critics were much more vocal than they had been at the time of John Paul II's tour nearly three decades earlier. The British Humanist Society and the National Secular Society launched campaigns to stop Pope Benedict coming, and an estimated 10,000 people joined a Protest the Pope rally in London. Attendees heard the prominent biologist and atheist Richard Dawkins denounce the pope as an 'enemy of humanity'.[7] Opinions about the pope and the Church he led were also coloured by the growing scandal of priestly abuse (which we cover in chapter 5).

Preparations for the visit were further marred by the leak of a Foreign Office document circulated in Whitehall with the headline 'The ideal visit would be...'. The ideas included inviting the pope to open an abortion clinic, bless a gay marriage and launch a range of Benedict-branded condoms. It also suggested that Pope Benedict should apologise for the Spanish Armada. In the event, it was the British government that was forced to apologise to the Vatican for what were politely described as 'far-fetched' proposals. The document had apparently been drawn up by relatively junior staff at the Foreign Office. To get preparations back on track, the Catholic Conservative peer Chris Patten was put in charge of arrangements for the papal visit.

On the eve of the visit, *Sunday* broadcast a BBC poll of Catholic opinion. The role of women in the Church, which has been such a theme of this chapter, provided the most striking result.

---

6 'Pope Benedict XVI UK visit a "mistake" says Ian Paisley', BBC News: https://www.bbc.co.uk/news/10484122 (2 July 2010, accessed 15 June 2023).

7 R. Dawkins, 'Ratzinger is an enemy of humanity', *The Guardian*: https://www.theguardian.com/commentisfree/belief/2010/sep/22/ratzinger-enemy-humanity (22 September 2010, accessed 15 June 2023).

Edward Stourton: *The BBC survey on the eve of Pope Benedict's visit was conducted earlier this week and involved interviews with 500 Catholics across the United Kingdom. The Church, of course, is not a democracy, but there is plenty here for its leaders to reflect on if they choose to. And we shall hear from the new archbishop of Southwark, Peter Smith, later in the programme. Here, though, is the assessment of the BBC's religious affairs correspondent Robert Pigott.*

Robert Pigott: *Well, I think the most telling finding was about the role of women, really, because sixty-two per cent, which is, I suppose, getting on for two-thirds of Catholics, felt they should have more authority and status in the Church, and only thirty [per cent] said they shouldn't. The percentage response for men and women, by the way, was identical. And young people, the bracket between eighteen and twenty-four, thought it was pretty obvious that women should have a greater role.*

Now, I think this does confirm what I've been gradually discovering over a period of time – especially looking forward to the pope's visit – that the sort of brewing discontent among women about their place in the Church is, I think, if anything, more damaging to the Church and keeping hold of congregations than even the sex abuse crisis. Pope John Paul II famously ruled out the ordination of women indefinitely, said it wasn't even to be discussed, but Benedict's declared that to be definitive. I just don't think that plays [out] well in a society where equality has become so potent.

And the other interesting figure I noticed was that many more Catholics think that compulsory celibacy should be dropped than those that don't. And women [were] notably more concerned about it than men...

Edward Stourton: *...A sense of a Church in which many people are pushing for change, then?*

Robert Pigott: *Yes. I think that there's not very much here that the Church can take comfort from. I think it does rather show not a really ringing endorsement of the way the Church is being led. I think it confirms the idea that Catholics are less deferential, less ready to accept Church tradition unquestioningly, and I think, tellingly, more uncomfortable with the way they feel that they fit as Catholics into mainstream society than once was the case. I think it was fifty-seven per cent said they felt*

*that their Catholic faith was not generally valued by British society...
And, you know, many Catholics will have picked up on the antipathy
felt [towards] the Vatican over sex abuse and simply the general
development of secularity.*

Later in the programme, Peter Smith, the archbishop of Southwark,
claimed to be 'slightly puzzled' by the idea of 'brewing discontent' among
Catholic women. While conceding that, 'OK, they can't be priests,' he
argued:

*I think the Church is very feminine. I've always said women have
always been the backbone of the Church. They're the ones who are the
most faithful to the practice of their faith, bringing up the children as
Catholics and so on... The Union of Catholic Mothers, I mean, they're
a great bunch. They're always there. You can always ask them to do
things. All right, these are not great dramatic things – it's providing
food and drink at diocese occasions and so on – but they're the salt of
the earth.*

Taking on the tea and sandwiches was probably not what most
Catholics had in mind when they voted to give women 'more authority
and status'.

The survey did produce one piece of good news for the archbishop
of Southwark and the Catholic hierarchy, however. Nearly seventy per
cent of Catholics declared themselves in favour of Benedict's visit going
ahead, and said they believed it would be good for the Church. In his
interview for *Sunday*, the archbishop seized on the figure:

*Well, I'm delighted to hear it. What I'm hoping for with Pope Benedict
coming is that people will begin to see a lot more of the real Benedict.
Because as we know from the beginning, when he was elected, there
has been quite a lot of negative press about his German origins; that
he was the Rottweiler of the Vatican and all that sort of thing. And
of course, he's totally different from John Paul II, who was a very
charismatic, huge man. Benedict is of slightly less stature physically,
but he's got a heart as big as John Paul II. And then when people*

see him and meet him, the whole attitude changes. It becomes very positive.

On that point he was proved right. Benedict's visit to Britain was much more successful than most had predicted, with large crowds attending his big open-air services at Bellahouston Park in Glasgow and Cofton Park in Birmingham. His thoughtful speech to the joint Houses of Parliament was widely praised.

More change ahead

But Benedict's pontificate was overwhelmed by scandals involving priestly abuse, money and, most weirdly, a crime committed by his butler. Paolo Gabriele was found to have a huge stash of papal documents cached away in his Vatican apartment, and he was accused of leaking the contents to an Italian journalist.

On 11 February 2013, Pope Benedict announced that he was resigning: the first pope to leave office in this manner since the thirteenth century. The veteran BBC Rome correspondent David Willey reflected on his decision for *Sunday.*

David Willey: *It's not been a very happy ending to this pontificate, because of course there's been a lot of scandal in the Church, including in the pope's private apartment, with the not-very-edifying story of his former butler who stole a lot of documents and got sent to prison for his pains. The pope himself has said that he finds the whole story incomprehensible. There's been a whiff of scandal and there's also been a lot of infighting among the Italians. My impression is that the pope may well have decided, in his current state of failing health and knowing that when a pope leaves his post, either through death or resignation, everybody in the Vatican loses their job. This is a time for a real cleanout and a whole new series of appointments by the next pope. So we could be looking at a very different sort of Vatican after the election.*

Edward Stourton: *David, you've been covering the Vatican for many years. Have you ever known anything quite like a week like this?*

David Willey: *No, no. Absolutely nothing. It's been amazing. And I think* *that there is great hope for renewal in the Church, after a period when clearly the leadership of the Pope has left a lot to be desired. [I think] we had the amazing papacy of Pope John Paul II, this really has been a papacy of transition, and we now have to look forward to the future.*

On the same programme, Clifford Longley, lead writer for the liberal Catholic weekly *The Tablet*, which had often been critical of Benedict and his reign, praised the manner of his departure:

It does seem to me that he has brought great credit to himself, and he has given the kind of grace to his papacy by withdrawing for the reasons he's given and the way he's done it. And I think there's been a surge of affection for him, but the fact is that he was facing absolutely formidable problems – particularly right at home on his own doorstep inside the Vatican – which was going to take an enormous amount of energy. And he just didn't think he had it.

Benedict's successor, Jorge Bergoglio or Pope Francis – formerly the archbishop of Buenos Aires, and the first pope from outside Europe – was inaugurated two days before Justin Welby was installed as archbishop of Canterbury, and, on 17 March 2013, *Sunday* took advantage of this neat symmetry with a programme that focused on the character and ambitions of the two new leaders. It included stark reminders of what divided the two Churches, but also illustrated what they had in common.

Women priests were now a well-established part of the Church of England's life and ministry, and its General Synod had moved on to the issue of women bishops (see chapter 6). This, of course, made the prospect of reconciliation between the Church of England and the Church of Rome even more remote, so when Justin Welby was asked about the relationship, he chose his words with care.

Trevor Barnes: *And of course, we can't not mention the pope, whose tenure coincides with your own. How do you see the future of Catholic–Anglican relations developing?*

Justin Welby: *I think, as we both think through the issues at the theological level, and live the issues at the practical and the prayerful* *and spiritual level, I am extremely optimistic about the future of our relationships.*

When Justin Welby visited Rome later that year, he wore the ring Pope Paul had given to Michael Ramsay as a symbol of the links between the Churches. But the vague talk of being 'optimistic about the future of our relationships' was a far cry from the ringing call for intercommunion made by Donald Coggan more than three-and-a-half decades earlier. However, when he was asked about some of the political issues we covered in the previous chapter, Archbishop Welby paid a generous compliment to Rome's intellectual legacy:

The point is, the Church does not stand for a party; not least because church members come from a wide range of political parties. And there isn't a party political programme in the Bible. What there is, is a clear and absolute imperative of the common good, of solidarity, of subsidiarity; the great heritage that we have of Catholic social teaching that's come from Rome. And we have to hold on to that. That will overlap with party political programmes at some point. It's political, not party political.

A pope for the poor

Justin Welby's generous acknowledgement of the Church of England's debt to Catholic social teaching indicated one area where he and Pope Francis had a similar agenda. Even at this very early stage of his pontificate, Francis's commitment to the poor was apparent.

Speaking to journalists at an audience immediately after his election, Pope Francis used a phrase that immediately became a headline. He declared that he wanted the Catholic Church to be 'a poor Church for the poor'. The American commentator Fr Thomas Reese – like the new pope, a member of the Jesuit order of priests – told *Sunday* it was much more than a slogan.

Thomas Reese: *I think this is a man who's lived that as bishop in Buenos Aires. You know, he was a bishop that went down into the slums, went* *down and was with the people baptising their children, being with them, preaching on street corners. This is, you know, living a very simple lifestyle. I think that brings something wonderful to the Church... a Church that is for the poor is exactly what we need. I mean, this is not a pope who's going to be comfortable wearing furs and silk. This is a pope who comes from a working-class background, and he's seen how poverty affects people.*

Pope Francis's first pastoral visit, made within weeks of his election, was to a refugee camp on the Greek island of Lesbos. 'He came,' a worker from the Catholic charity Caritas told *Sunday*, 'to give a sign of solidarity, of hope to all of us.' The treatment of refugees and migrants was another area where Pope Francis shared an agenda with the archbishop of Canterbury and, as we reported in chapter 1, this is an issue that brought Justin Welby into direct conflict with the British government.

At the time of writing, it seems unlikely that Pope Francis will follow in the footsteps of his two predecessors with a visit to Britain. He was expected at the COP26 meeting on climate change in Glasgow in 2021, but pulled out at the last minute. Though he has visited developed countries with significant Catholic populations (France in 2014, the United States the following year, Ireland two years after that), much of his travelling has been to the Global South. One of his ambitions has been to focus on the Church on what he calls 'the periphery'.[8]

It is, however, perhaps worth noting that one of Pope Francis's most vocal champions was English cardinal Cormac Murphy-O'Connor. He was too old to take part in the conclave of 2013, but in the run-up to the vote he lobbied fiercely on behalf of Argentinian archbishop Jorge Bergoglio, whom he had come to like and admire during their meetings in the Vatican. The dreams that he and so many others had nurtured back in 1982, when he greeted Pope John Paul at Gatwick, had been disappointed. But he had the consolation of seeing his candidate elected to the throne of St Peter, and he gave his reaction to *Sunday* with characteristic enthusiasm:

---

8   M. J. Clark, 'Pope Francis asks theologians to remember the marginalized. Here's how one global project is responding', *America* magazine, February 2023.

I think it's wonderful. And he took the name, as you know, of Francis: the poor man, the poor servant. He's a very simple man, a very intelligent man, a shrewd man. But above all, I think he's a man of the gospel. And I think the fact that he happens to come from Argentina, South America, is, of course, something that's never happened before. So that also is good, because he's got to be not only bishop of Rome, which he emphasised in his few words, but also bishop for the world. I'm very happy. I think it's been an inspired choice.

3

Saint-making

On the evening of 24 March 1980, Oscar Romero, archbishop of San Salvador, was shot with a single high-velocity round while saying Mass; the first archbishop to be killed at the altar since Thomas Becket was cut down by Henry II's knights in 1170. He was not formally recognised as a saint until nearly four decades later, but he immediately became the focus of a local cult – canonised by the veneration of his followers, if not by the Vatican.

The archbishop had made his home in the Salvadorian capital in a hospital complex run by nuns, and his unassuming bungalow – just across the hospital driveway from the chapel where he was assassinated – very quickly became a shrine. This description dates from the 1990s:

> *In the modest sitting room, a glass case contains the bloodied surplice and vestments he was wearing when he was shot, together with an assortment of cufflinks, photographs and episcopal skullcaps. There is a battered typewriter on the plain table in his bedroom where he wrote his sermons and his diary. Dozens of small marble tablets have been inset in the wall just outside the front door inscribed with 'thanks to Monsignor Romero for a miracle granted' – the nun who showed me round said they had been placed there by people from all over the Americas who felt their prayers had been answered through his intercession. A plaque next to his bust describes him as 'Martyr and Prophet'.[1]*

Over time, some of these relics began to degrade, and the Church in El Salvador turned to Britain for help in preserving them. In August

---

1   E. Stourton, *Absolute Truth: The Catholic Church in the world today* (London: Viking, 1998), p. 109.

2008, Jan Graffius, the curator at Stonyhurst – the Jesuit community and school in Lancashire – told Helen Grady (then a producer on *Sunday*, later the programme's editor) how she came to be approached about the task. She began by describing some of the items in Stonyhurst's collection of relics.

Jan Graffius: We have some very stark reminders of the brutality of religious persecution… Here we have what looks like a very pretty little beaded box, beautiful flowers on the top. But when you open it and look inside there's human bone. It's the shoulder blade and upper arm of one of four young priests who were hanged, drawn and quartered in Durham in 1590. And somebody was brave enough to reach into the pot – because they boiled the bits before they hung them up around the town – to rescue this as a reminder of their bravery and also an encouragement to future Catholics.

Helen Grady: You've also got items of clothing, I noticed.

Jan Graffius: Yes. We have a large collection of vestments, which were rescued or sent across by Catholics in the seventeenth century. This beautiful fifteenth-century chasuble here with its very elaborate embroidered crucifixion on the back. And [on] a slightly more domestic note, this little pink and gilded hat. It's like a beanie. You just pull it on and it's a nightcap, and it belonged to St Thomas More. And it is probably because of these types of artifacts that I was privileged enough to be asked to go over to El Salvador and advise on the conservation and display of the vestments that Oscar Romero was wearing when he was murdered.

It was, she explained, an unusually challenging task.

Jan Graffius: The people of El Salvador value this man and value these things so highly. The conditions in El Salvador environmentally are very challenging. It's hot; thirty-five, thirty-six, thirty-seven degrees all year round. Humidity is incredibly high. When I was there, on the last day I measured it. It was ninety-seven per cent. The problem with restoring something is that, generally speaking, you want to take away dirt. With these vestments the blood that's on them is an integral part of it, and you don't want to touch that.

Helen Grady: You're used to working with religious relics, but some people don't see a need for them. They'd say if you want to know and understand Oscar Romero, read his books, listen to his speeches, know him by his actions.

Jan Graffius: Sometimes you can learn things that you're not expecting to learn. One of the most important things that came out of this for me was dealing with the trousers that he was wearing under his vestments when he was murdered, saying Mass. There were white marks around the knees, and I assumed that it was mould or mildew, and then realised that these were salt crystal stains, sweat. According to the sisters who were there [the congregation included several nuns], he saw the sniper lining him up in his sights while he was saying the prayer over the gifts. And he flinched. And then he went on with the Mass, knowing that in the next few seconds he was going to be shot. And in that moment, he knew he was going to be killed. He knew he was about to die, and had [to decide] to duck, to run, to flee or to stand his ground. He just sweated profusely, and the physical stains of the sweat are a very permanent reminder of his bravery and also his human reaction to the fact that he was about to die. And that's terribly moving, and I think very important that that be preserved.

Missing remains

That focus on the remains of holy men and women, and the physical objects they left behind, is a distinctly Catholic trait, and one many non-Catholics find difficult to understand. It led to a curious twist in the story of the other modern saint who has often featured in *Sunday*'s broadcasts: the nineteenth-century theologian and convert Cardinal John Henry Newman.

For the last years of his life, Newman lived at the Birmingham Oratory – a community of priests he had established in England's second city – and when he died in 1890 he was buried at Rednal, a rural area just outside the city limits. His resting place was chosen in obedience to his wish to share a grave with his close friend Ambrose St John, a Catholic priest who had, like Newman himself, converted to Catholicism. Those wishes were spelled out in unequivocal terms in an essay titled 'Written in the Prospect of Death', which included the declaration: 'I WISH, with all my heart, to be buried in Father Ambrose St. John's grave – and I give this as my last, my imperative will.'[2]

But in 2008, as his journey to canonisation looked increasingly secure, the Vatican ordered that the joint grave should be dug up so Newman's remains could be moved to the oratory that had been his home, available for veneration by the faithful. Roger Bolton explained what happened next in the *Sunday* broadcast on 9 November that year:

> *Last Sunday, an historic mass was held in Birmingham to mark the return of some of the remains of Cardinal John Henry Newman to the oratory there. This is widely seen as a step on the way to making the cardinal a saint. The exhumation of his remains was controversial, since Newman had asked – almost begged – in his will to be buried next to the person he loved more than anyone else, Fr Ambrose St John. They were united in life – why disturb them in death? Nevertheless, the Church ordered the exhumation to go ahead, and at last Sunday's service, relics of the cardinal were indeed displayed. But there were no remains. Nothing of his body has been found.*

The only items that survived in the grave were pieces of the 'coffin furniture' – handles and the like. Everything else had simply disappeared. The Church insisted that this could be explained by the acidic soil in which the cardinal was buried, and a report from the *Birmingham Post* at the time of his death suggests he may even have contributed to it himself. The paper recorded that:

> *The coffin was covered with mould of a softer texture than the marly stratum in which the grave is cut. This was done in studious and affectionate fulfilment of a desire of Dr Newman's which some may deem fanciful, but which sprang from his reverence for the letter of the Divine*

---

2 'XVI. The Sacred Heart', The National Institute for Newman Studies: https://www. newmanreader.org/works/meditations/meditations12.html (accessed 15 June 2023).

Word; which, as he conceived, enjoins us to facilitate rather than impede the operation of the law 'Dust thou art, and unto dust shalt thou return'.

But not everyone was willing to accept the official explanation for the mysterious disappearance of the body. *Sunday* broadcast a sceptical interview with a forensic archaeologist, Professor John Hunter.

John Hunter: *Well, it takes very exceptional burial circumstances to completely degrade human hard tissue. I'm an archaeologist. I've been an archaeologist for thirty-five years. And during that time, I've excavated human remains which have been in longer archaeological timescales and more recent forensic ones, as well as mass graves, where you get very different types of, very extreme types of, body preservation and decay. Very, very rarely do you find situations where the hard tissue has gone completely.*

Roger Bolton: *And in those circumstances – we're talking now just over 100 years, perhaps 120 years – is it too short a time for the unlikely case that everything disappears?*

John Hunter: *Well, it's not so much the timescale as the nature of the soils down there. You really need a very, very acidic sand – preferably with a lot of groundwater running through it – to decay the body completely. What normally happens is that the first things to go, if you like, are the wooden coffin and the soft tissue, followed by the metal attachments to the coffin and the fabrics. And then that gets down to the hard tissue, the skeleton itself. And that's what usually survives.*

Roger Bolton: *So the metal goes before the bone. So they found bits of the metal and they haven't found the bones, and you think that's significant?*

John Hunter: *Well, I think it's significant. I think it's rather, rather odd that the metal coffin plate and the handles which apparently survived should have survived and the skeleton has not survived.*

Newman and Romero could not, in many of the characteristics that made them famous, have been more different. The cardinal was an intellectual and a poet; the author of sublime works of the imagination such as *The Dream of Gerontius*, as well as learned theological polemics.

The archbishop was a reluctant revolutionary, and although he too had a great gift for words, he used them in a very different way; preaching the fiery sermons that almost certainly cost him his life. Newman spent much of his career in the academic ivory tower of Victorian Oxford (although he also quietly attended to the pastoral work required of a good priest), while Romero lived a grittier life, on intimate terms with the poverty and violence of Central America in the 1970s.

But both men were controversial in their lifetimes, and both remained so after their deaths. And the interviews broadcast on *Sunday* as they progressed through the Vatican system towards sainthood demonstrate that saint-making is a highly political process.

Sunday's coverage of the Romero story drew heavily on the views and experience of Julian Filochowski, who was the director of the Catholic charity CAFOD for twenty years, and came to know the archbishop through his early development work in Latin America. He became chair of the Archbishop Romero Trust, which campaigned for the archbishop's canonisation, and in one of his many appearances on *Sunday* he presented this appealing picture of the man he so much admired:

He was very self-effacing. He was very simple. He was very straightforward. But he was a man who was very close to the poor communities for whom he sought not only to be a good pastor but, as their causes were repressed, he sought to defend them and he preached the gospel. And he was a wonderful preacher, a wonderful orator, and he became a voice of truth; the person who articulated the truth of what was going on in his country.

When Romero was chosen to lead the Church in El Salvador in early 1977, his appointment was welcomed by the government and its allies in the military, and by the country's rich landowners. He was widely regarded as a conservative priest who would stay out of politics.

But in the March of that year, his close friend Fr Rutilio Grande, a Jesuit priest and prominent campaigner in defence of the rights of the poor, was murdered by a death squad. Two of Fr Grande's parishioners, who were with him in his car when it was attacked, were also killed. The deaths had a profound impact on the new archbishop.

Julian Filochowski: He was a conservative figure, and he'd been appointed because he would probably stop and halt the social involvement of the clergy. But he was going through a process of change himself; coming to terms with the poverty and repression he'd begun to see clearly. And Rutilio was a friend of his, a good friend of his. And the killing of Rutilio really jiggled this process of change into place. It suddenly became much clearer, and he was overwhelmed by it... He said, 'If they've done this to Rutilio, I must follow the same path.' It became a kind of turning point.

Thereafter, Romero deployed his skills as an orator in a series of sermons broadcast across the country on the Church's radio station. The last, on 23 March 1980, was especially powerful. 'I would like to make an appeal in a special way to the men of the army,' he declared, 'and in particular to the ranks of the *Guardia Nacional* [National Guard], of the police, to those in the barracks. Brothers, you are part of our own people. You kill your own *campesino* ['peasant'] brothers and sisters. And before an order to kill that a man may give, the law of God must prevail. It says, "Thou shalt not kill." No soldier is obliged to obey an order against the law of God.'[3]

In the febrile political circumstances of the time, with the country sliding into a long civil war between a right-wing government and leftist guerrillas, that was dynamite. The archbishop was effectively inciting mutiny in the name of God. He was assassinated the following day.

Beatification beckons

A cause for his beatification was opened in 1993, and in 1997 Pope John Paul declared him to be a 'Servant of God'. But Romero's progress towards canonisation became bogged down. Part of the problem was purely bureaucratic. The Church's saint-making rules required that the Congregation for the Causes of Saints (CCS), the Vatican body that oversees the process, should trawl through the extensive body of written material – mostly diaries and sermons – the archbishop had left behind.

---

3   E. Stourton, *Absolute Truth*, p. 107.

The CCS had to certify that he was free of heretical opinions before his cause could be advanced.

But Romero's campaigning for the rights of the poor also meant that the cause for his sainthood became caught up in the raw-edged Vatican debate over what was known as liberation theology. The idea that the gospel dictates a 'preferential option for the poor' (see chapter 2) was interpreted by many priests in Latin America as a licence to engage in secular politics – indeed, some even took up arms in left-wing guerrilla movements. For Pope John Paul, moulded by his own bitter experience of communism in Poland, left-wing politics of any kind were neuralgic.

Julian Filochowski reflected on the slow progress of Romero's cause in a 2015 *Sunday* interview with Mike Wooldridge, a BBC foreign and religious affairs correspondent who sometimes presented the programme.

Julian Filochowski: Yes, there were people that delayed it. There were self-appointed devil's advocates, mostly in the Curia [the Vatican civil service] *in Rome, who did all kinds of bureaucratic obstruction to the process going forward...*

Mike Wooldridge: Was he, in fact, as you saw it, a follower of the doctrine of liberation theology? I mean, many people thought that, initially at least, he was something more of a sort of quiet conservative himself.

Julian Filochowski: He was a man who made an option for the poor. That happened very clearly throughout those three years as archbishop. His theology has been described as a theology of the Beatitudes; some say theology of liberation. But he was not a proponent of liberation theology. Liberation theology claims him and sees him as a hero and icon. That was part of the reason for the blockage on his beatification. People felt that beatifying Romero was beatifying liberation theology – people who [had] spent much of their episcopal lives trying to stamp it out.

Romero was an equally divisive figure in the geopolitics of the Americas. The man identified by the United Nation's Truth Commission as the mastermind behind the archbishop's assassination, Roberto D'Aubuisson, was also a prominent far-right politician. He founded and led the ARENA party, and served as president of El Salvador's Constituent Assembly.

In 2011, the annual Oscar Romero Lecture in Britain was given by

Fr Juan Hernández Pico, a Jesuit theologian teaching at the Central American University in El Salvador. He had known Romero personally, and when he spoke to Jane Little on *Sunday* in the March of that year, he argued that Salvadorean politics had been a significant factor in the blockage of his friend's cause.

Juan Hernández Pico: I don't think his liking of the theology of liberation would have been an obstacle. I think the obstacle has been really the political earthquake that would have to take place for Romero to be canonised. It would mean that the founder of ARENA, the rightist party in power for twenty years, would have been declared the murderer of a saint.

Jane Little: Of course, America was very involved in this period. And I'm wondering what you think of President Barack Obama's visit to the site where Oscar Romero was gunned down this week. Was that a symbolic moment for you?

Juan Hernández Pico: Yes, I think so. The symbolic value for the people of El Salvador and, in general, for the people of Latin America and many parts of the world... of Obama having asked to be led to the tomb in the cathedral of Monsignor Romero and lighting a candle honouring him – I think it was a gesture of tremendous value. That was the nearest you could have hoped to a kind of apology for what Reagan's government and Bush Father's government did to prolong the war in El Salvador by aiding one part of it militarily.

Jane Little: Do you think President Obama's visit will also be a boost to the campaign to make Oscar Romero a saint?

Juan Hernández Pico: I think it will, although I don't think it's that important for that kind of issue, because the real opposition to Romero's canonisation is both in El Salvador and in the corridors of the Vatican, where there are streams of opinion that think that Romero is dangerous for the well-being of the Church in Latin America.

Another untimely death

In March 2005, the Vatican official responsible for Romero's cause announced that the candidate had come through the theological audit of his writings, and that this should have cleared the way for beatification; the next big step towards becoming a saint. But Pope John Paul died a few weeks after that announcement and the momentum was lost. Pope Benedict XVI, who succeeded John Paul, was an uncompromising opponent of liberation theology, and there was little progress during his time in office.

It was not until Pope Francis acceded to the throne of St Peter in 2013 that things really began to change. In August 2014, he stated in blunt terms that Romero's cause had been 'blocked for "prudential reasons", so they said' by the Congregation for the Doctrine of the Faith – the Vatican's doctrinal watchdog. 'There are no doctrinal problems,'[4] Francis declared, and ordered that Romero's progress to beatification should proceed apace. The archbishop was beatified in May 2015 and raised to the altars as a saint in October 2018.

The manner of Romero's beatification had important theological implications, which went well beyond his own cause. The traditional Catholic understanding of martyrdom was tightly drawn. Only those who chose to die rather than deny their faith were judged deserving of the title of 'martyr'. Romero, of course, had not explicitly made that choice, and he was assassinated for what were arguably political as much as religious reasons.

In a *Sunday* edition marking the beatification ceremony, Julian Filochowski laid out the significance of declaring Archbishop Romero a martyr. 'Pope Francis,' he said, 'I think wanted it clarifying… that being killed for doing what Jesus told us to do was not less valid and valuable than being killed for reciting the creed.'

Filochowski argued that the beatification was a 'recognition of his [Romero's] ministry and his preaching and teaching, which brought about his martyrdom' and pointed out that 'today, during the ceremony, one of the homilies said very clearly he was *defensor pauperum* ['defender of the poor']. He would be known as a defender of the poor, and thereby a model for bishops and for Christians everywhere.'

From his first days in office, Francis sought to redefine the Church's

---

4 'In-flight Press Conference of His Holiness Pope Francis from Korea to Rome', Vatican: https://www.vatican.va/content/francesco/en/speeches/2014/august/documents/papa-francesco_20140818_corea-conferenza-stampa.html (18 August 2014, accessed 15 June 2023).

priorities. Making Oscar Romero a saint was a very powerful way of signalling the kind of Church he wanted to create. In January 2022, he hammered the message home by beatifying Fr Rutilio Grande, the priest whose murder inspired Oscar Romero's campaigns for social justice. The two lay people who died with him were also declared 'Blessed'.

Newman's turn

If Oscar Romero was a saint made for the Francis Church, John Henry Newman was in many respects an equally good match for the reign of Pope Francis's predecessor, Benedict XVI. Like Newman, Joseph Ratzinger (as he was known before his election) spent much of his early life as an academic, and both men were admired for their learning and skill in theology. Even Cardinal Ratzinger's opponents during his years as prefect of the Congregation for the Doctrine of the Faith conceded his high intelligence. Cardinal Newman was the most famous convert from Anglicanism of the nineteenth century, which of course recommended him to a pope much concerned with the ebb of the Catholic faith in its European heartland.

English Catholics had long championed Newman's cause, and the Vatican first opened a file on the cardinal convert in 1958. His life and works were, like Romero's, subject to close scrutiny by the Congregation for the Causes of Saints, and in 1991 Pope John Paul declared him 'venerable'. But to be beatified, the next stage on the road to sainthood, Newman needed a proven miracle.

That requirement raised a problem. Newman's writings suggest he was sceptical about modern miracles. He questioned whether they were really necessary in a world that is already full of wonders: 'Now what truth would a miracle convey to you which you do not learn from the works of God around you?' he challenged his readers. 'What would it teach you concerning God which you do not already believe without having seen it?'[5]

Newman did not deny that miracles were possible, but he argued that events which had been judged miraculous in earlier and less scientifically

5   J. Cornwell, *Newman's Unquiet Grave: The reluctant saint* (London: A&C Black, 2011), p. 240.

advanced times might, in fact, have been natural phenomena. 'I frankly confess that the present advance of science tends to make it probable that various facts take place, and have taken place, in the order of nature, which hitherto have been considered by Catholics as simply supernatural.'[6]

'One wonders against this background,' writes the Newman biographer John Cornwell, 'what Newman would have made of the miracle in support of his own beatification.'[7] It was reported by Jack Sullivan, a deacon from Boston, who suffered a severely painful back condition. Mr Sullivan, who was in his seventies, explained what had happened to *Sunday*'s presenter Roger Bolton.

Jack Sullivan: There were five vertebrae in four discs between them that were squeezing my spinal cord, as well as the nerves to my leg. The MRIs revealed that there was a bulge in my spinal cord above and below this affected area. So I was in severe pain.

Roger Bolton: Now, when you were in intense pain, why did you pray to Cardinal Newman?

Jack Sullivan: I was in my second year of a four-year formation process to become a deacon in the Catholic Church. I was told earlier in the afternoon of the particular day in June of 2000 that I couldn't return to classes because I would need immediate surgery, and my recovery period would be many months. Being very despondent, I returned home and put on the television set to get my mind off this, and I turned on to a programme and there were two priests. One of them, Ian Ker, was talking about Cardinal Newman, and I knew something about him, so I listened to it. At the end of the programme, they put a, you might say, a sign on the screen [saying] that if you receive any divine favours from the intercession of Cardinal Newman, please contact the postulator for the cause in Birmingham, England. I wrote it down and inasmuch as I wrote it down, I thought, 'Well, I should pray to him.' I prayed that I might be able to return to classes and be ordained a deacon.

---

6   J. Cornwell, *Newman's Unquiet Grave*, p. 241.
7   J. Cornwell, *Newman's Unquiet Grave*, p. 242.

Roger Bolton: *So how quickly, after praying to Cardinal Newman, did you cease to feel pain?*

Jack Sullivan: *I got up the following morning without any pain whatsoever. So I returned to classes, and for eight months I felt no pain whatsoever. The interesting thing is that my condition hadn't changed, but yet I had no pain.*

Roger Bolton: *So has your condition changed now?*

Jack Sullivan: *OK. After my last class, the following day, the pain returned in full fury. I had the surgery in the August of 2001. I was told that, again, don't even consider returning to classes in about a month's time, because my recovery period would be eight months to a year. Within four days after the surgery, I prayed to Newman the same prayer I had before. And at that moment I felt an intense heat, a tingling feeling all over, that lasted for about ten minutes; a tremendous sense of confidence and a sense of peace. Immediately, the pain went away and I was able to walk perfectly. I was discharged that very moment.*

Roger Bolton: *Has the pain ever returned?*

Jack Sullivan: *No.*

Roger Bolton: *And if an MRI scan was carried out now, today, what would it show?*

Jack Sullivan: *It would show that I have the spine of a thirty-year-old man.*

Roger Bolton: *With no trace of any problems at all?*

Jack Sullivan: *No.*

It is worth underlining that the youthful condition of Mr Sullivan's spine was down to the surgery he'd had in 2001, and he did not credit Newman with the repair work done by his surgeon. Newman's miracle, if a miracle it was, lay in pain relief rather than surgery. That fold in the story notwithstanding, the Vatican's medical experts declared in 2008 that what had happened to Mr Sullivan was 'inexplicable', and Pope Benedict duly set Cardinal Newman on course for beatification.

Separated in death

It was at this point that the Church took the decision to exhume Newman's body and move it to the Birmingham Oratory. The row which then blew up – even before the work that revealed the puzzle of the disappearing bones begun – must surely have blindsided the Vatican. Pope Benedict was, notoriously, somewhat other-worldly about the social changes of the twenty-first century. The following discussion on *Sunday* was broadcast in August 2008.

Roger Bolton: Cardinal John Henry Newman is well on his way to becoming a saint in the Roman Catholic Church, and the Vatican wants to move his body to a splendid new tomb in the oratory in Birmingham. But there's a problem. Newman is buried in the same grave as his great friend Ambrose St John, and they share the same headstone. Newman wrote just before his death that 'this was my last, my imperative will'. There is no doubt that Newman loved St John above everyone else, and he wrote after his friend's death that: 'I have ever thought no bereavement was equal to that of a husband's or a wife's. But I feel it difficult to believe that any can be greater, or anyone's sorrow greater, than mine.'

So should Newman and St John be separated in death? Peter Tatchell, the gay rights activist, says not. He believes to do so would be an act of shameless dishonesty and personal betrayal by the gay-hating Catholic Church. I'm now joined by Mr Tatchell and by the Catholic journalist and former adviser to Cardinal Cormac Murphy-O'Connor, Austen Ivereigh. Good morning to you both. Austen Ivereigh, why do you think the Church is so intent on moving Newman's body?

Austen Ivereigh: Well, it's not making a great exception for Newman. Part of the process of the journey towards canonisation is that normally the remains of the saint [are] transferred to a suitable place – usually a church in a city where pilgrims can easily come and venerate the saint-to-be.

Roger Bolton: So do Newman's own wishes, clearly expressed in a note written before his death, count for nothing, then?

Austen Ivereigh: I'm afraid so, yeah. The process of becoming a saint involves all kinds of new departures. I mean, Pope John Paul II asked to be buried in Poland, but I don't think he seriously expected that to happen.

Roger Bolton: Now, Peter Tatchell, you think there's more to it than that, don't you?

Peter Tatchell: *Well, this isn't a* gay rights *issue, it's a* human rights *issue. I'd ask any of your listeners to imagine how they would feel if the Church demanded that the body of their deceased loved one was moved on its orders, against that deceased person's wishes, they would be horrified, and I think that we owe it to Newman to ensure that his wishes are carried out. He wanted to be buried for eternity with the man he loved, Ambrose St John, and the reason the Catholic Church is doing this is because they don't want to acknowledge that Cardinal Newman loved a man.*

Roger Bolton: *Austen Ivereigh?*

Austen Ivereigh: *Well, it's just nonsense. I mean, I don't think anybody disputes that Cardinal Newman deeply loved Ambrose St John as he did, particularly him. But there were also two other companions who were with him in the early days, whom he always remembered and always felt very, very close to. And indeed, the quote, Roger, that you gave at the beginning; I mean, he did say after St John died – he predeceased him by some fifteen years – the grief is comparable to that of a husband losing a wife or a wife losing a husband. But by that, he did not mean that the relationship with Ambrose St John was a marriage, or was like what we would now call a same sex-relationship or a gay relationship. And it's just simply wrong to read back from today's categories into the Victorian period, where these kinds of very intense, very passionate, but totally celibate, relationships between people in Oxford and members of the clergy, particularly the Anglo-Catholic clergy, were very common.*

Roger Bolton: *Peter Tatchell, is there any evidence that the relationship was a sexual one, a physically expressed one?*

Peter Tatchell: *Being gay is not just a sexual orientation; it's also an emotional and psychological orientation... We don't know whether Ambrose St John and Cardinal Newman had a sexual relationship. What we do know is that they lived together for half a century. They loved each other. They acted like a husband and wife. Their love for each other was absolutely extraordinary. And the expressed wish of Cardinal Newman was that he'd be buried for eternity with Ambrose St John. We cannot go against that. Well, we can, and the Vatican Church is trying to go against his wishes. But I think morally and ethically we have a duty to carry out and ensure that Cardinal Newman's wishes are respected.*

That's just elementary human decency for anybody who has died, and for anyone who has expressed a view about what should happen to their body after their death.

Austen Ivereigh: *But come on, this is opportunistic, isn't it? I mean, Peter Tatchell is only taking up cudgels on behalf of Newman and saying that his will should be respected because he's trying to make this into a gay relationship. I mean, that's what the purpose of Peter Tatchell's intervention is all about, and it's simply wrong to try to claim every intense, non-heterosexual relationship as being gay. I mean, of course people know spinster aunts who live together. People who lose, indeed, a loved pet can often experience a grief which is very, very profound. And nobody questions, and certainly not the Catholic Church, that this was a very deep and very, very profound friendship. But it simply was not a gay relationship. It was not a same-sex relationship. And Newman himself would simply not have recognised that idea. I mean, a gay relationship in today's terms means something which consciously emulates a marriage between a man and a woman, or that kind of relationship. That's not what Cardinal Newman had, and I think he can do without this kind of 'fellow traveller' opportunism on his way to sainthood.*

Peter Tatchell: *I haven't raised this issue. This issue has been raised by the Catholic Church, which has decided to pursue a cruel, insensitive act of grave robbery and desecration to violate a person's will. What I'm saying is that a person's will, as clearly expressed, should be respected. And the Catholic Church is not doing that. And I'm sure that even the majority of Catholics find this very offensive. I don't know what the Catholic view is, but the* Church Times *is currently conducting a poll, which so far isn't complete. But so far over eighty per cent of readers of the* Church Times *say that this is wrong for the Vatican to disinter Cardinal Newman against his expressed wishes. That's a Christian point of view, briefly.*

A special ceremony

Newman was beatified the following year, and the ceremony was the high point of Pope Benedict's visit to Britain that autumn (see chapter 2). *Sunday* marked the moment with an outside broadcast on the morning of 19 September 2009.

Saint-making

Edward Stourton: *Welcome to Cofton Park, the scene later this morning for an unprecedented event in British history. For the first time on British soil, a pope will preside at a service of beatification. John Henry Newman will be accorded the title 'Blessed'. It's the Roman Catholic Church's way of saying that it believes he has secured a place in heaven. There's been a light rain falling early this morning, but the clouds are breaking up in a promising way. And I've been watching an apparently never-ending procession of coaches bringing pilgrims up the road just over there at the side of the park. A heavy-hitting line-up of theologians, bishops, historians and commentators will be joining me here... and we'll be discussing the legacy of Cardinal Newman, the figure at the heart of today's events. But first, let's join Jane Little, who is deep in the throng of the congregation. Morning, Jane.*

Jane Little: *Morning. I am indeed, Edward. I'm actually perched on a small hilltop, competing for shelter under a cluster of trees here alongside thousands of other people who began arriving in the dark as early as 3 a.m. Up to 60,000 are expected here today. So far, a very civilised crowd seated on camping chairs and opening tinfoil with sandwiches in them, eating their breakfast. We're looking down upon a large white stage, and at the centre of it [is] an eight-foot-high papal chair designed and made by the teachers at Cardinal Newman [Catholic] School. It is very much his day. And I'm joined now by Fr Daniel Seward of the Oxford Oratory, one of three English oratories inspired by Newman.*

Fr Seward, a big day for a man who surely shunned the idea of becoming a saint.

Daniel Seward: *I suppose that's part of the qualification. Newman didn't think that he was a saint, but in the end he's the son of the Church. And so he'd be happy to do what the Church says by being beatified today.*

Jane Little: *And how important is it for you today?*

Daniel Seward: *Well, Newman founded the English Oratory, and he's the towering figure of nineteenth-century English Catholicism. And so he gives us heart today to be able to be bold in speaking our faith, as he was in his time.*

Newman may have deprived his oratory of bodily relics by disappearing so completely into his grave, but the community there made a shrine of

65

his room as soon as he died – just as Oscar Romero's study half a world away in San Salvador was preserved. The *Sunday* outside broadcast included a recorded item from the Birmingham Oratory.

Edward Stourton: At the Birmingham Oratory, where he spent much of his later life, they've kept his room exactly as it was when he died. Father Richard Duffield, who's currently in charge at the oratory, took me there... And here we are. It's quite dark. The curtains are all drawn. There are bookshelves lining the side of the fireplace here on my right, and in the middle of the room, a desk. And this is exactly as it would have been when he died.

Richard Duffield: Yes, it's exactly as it was. We've dusted, but otherwise we've not done very much.

Edward Stourton: What's the paper stuck to the cupboard over here?

Richard Duffield: It's a newspaper cutting from the Birmingham Post *of September 1884, and it shows General Gordon's campaign in Sudan* [Charles Gordon, a British army officer, was killed when Khartoum fell to the Muslim religious leader known as the Mahdi], *which Newman was following, like almost everybody else, with wracked fascination. But what Newman didn't know was that General Gordon was also interested in Newman. And he had in his pocket – in fact, it was there, I think, when he was shot – a copy of* The Dream of Gerontius. *So after Gordon died, the copy of* The Dream of Gerontius *was sent back here to the oratory.*

Here, beside his altar on the right, you can see lots of pictures of his friends who'd died. And he kept them there so that he only had to turn his head when he was saying Mass to bring them to mind.

Edward Stourton: What do you make of some of the controversies that have been about his friendship with Ambrose St John, in particular?

Richard Duffield: To eroticise any kind of friendship in the way that some people would like to, say about Newman and St John, is very diminishing of what friendship is all about.

Sunday's 'heavy-hitting line-up' of commentators had very different views on the meaning of Newman's beatification. The Cambridge scholar Professor Eamon Duffy dismissed Jack Sullivan's pain relief as 'a strange miracle', but said that 'for most people who have a devotion to Newman, the miracle doesn't matter'.

Eamon Duffy: I think what's being done today is the beatification of the most luminous Christian intelligence of the last 300 or 400 years. Some years ago, the English bishops attempted to have Newman made a 'doctor of the Church', bypassing the process of canonisation – because canonisation, in a way, wasn't Newman's style. I have no doubt that he's in heaven and that he's a transcendentally good man, though he wasn't always a very agreeable man. But he disliked this style of religion himself. When he first became a Catholic, he did his best to fit in with it. He went off to Naples and was very interested in the liquefaction of a Neapolitan saint's blood [the fourth-century martyr St Januarius is the patron saint of Naples, and a sample of his blood, preserved in an ampoule, is said to return to a liquid state three times a year]. *But it just wasn't his style. He found it all, in the end, a bit Italian. And what he liked was a more sober, moderate kind of Catholicism.*

Because Newman had been such a significant figure in the Anglican Church before his conversion to Catholicism, the panel included a Church of England scholar. Dr Frances Knight, associate professor of Religious Studies at the University of Nottingham, noted that the beatification was taking place at a time when a number of Church of England priests were considering conversion to Catholicism (over the issue of women's ordination, see chapter 6). Her suspicions were emphatically rejected by Kieran Conry, then the Roman Catholic bishop of Arundel and Brighton.

Frances Knight: I think there is a feeling among some Anglicans that there is politics behind this – to present Newman as the kind of, you know, model for Anglican converts at a time when there are obviously large numbers, or some numbers, of people who may be thinking of moving. But I think the point to make is actually that the campaign to beatify Newman really predates recent moves.

Edward Stourton: Well, let's ask Bishop Kieran Conry about that. Is there, somewhere in the back of the minds of the Vatican, the idea that Newman might lead other Anglicans over?

Kieran Conry: I guess I would say the two issues are not connected at all.
Edward Stourton: [It] just happens to happen at this particular moment…
Kieran Conry: I don't think the Vatican plots and plans that carefully.

Bishop Conry suggested that for many of those who had come to watch the ceremony, 'Newman is quite a distant figure.' He argued that the pope, and not the soon-to-be Blessed theologian, was the real star of the day's show. 'I don't think many people have access to Newman at all in their hearts and minds,' he said. 'If the pope weren't here – because the pope doesn't normally beatify people, he'd send some cardinal to do it – …we wouldn't have 60,000 pilgrims here.'

Eamon Duffy, however, who made the final contribution to the discussion, set Newman's significance rather higher. He sketched a picture of Blessed John Henry as a prophet, and perhaps unsurprisingly – he was of course an Oxbridge don himself – praised his scholarly character:

I think that Newman's importance is that many of his key ideas came to fruition in the twentieth century. He anticipated a great deal of the reconfiguring of Catholicism; its rediscovery of the laity, for example, the importance of the people of God. And so what's being done is, he's getting the stamp of approval on a questing intellect, which is also profoundly Catholic. It's unafraid to explore, but from the firm base of commitment to the Church.

Newman completed his journey to the altars in October 2019. He was canonised in St Peter's Square a year, almost to the day, after Oscar Romero.

4

Zimbabwe's long struggle

In 1963, Revd Ndabaningi Sithole helped to found the Zimbabwe African National Union (ZANU) to fight for an end to white minority rule in what was then called – on British colonial maps, at least – Southern Rhodesia. It was a hugely consequential moment in Zimbabwe's long struggle. One of Revd Sithole's co-founders was Robert Mugabe, who later ruled the country for thirty-seven years, and ZANU-PF (Patriotic Front) – formed after a split with the original ZANU – is still the dominant force in Zimbabwean politics today.

Revd Sithole, who was ordained a Congregational Methodist Church minister after studying in the United States, paid dearly for his involvement in politics. ZANU was banned by Ian Smith's white minority government in 1964. Sithole was arrested and spent ten years in jail, sharing a cell with Mugabe for a period.

In 1965, the Smith regime made its notorious Unilateral Declaration of Independence, refusing to bow to British and international pressure to move Southern Rhodesia towards majority rule, and the country descended into fifteen years of civil war. Britain and the United Nations imposed sanctions, and the Smith regime was eventually forced to accept that white minority rule could not be sustained. In 1978, Sithole – a free man again – agreed to serve in a transitional government with his old adversary, and in May that year he visited the United Kingdom.

Zimbabwe has been covered often and extensively by *Sunday* over the past half-century, and Revd Sithole's interview during that visit is the earliest surviving item on the story in the programme's archive.

Clive Jacobs: Since Mr Sithole spent a decade in prison at Mr Smith's behest, some express no small surprise that he was prepared to join

69

him in government. *Ted Harrison took the opportunity of his visit here to ask Mr Sithole if, as far as he was concerned, all had now been forgiven.*

Ndabaningi Sithole: *It is futile to spoil the good future of the country because of the past. By nature, and by my own Christian profession, I am not a man who lives in the past. I recognise [that] Mr Smith and I have been fighting very hard in the past, but that is all over. What is most important is for us to bury the past, accept the present and guide the country as well as we can to full independence on the 31st of December 1978.*

Ted Harrison: *Looking back in the past, what do you think was really the darkest moment that strained your own faith most?*

Ndabaningi Sithole: *Well, I would say the darkest moment in my life was being kept for so long in solitary confinement in prison. But I must say that, although materially I came out poorer... spiritually I came out a much richer man. I must say, if someone has no real vital faith under those circumstances, there is every chance that he would break down. I'm glad to say that my own faith sustained me during the dark years when I was in prison for ten years.*

Ted Harrison: *Did you in any way go into prison as a man with hatred in your heart and come out as a man prepared to look for an agreement and compromise?*

Ndabaningi Sithole: *No. I must say, hatred is a stranger in my heart. This is one of the things people often ask me. They say, 'Revd Sithole, how is it that you are able to sit across the same table with Mr Smith? Don't you feel bitter when you see him?' The truth is, I don't. We were fighting. It's a political fight. Now it's over, and we are getting on very fine.*

Ted Harrison: *Do you ever pray together?*

Ndabaningi Sithole: *We have not prayed together... partly because we do not meet under circumstances that warrant that.*

Ted Harrison: *Do you pray for each other?*

Ndabaningi Sithole: *We pray indeed for each other. There can be no doubt about that. After all, a human life is more than a particular individual. We belong together. We belong to the same human family. And one of the things I like most with our policies is that we believe – in thought, word and deed – in non-racialism. We believe human beings are human* *beings, first and foremost. We believe everyone was made in the image of God. We believe that we derive our very humanity from that very fact that all of us were made in the image of God, and that God is the universal Father, and that we are universal brothers.*

Revd Sithole was not the only leader from this period to mix religion and politics. Abel Muzorewa, who served as prime minister in the transitional government, was a bishop of the United Methodist Church. Another Methodist minister, Revd Canaan Banana, became the country's first black president. Robert Mugabe himself had been educated by Jesuits, and remained a committed Catholic until his death.

Two Brits killed

Between eighty and ninety per cent of Zimbabweans are Christian,[1] and the prominence of ministers and bishops among Zimbabwe's black leadership reflected a long history of missionary activity in southern Africa. The month after that interview with Revd Sithole, *Sunday* broadcast a poignant reminder of the close ties between the region and religious organisations in Britain.

Many of Revd Sithole's former comrades refused to accept the legitimacy of the 1978–79 transitional government he joined, and both Robert Mugabe and Joshua Nkomo, who led the Zimbabwe African People's Union (ZAPU), continued to prosecute the war. On 7 June 1978, two British women were killed in a guerrilla raid on a Salvation Army institute near Bulawayo, the country's second city. This is how *Sunday* covered the story.

Clive Jacobs: On Friday, a Salvation Army official and the parents of the two Salvation Army women killed in Rhodesia left Heathrow to attend the funerals on Tuesday. In a rather emotional atmosphere, a number of senior army members went to the departure hall at the airport to give

---

1 '2020 Report on International Religious Freedom: Zimbabwe', U.S. Department of State: https://www.state.gov/reports/2020-report-on-international-religious-freedom/zimbabwe (12 May 2021, accessed 16 June 2023).

those parents their support. *They were Mr and Mrs Thompson, whose twenty-eight-year-old daughter Barbara* [Diane Barbara Thompson, referred to in the following interview as Diane] *was murdered this week, together with twenty-five-year-old Sharon, the daughter of Mr and Mrs Swindells. Both women were teachers at a missionary school in Rhodesia.*

According to one report, the six mission staff were ordered out of their houses, lined up, and then the guerrillas – thought to be members of Mr Nkomo's Zimbabwe African People's Union – opened fire indiscriminately. Barbara Thompson and Sharon Swindells died immediately. Just before he left Heathrow, Sharon's father, William Swindells, talked to Ann McNamara.

William Swindells: *My daughter was… just a wonderful daughter. Her whole life was so that she could serve or help others. She wanted to radiate, really, the experience that she had gained as a Christian.*

Ann McNamara: *Before she went out to Rhodesia, what was her work in Northern Ireland?*

William Swindells: *She was a teacher. She has a Bachelor of Education degree, specialising in religious education, sciences, mathematics. She taught for two years in one of the local schools in Belfast, and we really have been overwhelmed by the response of both the teachers and the pupils from the school… The school closed, and on Tuesday morning they will be holding a small service of their own on the day of the funeral in Rhodesia. The young people of the Salvation Army [in Rhodesia] and in Ireland will also be holding a remembrance service for her on Tuesday. In our absence, they have decided that they must give some recognition for the work and the association that she had as one of their colleagues in the work for the Lord.*

Ann McNamara: *How did she get the call to go and work in Rhodesia?*

William Swindells: *She wrote to the Salvation Army to offer her services as a teacher. Now, the Salvation Army have schools right around the world. She felt when she was at college that the Far East was her calling. But having written to the Salvation Army, they came back and said would she not consider Rhodesia because there was a desperate need. And she said no. She felt the Lord wanted her to go to the Far East, and three times she turned them down. Three times she refused, and the fourth* *year she just couldn't; she said it was definitely the right calling. So that, basically, is how Sharon got there. And it is our intention – as it is the intention of the other couple – that we leave both Sharon and Diane in Rhodesia, because they had both adopted the country as their own. The girls at the school – that was their family.*

Ann McNamara: *So obviously, you feel very distressed at what has happened. Are you bitter about how it has turned out?*

William Swindells: *Let me be very sure and let me, let us, tell the world that we're not bitter. No, no, we must not be. The unfortunate part for these young people that have been involved with this shooting of my daughter, they have not found the love, the greatness, that she was able to find...*

Clive Jacobs: *William Swindells. The deaths of Sharon Swindells and Barbara Thompson bring the total number of white missionaries killed in the Rhodesian civil war to nineteen.*

A temporary impasse

The fighting was finally brought to an end at the 1979 Lancaster House Conference in London. Mugabe and Nkomo agreed to a ceasefire in return for the right to participate in elections. Their country was temporarily returned to the status of a British colony, and a British governor, Sir Christopher Soames, was appointed to oversee the electoral process.

There were serious allegations of voter intimidation during the campaign, and Robert Mugabe's opponents called for his disqualification. Soames, however, refused that sanction on the grounds that it would make an orderly transition to black majority rule impossible. In February 1980, Mugabe was elected prime minister with sixty-three per cent of the vote.

The country's capital, Salisbury, was renamed Harare. Statues of Cecil Rhodes, the imperialist and diamond magnate who gave his name to Rhodesia, came down. But during his early years in power, Mugabe pursued moderate economic policies and stuck to the Lancaster House Agreement on the contentious issue of land reform. At independence, nearly forty per cent of Zimbabwe was held by some 6,000 white farmers. Mugabe agreed that for at least a decade there would be no forced seizure of white-owned land.

The first serious evidence of his dictatorial instincts came with what is now known as the *Gukurahundi*: a crackdown on dissent that began in 1982. The operation was conducted by his notorious Fifth Brigade, trained by North Koreans, and was directed at the people of Matabeleland – Joshua Nkomo's powerbase. *Gukurahundi* means 'the early season's rain that washes away the chaff' in Shona. It is now widely regarded as a genocide, and estimates put the number of dead at 20,000.

Robert Mugabe became Zimbabwe's president in 1997, and remained in power for the next twenty years. His regime grew increasingly repressive as time went on. In the 2002 parliamentary election, his party faced a serious challenge from the Movement for Democratic Change (MDC), led by Morgan Tsvangirai. The Zimbabwe Human Rights Forum reported that during the campaign of intimidation against MDC voters twenty-seven people were killed, there were some 2,500 assaults, and 10,000 people were displaced by violence.

Zimbabwe's economy began to falter in the 1990s, and the decline was exacerbated by violent invasions of white-owned farms, which began in the early 2000s and soon became a campaign, supported by President Mugabe himself. Dozens of white farmers were killed and many others abandoned their farms, which inevitably had an impact on agricultural production. In October 2003, Human Rights Watch reported that half the population was 'food insecure'. Zimbabweans began to leave the country in significant numbers, many of them seeking refuge in neighbouring South Africa.

In March 2007, Roger Bolton introduced a *Sunday* item on Zimbabwe as follows:

'*We Africans should hang our heads in shame. How can what is happening in Zimbabwe elicit hardly a word of concern, let alone condemnation from us, leaders of Africa?*' *That was Archbishop Tutu speaking this week after the assault on the opposition leader in Zimbabwe* [Morgan Tsvangirai] *at a prayer meeting, which left him in hospital with stitches to his head. Apart from the constant violations of human rights, most Zimbabweans are living on less than $2 a day. Eighty per cent are unemployed. Inflation is heading for*

4,000 per cent. In addition, twenty per cent of adults have HIV, one of the worst epidemics in the world.

Quiet diplomacy

Desmond Tutu's *cri de coeur* was directed first and foremost at his own government. Many capitals around the world were outraged by the conduct of the Mugabe regime, but South Africa's president, Thabo Mbeki, refused to condemn it publicly, preferring what he called 'quiet diplomacy' in the hope of persuading his Zimbabwean counterpart to change his ways.

Roger Bolton's guest on *Sunday* that morning took a rather different view of the South African leader's motivation. Rubin Phillip, bishop of Natal, was the first person of Indian heritage to hold that position, and had been a close friend of the anti-apartheid activist Steve Biko, killed in police custody in 1977.

He told Roger Bolton: 'I think it's a tragedy that he [President Mbeki] hasn't been speaking more forcefully. His so-called [quiet] diplomacy has certainly not helped the situation. If anything, there's greater poverty there, there's more violence, there's a greater sense of hopelessness.'

Roger Bolton: Do you know why he hasn't spoken out? Because the rest of the world, and the British government of course, have been asking him to take the lead in asking the African Union to take the lead on this. Why do you think that President Mbeki has not spoken out before now in a much clearer way?

Rubin Phillip: I wish I knew, but I think part of it has to do with the fact that Mugabe was a liberation icon. But the other part has to do with the fact, I think, that Mugabe is black. And given Mbeki's stand on black development, I think [he feels] if he criticises Mugabe, then he is being disloyal to that African cause.

Roger Bolton: Despite the evidence that, far from development going on in Zimbabwe, everything is regressing? Every statistic you look at is a disaster. Unemployment eighty per cent, life expectancy down dramatically.

Rubin Phillip: *It is more than that. We have over a million Zimbabwean refugees living in our country, and our Department of Home Affairs is not treating them with any sort of justice. I mean, these are people who also suffer in this country. So the situation is not only bad in Zimbabwe itself, but has serious implications for our own country and other neighbouring countries.*

Roger Bolton: *And do you think the churches themselves in South Africa can play a larger role? Can you take an initiative which will help end this torture of the people of Zimbabwe?*

Reuben Phillip: *Yes, we can. Unfortunately, the Church in South Africa – and it saddens me to say this – has tended to mouth government policy, and that's a great sadness. It needs to break ranks with the government. It needs to be more prophetic in its pronouncements. It needs to say, 'Whatever the politics of it all, there are people – our sisters and brothers, our neighbours – who are suffering. And as a Church we can no longer remain silent or have our hands tied behind our backs.' The world knows that the Church played such a critical role in this country in bringing about a new political dispensation. And it needs to rise once more from its lethargy and its compliance with existing governments, and begin to do something about the situation.*

Desmond Tutu had recently retired as archbishop of Cape Town by this stage, but he was, unusually, awarded the title 'archbishop emeritus', as his role during the struggle against apartheid had given him enormous moral authority. He turned his fire on the Anglican Church in Zimbabwe as well as his own government. Two months after Bishop Phillip's interview, Desmond Tutu was in Britain to unveil a stained-glass window commissioned in honour of Archbishop Trevor Huddleston, one of the giants of the anti-apartheid movement, and he spoke to *Sunday*'s Trevor Barnes.

Desmond Tutu: *Yes, I am sad. And I think a lot of people would be distressed that we have seemed to forget the tradition of our Church. I mean, the Anglican Church in the old Rhodesia was one of those in the forefront of opposition, and some of the bishops were... incredibly*

76

courageous people. And you would have thought that people would say, 'We want to emulate them.' But one wishes that the Anglican Church out there had been slightly more vocal.

Excommunication for pro-government bishop

The Anglican Church in Zimbabwe during this period was preoccupied with its own internal divisions, which had been created by the pressure of the Mugabe regime. Nolbert Kunonga, appointed bishop of Harare and Mashonaland in 1997 (the year of Mugabe's elevation to the presidency), was an enthusiastic Mugabe supporter, and tried to withdraw Zimbabwe's Anglican Church from the Province of Central Africa, where the regime faced frequent criticism.

He was officially excommunicated by the province in 2008, but continued a bitter fight in the Zimbabwean courts to secure ownership of the Church's assets. In January 2008, *Sunday* broadcast an interview with a senior member of the Zimbabwean hierarchy.

Roger Bolton: There are fears this morning in Zimbabwe that Anglican services will once more be interrupted, and priests and parishioners arrested. That is what happened in more than twenty churches last Sunday to some of those who opposed the former bishop of Harare and supporter of President Mugabe, Nolbert Kunonga. He ceased to be bishop of Harare in the eyes of the Anglican Communion when he attempted to withdraw his Church from the Anglican Province of Central Africa. He has since announced the creation of a new independent Anglican Church of Zimbabwe, naming himself as archbishop. Earlier this week, the archbishop of Canterbury, Dr Rowan Williams, condemned the use of state machinery to intimidate Kunonga's opponents and pledged support for his replacement.

Last night I talked to the bishop of Central Zimbabwe, Ishmael Mukuwanda, who is on a visit to this country. I asked him why he thought the riot police intervened last week.

Ishmael Mukuwanda: I think it's quite clear that it happened because many people have made up their minds where they want to belong.

77

And I think the majority of parishes in Harare have decided to belong to the Church of the Province of Central Africa, but they are now being forced, as we see it, to follow Bishop Kunonga. But you can't force people to follow whom they don't want to follow. And I think we are waiting to see what will happen tomorrow, and the few Sundays following, and see whether they will continue to force people to go against their will.

Roger Bolton: *And has Bishop Kunonga himself, has he been appearing in churches and saying effectively, I am still the bishop?*

Ishmael Mukuwanda: *Yes, that's what he is saying. And that's the statement he has made. And he still he continues to visit churches as if nothing has happened. As far as he is concerned, he is the one who is in charge.*

Roger Bolton: *And what will happen to the Church property? Will he be able to effectively take possession of all the churches in Zimbabwe?*

Ishmael Mukuwanda: *That is the bone of contention at the moment, because that's the issue that is in the courts, and we have to wait and see what will happen. He contends that he owns the property, but the property belongs to the Church of the Province of Central Africa.*

Roger Bolton: *Now, the archbishop of Canterbury, Rowan Williams, has pledged his solidarity with Christians in Zimbabwe, and those opposed to Bishop Kunonga. What other support do you think could be given by the wider Anglican Communion?*

Ishmael Mukuwanda: *I think somebody somewhere needs to declare that the province that he has formed has got no relationship with the Anglican Communion.*

Roger Bolton: *Now, it's obviously a very difficult and dangerous situation for Christians within Zimbabwe. As the bishop of Central Zimbabwe, what do you say to your members, to your congregations? Do you say to them they should actively oppose the president, or what?*

Ishmael Mukuwanda: *I always want to make a division between politics and the Church. And what I normally tell the people of Central Zimbabwe is that, you know, they really need to live by their faith and by their Christian beliefs.*

Roger Bolton: *But putting that into practice in the particular circumstances in Zimbabwe at the moment, does that mean standing up for things which the president opposes?*

Ishmael Mukuwanda: Yes. I think that, in a nutshell, that's what it means.

Wrenched from the altar

In the first round of that year's presidential election, Morgan Tsvangirai of the MDC won more support than Mugabe, but since neither secured over fifty per cent of the vote, the contest went to a second round. The intimidation of MDC supporters became so intense that on 22 June, just five days before the final ballot was due to take place, Tsvangirai decided not to contest it.

The Anglican Church, now clearly identified as part of the opposition in Zimbabwe, became caught up in the violence. Here's Rowan Williams, then archbishop of Canterbury, speaking to *Sunday* early that June about the attacks on Anglican churches.

Rowan Williams: I think in the last two weeks it's really got quite a bit more serious. We've heard news of... a Mothers' Union meeting being broken up with violence. We've also, of course, heard of the continuing barricading of churches against the legitimate congregations there by, one supposes, government-backed forces.

I spoke earlier in the week to a couple of bishops in the region, and it's very clear that the situation has deteriorated for the Church – the Anglican Church – very, very sharply in the last couple of weeks. And they're very eager that we should let people know that this is happening.

Trevor Barnes: And you've framed your request in terms of individuals being wrenched away from the altar rail. Is it that bad?

Rowan Williams: Well, that's what we hear... And certainly, the breaking up of the Mothers' Union meeting that I referred to had that element to it. And there was physical violence involved.

Trevor Barnes: Is there anything that the Anglican Communion, either in Africa or worldwide or here in Britain, can actually do?

Rowan Williams: The bishops in Zimbabwe are now, of course, appealing for rather louder support from elsewhere, and that's where, of course, the Church in South Africa has been and continues to be very important. That's why I contacted this week the archbishop of Cape Town to see if he and I could speak together on this, simply because he's there in the region. And his predecessor and he himself have been very active in keeping people's attention focused on the Zimbabwean situation. Now, it would be good also if some of the other African primates could weigh in on this, because it's so easy for it to be represented as just a colonial matter – as President Mugabe is always eager to do. So it's of the greatest importance that people in the region, in the continent, say what they have to say about this.

The Roman Catholic Church in Zimbabwe represents only a small minority (less than ten per cent of the population, while nearly seventy per cent are members of Protestant denominations), but by far the most effective religious voice against Robert Mugabe in the early years of this century belonged to the Catholic archbishop of Bulawayo. As a member of the Ndebele people – the group targeted by Mugabe's *Gukurahundi* genocide – Pius Ncube was an instinctive opponent of the regime, and he began speaking out publicly not long after his installation as archbishop. *Sunday* broadcast this profile by the BBC reporter Shazia Khan in 2007.

Shazia Khan: *For years he's been a fierce critic of Robert Mugabe. In the early eighties, Pius Ncube witnessed the massacre of 20,000 people in Matabeleland, and later watched with horror as his country descended into dictatorship. He became archbishop of Bulawayo in 1998, and soon decided enough was enough. He would have to speak out. He explained the turning point for him in a Radio 4 interview four years ago.*

Pius Ncube: *Around the year 2000, round about April, a farmer was killed not far from Bulawayo whose funeral I attended, and I felt that Mugabe had become now evil. I brought together my priests. I told them, 'I'm taking a stand now.'*

Shazia Khan: *Pius Ncube regularly challenged Robert Mugabe and attacked him as a murderous and corrupt dictator. Kate Hoey, Labour MP and chair of the All-Party Parliamentary Group on Zimbabwe, says Ncube's contribution as a voice of resistance cannot be underestimated.*

Kate Hoey: *He's been a figurehead for people who have not been involved in party politics, and he's been someone who the Churches internationally* *have been able to look to as a voice who has been standing up to Mugabe. I think he symbolised, for me, the bravery of people to stand up to the regime.*

In the run-up to the 2005 parliamentary election, Ncube accused the Mugabe regime of deliberately denying food aid to rural supporters of the opposition party, MDC. Predicting that the poll would be fixed, he declared: 'I hope people get so disillusioned that they really organise against this government and kick him [Mr Mugabe] out by non-violent popular mass uprising,'[2] and he cited the Orange Revolution in Ukraine as an example to be followed. Mugabe's information minister responded by calling the Archbishop a 'mad, inveterate liar'.[3]

Stitched up?

Two years later, Ncube suffered a spectacular fall from grace. He was sued for adultery and, in September 2007, images said to show him in his bedroom with his lover were broadcast on Zimbabwean television and published in the press. Many observers believed he had been deliberately stitched up by the regime.

Basildon Peta, a reporter based in South Africa, told *Sunday* that when lawyers for the aggrieved husband in the case served a summons on the archbishop, they were accompanied by the state media: 'Immediately after they handed over the summons, they produced the videotapes, which they played on a laptop. It all showed that they had been working on this for a very, very long time.'

Whatever the truth of the story, Pius Ncube concluded that his position was untenable, and resigned. Immediately afterwards he gave a defiant interview to the BBC World Service reporter Dan Damon, which was broadcast on *Sunday* on 23 September 2007.

2   A. Penketh, 'Mugabe condemns Archbishop who called for mass uprising as "halfwit"', *The Independent*: https://www.independent.co.uk/news/world/africa/mugabe-condemns-archbishop-who-called-for-mass-uprising-as-halfwit-530322.html (29 March 2005, accessed 16 June 2023).

3   J. Vasagar, 'Mugabe attacks 'half-wit' archbishop', *The Guardian*: https://www.theguardian.com/world/2005/mar/29/zimbabwe.jeevanvasagar (29 March 2005, accessed 16 June 2023).

Pius Ncube: *This was the evil plan of the government to try and isolate me and cut me off from the human rights drive in the country. They're trying to break me. They're trying to hurt me. That hasn't succeeded; their evil plans of trying to break me. I will not fear them. I refuse to be threatened by them. I refuse to be intimidated. I refuse to bow to their pressures in any way, because when you bow to that person, that tells you they... have got you where they want you. So this is my country. I'm free to speak and to criticise the evil things which are... causing so much trauma among the people.*

Dan Damon: *When you talk about 'evil plans', what do you mean? What have they done to you?*

Pius Ncube: *They've accused me of adultery. They haven't proved it.*

Damon challenged the archbishop over the apparently incriminating video. Ncube insisted he couldn't discuss it because 'it's under law and my lawyers are still dealing with it'. He also refused the invitation to issue a flat denial of the allegations against him. But he insisted:

> *There is no loss of moral high ground. The thing is that, for them, they are trying to divert people's attention because people are extremely angry. People are starving here. More and more people leave the country. Fuel has become impossibly expensive, and there are very few cars on the road. The very essentials of livelihood are not there. And so, because they are failing to provide this, they must then try and get people's attention diverted to things that are unessential.*

In 2016, Nehanda Radio, a Zimbabwean station based in the United Kingdom, reported that Ncube was 'set to bounce back'. A group of Bulawayo citizens were pushing to have him made an archbishop emeritus – giving him the status enjoyed by his Anglican colleague, Desmond Tutu. But he never did regain the 'moral high ground' he had once enjoyed.

Mugabe out

Mugabe held on to power for a full decade after the Ncube affair. When he was finally forced out, the deed was done by members of his own ZANU party, not by clerical critics.

In November 2017, Mugabe sacked his senior vice-president, Emmerson Mnangagwa, fuelling speculation that he intended to name his wife Grace as his successor. It proved a step too far for the rest of the ZANU leadership, and on 15 November the president was placed under house arrest. The news brought the people of Zimbabwe out onto the streets in celebration the following day. Dr Shingi Munyeza, then the senior pastor at the Faith Ministries Centre Church, a Pentecostal church in Harare, described the scene for *Sunday* on 17 November 2017.

Shingi Munyeza: *Yesterday was an unbelievable day. I was part of those who walked from Highfields, which is one of the townships in Harare, to the city centre. It was… just like a sea of people. And we were all just marching and celebrating and declaring that we need a fresh start. And I saw a lot of hope being ignited amongst the people, young and old. I mean, we had old people, old ladies, walking. And actually, they're going to have to walk back the same distance, which is about ten kilometres…*

Edward Stourton: *It's still a bit uncertain exactly what's going to happen. What are you going to say during today's service?*

Shingi Munyeza: *I think that for us as believers it is that this whole matter is in the hands of God. I don't believe that God would have allowed what happened yesterday only to reverse this momentum. I don't believe that. So that's the position that we are taking.*

The BBC's correspondent in Harare, Shingai Nyoka, told the same morning's *Sunday* that the president's fate would be settled at a meeting of the ZANU leadership:

The central committee is expected to meet, where they will recall him and strip him of the title of president of the party and also recommend that he be stripped of his position as the head of state. And so, over the next few days, we are likely to see a process. And if he doesn't resign, the parliament, ZANU-PF in parliament, will begin the process of impeaching him. They have stressed that they wanted to give him a dignified exit, but they say that if he does refuse to resign, his exit might be less dignified.

Nyoka also reported that the president had called on his Catholic contacts in his hour of need.

Shingai Nyoka: President Robert Mugabe is a practising Catholic. He and his family normally travel to Rome to take part in Communion services, and he takes his religion – the practice of his religion – very seriously. A Fr Fidelis Mukonori has been roped in to mediate between the generals and President Mugabe. This is the second meeting that he is mediating in. He is also the family chaplain. He celebrates Communion… and also takes President Mugabe's confession. He's been very close with the family. He has strong ties to the state, and he is also very close to many political figures in the country. He is authoritative and is seen as somebody who might be able to broker some kind of agreement between the two warring parties.

Edward Stourton: Is that a purely personal thing, or is the Catholic Church, as an institution, involved at all?

Shingai Nyoka: It appears as if it's personal – that he was brought in because President Mugabe trusts him. He's been an adviser to the president before, and he was seen as the one person who might be able to broker an agreement, and who President Mugabe would listen to.

It is not clear whether Fr Mukonori – a Jesuit who had known Mugabe since the mid-1970s – was responsible for the deal that was finally done. Mugabe resisted resignation right up until the moment that impeachment proceedings began in the Zimbabwean parliament. He secured immunity from prosecution for himself and his family, the right to preserve his business interests and a pay-off reported to be as much as $10 million. Mugabe died in hospital in Singapore in September 2019.

5

Abuse and the Irish Church

The sheer weight of material relating to reports of abuse in the *Sunday* archive tells its own sorry story. The way that children and young people have been subjected to violence and abusive sex within religious organisations has often dominated the programme's agenda since the turn of the century.

And the same themes constantly recur in the coverage. Victims were not listened to, and leaders lied and covered up. Institutions resisted change, and sometimes sought to minimise compensation payments. In many cases, the truth was dragged out by the press and the secular authorities in the face of determined opposition from the Churches, and the often agonisingly slow process caused further pain and deepened distrust. The damage done has been incalculable; touching not only the individuals and organisations concerned, but the standing of religion itself.

The Catholic Church in Ireland was overwhelmed by a veritable tsunami of abuse scandals, and this chapter will focus on Ireland because it so clearly illustrates many aspects of the wider abuse story – including both the seriousness and extent of past crimes, and the deep and enduring changes the scandals have brought in their wake. Ireland's religious and political landscape has since been transformed.

The dam began to break in 1991, when four siblings in Belfast's profoundly Catholic Falls Road reported abuse by Fr Brendan Smyth, a priest in the Norbertine Order. He was arrested by the Royal Ulster Constabulary (as Northern Ireland's police service was then known), but absconded from bail. He headed across the border and sought refuge in his order's Kilnacrott Abbey in County Cavan. The authorities in Northern Ireland applied for his extradition, but the case was so badly handled that it led to the fall of the Labour–Fianna Fáil coalition government in 1994. As a result, clerical abuse became a political issue very early in the Irish story. Thereafter, the Dublin government became a central player in deciding how abuse allegations should be managed.

When Brendan Smyth finally appeared in court in Belfast, he was convicted of forty-three cases of sexual assault on children and sentenced to four years in jail. A subsequent conviction for a further twenty-six charges led to a three-year sentence, which he was able to serve concurrently. On his release he was immediately rearrested and extradited to the Irish Republic, where, in 1997, he was convicted of seventy-four cases of abuse over a thirty-five-year period. He died of a heart attack that same year, just a month into his twelve-year sentence but, as we shall see, his grim record continued to haunt the Catholic hierarchy.

The Ryan Report

Most of the material in the *Sunday* archive relates to the turn of the first and second decades of the century. Without a doubt, 2009 was an *annus horribilis* for the Catholic Church in Ireland, because it was marked by the publication of two weighty, government-commissioned reports into abuse.

The first, the Ryan Report, looked at abuse in government institutions for children – which meant reformatory schools for young people who had got into trouble and so-called industrial schools for destitute orphans and children. Because the Church was so central to every aspect of life in the Irish Republic, all these institutions were run by religious orders such as the Sisters of Mercy and the Christian Brothers. The report into their management of the schools was compiled by the Commission to Inquire into Child Abuse, established by Bertie Ahern's coalition government in 2000.

The decision to set up the commission was driven largely by a steady drip of media revelations in the 1990s – notably in the *States of Fear* television series made by the writer and journalist Mary Raftery for the state broadcaster *RTÉ*. She spoke to *Sunday* on 17 May 2009, when the programme previewed the Ryan Report, which was due to be published the following week.

Roger Bolton: *How widespread was the abuse?*

Mary Raftery: *Well, it was very widespread, is the simple answer to that. I mean, at this stage, hundreds of individuals have come forward and spoken of the trauma they suffered growing up in these institutions. These were not ordinary day schools. They were residential institutions, where children who were in need of care – who were destitute or who were orphaned – were put. And a system grew up in Ireland, in the middle decades of the twentieth century, that locked up vast numbers of these children. There were thousands and thousands of children within the system at any one time. It was one of the ways that the religious congregations and orders could actually get money from the state, because the state funded the system. But it was run entirely by Catholic religious orders.*

Roger Bolton: *And is it fair to say that in some ways these Catholic schools were institutionally abusive; that violence was sort of built into the system?*

Mary Raftery: *Absolutely, yeah. I mean, there was an extraordinary kind of psychological effect operating. The only kind of explanation that those of us who have looked at this have come up with, the only plausible one, is that the religious orders running these institutions regarded these children as in some way different and undeserving of the normal kind of treatment that children would have within the community. And this separated them. And what they did was, they trained them to be sort of menial workers. And that effectively involved, you know, either domestic servants or farm labourers that effectively involved breaking their spirits.*

Roger Bolton: *So this is not a case, as we've had in the past, of aberrant priests committing sexual abuse. There may be some of that. But it's more about the attitude of... religious orders to children. This is difficult to get a hold of now, to understand how that could have been tolerated.*

Mary Raftery: *Exactly. It's a huge difficulty for us all here in Ireland to actually understand, because it was so pervasive... As you say, it wasn't just sexual abuse, it wasn't just violent physical abuse, which was there; it was an absolutely endemic emotional and psychological abuse. These children were terrorised in every possible way. And there are very, very, very few children who went through the system who describe any kind of a positive experience.*

Roger Bolton: *And are you confident that this report, when it comes out on*

Wednesday, will not pull its punches? It's not going to name individuals, as far as I understand. But I mean, there have been attempts to block it. There are stories that the Department of Education wouldn't cooperate properly with it. I mean, do you think it's going to get out the truth?

Mary Raftery: Well, we're hoping it will. It's been described to us as being between 2,500 and 3,000 pages long. It's coming at us in five volumes. And realistically… even though nothing has [been] leaked about it… the only way we think it could be that length is by going into the detail of the abuse. Three thousand people have testified before this particular commission. Almost 2,000 wanted their stories fully investigated. Its task has been mammoth, which is, I think, probably why it's taken it so long, and it's inconceivable that it wouldn't actually give us full chapter and verse on the scale of the abuse, and indeed go some way towards explaining: how could this possibly have happened? How could people who dedicated their lives to the opposite of what they actually did in terms of terrorising and brutalising these children, how could they have not questioned their own consciences in terms of this kind of activity?

Roger Bolton: And very briefly, Mary, how will the Churches respond to what is going to be a devastating report?

Mary Raftery: Well, that's an intriguing question, because most… of the religious orders continue to remain in some element of denial. They feel that many of the people are making up the stories about them. They've said very nasty things about people; that people are only looking for money by describing the abuse they've suffered. Now, as I say, not quite all the religious orders. I think the Sisters of Mercy have come to terms more with their past than perhaps any of the others. But certainly, a lot of the orders who dealt with the boys – and this is where most of the really severe sexual abuse happened – the Christian Brothers have not been able to deal with this in any significant way.

When it appeared the following Wednesday, the Ryan Report proved every bit as devastating as Mary Raftery had predicted. The *Irish Times* described it as a 'map of an Irish hell',[1] while the *Belfast Telegraph*

---

1 'The savage reality of our darkest days', *Irish Times*: https://www.irishtimes.com/opinion/the-savage-reality-of-our-darkest-days-1.767385 (21 May 2009, accessed 16 June 2023).

characterised the story it told as 'Ireland's shameful holocaust'.[2] Some of the abuse it described was extreme – including rapes, forced oral sex, beatings and, sometimes in boys' homes, naked beatings in public. Sexual abuse in boys' homes was endemic, and the use of corporal punishment as a means of control was systematic. All this took place despite the fact that the institutions were theoretically subject to government supervision.

Ireland's president, Mary McAleese, condemned the abuse detailed in the report as 'an atrocious betrayal of love'.[3] Cardinal Seán Brady, leader of the Catholic Church in Ireland, said he was 'profoundly sorry and deeply ashamed that children suffered in such awful ways in these institutions'.[4]

Uncovering the cover-up

The report did not, however, provide a basis for prosecutions, because one of the religious orders at the heart of the scandals, the Christian Brothers, had gone to court to prevent those accused of abuse from being identified. By the time *Sunday* returned to the story the weekend after publication, the fact that no one was 'named and shamed' had become the focus for much of the media and political reaction.

Roger Bolton: *Last Sunday, we previewed the publication of an official report into the abuse of children in Catholic-run institutions in the Republic of Ireland. That report was published on Wednesday and detailed the systematic and violent abuse of thousands of children over a sixty-year period. It found that sexual abuse was endemic in boys' institutions, and that Church leaders knew what was going on. The head of the Catholic Church in Ireland, Cardinal Seán Brady, has since apologised to the victims. However, many of those victims, some now in*

---

2 D. Moore, 'Child abuse scandal was Ireland's nightmare from hell', *Belfast Telegraph*: https://www.belfasttelegraph.co.uk/opinion/letters/child-abuse-scandal-was-irelands-nightmare-from-hell/28505737.html (23 May 2009, accessed 16 June 2023).

3 'McAleese: Abuse victims suffered "betrayal of love"': *Irish Examiner*: https://www.irishexaminer.com/news/arid-30411723.html (21 May 2009, accessed 16 June 2023).

4 H. Chu, 'Children abused at Catholic-run schools in Ireland, report says', *LA Times*: https://www.latimes.com/archives/la-xpm-2009-may-21-fg-irish-abuse21-story.html (21 May 2009, accessed 16 June 2023).

their fifties and sixties, are angry that the names of those responsible for the abuse have not been included in the report. Alan Shatter is shadow minister for Children and Youth Affairs in the Dáil, the Irish Parliament, and a member of the Fine Gael party. I asked him whether it was inevitable that anonymity be granted to the abusers.

Alan Shatter: *No, I don't think it was inevitable. The anonymity that was granted essentially arose out of court proceedings that the Christian Brothers took against the commission that was conducting the hearings and the investigations into what happened in the past. And in order to bring those court proceedings to a conclusion, and to facilitate the commission continuing its work, it was agreed that anonymity would be granted.*

Roger Bolton: *Well, John Walsh of the Irish Survivors of Child Abuse said he felt cheated and deceived by the lack of prosecutions. Do you understand that?*

Alan Shatter: *I think that anyone who's been a victim of the horrendous events that took place within our residential institutions could feel no other way about those who perpetrated abuse and who haven't been subjected to the criminal law. Of course, some of those have passed away. There are others who aren't publicly known and whose names were apparently concealed in files in Rome, and subject to Church procedures within the congregations of which they were members. And it's very, very regrettable that more prosecutions haven't taken place over the years.*

Roger Bolton: *Do you think that prosecutions... are both possible and necessary?*

Alan Shatter: *Well, I don't know whether that will happen, but I think there's a very particular and obvious issue, which is the extent to which congregations concealed the identit[ies] of those who abused and wished to keep their names out of the public domain. And that is something that the Ryan Commission makes reference to. And I, for my part, I believe there should be more prosecutions. But whether that proves feasible in the context of the information available, I can't answer that.*

Roger Bolton: *Now, when the report came out, you issued a press release in which you said it was scandalous that some religious organisations – you named the Christian Brothers and the Brothers of Charity – continue to deny what you call 'congregational responsibility' for such abuse. Has*

*that changed? Have the organisations now acknowledged that there
was... an institutional problem?*

Alan Shatter: *Well, of course the Ryan Commission also made reference
to this, and I found it quite extraordinary and unacceptable that
institutional congregational responsibility hadn't been accepted. I think
the weight of this report, the terrible incidents and events that are
depicted in it and the public reaction to that, resulted by Thursday
evening in some of the congregations and orders finally accepting that
this was not just a few bad apples, but something that was endemic
to their congregations and something that was covered up by them.
I cannot fathom how that wasn't accepted many years ago. Those who
were in positions of leadership within these congregations knew the
extent to which there had been a cover-up.*

Unwilling to 'redress'

Sunday returned to the story two weeks later.

Edward Stourton: *We begin with the continuing fallout from the Ryan
Report into the abuse of children in Church-run institutions in Ireland.
Cardinal Seán Brady, the archbishop of Armagh, flew to Rome to brief
the pope about developments. And at a meeting with the Taoiseach
[prime minister], Brian Cowen, the eighteen religious orders involved in
the scandal came under pressure over the amount of money they should
offer to the victims. Joe Little is the religious affairs correspondent of the
Irish national broadcaster RTÉ, and joins us now.*

Edward Stourton: *Where are we, Joe, on the money front?*

Joe Little: *I think, first of all, we have to recognise [that] the public
opinion here has been transfixed by the findings of the child abuse
commission of last Wednesday fortnight. And the public has been
alarmed to learn [that] it was known before in political circles, and
had been argued in parliament, that it's stumping up nine-tenths of
the bill for compensation or, as it's called officially here, 'redress' for the
survivors of fifty industrial schools: the survivors of a cohort of about
170,000 young people, most of whom were sent to these industrial
schools because they were needy, and in which it has been found there*

was systemic abuse, endemic sexual abuse in the boys' school, and horrific sadistic punishments were meted out on a regular basis by the Catholic religious managers and owners of those schools under the noses of inspectors from the Department of Education, who did little to help the inmates.

Edward Stourton: *So the feeling is that while the state does bear some responsibility, because the state was responsible for the children concerned and sent them to the schools, it doesn't bear nine-tenths of the responsibility, which is the proportion that is reflected in the way the money's currently apportioned.*

Joe Little: *Indeed, and although there was controversy about the striking of a deal limiting the exposure of the religious orders in 2002, there's now uproar over the terms of that deal for two reasons. The deal put an absolute ceiling of €127 million and the liability on the eighteen religious congregations and orders concerned. And the bill has turned out to be about €1.3 billion. So that wasn't known at the time, that the 14,000 people who would apply for redress would be quite as numerous. But the actual amount of the bill has climbed beyond all predictions. And yet the religious [orders] not only got to limit their contribution to that scheme, but they also secured indemnity in the sense that anybody who took a civil action against the state and the religious for their mistreatment, they ended up getting their civil award paid by the state, and the religious paid nothing towards those awards...*

Now the government, following a unanimous motion... in the lower house of parliament, the Dáil, the government has rather belatedly, in the eyes of many, squared up to the religious and called them in this week and challenged their reluctance to give any more to survivors, and has said that they must do so, and they must contribute substantially more. And the religious have opted for a trust fund which would be independent of them, which they are now willing to contribute to, following independent audits of what they have available to them.

Edward Stourton: *That's the scene on the Irish Republic side. What about the meeting in Rome? Do we know what was said between the cardinal and the pope?*

Joe Little: *We do know that Pope Benedict was very distressed by what he heard from Cardinal Seán Brady and from the archbishop of Dublin,*

Diarmuid Martin, who was also in Rome on business last week, and who joined the cardinal for the meeting. And we don't know precisely what message the pope has given them to bring back to the hierarchy. The summer meeting of the hierarchy, the three-day meeting, begins tomorrow in Maynooth, and it remains to be seen what precisely the pope has said. But we do know that the pope must be looking at the reputation of the worldwide Church, which is going to be affected by this, because the Irish Christian Brothers, the congregation which provided most of this so-called care, and the Mercy Sisters, are known throughout the English-speaking world, and their reputations are in tatters now.

The Murphy Report

There was more reputation-shredding to come. The Ryan Report was followed in short order by the Murphy Report into the handling of abuse cases in the Archdiocese of Dublin. Like the Ryan Report, the Dublin investigation was prompted by media revelations. The television programme *Prime Time* broadcast a special report called 'Cardinal Secrets', which alleged that complaints of abuse by priests in the diocese had been repeatedly ignored by the Church's leadership.

Judge Yvonne Murphy began work in 2006, expecting to complete her report within eighteen months, but the volume of evidence proved overwhelming, and the timetable was extended. *Sunday* previewed her findings on 26 July 2009.

Roger Bolton: *Yet another report on child sex abuse perpetrated by members of the Catholic Church in Ireland has just been handed to the Irish government. When published, it will 'shock... us all', says the archbishop of Dublin. Dr Diarmuid Martin went on: 'It is likely that thousands of [children or] young people across Ireland were abused by priests in the period under investigation.'[5] One of those who's been abused by a priest is Marie, who was assaulted when she was twelve. I asked her how long it was before she could talk about it.*

---

5 H. McDonald, 'Ireland archbishop admits child abuse report "will shock us all"', *The Guardian*: https://www.theguardian.com/world/2009/apr/10/child-abuse-catholic-church-ireland (10 April 2009, accessed 16 June 2023).

Marie: It took me about thirty years, during which time I suffered a lot of psychological problems, depression. I had three or four years of agoraphobia, and I couldn't leave my house. And it was during the treatment for all those problems that eventually I came into contact with the doctor who started to look at my childhood, and at that point began to get me to the point where I could see that it wasn't my fault; that it had been done to me by somebody else. This was not something that I had any blame for or should have any guilt for.

Roger Bolton: And how did the Church react when you raised these issues?

Marie: Well, the first time I actually reported to the Church was to my local curate, and he told me it was probably my fault, and I could now go away as he'd forgiven me.

Roger Bolton: How long ago was this?

Marie: This was in 1985. And as you can imagine, after I'd spent time with a doctor convincing me it wasn't my fault, I was then thrown by this, back into a whole pit of despair. And it took me another ten years to approach the Church again, which I did in 1995.

Roger Bolton: And this time, did you get a different sort of a response?

Marie: Well, I approached the cardinal [Cardinal Desmond Connell was then archbishop of Dublin], and his response was not good at all. He wouldn't cooperate with the police.

Roger Bolton: Do you think the hierarchy did not understand what was happening or know? Or... were they trying to protect the institution?

Marie: I think it wasn't that he didn't believe it had happened. He just didn't see that there was any necessity to do anything about it. And I think the scandal to the Church was far more important than the safety of children.

Roger Bolton: Can I ask what this experience has done to your faith? Were you a Christian? Are you a Christian now?

Marie: I was a normal, average Catholic. I was a practising Catholic going to Mass every Sunday. And the extraordinary thing is, the abuse that happened to me as a child didn't affect my religion in any way. I was still a Catholic for thirty years. My son was an altar boy, etc. But after three years of dealing with the hierarchy and seeing how they actually misled people – said they were dealing with this situation properly, said they had perfect child protection guidelines in place – I've *become completely disillusioned with my Catholic faith, and I'm now detached. I'm not a practising Catholic. I am still a Christian, and I still have a belief in God, and I have my spiritual relationship with God. I hope I can still pray, but I don't use the Catholic Church as my intermediary.*

The whole truth

Roger Bolton told the audience that *Sunday*'s request for an interview with someone from the Dublin Archdiocese had been turned down, and the programme turned once again to RTÉ's religious affairs correspondent Joe Little. Bolton asked whether the public could be confident that the report told 'the whole truth'.

Joe Little: *Although the report deals exclusively with the Dublin Archdiocese, the largest by far in the country, it was commissioned by the government. And I think that it has a very good chance of getting to the source of the problems in the archdiocese, which I think stand a good chance of being defined as endemic – as was the abuse in institutions for children by the report which came out late last May. People might easily confuse those two reports, but the one on the archdiocese is concentrating on sample allegations of abuse, by priests, of children. Sexual abuse.*

Forty-six of those sample allegations have been pored over for over three years by Judge Yvonne Murphy and her two associates on the Commission of Inquiry. And because that inquiry, by the way, was conducted behind closed doors, we don't know how the dozen or so bishops who still live, and who had responsibility for handling those allegations in the three decades after 1975, explained their stewardship on those issues. But we did get a clue when the last archbishop, now Cardinal Desmond Connell, went to the High Court to challenge his successors' right to hand over many thousand[s] of documents to the inquiry on the basis that they were legally privileged.

Joe Little explained one obstacle to the immediate publication of the report. It covered abuse allegations against three priests from the Dublin

Diocese who were facing prosecution at the time, so there was a risk their trials might be prejudiced. When the report was published at the end of November 2009, it was redacted to avoid that.

The Murphy Report presented more sickening evidence of the way children had been abused, but it also – as Joe Little had hinted – highlighted the failure of the Catholic hierarchy to deal with abuse when complaints were made. Four archbishops of Dublin – in a line going right back to 1940 – were censured. Cardinal Connell, the only one still alive, expressed 'bitter regret' for the failures – despite his attempts to keep documents from the inquiry. The Irish police, the Gardaí, were also criticised for helping to cover up the scandal.

A Roman summons

The report was published on 26 November. On 6 December, Roger Bolton reported on *Sunday* that: 'The Catholic Primate of Ireland, Cardinal Seán Brady, has been summoned to Rome next week to meet the pope.' Diarmuid Martin, the archbishop of Dublin, went with him.

To preview the meeting, *Sunday* again turned to the journalist Mary Raftery, who provided her brutal and concise interpretation of the Murphy Report's findings:

> *It has produced a cataclysm, really, in this country in terms of revulsion and absolute disgust; not just at the crimes that were committed against children, but particularly at the level of cover-up. Because what the report detailed was bishop after bishop knowing what was going on, and the fact that there seems to be, in the week since the report has been published, an incapacity really from any of them to step up to the mark, to even come clean about what they actually did and what they failed to do.*

The following weekend, *Sunday* reported the outcome of the meeting between the two top Irish bishops and the pope.

Roger Bolton: *This weekend, the pope said that he shares, and I quote, 'the outrage, betrayal and shame felt by so many of the faithful in*

Ireland [over] these heinous crimes'.[6] He was referring, of course, to the Irish Church sex abuse scandal, or should I say scandals, since – as well as appalling abuse by priests and institutions – there has been an extensive cover-up of their crimes by the Irish bishops, who put what they perceived as the interests of their Church above those of the abused. The pope is clearly furious and, after his meeting with the Holy Father, the archbishop of Dublin, Diarmuid Martin, said: 'I think [that] we are looking at a very significant reorganisation of the Church in Ireland.'[7] To discuss the implication of the Vatican summit, I'm now joined by Joe Little, the religious affairs correspondent of the Irish state broadcaster RTÉ... There's no doubt, is there, that there's real anger in the Vatican about this?

Joe Little: *Yes. And I think that anger percolated up from Archbishop Diarmuid Martin and Cardinal Seán Brady, who emphasised in the last ten days that there had to be much stronger leadership within the Irish Church. Archbishop Martin has been bringing a particular brand of strong leadership to the Church in the Archdiocese of Dublin since he replaced Cardinal Desmond Connell as the archbishop in 2004. And he has brooked opposition when insisting that the Church be totally frank with the Commission of Investigation, which produced this latest report on the Archdiocese of Dublin, and which was given all Church files that were available to Archbishop Martin, despite the opposition by Cardinal Connell to that particular move...*

Roger Bolton: *Well, if the archbishop of Dublin is a credible figure, is Cardinal Seán Brady still capable of leading the Irish Church?*

Joe Little: *Yes, I think Cardinal Seán Brady has emerged from this scandal as a very significant leader. He has a much gentler manner. He is a country man, as opposed to Diarmuid Martin, who is a Dubliner, a city man and more direct in his manner. But I think Cardinal Brady will bring with him the more conservative elements in the Church in bringing about a restructuring, perhaps accepting that many bishops*

6 P. Turle, 'Pope questions Irish bishops over abuse scandal': RFI: https://www.rfi.fr/en/europe/20100215-pope-questions-irish-bishops-over-abuse-scandal (15 February 2010, accessed 16 June 2023).

7 'Child abuse crisis to spark Irish Church shakeup', reuters.com: https://www.reuters.com/article/pope-abuse-irish-reorganisation-idUSGEE5BA1WX20091211 (11 December 2009, 16 June 2023).

may have to stand down because of their association with this process of cover-up.

When Cardinal Brady was asked about one of the bishops named in the report, he made a statement that would, as we shall see, come back to haunt him: 'If I found myself in a situation where I was aware that my failure to act had allowed or meant that other children were abused,' he told the Irish broadcaster RTÉ 'then I think I would resign.'[8] Later in December, four senior bishops – all of whom had earlier served as auxiliary bishops in the Dublin Archdiocese – did indeed resign.

A common position

By the end of 2009, the Irish Church was in a kind of meltdown, despite the best efforts of Archbishop Martin and Cardinal Brady. In February 2010, all its bishops were summoned to Rome by Benedict XVI. 'Depending on who you believe,' William Crawley told the *Sunday* audience, 'the meeting is either an opportunity for the bishops to advise the pope on what should be said in his pastoral letter to the Irish Church in the wake of the Dublin child abuse scandal, or it's an unprecedented papal carpeting for the Irish hierarchy.' The BBC's Mary Harte reported for the programme from Dublin.

Mary Harte: *Here in Dublin the air is thick with tension ahead of the bishops' visit, with some unseemly rows breaking out among the bishops and clergy, playing what can only be described as a blame game. At a meeting of priests in the diocese last month, Archbishop Martin was criticised over his handling of the fallout from the Murphy Report. And there have been public spats between the archbishop and his fellow bishops.*

Garry O'Sullivan, editor of the Irish Catholic newspaper, says that, more than anything else, the Vatican will want to put an end to the squabbling.

---

8 'Murray is "reflecting on decision"', RTÉ: https://www.rte.ie/news/2009/1205/125052-abuse (5 December 2009, accessed 16 June 2023).

Garry O'Sullivan: *I would imagine the Vatican is quite concerned at the public disunity of the Irish bishops. So the fact it's been brought to Rome, I think people see that as Rome trying to pull them into a room together. They'll be there for a day and a half, basically, and what hopefully will emerge is a common position, and they will come back down on Ash Wednesday, I suppose, to promote that common position.*

Mary Harte: *That may be so, but Irish lay people want a lot more. Theologian Gina Menzies says the whole story of what happened in the Dublin Archdiocese has yet to come out.*

Gina Menzies: *I think we need a root-and-branch excavation of what went on. Because if you're very ill and you go to a doctor – unless the doctor really can diagnose your condition, he may be prescribing the wrong medicine, the wrong treatment. So I think the first thing you have to do is really diagnose what happened. And I don't think we've got to the bottom of that. I think people are still wondering how in this Christian Church, which follows the gospel of Jesus, how did it go so pear-shaped?*

Mary Harte: *The pope has promised a pastoral letter. It's almost unheard of for a pope to address such a letter to an individual country rather than to the Catholic Church more generally. Fr Gerry O'Hanlon of the Jesuit Centre for [Faith] and Justice has published his own wish list for the letter.*

Gerry O'Hanlon: *What I suggested as an end product, if you like, for Ireland, was something like a national assembly or a national synod. But really, I don't think people are just going to come together for the sake of talking. They need to feel and be convinced that they're really going to be listened to. And it seems still that we have a situation where the Church is too easily identified with bishops, with the pope, with the priest. And the lay person who, by baptism, is called to be a full member of the Church and to exercise full ministry, is very much still at the receiving end rather than active.*

Mary Harte: *Robert Mickens is Vatican correspondent for the Catholic weekly* The Tablet. *He's not convinced that anything significant will result from the pastoral letter.*

Robert Mickens: *You have to understand that Benedict XVI is very different from his predecessor, John Paul II, who was really a master of gestures. Benedict XVI, on the other hand, puts a lot of stock in the written word.*

So if it is supposed to be a letter to ask forgiveness, to call for repentance, to give consolation, to encourage Catholics, I think people are looking for something much more concrete.

Mary Harte: And what of those who suffered abuse in the Dublin Archdiocese? They've written a public letter to the pope saying they've been excluded from discussions about renewal and healing. Marie Collins from the victims group One in Four says the clergy are still able to hide behind canon law; not just in Ireland, but across the world. That's a problem that the pope needs to address.

Marie Collins: I don't think it was just the leadership in Dublin. I think reading the report, and looking at the policies that the leadership were following, and the canon law dictates that they were following, they are all worldwide. So I think it was a universal policy of protecting abusing priests because of this thing in canon law of good name and reputation. I think it's a universal thing. It's part of the structure of the Church, and it's a part that needs to be changed worldwide.

A 'heinous crime' and a 'grave sin'

Sunday reported the outcome of the meeting the following weekend, on 21 February 2010.

Edward Stourton: For two days this week, Ireland's twenty-four bishops met the pope in Rome to discuss the failure of their Church in dealing with cases of sex abuse by its priests, monks and nuns. The word 'failure', incidentally, isn't mine. It's the word the Vatican itself used in its statement on the meeting; a statement which described the present state of the Irish Church as a grave crisis. Here's the pope's spokesman, Fr Federico Lombardi.

Federico Lombardi (statement): The Holy Father observed that the sexual abuse of children and young people is not only a heinous crime, but also a grave sin which offends God and violates the dignity of the human person created in his image. While realising that the current painful situation will not be resolved quickly, he challenged the bishops to address the problems of the past with determination and resolve, and to face the present crisis with honesty and courage.

Noël Treanor, the bishop of Down and Connor (in Northern Ireland), was among those who were present at the Vatican summit.

Edward Stourton: Tell me about the atmosphere at your meeting – meetings, I should say – with Pope Benedict this week. Were you being given a dressing-down?

Noël Treanor: The atmosphere was one of very straight talking and open dialogue. I would consider that the meeting itself is a measure of the importance that Pope Benedict XVI and the Holy See gives to this problem, which has so infested the life of much of the Church in Ireland, and is... a problem which passes the borders of this country. And indeed, of course, as we know, passes the frontiers of the Catholic Church itself. A dressing-down is a rather dramatic expression, certainly...

Edward Stourton: Well, these are dramatic times.

Noël Treanor: Yes, of course. A clear statement that this issue has to be addressed root and branch, and that was the clear message. If you call that a dressing-down, so be it. I would say it was a meeting which, on both sides – that is to say on the side of the Irish [Catholic] Bishops' Conference and the Holy See – registered the total determination to address this issue. And this, in fact, was clear in the opening words of the pope to us on Monday morning.

The programme also sought a verdict on the week's events from Colm O'Gorman, who was himself a victim of priestly sex abuse. Mr O'Gorman began by describing what had happened to him.

Colm O'Gorman: Everything I did revolved around church. And at the age of fourteen I was attending a youth group event, and at the event was approached by a priest in his late twenties, who chatted to me for a little while. Nothing unusual about that. But two weeks later he arrived at my family home. As he was a priest, he was invited in. He sat down in front of our fire at home and had tea, and chatted away to me for a couple of hours. And in the course of the conversation he talked about the things that I might be interested in. [He] talked about his own parish – he'd been newly appointed to a new parish – and he asked me to help him get his youth group and his folk group – his choir – up and running in his parish. At fourteen years of age I was enormously flattered that somebody as important as a parish priest believed I had something significant to offer.

Two weeks later, with my parents' consent, he arrived to take me down to his parish. And as I found out very quickly, he was not remotely interested in what I might contribute. On the first weekend that I was there, he sexually assaulted me. And then, using my own confusion and guilt and fear, blackmailed me into returning. And the abuse continued for two-and-a-half years.

Edward Stourton: *And it was very many years before you felt able to talk about it.*

Colm O'Gorman: *Well, all the time it was happening, outside of the moments where I was being assaulted or raped, I simply pretended that it wasn't real. It existed in some parallel universe that I only had to deal with in the moment that these things were happening.*

Then I moved to London in 1986. It was 1994, living in London, when I think the best way to describe it is I'd started to stop running, and a sense that there was this stuff from my past that I needed to deal with in some way emerged.

And then, through a variety of just family coincidences, I became aware that he was still very much a priest. He was officiating at a wedding of a cousin, and one of my sisters told me he was there and was surrounded by young boys, and that threw up for me the fear that this might still be happening. And at that point I realised that I had to do something. And then, with the support of my family, I reported it to the Irish police in... [the] February of 1995.

Edward Stourton: *It's probably true to say, isn't it, that your story and your decision to go to the police is one of the things that made this whole terrible saga unravel in the way that it's done? In the light of that, what's your verdict on the way Pope Benedict acted this week?*

Colm O'Gorman: *Well, I think there [are] a few things that we need to put in context before we can possibly assess his performance and the things that he's said and done over the past week. The first is that as prefect of the Congregation for the Doctrine of the Faith, he was for twenty years responsible for overseeing, at a Vatican level, how this issue was handled in Catholic dioceses across the world.*

In 2001, as head of the congregation, he wrote to every Catholic bishop in the world. And in that letter, he told them that all cases of priests who abuse children were to be reported to his department, which would, and I quote, 'Continue to have exclusive competence for how such cases were to be handled.' Two [elements] are important there, I think: 'continue', as in, it already had, and 'exclusive competence'.

So this is a man who, more than anybody else on the planet, possibly, fully understands the nature of this problem, the scale of this problem... as a problem of the global Catholic Church. But it was extraordinary to hear that after two days of great drama and ceremony, the sum of the statement that he had to make was that the abuse of children is a 'heinous crime'. But even more disgracefully, in my view, was his assertion that a significant contributing factor to the abuse of children has been a weakening of faith.

Too little, too late?

The pope's letter to the Irish Church was published in mid-March.

Edward Stourton: 'You have suffered grievously and I am truly sorry' – thus does Pope Benedict address the victims of abuse in Ireland in his pastoral letter to the country's Catholics. 'I openly express the shame and remorse that we all feel,' he goes on.[9] The letter probably goes further than anything we've so far seen from the Vatican in recognising the gravity of the abuse scandal confronting the Catholic Church.

To put the letter into its historical perspective, *Sunday* turned to the veteran Catholic commentator Clifford Longley and Diarmaid Ferriter, professor of Modern Irish History at University College Dublin.

Clifford Longley: It's unique in the history of the Catholic Church. It doesn't contain any of the pleasantries that you usually come across in documents of this kind. It's condemnation, frankly; a very severe condemnation to come from the pope towards one of the heartlands of the Catholic Church. There isn't anything like it... No words the pope can say are ever going to meet the degree of hurt and disappointment and estrangement that the behaviour has caused. But frankly, what else could the pope have said? I mean, it's an extraordinarily outspoken document.

Edward Stourton: *Well, I suppose, Professor Ferriter, that raises the question of whether the Catholic Church in Ireland is beyond the point where even a very direct intervention of this kind from the pope himself can undo the damage that's been done.*

Diarmaid Ferriter: *That was one of the interesting things about waiting to see the kind of language that the pope would use. I mean, it is less legalistic and officious and formal, perhaps, than some previous letters. What a lot of victims wanted was a very abject apology. They wanted him to follow his gut pastoral instinct rather than being overly influenced by his Vatican officials.*

Edward Stourton: *It was pretty abject, though, wasn't it?*

Diarmaid Ferriter: *And it was. I mean, I think Clifford's right; it is quite unique in that sense. And there's an acknowledgement about the trust of those children having been betrayed, and their dignity being violated, and the fact that so many of them, when they were courageous enough to look for answers as to why this had happened, were ignored or met a wall of silence. So in that sense, that will please some people that it's actually quite an emotional letter.*

Having said that, is it too little, too late? There's going to be a mixed reaction to this, particularly when you consider what we have in Ireland now, which is a constituency of abused people who are very articulate, who are very angry, and who will want to see more attention devoted to the Vatican itself, which isn't really addressed in the letter. Why did the Vatican not play its part in trying to undo this damage? And there are people who believe that this is too little, too late; that the Church is beyond redemption in this whole area of child abuse, and that until those... in senior positions in the Church who are associated with that era in Ireland are gone, the Church cannot begin a meaningful process of renewal.

Less than a week after the pope's letter, the Vatican accepted the resignation of the bishop of Cloyne, John Magee. Magee was a big figure in the Irish Church, having worked in the Vatican Curia for many years before being appointed to the Diocese of Cloyne in 1987. He had the distinction of being the only cleric to serve as private secretary to three popes (Paul VI, John Paul I and John Paul II).

His resignation was driven by yet another set of revelations exposed in the media (this time by the *Sunday Tribune*) and growing evidence that abuse had been covered up in the Cloyne Diocese, just as it had been in Dublin. The team under Judge Murphy that had produced the Dublin report was asked to turn its attention to Cloyne.

'A problem for everyone in Ireland'

April 2010 brought an unwelcome reminder of the way the Irish Church now looked to those beyond Ireland's shores. On 4 April, *Sunday* reported a story that had been kicked into life by another Radio 4 programme.

William Crawley: *It is the religious equivalent of a diplomatic incident. The archbishop of Canterbury, Dr Rowan Williams, is the guest on tomorrow's edition of* Start the Week *on Radio 4, but he certainly wasn't expecting to start a row. Dr Williams has been talking to Andrew Marr* [then host of *Start the Week*, and a former BBC political editor] *about the crisis facing the Catholic Church in Ireland.*

Rowan Williams (in a recording from Start the Week): *It's quite difficult in some parts of Ireland to go down the street wearing a clerical collar now, and an institution so deeply bound into the life of the society... suddenly losing all credibility... that's not just a problem for the Church. It is a problem for everybody in Ireland.*

William Crawley: *That comment from Rowan Williams triggered an avalanche of criticism from both Anglican and Catholic bishops in Ireland, including a clearly unsettled Catholic archbishop of Dublin, Diarmuid Martin.*

Diarmuid Martin: *To say that the Catholic Church in Ireland has lost all credibility, and to hear that booming out on the BBC World Service to every corner of the world, I was stunned. I was also discouraged. We* *cannot put the past aside. We can't put it to sleep. We have to recognise the damage that was done to people who were abused. And that was made more difficult by the way the Church managed and covered up these things. But I really felt, you know, I felt that those people are putting so much effort into renewing the Church – to move away to a more gospel-led Church, to a less arrogant Church – to have all of them lumped in together into a Catholic Church in Ireland which has lost all credibility! I think that was, that's damaging. It's a very sweeping statement, 'lost all credibility'. And the only evidence that he produces for it are comments that he has received from a friend of his in Ireland. I rarely felt so discouraged as I felt this morning when I hear that being said; not just in an interview, but it's being sent out around the world...*

Speaking on *Sunday*, Linda Hogan, professor of Ecumenics at Trinity College Dublin, defended Rowan Williams on the grounds that 'his comments really do articulate to a certain extent the depth of the crisis in Ireland and its impact. And I think much of what he said really does capture what some people do really think about where we are at the moment.'

And even Donal McKeown, an auxiliary bishop of the Northern Irish diocese of Down and Connor, accepted that Dr Williams was not entirely wide of the mark:

I think in the past there was a large degree of trust between clergy and people that applied, I suppose, across all churches and in a particular way in Northern Ireland, where I've been living for so many years. And that trust certainly has been damaged. In other words, people are asking, even in parishes, 'Will my local clergy be in court next? Will my aunt or my uncle be accused of something? Has any bishop at all got a clean record?' And I think what really is changing, and Rowan Williams was suggesting this throughout his piece, we're having to discover a new language for talking about who we are as the Church in Ireland.

That actually is a good situation to be in, because we were living, in some ways, in what you might call a heresy of clerical perfection, and a very simplistic understanding of where the Church in Ireland was coming from and was going to. And I think, like the people of the Old Testament, we have to rediscover a new way, with the aid of the prophets, to speak a new story about who we are, where we're coming from and, equally importantly, where we're going to. Because many people haven't got a good language yet to defend where we are. They recognise [that] mistakes – terrible mistakes – were made.

But I think Archbishop Diarmuid Martin is quite right. We're also a people who are trying to build a future for the Church, to build a future for faith within Ireland, in a very new country and playing a very new role. But I think it's important that those who are struggling to build a new role for faith in a very multicultural Ireland should at least be given recognition for the effort they're putting into it.

Magdalene Laundries

The Irish Church really was reeling under these relentless blows (and our apologies to the reader if this chapter feels relentless, too). As well as the rash of allegations and resignations in 2009–10, Ireland was still absorbing the reality of a parallel scandal over what were known as 'Magdalene Laundries'. Originally established in the eighteenth century for so-called 'fallen women', these institutions were, like Ireland's reformatory and industrial schools, run by religions orders.

They grew into successful businesses on the back of the free labour provided by the inmates, and in the course of the twentieth century, all sorts of women were drawn into the system: unmarried mothers, those suffering from mental illnesses, young women who had emerged from reformatory schools, women convicted of petty crimes, girls rejected by their families and others who were simply destitute.

The truth about the laundries began to emerge at the turn of the century. In the summer of 2011, following evidence from campaigners, the cause was taken up by the United Nations. The following item was broadcast on 12 June.

Edward Stourton: *It is an extraordinary fact that the last of the Irish institutions known as Magdalene Laundries closed as recently as fifteen* *years ago. The laundries were run by four orders of nuns, and all sorts of girls and women were sent to live and work in them. Some were accused of loose living. Some simply couldn't look after themselves.*

This week the UN's Torture Committee, no less, produced a report on the way they were treated, and it accuses the Irish state of failing to protect them from physical and emotional abuse. Mary Currington was among those who gave evidence to the committee. She was put into the care of nuns when she was five, and then sent on to a laundry when she was eighteen.

Mary Currington: *I was very nervous. I cried for months after I went into that place... and my hair was cut short as well. My clothes were taken off me. My name was taken from me. My whole identity was taken from me.*

Edward Stourton: *And what about work? How hard did you have to work?*

Mary Currington: *I was to go into the sewing room, because I was very good at sewing. I am to this day. I probably had a cushy number there because I was sitting down all day. Well, that wasn't easy either, because we worked very, very, very long hours and we had to do so much work a day. And we earned pots and pots of money for those nuns. We never saw one penny of it. We didn't know that we were supposed to be paid, you know.*

Edward Stourton: *Did anybody say to you that, if you wanted, you could leave? Or were you given the impression that you were in some way imprisoned in there?*

Mary Currington: *Never could we leave. I ran away with my little friend, and we were gone only two hours. We managed to escape down the little narrow lane from the convent down into the city of Cork. And she decided to go into the arcades and see if she could find pennies to play on the machines. And then this guard [police officer] came along and he said, 'Oh, hello.' And he said, 'Are you on your own?' I said, 'No, my friend's in there playing on the machines.' And he said, 'Can you come in and show me where she is?' Of course, me, I'm so stupid. I went in and said, 'Oh, there's my friend.' He said, 'Come on. You come with us now.' Now, if I wasn't a prisoner up there, would I be taken back by the guards? There you go... We were not free to leave.*

Edward Stourton: And what do you think the nuns thought they were doing? Do you think they thought they were genuinely helping people like you, or were they being deliberately cruel? What was motivating them, do you think?

Mary Currington: As far as I can remember, they enjoyed being cruel, especially on the children's side. We had nobody to tell our stories to, after all. And they knew this, you see, so they could whip us to [within] an inch of our lives and we would have no one to talk to about it.

Edward Stourton: So you were physically punished and abused?

Mary Currington: Of course.

Edward Stourton: As an adult?

Mary Currington: That was their job, wasn't it? After all, that's what they say these days. It was the system. I don't see it as the system. I see we were little battering rams for them. We weren't all as clever as one another. And if I was trying to help a little girl beside me in class, I'd be punished... A nun would pluck me out of the school, send me outside, and then I was beaten to [within] an inch of my life with a sewing machine strap. And that was made of rubber. And it was never a single strap; it was always doubled. And you were beaten across the bare bottom.

Edward Stourton: And that sort of thing continued when you went to the Magdalene Laundry when you were an adult?

Mary Currington: It wasn't as physical as that. The punishments were more cutting your hair, going without food, going without recreation. It's very hard to talk about. I mean, I was sexually abused in the school as well – by the big girls, you know – and the nuns [turned] a blind eye to that. I told one of the nuns about it one day, and I got beaten because they said I was telling lies. And it's ruined my whole life. I got married so I could have a little child, and my marriage hasn't turned out as well as I would have liked it to turn out because of the sexual abuse. It's totally ruined my life. And I have very, very dark days at times. And my son or my husband say, 'What you're crying for now, Mary?' And I say, 'I can't help it, you know. I'll be OK in a minute, you know.' It just comes on.

Edward Stourton: I completely understand. And as I say, it's very kind of you to go through such a painful set of memories for us. I won't keep you much longer. Can I just ask you a couple of things about the state, particularly the Irish state? Because the question of the degree to which they colluded in what happened is something that the UN committee has raised. What's your view of that?

Mary Currington: *The state, of course, knew everything that was going on in the school, and also in the Magdalene situation. They're claiming that we were residential there. We were not residential there. We were put in there against our will, and all the money the laundry made, the nuns made out of every one of us. Where did all that money go to? Of course, the government had to have some claim on that money. They couldn't have kept it all for themselves.*

Edward Stourton: *The UN committee also says that now the state, the Irish state, should investigate all the allegations that have been made and punish those who were guilty of them. Is that your view? Should that happen now, do you think?*

Mary Currington: *Well, most of the nuns are dead. There's only one I still know of, [whom] I won't mention the name of. I don't see punishment would do any good at all. It's over and done with. They knew what they were doing to us at the time. They got away with it, yes. But no, I don't think punishment would do them any good. They're too old now.*

Edward Stourton: *So is there anything either the Church or the congregations of sisters or the Irish government could do now that would help you?*

Mary Currington: *Money never solves the whole situation. It's embedded in your mind. It will never, never leave us. Our lives were ruined in there by the nuns and by the state. The state knew what was going on. They are just as much responsible as the nuns are, the government are.*

The Cloyne Report

Judge Murphy's commission, meanwhile, had completed its work on events in the Diocese of Cloyne. Their findings were published in the summer of 2011, and *Sunday* reported the story on 17 July. As Jane Little pointed out in her introduction: 'Unlike earlier reports of cover-up and foot-dragging, this one documents active obstruction in the face of the Church's own guidelines – guidelines that were introduced in 1996 to ensure that concerns for priests and the Church never again trumped those for victims or alleged victims of abuse.'

The BBC's Ruth McDonald told the programme:

The report pulls no punches. As few of these reports do, it gets straight to the heart of the matter. The former bishop of Cloyne, Bishop Magee, is pinpointed for attempting to blame others for his failures, for not taking proper responsibility, for delegating a lot of responsibility to his second-in-command in the child protection area, a Monsignor Denis O'Callaghan – who didn't appear to approve of the Church's protection guidelines; in particular, perhaps, the need to call the police when an issue arose. And essentially, there was a stymying of child abuse policy.

The report also confirmed that Bishop Magee – who had, of course, resigned the previous year – had even misled the Church's own safeguarding watchdog, the National Board for Safeguarding Children (NBSC), when it carried out an earlier investigation. Ian Elliott was head of the NBSC, and he told Jane Little:

The same statements were made to me by Bishop Magee that essentially all policies and procedures were being followed, and everything was very good within his diocese and so on. But the investigation that we undertook was evidence-based. In other words, we had to look at records, we had to establish the facts of the matter. And the facts didn't lie. It was quite clear when we did that he was not reporting accurately and honestly.

The programme also heard from Fr Brian D'Arcy, a high-profile priest and a longstanding anti-abuse campaigner.

Brian D'Arcy: Everybody is absolutely fuming throughout the rest of the country. Those who have a connection to the Catholic Church, those who haven't a connection to the Catholic Church. But most of all, those who spent night after night and day after day, and suffered rejection and abuse – as most of us have for the last fifteen, sixteen, seventeen years – trying to get justice for the decent, good people who were offended and abused by powerful people who should have known better. And we had got guidelines in that had been painstakingly drawn together, and it was on a plate for people. This is what you do. The abused person comes first.

It is not up to the Church to examine criminal matters. That's up to the civil authorities. If canon law wants to come in after that – and it should come in after that – then let it do so. But you can't do these things behind closed doors. And... that's precisely what was happening in this diocese, where a man with great influence in Rome, Bishop John Magee – a man who was a secretary to three popes – guided by a former professor of Moral Theology at Maynooth College, Monsignor Denis O'Callaghan... were driving a coach and four through the regulations that should have been done. And the poor people were abused and continue to be abused, and got no satisfaction because of this. It's a horrific scene.

Jane Little: *And the report says the Vatican was 'entirely unhelpful' here. I mean, do you think that's fair on the Vatican?*

Brian D'Arcy: *Well, all I can say is that Judge Yvonne Murphy has been a terrific and wonderful person. She has done it magnificently here. She has already said in the Murphy Report that, from her examination of the Dublin Diocese, there is not a question in the world, but – and this is a wonderful phrase – there is a 'systemic failure' in the Catholic Church, reaching to Rome, to make sure that this problem has not been faced. Here she puts it more clearly. As you say, again, she says that the Vatican, in the phrase that you used, was not only less than helpful, but actually was an obstacle to the proper running of this. One would hope that... the Vatican's attitude has changed since that time.*

The Cloyne Report covered such recent events that it inevitably raised questions about the Irish Church's willingness to reform, so it brought the scandal closer to those who were then leading it. Cardinal Seán Brady, the primate of All Ireland, had initially attracted good reviews for his handling of the abuse crisis, but his reputation suffered a serious blow when it emerged that, as a young priest back in the 1970s, he had been involved in an internal Church investigation into Fr Brendan Smyth, the paedophile priest who had, for many people, become a symbol of the whole abuse affair.

In 2011, the Vatican conducted an Apostolic Visitation (a high-level investigation) to find out what had gone so badly wrong in the Irish Church. The subsequent report, published the following spring, included an exhortation that the Irish Church should 'make its voice heard in the media and... establish a proper relationship with those active in this field, for the sake of making known the truth of the Gospel and the Church's Life'.[10]

A 'gaping wound'

In March 2012, Cardinal Brady agreed to be interviewed by *Sunday*. The cardinal was already facing a growing clamour for his resignation, and his encounter with William Crawley turned testy.

William Crawley: You and other bishops have lost the trust of many Catholics in Ireland, haven't you? I mean, why would a Catholic in Ireland believe that the hierarchy is now in a place, intellectually and spiritually, to do this job, to make these reforms?

Seán Brady: Well, they just will have to judge us... as they meet us, and see us as we go around humbly listening to God's word, as the report asks us to do, and listening to what the Spirit is asking and providing to us.

William Crawley: Michael Kelly from the Irish Catholic *newspaper has said Cardinal Brady is a 'gaping wound' in the Irish Catholic Church. That's a pretty devastating criticism of your leadership by an influential lay Catholic in Ireland. Are you really, personally, Cardinal, the person to lead the Catholic Church through these reforms?*

Seán Brady: I don't know. But I'm the person who finds myself in the position of leading the Catholic Church, along with other people. And I will continue to try to do that to the best of my ability, wounded as anyone may consider me. But this report is an opportunity for all of us to express sorrow, which I definitely do, but also to... do our best to lead where Christ wants us to go.

William Crawley: If you were convinced, Cardinal, that the Catholic Church in Ireland had a better chance of reform with another leader at the top, would you consider resigning?

Seán Brady: If I were so convinced, yes, but I am not so convinced at this moment. Nobody has, apart from what you are saying there, told me that.

---

10 'Summary of the Findings of the Apostolic Visitation in Ireland', Vatican: https://www.vatican.va/resources/resources_sintesi_20120320_en.html (20 March 2012, accessed 16 June 2023).

Following this interview, Cardinal Brady complained to *Sunday*'s editor, Amanda Hancox, because he did not think he should have been pressed on whether he would resign. He evidently believed there should be limits to journalistic investigation into 'the truth… of the Church's life'.[11]

Two months later, the ghost of Brendan Smyth returned with a vengeance. In May 2012, the BBC's *This World* programme broadcast explosive new evidence about Cardinal Brady's role in the Church's management of Ireland's most notorious paedophile priest. *Sunday* reported the story on 6 May.

Samira Ahmed: *Now, it's been a devastating week for the leader of the Catholic Church in Ireland, Cardinal Seán Brady. Leaders of almost every political party in Ireland, both North and South, have called on him to consider his position after the BBC's* This World *programme revealed how, in 1975, he had names and addresses of children being abused by Ireland's worst paedophile priest, Brendan Smyth, but he didn't pass on the information to the police or their parents. One police officer who worked on the case of Brendan Smyth told an Irish paper that up to thirty victims of abuse could have been saved if this had been dealt with in 1975. When a government inquiry in 2009 revealed the extent of clerical child abuse, the cardinal said that he himself would resign if he found that a child had been abused as a result of any managerial failure on his part.*

The programme then replayed the cardinal's 2009 commitment to resign if 'I was aware that my failure to act had allowed or meant that other children were abused', and contrasted that with his statement that the *This World* revelations were 'not a resigning matter'. Michael Kelly, deputy editor of the *Irish Catholic* newspaper, had a rather different perspective.

Michael Kelly: *I suppose the first important thing to say, really, is that the name Brendan Smyth, I mean, he's the most notorious paedophile in Ireland, really. This is a man who abused children from the 1940s into*

11 'Summary of the Findings of the Apostolic Visitation in Ireland', Vatican.

the 1990s, when he was finally imprisoned. So the very name strikes fear and terror into the people of Ireland. He's a very potent symbol of this entire crisis.

What we know is that Cardinal Brady – obviously before he was cardinal, when he was a parish priest in 1975 – he met with children who alleged that they were abused by Fr Smyth. He was involved. He was what they call, in canon law, the notary. He interviewed the children. He questioned them about the abuse that they had suffered. And he prepared that for his own superiors and passed that up the line.

Crucially, during that process, he was given the names of other children who these children believed were being abused by Fr Smyth. He didn't pass those names on to the civil authorities, nor did he contact the parents of those children – some of them had already been abused by Fr Smyth, and others [who] were in danger of being abused by him. The cardinal, I think, assumes that… he did what his superiors asked of him to prepare the note, to interview the children. And he didn't obviously believe his responsibility went further than that.

Samira Ahmed: Well, it has been interesting hearing him explain himself in terms of following, sort of, the letter of his instructions of what he was supposed to do. I mean, what's been the reaction in Ireland this week to this?

Michael Kelly: Well, the reaction for the cardinal has been devastating, frankly, because his attitude or some of the statements he's been making seem to border along the line[s] of, 'Well, I was only following orders.' I mean, no one doubts that he did his duty, from the point of view of canon law, in a very efficient and very proficient manner. That's never been in doubt or never been in question.

What has really caused great alarm among people is, though, how he could be given information about dozens of children who were being abused by this, frankly, monstrous man – things that people knew even in the mid-1970s were criminal matters – and he didn't report this to the civil authorities on either side of the border. And as a result of that, Fr Smyth went on to abuse children in Northern Ireland, in the Republic of Ireland, in the United States for another twenty years.

So, frankly, many people feel the cardinal's moral authority has vanished. In fact, Fr Vincent Twomey, a very prominent conservative *theologian here in Ireland, said as much this week. He said that he wasn't in the business generally of coming out to criticise senior churchmen, but he thought the cardinal's moral authority had evaporated and, as a result, he should resign. Now, that's quite something coming from a conservative theologian like Fr Twomey.*

Samira Ahmed: *And from politicians in Ireland, do they all feel the same?*

Michael Kelly: *Very much so. This has been something expressed on both sides of the border, and perhaps the leader of the SDLP [the nationalist Northern Ireland party, the Social Democratic and Labour Party], Alasdair McDonnell, I think, put it in the most heartfelt fashion because he was talking obviously about the need for victims and survivors to have healing and for justice to be done, and to be seen to be done. But also, he made the point that many ordinary Catholics are really sick, sore and tired of their Church leadership's inability to get this issue right; to show that they have credibility on this issue.*

Cardinal Brady hung on until close to his seventy-fifth birthday – the usual retirement age for Catholic bishops – before offering his resignation. The pope often delays before accepting the retirement letters of senior clerics, especially if they are popular, but Pope Francis accepted Cardinal Brady's offer immediately.

Part 2

REVOLUTION AND REACTION

6

The ordination of women

On 26 January 2014, *Sunday* broadcast an item to mark the seventieth anniversary of the ordination of Florence Li Tim-Oi, the pioneering woman priest who ministered to Christians in Macau during the Japanese occupation of Hong Kong in the Second World War. Although she gave up her licence at the end of the war (see Introduction), she continued her Christian ministry in China after the communist victory of 1949, and felt the full force of Maoist persecution, especially during the Cultural Revolution. Christina Rees, a leading campaigner for the ordination of women, described her life and achievements for *Sunday*.

Christina Rees: Her life story is the making of an adventure story, really, because for thirty years she lived in Maoist China and could not only not behave as a priest; they also made her cut up her vestments into shreds in front of them with scissors, and then they put her out to feed the chickens. So she could not minister as a priest. She couldn't even express her faith openly. And she talks about how she used to go up on top of a hill and pray in silence...

Everywhere she went, she brought people hope. So she ministered as a Christian throughout times of extreme deprivation and hardship and depression. It was awful. And then, when the Bamboo Curtain was lifted, she took up her priestly order, you know, her licence again, and carried on ministering, and then joined her family, who had moved on to Canada, and ministered for many more years.

'Who am I to say who God can or cannot call?'

Florence Li Tim-Oi visited Britain during the 1980s, when the Church of England was agonising over the issue of women priests, and met the then archbishop of Canterbury, Robert Runcie. 'He was at that time undecided about whether it was the right thing for women to be ordained as priests,' Christina Rees told *Sunday*, 'and after meeting Florence Li Tim-Oi, he said, "Who am I to say who God can or cannot call?"'

The Movement for the Ordination of Women (MOW), the main campaigning group for women priests, was founded in 1979. After a long and sometimes bitter internal battle, the Church of England's General Synod finally voted to allow the ordination of women to the priesthood in November 1992. Those who opposed women priests were given the option of submitting to the authority of so-called 'flying bishops' who shared their views. This gave them a kind of 'protected status' in a Church now committed to what many of them saw as a heresy.

An unexpected mirage

In March 1994, thirty-two women were ordained in an emotional ceremony at Bristol Cathedral. The first of them, Angela Berners-Wilson (they were ordained in alphabetical order), recalled her feelings that day in a *Sunday* interview many years later:

'I'd had eight years as a deaconess and then seven as a deacon, and finally, on that amazing day... to finally be ordained as a priest in the Church of God, and to be able to take my place behind the altar and to celebrate the Eucharist, to give the absolution and the blessing at last, was just wonderful.'

Some commentators predicted that the first women bishops would follow in short order, but any idea that the argument over the role of women in the Church of England was settled on that spring day in Bristol was to prove a mirage. At the time of Christina Rees's interview about Florence Li Tim-Oi (in early 2014), the Church still had not taken that final step on the road to full gender equality. Christina Rees's contention that 'It's been really hard for women in the Church of England. I think it has been such a bastion of patriarchy and male hierarchy' seemed difficult to fault.

Sunday's coverage of the 1980s debate about women's ordination has not survived, but the programme regularly discussed and reported on the subsequent argument about women bishops. The evidence of the archive suggests the proud Anglican tradition of compromise evaporated very early on. Both sides seemed determined to fight this battle to the finish – and sometimes beyond.

The General Synod first considered the matter in 2000, and four years later the bishop of Rochester, Michael Nazir-Ali, produced a report that outlined a range of options for the Church. Although in the Church's evangelical tradition, Dr Nazir-Ali was a supporter of women priests, and his report concluded that the status quo placed the Church at odds with the society it served:

> It seems certain that, for the foreseeable future at least, acceptance of gender-blind equality of opportunity will remain a central feature of western society. This means that the Church's position will appear increasingly isolated and anachronistic, and there will be continuous pressure on the Church to reconsider its decision... the Church of England will not be able to commend the gospel effectively if its structures embody sexism in a way that contemporary society no longer finds acceptable.

One of the possible future models outlined in the report was the creation of a new Church of England province – to sit alongside those of Canterbury and York – which would provide a home for those who could not accept women bishops. This idea was eagerly embraced by some opponents of women bishops, and equally fiercely rejected by the champions of change.

'Women bishops can't be that'

This sometimes ill-tempered *Sunday* exchange, broadcast in October 2004, provides a flavour of the atmosphere in which the debate unfolded.

Roger Bolton: *The long-standing row about whether women should be able to become bishops in the Church of England, and whether one day there might be a woman archbishop, is coming to a head... For Forward in Faith, the organisation that opposes the ordination of women as bishops, or indeed as priests, there are only two options, which they will* *outline in their own report to be published next Friday. These are either to maintain the status quo, where all bishops are men, or to set up an independent or free province of the Church for those who cannot accept women bishops. Geoffrey Kirk is the national secretary of Forward in Faith UK. I asked him why the issue of women bishops was so crucial.*

Geoffrey Kirk: *Bishops exist, amongst other things, to be a focus of unity within the Church. It's quite clear that women bishops can't be that.*

Roger Bolton: *Does that mean that a person like yourself could not accept a priest working with you who had been ordained by a woman bishop?*

Geoffrey Kirk: *Yes.*

Roger Bolton: *Because you think he or she would not be a priest?*

Geoffrey Kirk: *Well, she hadn't been ordained by a bishop, or he had not been ordained by a bishop, because the person who had ordained them was not a bishop.*

Roger Bolton: *Granted that view, is there any option for you in the future other than… a so-called independent or free province of the Church? You don't leave the Church of England, but you have a separate province for people like yourself.*

Geoffrey Kirk: *I've got to say that, no, I don't think any of them, apart from that, is viable…*

Roger Bolton: *Can I bring in Christina Rees now, who is chair of the organisation, WATCH* [Women and the Church, a successor organisation to MOW, which was dissolved when its objective had been achieved]? *And could we ask you about this principle first? In principle, if this is the only way to keep people like Geoffrey Kirk in the Church, would you agree that there should be a separate province?*

Christina Rees: *Well, I think if Geoffrey and people who feel the way he does want to have their own Church without women priests, women bishops, and have only priests who have not been tainted by women, in his point of view, then that's fine. That's a great idea. Let them have their own Church. But it won't be part of the Church of England. It will be another province; it will be a separate Church. And the Anglican Communion allows for different provinces to be independent, autonomous and make up their own rules. But it will not be part of the Church of England, because for twelve years the Church has said yes to women priests, and for the last ten years it's had the ministry of women priests.*

And I have to disagree with Geoffrey when he says that significant numbers wouldn't accept women priests. Significant numbers do – to the tune of about eighty-five or ninety per cent – accept women priests. And very nearly the same amount are looking forward, very much enthusiastically, to women bishops.

The General Synod voted in favour of women bishops in 2005, and reaffirmed that position repeatedly in subsequent years. It could not, however, agree on that critical question of how to provide for those who opposed reform.

The debate was, in many ways, a rerun of the one that led to the creation of 'flying bishops' to care for those who could not accept women priests, but settling on a mechanism to satisfy those who opposed women bishops proved even more contentious. This was partly because the leadership role of bishops raised new questions (thus Fr Kirk's objection that even a male priest ordained by a woman bishop would not really be a priest at all), and also because those campaigning for change feared that the status of women bishops would be undermined by over-generous compromise to appease their opponents.

'Trust us'

Both sides became entrenched in their positions, and increasingly questioned one another's good faith. As a result, progress was agonisingly slow. When *Sunday* returned to the subject in July 2008 –four years after that discussion between Fr Kirk and Christina Rees – very little seemed to have changed.

Roger Bolton: The Church of England's latest decision on women bishops has left many so-called traditionalists wondering if there is any future for them in their present Church. The Synod vote last Monday was to decide the conditions under which women could be consecrated as bishops. The sticking point was what provisions should be made for the minority who could not accept the authority of women bishops. Synod members rejected the pleas of its two leaders, the archbishops of Canterbury and York, and refused to put in place safeguards, such as allowing male 'super bishops' to cater for those who opposed change. Instead, it voted for a code of practice, a draft of which will be put before the Synod next February. In effect, it said, 'Trust us.' There's not much trust about, and that's failed to satisfy a significant minority from both wings of the Church.

Roger Bolton's reference to 'both wings of the Church' reflected the fact that the issue had created a common front that included evangelicals and Anglo-Catholics. Evangelicals objected that the ordination of women ran contrary to Scripture (particularly to the writings of Paul) while Anglo-Catholics were concerned that the Church of England was taking a unilateral decision that put it at odds with the broader Catholic tradition.

Both sides were represented on that edition of *Sunday*. Revd David Banting, a member of the evangelical group Reform, suggested that some congregations were considering withholding the fees they would normally pay to support their diocese – effectively a unilateral declaration of independence.

David Banting: *We're not going to react precipitately, but I've heard people talk about the possibility of having to find our own bishops. If we're not going to be granted them within the Synod procedure, we need to seek them out ourselves. I'm even hearing some people saying if, in the end, the only thing that the Church will listen to is money, maybe we need to play that card. Every parish has to pay a quota to the central authorities in the diocese. Some people are already talking about channelling that ourselves to support the ministry that we really want. We should do so with immense reluctance, but if it's the only thing that'll make people listen, well, so be it.*

Roger Bolton: *David Banting of the evangelical organisation Reform. And there's equally, if not more, disquiet among the Anglo-Catholics who oppose women bishops. Fr David Holding was one of their leaders at General Synod. He feels hurt and angry.*

David Holding: *How could the General Synod do this? It seems as though the Synod made this decision deliberately in order to exclude the Catholic side of the Church. If the Church is determined to push us out, then we will inevitably, at some point, have to find a new home. And obviously that will lead us in the direction of the Church of Rome. I don't think* *we've quite reached that point yet, so I think what we have to do now is to stay calm. I think a way forward can be found. I think it's going to be quite difficult, but I'm not yet in a position to give up.*

A Catholic welcome for disaffected Anglicans

The Catholic Church, meanwhile, was taking steps to make it easier for Anglicans who, like Fr Holding, felt led 'in the direction of Rome'. A significant number of Anglican vicars had left the Church of England because of the original 1992 decision to ordain women as priests (though not the flood that some had predicted), and Cardinal Basil Hume, then archbishop of Westminster, did everything in his power to ensure they were given a warm welcome by the Catholic Church. In a break from Catholic tradition, married Anglican vicars who converted were allowed to practice as Catholic priests.

As the Church of England's struggle over women became more intense, Pope Benedict XVI took Hume's approach to another level. In 2009, the Vatican announced its intention to create a system of 'personal ordinariates', which would allow Anglican converts to worship as Catholics while preserving elements of their 'distinctive Anglican patrimony'. The Ordinariate of our Lady of Walsingham was established on 15 January 2011, and the story was introduced on *Sunday* as follows.

Jane Little: Three former Anglican bishops awoke this morning as Roman Catholic priests in what is a radical departure, both for them and for the Church they have joined. Frs Keith Newton, Andrew Burnham and John Broadhurst have become the first former Anglican bishops to take advantage of a new structure the pope created to accommodate disaffected Anglicans. Because the Vatican doesn't recognise Anglican orders, they were ordained yesterday at Westminster Cathedral in a ceremony presided over by Archbishop Vincent Nichols, the leader of the Roman Catholic Church in England and Wales.

Archbishop Nichols (not yet the cardinal he later became) appeared live on the programme to address some of the practical issues thrown up by the creation of the ordinariate; not least the question of where its members would hold their services when they had lost the use of their C of E parish church.

Vincent Nichols: Well, they will meet in the places that will welcome them. And I have said that I expect the simplest solution to that will be in their local Catholic church. There might be some exceptions to that, but in a way the place is less important than the faith that they celebrate. And the faith they celebrate will be the faith of the Catholic Church. They are coming into full communion with the Catholic Church. They're becoming Catholics.

Jane Little: You're also taking on board the funding of them as well. Of course, these former Anglican bishops have lost their homes and their pensions. How are you going to fund it?

Vincent Nichols: Well, there will be generosity on our part, and I think that's already been publicised. And there is also the expectation that the ordinariate will take care of its own responsibilities. So it will be, how can I put it, like a non-territorial diocese. So just as each diocese in the Catholic Church, and through the generosity of its people, makes provision for its needs, so the ordinariate in time will be able to do that.

And we will find we will work our way through these things. What is very helpful, from our point of view, is that those who are coming into full communion are nicely spread across many of our dioceses. So there's not too much burden on any one diocese. And we can work together and find houses and find some initial places for them to get settled and find a principal church for them. Probably here in London.

Jane Little: They're going to be able to preserve their liturgies and practices that are, quote, 'concordant with Catholic teaching'. So what will go and what will stay?

Vincent Nichols: Well, you know, I don't think it is largely a question of liturgy. There might well be some of that, but most of the groups who come are well acquainted with the Roman rites of the Mass. I think it's in other things that they bring characteristics of their Anglican tradition. I think there are some particular aspects of the theological formation, there are some particular emphases within their spiritual

126

tradition, and there are some matters of governance as well. So the ordinariate, for example, will have a council of priests that has a stronger role within the running of the ordinariate than it would do in a normal Catholic diocese. So there are different things. And I know this is the vision of the Holy Father; there will be mutual enrichment here.

What this does in the longer view is it shows in practice how aspects of the Anglican tradition enrich and strengthen the Catholic tradition in this country and in other countries, too. I think Pope Benedict has a very open sense of the Catholic Church and its faith, and is not at all afraid of a richness of expression.

The Church of England did lose some priests and parishes to the ordinariate (in 2019 it was estimated to have slightly fewer than 2,000 members), but it was also under pressure over those who chose to leave because they were frustrated by the slow pace of change.

Helen Hamilton's journey

In the summer of 2012, Scotland acquired its first woman bishop. Helen Hamilton left the Church of England for the Open Episcopal Church because of – this is how Samira Ahmed put it on *Sunday* – 'its equal treatment of women and lesbian and gay people. It says it aims to provide a community that has no walls, barriers or exclusions. Its roots are in the Netherlands, and it has just twelve dioceses in Britain.' Just before her consecration, the soon-to-be Bishop Hamilton gave the programme an account of her journey.

Helen Hamilton: *I felt called to be a priest, but because of the regulations concerning the Church, I knew that this was impossible. But I believed that eventually it would happen. And so I sought for ways to serve God and people in a pastoral capacity. And to do that, I eventually, first of all, trained as a teacher, and worked with disturbed adolescents in Northern Ireland and then in England, and then moved on to the prison service.*

Samira Ahmed: *And when did you make the move into the priesthood,* *and how did it come about when you felt you had to leave the Church of England?*

Helen Hamilton: *Well, I first of all, after working as a prison governor, I went and became an Anglican nun, because that was the nearest thing I could do to being a priest in the Anglican Church at that time. And after about five years in the community, the community of St Mary the Virgin at Wantage, the Church of England decided that women could become priests.*

I went and asked whether I could actually go forward for the priesthood, and I was accepted. And I trained as a priest for a year at Westcott House. However, I was so disturbed by what I saw about the Church's attitude to women still within that Church that I felt I could not go forward. And consequently, I left and continued with my studies at Cambridge University.

Samira Ahmed: *What disturbed you so much that you felt you had to leave?*

Helen Hamilton: *I just felt very strongly that it was wrong that women were continually being disempowered, though they were being used in the priestly capacity. They could not be recognised for the gifts that they had in the high echelons of the Church.*

Second-class status

In the month following that interview, the Church of England's debate about women bishops descended into a chaos that even its greatest fans and friends found difficult to defend. The meeting of the General Synod in York in July 2012 was widely heralded as the moment when the Church of England would, at long last, make women bishops a reality. A new set of proposals for providing for those who could not accept the change were sent out for consultation earlier in the year, and they were endorsed by forty-two of the Church of England's forty-four dioceses.

But at the eleventh hour, the archbishops of Canterbury and York, Rowan Williams and John Sentamu, proposed two amendments that threw the whole issue into doubt again. To anyone unfamiliar with the intimate detail of this debate, they were completely impenetrable.

The amendments related to the way women bishops should delegate authority to an alternative bishop when a parish in their diocese declared that it could not accept a woman bishop. And some detected, buried away in all the legalistic language, a change that would reduce women bishops to second-class status.

Some champions of women bishops felt so strongly about the issue that they vowed to vote *against* the overarching Synod motion that would open the way to the reform they had fought so hard for over many years. *Sunday* broadcast the following discussion in June 2012.

Samira Ahmed: *It looked as though this summer legislation might finally be passed in the General Synod to allow women bishops. But after years of meetings, reports and debates, two amendments to the draft measure have been tabled by the House of Bishops, which have caused huge controversy. Many supporters of women bishops believe they're so significant that they themselves may vote 'no' in the debate. Amendment 5 allows parishes which object to women bishops to be supervised by a male bishop who shares their theological principles and Amendment 8 qualifies the authority of bishops' office and ordination.*

Well, I'm joined by the Revd Pete Broadbent, the bishop of Willesden, and Canon Dr Judith Maltby, who's chaplain and fellow of Corpus Christi College, Oxford, and a member of the House of Clergy of the General Synod. So we'll have a vote on the issue. Judith Maltby first... How are you going to vote in this motion and why?

Judith Maltby: *Well, at the moment I feel I'm going to vote against it. It's absolutely essential to understand that the measure before it was amended by the bishops at this eleventh hour was a compromise. A 'no' vote in July will not be because many of us are unwilling to compromise. We feel that we have now gone a step too far in terms of compromising the legislation on women bishops.*

Samira Ahmed: *Let me put that to the bishop, Pete Broadbent. You supported the amendments, didn't you? Do you recognise that they seem to have gone too far for many people?*

Pete Broadbent: *Well, it's a very long story.*

Samira Ahmed: *Well, tell us briefly, then, why you're still supporting them.*

Pete Broadbent: A bunch of people didn't want any kind of compromise at all – what was called a one-clause measure, which says women can be bishops – on the one hand, and folk who are against saying they wanted a separate Church on the other. We have got a compromise. Judith is absolutely right. The compromise we've reached is to try to accommodate people.

It did not help that the amendments were put forward without any debate or consultation. The House of Bishops supported them, but neither of the Synod's two other constituent bodies, the Houses of Clergy and of Laity, had been given any sight of the proposed changes.

Pete Broadbent: Well, we've said publicly as the Church of England that there is an honoured place for people who are against. I'm totally in favour of women bishops. I don't agree with the theology of those we're trying to help, but I do believe we have an honoured position which says we want these folks to stay in the Church, and we're going to try our best to make it happen. And actually, the compromise we've now reached gives women full authority in their dioceses as women bishops, but also respects the integrity of those who can't cope with them.

Samira Ahmed: Judith Maltby, is that how you see it?

Judith Maltby: No, that's not how I see it. And the measure that we already had, the measure that went around all forty-four dioceses of the Church of England and passed forty-two of them, made exactly that provision for the opponents. It's this additional provision which has caused so much trouble. And it's also a process question, I think. We went through this long, long process of consulting the wider Church, and the bishops, I think, really have acted with some bad faith at amending the legislation at this late hour. All the other Houses of the General Synod meet publicly. We meet in the open. The House of Bishops meets behind closed doors, and I think that's a very serious issue here.

When the Synod gathered in York over the weekend of 7–8 July 2012, the outcome of the vote was still in doubt. One member who supported women bishops, Revd Sandra Millar, told *Sunday*:

I think we're caught between a rock and a hard place on this one. I wish we could move forward on the issue of women bishops, because I think there are many, many other issues that the Church needs to be addressing. But at the same time, I don't want us to pass a piece of legislation that enshrines in law something that says that women's ministry is somehow inferior or second-rate, and then people for generations to come have to live with that.

The Synod's discussions over that weekend seemed, to most of those watching from the outside, arcane in the extreme. Ruth Gledhill, the religious affairs correspondent at *The Times*, told *Sunday*:

I think ordinary Church of England members are baffled by the fact that there still aren't women bishops... And I think, beyond the Church, people in the country are bemused that the Church is still embroiled in arguments that most of, or a lot of, Western society has moved on from already.

Now, whenever you say something like 'the Church should move with the times' or 'adapt to the times', of course, you immediately get tons of bricks landing on your head from people saying the Church must remain true to traditional values and not change. I think that's all very well. But I think if you've then got an Established Church, when its laws come into conflict or are in apparent dissonance with the laws of the land, I think that's when you're in trouble.

For a 'view from the pew', *Sunday* turned to the *Daily Mail*'s parliamentary sketch writer Quentin Letts, who complained that: 'Being an Anglican can feel like being driven at fifty-five miles an hour down the middle lane of the M4. Traffic zooms past [on] both sides. You slightly wish someone would put his or her foot down and let the rest of us crack on with this journey of life.' Letts's view of the Synod's style of debate was less than flattering:

Watching occasionally from the press bench, I've been struck by the oratory; it's a match for the House of Commons. And by the paperwork for every proposed line of law, every tiddly subclause and crossed 't', wads of footnotes. Synod's minutes make the New Testament look like an executive summary.

But to fill the pews, does policy on female bishops matter as much as, say, finding a competent organist or giving everyone a glug of Amontillado after matins? ...I love the Church of England for being so open to discussion. But the more that Synod talks, the more it costs and the more they dance on the pinhead.

On Monday 9 July, after four days of debate, Synod voted to put off a final decision yet again. The debate was adjourned until the body's next meeting.

Another twist in the tale

And this long saga still had one more twist in store. When the General Synod met in November there was a widespread expectation – just as there had been in the run-up to the meeting in July – that it would, at last, settle matters. But it was not to be. This is how *The Guardian* reported what happened:

The Church of England has been plunged into its gravest crisis in decades after legislation that would have allowed female clergy to become bishops, and swept away centuries of entrenched sexism, was rejected by just six votes.

In dramatic scenes at Church House in Westminster, a long-awaited measure that was the result of 12 tortuous years of debate and more than three decades of campaigning was defeated by lay members, prompting one bishop to warn that the established church risked becoming 'a national embarrassment'.[12]

The November vote tipped the Church's internal argument over women bishops into a broader debate about the Church of England's place in the nation's life. The warning given by Bishop Nazir-Ali back in 2004 – that

---

12 L. Davies, 'Church of England votes against allowing women bishops', *The Guardian*: https://www.theguardian.com/world/2012/nov/20/church-of-england-no-women-bishops (21 November 2012, accessed 25 April 2023).

the Church would become 'isolated and anachronistic' if it resisted change – suddenly looked ominously prescient.

The values of the nation ·

Two days after the vote in the General Synod, the issue was raised in parliament. The Tory MP for Banbury, Sir Tony Baldry, was the second church estates commissioner at the time, and so had the task of answering questions in the Commons. The exchanges, recorded in *Hansard*, reflected real anger over the Church of England's deadlock.[13]

Tony Baldry: The really important point is that the whole House wants the Church of England to get on with this matter. It cannot be parked, and work needs to be done urgently to try to ensure that it is resolved as quickly as possible. In fairness, the House of Bishops gave the greatest possible leadership in the General Synod. However, as I sat there, the analogy that struck me was that it was a bit like Government Whips trying to talk to the Eurosceptics; there were those in the General Synod who, whatever the bishops said to them, were just not going to listen. So, in fairness, the House of Bishops in an episcopal-led Church was very clear about the need to make change. Those bishops work every day with women clergy in their dioceses and see the fantastic work that they are doing in the Church of England. That work must be valued and cherished, and we need to ensure that any changes do not square the circle by bringing forth proposals for women bishops who would be second-class bishops. I have made it clear to the General Synod on a number of occasions that Parliament simply would not approve any Measure that introduced women bishops as second-class bishops.

Eleanor Laing (Conservative MP for Epping Forest): I am sure that the hon. Gentleman will appreciate that the whole House has sympathy with his position and great respect for the hard work that he has done in trying to resolve this matter. Does he agree that when the decision-making body of the established Church deliberately sets itself against

---

13 'Women Bishops: Volume 553: debated on Thursday 22 November 2012', UK Parliament: Hansard: https://hansard.parliament.uk/Commons/2012-11-22/debates/12112237000010/ WomenBishops (accessed 25 April 2023).

the general principles of the society that it represents, its position as the established Church must be called into question?

Tony Baldry: The hon. Lady makes a perfectly good point, and it is one that I have repeatedly made. As a consequence of the decision by the General Synod, the Church of England no longer looks like a national Church; it simply looks like a sect, like any other sect. If it wishes to be a national Church that reflects the nation, it has to reflect the values of the nation.

The veteran Labour MP (and former member of the General Synod) Frank Field tabled a bill in the Commons to remove the Church's exemption from equalities legislation. 'What we would be saying is that from now on, the vast majority would be able to make their views felt,' he explained to *Sunday* listeners on 25 November, 'because the Church would be open to legal action for continuing to discriminate against half the population in this fashion.'

'A slow-motion train crash'

On the same programme Pete Broadbent, the bishop of Willesden, delivered this damning verdict on that week's Synod meeting.

Pete Broadbent: It felt like a slow-motion train crash... And we could have predicted it. Nothing changed. During the debate, I didn't feel people were moving at all in their opinions. And there always was this sense that the House of Laity [was] going to scupper it. What I think was unfortunate was that we did all that in public, and we just looked like complete idiots. And the Church of England is in disrepute because of that.

Although parliament gave the Church of England the power to run its own affairs in 1919, it still formally approves all Church legislation, and the threat of parliamentary action to force the Church of England's hand had a significant effect on the General Synod's thinking. Justin Welby, who succeeded Rowan Williams as archbishop of Canterbury in early 2013, turned the screws further on the naysayers with plans to dissolve the Synod and hold fresh elections if the House of Laity continued to hold out against the reform. In July 2014, the Synod at last voted the measure through, with significant majorities in all three houses.

Speaking to *Sunday* later that year, Archbishop Welby defended the Church's record:

> *It takes people a long time to get their mind around things. Sometimes you need to hammer out all their concerns. Part of being a Church and not a political party or a business is you don't just say, 'This is it, and if you don't like it, quit.' You listen to people. You pay attention to them. You hope that they will listen to you. And between you, you work it out and, in prayer and reflection, discern how God is calling the Church forward.*

In the same programme, Revd Angela Berners-Wilson, the first woman to be ordained back in 1994 and now chaplain at the University of Bath, paid tribute to Justin Welby's skill in piloting the measure through, declaring herself 'enormously impressed by the way he has handled it'. In what sounded like a reflection on the scars left by the long years of trench warfare, she added her view that women bishops would 'change the Church in subtle ways' because 'I think, on the whole, women are... perhaps more conciliatory'.

7

Sexuality

In the summer of 2013, on the plane back to Rome at the end of his week-long tour of Brazil – the first of his pontificate – Pope Francis startled the travelling press with a rhetorical question: 'If a person is gay and seeks God and has good will, who am I to judge?' It made headlines all over the world, and led the gay superstar Elton John to call for his immediate canonisation.

In the same week, the archbishop of Canterbury, Justin Welby, also made news (on a more modest scale) when he described the change in social attitudes to homosexuality as 'a revolution we must pay attention to'. The following weekend, *Sunday* took stock of the debate on sexuality in both the Catholic and Anglican Churches. William Crawley was in the chair:

Both the pope and the archbishop of Canterbury took the ongoing debate over Church teaching on homosexuality a notch further this week. On the plane back from Brazil, where he celebrated World Youth Day, Pope Francis spoke of gay people with a warmth rarely heard of in recent times at such an official level. And against a background of the upcoming same-sex marriage legislation [parliament passed legislation introducing same-sex marriage in England and Wales in July 2013], *Justin Welby similarly spoke of a revolution in society, which it would be foolish to ignore. But do the combined comments signal a change of mind as well as a change of heart?*

Trevor Barnes was dispatched to the pub in search of vox pops.

Trevor Barnes: Old Compton Street in London's Soho is arguably the epicentre of the metropolitan gay scene, where lunchtime drinkers are sceptical of the pope's apparent change of heart.

136

Vox pop: I think it's an attempt to be populist, to try and gain more followers – more political power – rather than… a genuine statement about personal beliefs.

Vox pop: I think this pope is trying to make ways in which to just sort of appease the gay community somewhat. But he had to put the riding factor on to say that gay sex was still immoral, and it shouldn't be practised, you know. And that is a little bit disappointing from such a compassionate man – as I see him – really.

Trevor Barnes: And that, according to William Naphy, professor of Church History at Aberdeen University, is pretty much spot on. A renewed but more heartfelt compassion towards those who have homosexual orientation, but a commitment still to traditional Catholic Church teaching – that any form of sexual activity outside or even within marriage which is not open to procreation is sinful.

William Naphy: They rely very heavily on the Old Testament understanding of what is 'natural' and 'unnatural' sex, and therefore it's quite straightforward: all 'unnatural' sex – in other words, sex that doesn't physically unite a couple in the confines of marriage, and isn't open to the possibility of creating life – is unnatural and wrong.

Trevor Barnes encountered similar scepticism when he turned to the position in the Church of England. 'I've not seen any sign of a change in the policy on sexual ethics from the archbishop of Canterbury,' the theologian and lecturer in Christian ethics Canon Andrew Goddard told him, adding: 'It looks like it is one of those questions that may prove even more difficult than the women bishops question for the Church of England.'

That assessment may startle readers who have just worked through the knotted twists and turns of chapter 6, but it proved well founded. At the time of writing – a decade after Canon Goddard made his prediction – sexuality remains a source of raw feeling and sometimes bitter controversy in most mainstream Churches, and the gap between official Christian teaching on homosexuality and social attitudes in most Western societies grows wider all the time.

The Wolfenden Report

So it is an irony that the Church of England was intimately involved in early efforts to liberalise the law on homosexuality in Britain. In 1957, the Wolfenden Report – or Report of the Departmental Committee on Homosexual Offences and Prostitution, to give it the dignity of its official title – recommended that 'homosexual behaviour between consenting adults in private should no longer be a criminal offence'.[1] The committee was chaired by a committed Anglican – Sir John Wolfenden later chaired the Church's Board for Social Responsibility – and the Churches were well represented among its members.

The fifteen-strong committee based its conclusion on the principle that 'It is not, in our view, the function of the law to intervene in the private life of citizens, or to seek to enforce any particular pattern of behaviour.' Only one member dissented. James Adair, a former procurator-fiscal for Glasgow, took the view – as reported in what was still known as the *Manchester Guardian* – that: 'The presence of adult male lovers living openly and notoriously under the approval of the law is bound to have a regrettable and pernicious effect on young people.'[2]

At the time, many people held similar views. The opinions of Church leaders carried more weight in the 1950s than they do today, and the fact that the archbishops of Canterbury and York, Geoffrey Fisher and Michael Ramsey, supported change was, given the social climate of the day, critically important – even though that support was heavily qualified.

Both archbishops picked up on the committee's distinction between what is legal and what is moral. According to the *Manchester Guardian*, Dr Fisher took the view that:

> *Because man's ultimate responsibility is to God alone... there is a sacred realm of privacy for every man and woman where he makes his choices and decisions, fashions his character, and directs his desires – a realm of his own essential rights and liberties (including, in*

---

1 'Wolfenden Report, 1957', British Library: https://www.bl.uk/collection-items/wolfenden-report-conclusion (accessed 16 June 2023).

2 'Easier laws for homosexuals', *Manchester Guardian*: https://www.theguardian.com/news/1957/sep/05/leadersandreply.mainsection (5 September 1957, accessed 25 April 2023).

the providence of God, liberty to 'go to the devil') into which the law must not intrude.[3]

Both archbishops also, however, insisted that homosexual sex remained a sin, a step along the road 'to the devil', to echo Dr Fisher's vivid phrase. On 27 September 1957, *The Times* reported that 'Dr A M Ramsey [the archbishop of York] has urged the Home Office to introduce legislation to give effect to the main recommendations of the Wolfenden Report', but the paper also quoted Michael Ramsey's view that 'Christianity abhors the indulgence of lust, whether by fornication, adultery or homosexuality'.[4]

'A horrible proposition'

When the Church Assembly (the precursor to the General Synod) met in November that year, a majority voted for the implementation of the Wolfenden Report's conclusions, but the body was deeply divided. The *Manchester Guardian*'s Anglican correspondent quoted an assembly member who 'made reference to the [committee's] proposals concerning homosexual practices between adult males in private as "a horrible proposition"'.[5]

A couple of weeks later, the same paper reported the view of the bishop of Chester, Dr G. A. Ellison, that a change in the law would 'lead to a general falling in standards of public morality, and the emergence of much homosexual behaviour which is at present latent, and which is possibly more widespread than any of us like to think'.[6]

It was another decade before the Wolfenden Report's recommendations were translated into law. The Sexual Offences Act, which made it legal for men over twenty-one to have consensual sex in private (there had never been any formal ban on homosexual acts between women), reached

---

3 'Dr Fisher on the Wolfenden Report: Distinction between crime and sin', *Manchester Guardian*, 25 September 1957, p. 2.

4 'Wolfenden Report: Archbishop of York urges legislation', *Manchester Guardian*, 27 September 1957, p.10.

5 'Church and Wolfenden Report', *Manchester Guardian*, 11 November 1957, p. 12.

6 'Bishop's Criticism of Wolfenden Report', *Manchester Guardian*, 9 October 1957, p. 8.

the statute book in 1967 (not long before *Sunday* first went on the air). Michael Ramsey, now himself archbishop of Canterbury, remained a champion of reform and played a significant role in helping to pilot the legislation through the House of Lords.

Social revolution

By this time, social attitudes had begun to shift. A 1965 poll in the *Daily Mail* found that nearly two-thirds of respondents supported reform (although more than ninety per cent believed that gay people were in need of medical or psychiatric attention). And the way that attitudes towards sexuality have developed since then represents perhaps the biggest social revolution of the past half-century. The polling organisation YouGov began a tracker poll of attitudes towards gay – or equal – marriage in 2019. It has shown a consistent level of over seventy per cent approval ever since, with the level of opposition hovering around the ten per cent mark.

Debate within the Church of England, however, remained, in many of its essentials, exactly as it was when the Sexual Offences Act went through. The liberal instincts and sense of humanity that underpinned Michael Ramsey's support for reform of course endured, but so too did the conviction – held by a significant body within the Church of England and the wider Anglican Communion – that gay sex is against the laws of God.

The issue was addressed in a seemingly endless stream of reports and so-called 'shared conversations', but the Church found it difficult to move beyond the apparent contradiction between two basic theological principles: the belief that we are all created in the image of God (and therefore deserve to be treated equally in his love); and the biblical evidence that the same God prohibits sexual relationships between people of the same gender.

Significant milestones

The *Sunday* archive does not really get going on this issue until the turn of the century, but there were two milestones towards the end of the twentieth century that continue to play a significant role.

The General Synod's first formal pronouncement on gay relationships – remembered now as the Higton Motion – was debated in November 1987. Revd Tony Higton, a firebrand rector from Essex, introduced a private member's motion to – in the words of *The Guardian*'s Synod report – 'oust practising homosexuals from the clergy'. Revd Higton told the Synod he was 'not calling for a witch-hunt or hasty accusations, but rather for Godly discipline which upholds the teaching of Scripture, including the teaching that all homosexual practice is an abomination and a perversion'. In his address to the Synod, he cited a list of what he called 'rampant' homosexual practices among clergy who 'take off their Christianity when they take off their clerical collars'.[7]

The rector's guns were skilfully spiked by Bishop Michael Baughen, who proposed an amendment softening some of the motion's more extreme language and, critically, removing the wording that would have mandated the sacking of gay clergy. Thus amended, the motion passed by 403 votes to eight. Though more moderately phrased than Tony Higton's original, it still affirmed that 'sexual intercourse is an act of total commitment which belongs properly within a permanent married relationship', and that fornication, adultery and homosexual acts 'fall short of this ideal'. Those who indulged in 'homosexual genital acts' were called to repentance, and the motion declared that 'holiness of life is particularly required of Christian leaders'.

The impact of this episode reflects recurring themes in the Church of England's long agony over this issue. The Synod was condemned by some sections of the press for being too liberal and out of touch with the social climate of the day. It was around this time that the Thatcher government passed the notorious Section 28 of the Local Government Act, which banned the 'promotion' of a gay lifestyle in schools. On the other hand, those who championed change would be forever hamstrung by the Synod's unambiguous condemnation of gay sex and its call to 'Christian leaders' (i.e. priests) to maintain 'holiness of life'.[8]

---

7 Quotes in this paragraph from 'Bishop's gambit lifts threat of ban on gays', *The Guardian*, 12 November 1987, p. 6.

8 'Presentation prior to the group work on case studies and GS2055', Church of England: https://www.churchofengland.org/sites/default/files/2017-11/bishop-of-norwich-presentation.pdf (15 February 2017, accessed 13 July 2023).

In a 2017 speech outlining the history of Church debate on sexuality, the bishop of Norwich, Graham James, stated that: 'Nearly everything that has happened in the Church of England on these issues since then has been in reaction to that motion.'[9]

Leaders of the worldwide Anglican Communion meet once a decade, and when they gathered for the Lambeth Conference of 1998 it was already apparent that sexuality might lead to schism. Western Anglican Churches – especially in North America – were moving increasingly towards more liberal positions, while the Anglican Churches of the so-called Global South – in Africa, especially – held fast to traditionalist beliefs. The 1998 conference voted through a resolution which rejected 'homosexual practice as incompatible with Scripture'.[10] This was the second milestone that has dictated the trajectory of the debate ever since.

It was against this backdrop that Rowan Williams became archbishop of Canterbury in December 2002. The issue of sexuality blew up into a crisis almost immediately.

In the spring of 2003, Jeffrey John, then canon chancellor and theologian at Southwark Cathedral, was chosen to be the bishop of Reading. John was in a long-term relationship with another Church of England priest, and he was the first person in such circumstances to be nominated as a bishop. The couple declared that their relationship was celibate, but the appointment still met with widespread opposition. Leaders from some parts of the worldwide Anglican Communion warned Archbishop Williams that there would be a schism if he went ahead and consecrated John as a bishop, and in circumstances that were not entirely clear – and that left some badly bruised feelings – the appointment was abandoned at a very late stage.

Bishops in the Episcopal Church of the United States are elected by diocesan conventions rather than being appointed, and later that year Eugene Robinson was elected as bishop in the New Hampshire Diocese. He was the first openly gay man to become a bishop in the Anglican Communion, and the election polarised opinion right across the Anglican

---

9 'Presentation prior to the group work on case studies and GS2055', Church of England.
10 'Section I.10 - Human Sexuality', Anglican Communion: https://www.anglicancommunion. org/resources/document-library/lambeth-conference/1998/section-i-called-to-full-humanity/section-i10-human-sexuality (accessed 16 June 2023).

world. When, in December 2003, *Sunday* took stock of Rowan Williams's first months in office, the issue of sexuality dominated the item.

Roger Bolton: *In February, Dr Rowan Williams was enthroned as the 104th archbishop of Canterbury. If he had any illusion that he would be able to ease himself gently into the job, it was very quickly shattered. This year has been a baptism of fire for the new leader of the Anglican Communion. Within weeks of taking up his post, war with Iraq was declared* [the invasion of Iraq by British and American forces began in March 2003]. *Three months later, the Diocese of New Westminster in Canada voted in favour of same-sex blessings. This was to start a sequence of events that would take the Anglican Communion to the brink of schism. Within a fortnight of the New Westminster decision, Canon Jeffrey John had been appointed bishop of Reading with the apparent agreement of Dr Williams, and Canon Gene Robinson elected diocesan bishop of New Hampshire in America.*

Both men are openly gay and living with partners. Both appointments were seen by many evangelicals, particularly conservatives, to go against a resolution signed by leaders of the Anglican Communion at the last Lambeth Conference in 1998. The resolution rejected homosexual practice on the grounds that it is incompatible with Scripture and also opposed the legitimising of same-sex unions and the ordination of gays. When I spoke to Canon Gene Robinson on the day of his election, I asked him whether he was worried about the effect his appointment might have on the Anglican Communion.

Gene Robinson: *Yes, I understand that this election today will be very disturbing to some of my brothers and sisters in Christ, both in this country and overseas. I believe that those who find this troublesome are following their call from God as faithfully and sincerely as they can. On the other hand, I am also following my call from God. I believe that there is room in our Church, in the Anglican Communion for all of us.*

Roger Bolton: *Others were not so optimistic. There was fierce opposition, and a number of Anglican primates called on Rowan Williams to intervene to prevent the Anglican Communion from splitting over this issue. In the end, Jeffrey John stepped down from Reading. But an unprecedented meeting of the primates gathered at Lambeth in October to discuss the imminent* *consecration of Gene Robinson. I asked one of the primates opposing the consecration, Archbishop Gregory Venables* [leader of the Southern Cone province of the Anglican Church, which includes six dioceses in South America], *what he would say to the supporters of Gene Robinson.*

Gregory Venables: *I think it's obvious that the majority of primates are saying, 'If you do that* [ordain a bishop in a gay relationship], *then we have a split.' I think that's the message we're hearing all over the world. So the message will be, 'Please do not do it. Please show that you're sorry that you've done this without full consultation and without working together as a Communion. Let's go back and please let's try to put it right, because if you go ahead, then it's going to be impossible to continue as a Communion as we know it.'*

Africa or America?

For an assessment of the seriousness of the strains on the Anglican Communion, the programme turned to a religious affairs correspondent of many years' standing.

Roger Bolton: *Earlier, I talked to Stephen Bates, religious affairs correspondent for* The Guardian, *and asked whether he felt this was the beginning of the end for the Anglican Communion.*

Stephen Bates: *I think it's maybe a little early to say that, but certainly they're in a more fractious mood than they've been for very many years, and certainly a number of the black churches in Africa, the developing-world churches, are very angry about what's been going on in America, especially, and are declaring themselves, in lofty tones, out of communion with the American Episcopal Church. So there are signs that all is not well.*

Roger Bolton: *Do you think, therefore,* [the archbishop of] *Canterbury is going to have to make a choice either to side with Africa – where there's a great expansion in Christian belief and converts are multiplying – either go with them or go with the American churches? Is that the sort of decision that Rowan Williams is having to make?*

Stephen Bates: *Yes, I think so. I think he's done as much as he can to keep things together. He doesn't want to be seen as the archbishop who let it* *all fall apart. And what he's trying to do at the moment is to straddle the two options by appointing a commission which will look into the whole issue of homosexuality... One of the American evangelicals said to me in the summer that it's a bit like two sides playing tennis on adjacent courts. We bat the ball over the net, but there's no one at the other side to bat it back. And really, the two sides have stopped talking to each other, and that's a significant problem for the archbishop of Canterbury in trying to keep things on the road.*

Gene Robinson's ordination provoked anger among some of his own flock as well as internationally, as Jane Little discovered when she reported from New Hampshire the following spring. In Rochester, a picturesque New England city with roots in the colonial era, she visited a parish where local leaders had handed back the keys to their church and walked out, setting up a breakaway parish organisation of their own. She found 'such bitterness that neighbours in this small town aren't speaking to one another'.

Jane Little: *Lisa Ball was one of those who walked out. She can't accept the authority of Gene Robinson because he's in a gay relationship, which she says contradicts the Bible. She's helped set up a breakaway church. They voted and chose the name St Michael's.*

Lisa Ball: *He slew the devil. He stood up for what he believed in. St Michael's means courage, strength and standing firm. And we wanted to continue that.*

Jane Little: *It's one o'clock and a dozen people worship in the newly incorporated St Michael's – or rather in a borrowed Baptist church, as St Michael's is currently homeless. There's palpable anger in the pews and in the pulpit.*

Don Wilson: *The Episcopal Church, as we know, has forgotten and rejected its roots. Scripture and tradition have been dismissed, subject to interpretation.*

Jane Little: *The Revd Don Wilson, retired, is serving as their priest, and they've started a building fund. They're the only people so far to leave the diocese en masse, but they're joining forces with conservatives from other states. The Revd Bill Murdoch is the dean of the New England*

Convocation, as it's called, which is part of the growing conservative Anglican Communion network.

Bill Murdoch: *We now represent twelve diocese, 1,100 clergy and all of the clergy in churches within the five convocations, totalling numbers larger than the Anglican province of Wales or the Anglican province of Scotland. So already the Anglican Communion network, size wise, is bigger than those two places within our Communion.*

Jane Little filed her despatch just as Archbishop Robin Eames (Anglican Archbishop of Armagh and Primate of All Ireland), who had been charged with finding a way through the crisis by Rowan Williams, was preparing to report his conclusions. His commission had not taken evidence from Gene Robinson himself, which Bishop Robinson told *Sunday* he considered an 'eccentric' decision – to put the matter at its mildest.

Gene Robinson: *I've very much wanted to talk with the Eames Commission, and there are people in the Diocese of New Hampshire who could have told the story of what happened in New Hampshire and why. And our requests to meet with the Eames Commission have all been answered with a fairly firm 'no'. And that's been a real sadness to us.*

Jane Little: *Why? What reason did they give?*

Gene Robinson: *They said that this was not about Gene Robinson or what happened in New Hampshire. It was really only about how we're going to live together as thirty-eight autonomous provinces of the Anglican Communion. That would be fine if I didn't see my name in virtually every paragraph written about the Eames Commission – even in their own press releases and so on. In one sense it's not about homosexuality or what happened in New Hampshire. On the other hand, would we have an Eames Commission had there not been an election in New Hampshire?*

The Lambeth Commission

Archbishop Eames and his commission – the Lambeth Commission, as it was known – finally delivered their report in the autumn of 2004. In early September, just before it came out, *Sunday* picked up on leaks suggesting the commission believed that the American Church should be disciplined.

Roger Bolton: *The Lambeth Commission, headed by Archbishop Robin Eames of Armagh, will deliver its report to the archbishop of Canterbury, Rowan Williams, at the end of this month. Reports over the last few days suggest it will recommend disciplinary action against the American Episcopal Church and against its Canadian neighbour unless they back down from authorising the blessing of same-sex unions. Martin Stott reports.*

Martin Stott: *Many would argue that the consecration of Gene Robinson made schism almost unavoidable in the 70-million-strong international Anglican Communion. Within weeks of that action, over a dozen Anglican provinces, including Nigeria, Uganda and Kenya, declared themselves out of communion with the American Church. The task of the Lambeth Commission is to find a way to restore and repair the torn fabric of the communion. The Times's religion correspondent Ruth Gledhill reported this week that its current draft proposals call for a hard line to be taken against the Americans.*

Ruth Gledhill: *Three or four people who are very close to the commission have given me some indication of key elements that it contains at present. I have been told that everything is still to play for. However, I've also been told, categorically, that it's disastrous for the lesbian and gay community, and that the report will have teeth; that it will not be the classic Anglican fudge which we've all grown to expect over the years. The teeth, as I understand it, will include some form of disciplinary action taken against ECUSA, the Episcopal Church in America.*

When the report was finally published, it called for the American Episcopal Church to apologise for choosing Gene Robinson as a bishop, and to refrain from appointing any more bishops in same-sex relationships. Those who consecrated Bishop Robinson were urged to 'consider in all conscience whether they should withdraw themselves from representative functions in the Anglican Communion.'[11] But the

---

11 'The Windsor Report 2004', Anglican Communion: https://www.anglicancommunion.org/media/68225/windsor2004full.pdf (accessed 16 June 2023).

report certainly did not settle the matter; instead, it merely inflamed liberal Anglican opinion.

An ambiguous position

While Rowan Williams wrestled with the international dimension of this crisis, he came under more pressure at home because of the way government policy was developing. In 2004, the Blair government introduced civil partnerships, which allowed gay couples to secure the legal status and protections enjoyed by married couples. Most bishops in the House of Lords voted for the legislation, but the Church's leaders then issued a statement reaffirming their belief that marriage itself could only be solemnised between a man and a woman.

The guidance given to priests on how they should treat civil partnerships was clearly intended to be a 'middle road', but anyone who tried to follow it was liable to get lost. The Religion Media Centre summarises the bishops' response to civil partnerships as follows:

> *The church would not create a service to bless civil partnerships, but clergy could respond individually with prayers to a partnership if they deemed it to be within the church's teaching (i.e. was celibate). Any priest wishing to enter into a civil partnership themselves had to promise their bishop they would not have sex. Lay Christians in civil partnerships would not have to promise the same before being baptised, confirmed or given communion.*[12]

The ambiguity inherent in the Church's position left a certain amount of wriggle room in the way the guidelines were followed, as Roger Bolton found out in an entertaining *Sunday* joust over a service – the precise nature of the event was itself disputed – at a London church in the summer of 2008.

Roger Bolton: *'Dearly beloved, we are gathered together here in the sight*

---

12 T. Wyatt, Factsheet: 'Sexuality timeline in the Church of England', Religion Media Centre: https://religionmediacentre.org.uk/factsheets/factsheet-sexuality-timeline-in-the-church-of-england (11 January 2022, accessed 25 April 2023).

of God and in the face of this congregation to join together these men in a holy covenant of love and fidelity.' That was part of what has been called the wedding service of two Anglican priests, the Revd Peter Cowell and the Revd Dr David Lord, which took place on the 31st of May this year in the Church of St Bartholomew the Great in the Diocese of London. They had previously gone through a civil partnership ceremony. The service, and the Act of Holy Communion which followed, was conducted by another Anglican priest... I'm now joined by the rector of St Bartholomew's, the Revd Martin Dudley, who conducted the service. Good morning. Thank you very much for joining us. Was this a gay church wedding?

Martin Dudley: No, it wasn't a gay church wedding. It was the blessing of two people who had contracted a civil partnership.

Roger Bolton: And yet it was a service based in large measure on the 1662 Book of Common Prayer. And it contained this: 'With this ring I thee bind, with my body I thee worship, and with all my worldly goods I thee endow.' And you yourself said to the people, 'For as much as David and Peter have consented together in Holy Covenant and have witnessed the same before God in this company and thereto have given and pledge their troth either to the other, and have declared the same by giving and receiving a ring and by joining of hands, I pronounce that they be bound together in the name of the Father and the Son and the Holy Ghost.' 'Bound together' as what?

Martin Dudley: Bound together as a couple committed to a relationship for life, which is exactly what a civil partnership allows them to be.

Roger Bolton: In church, with a Holy Communion service, with a service modelled on the wedding service. Well, it was as close as you can get, wasn't it?

Martin Dudley: I don't think it was as close as you can get. One can selectively choose the bits. Actually, the preface was a bit different from that, and actually it was quite a bit different from what Peter and David had brought to me originally.

Roger Bolton: Well, the mind boggles, because I've got lots of other bits I could quote. What did they want to do originally? What form of service were they asking for? An exact mirror image of the wedding service?

Martin Dudley: Yes. In essence, that's what they were looking for. But it

had to be words that I could use with integrity, that my fellow clergy who
assisted me could use, and that Peter and David felt expressed their love
for each other and their commitment to each other.

After sparring like this for several rounds of quick-fire question and answer, Roger Bolton pressed Revd Martin Dudley over why he had done something that seemed so clearly contrary to the express wishes of the Church of England's leadership.

His interviewee finally lost his patience. 'Let's get beyond that issue to the number of gay people there are in the Church and in the clergy,' he snapped back, 'and the total hypocrisy of trying to make out that they are not there, that they are not in civil partnerships.'

Bolton then turned to Colin Slee, the dean of Southwark, who criticised the way the presenter's questions had been framed and defended his colleague. 'I think that the way you've been representing the House of Bishops' guidelines makes them sound mandatory,' he challenged. 'You actually use the word "instructions", and they are guidelines. And clearly within them there is room for clergy to act when there are compelling pastoral reasons. So I would assume that Martin Dudley takes the view that there are compelling pastoral reasons in connection with this particular ceremony.' At the same time, the dean insisted that he would not allow a service of the kind the Revd Martin Dudley had conducted to be held at his own cathedral.

Roger Bolton reminded the audience that the service-that-wasn't-a-wedding in St Bartholomew's took place 'at a particularly sensitive moment'. The following week, dozens of conservative Anglican bishops and archbishops gathered in Jerusalem to set in motion the process of establishing a breakaway group known as the Global Anglican Future Conference (Gafcon).

The 'crisis over homosexuality'

A month later, in July 2008, Rowan Williams presided over another Lambeth Conference; one of those once-a-decade meetings of the whole Anglican Communion. Several conservative primates declined his invitation to attend. One of them, the leader of the Anglican Church in Uganda, explained his decision to *Sunday*, and he placed the blame squarely on Rowan Williams's shoulders.

Edward Stourton: *The archbishop of Canterbury got another piece of unwelcome news this week. The Anglican Church of Uganda announced that its bishops will not be attending this year's Lambeth Conference... The Ugandan bishops cited what they called the 'crisis over homosexuality'. I asked the Most Revd Henry Orombi, the archbishop of Uganda, whether anything would make them change their minds.*

Henry Orombi: *I think it's not a question of persuasion. I think what is very important to us as bishops, and also Christians, in Uganda is that we had requested that Lambeth should be delayed until the house, which is the Anglican Communion, can resolve the problem that we have. That request was not taken seriously... We believe that there is some kind of lack of seriousness to deal with the real issue of the Communion. And so we feel like, why are we going to be pretending, when seriously there is no communion and fellowship among us?*

Edward Stourton: *And when you say there is a lack of seriousness about dealing with this problem, do you aim that charge at the archbishop of Canterbury?*

Henry Orombi: *He is our leader. He is the one who should put us around the table as the primates that support him. We are wondering why some of these decisions are made without consulting with us as primates.*

In the hope of lowering the temperature at the conference, Rowan Williams declined to issue an invitation to Gene Robinson himself. He could not, however, prevent the bishop from travelling to the United Kingdom to publicise a book he had written about his beliefs. The New Hampshire bishop was something of a *Sunday* regular by this point.

Roger Bolton: *Now, you talked earlier about this issue of homosexuality being out of proportion. The Church was about far more than this. And yet you will be going to London and to Canterbury for the Lambeth Conference. You will not be attending directly, of course, but you [will] be in London. You will be in what you call the marketplace. Wouldn't the best thing to do [be] to stay home?*

Gene Robinson: *I believe the archbishop of Canterbury has gotten it just exactly right that this conference will have no legislation, no resolutions, and indeed it will be a place for prayerful conversation between bishops.*

Roger Bolton: *But with your presence... and I understand you're also going to preach while you're in this country, just before and during the conference – inevitably, your presence will ensure that this issue of homosexuality dominates.*

Gene Robinson: *Well, first, I will not be preaching unless, and until, I receive permission from the archbishop of Canterbury.*

Roger Bolton: *But you will, sir, take part in what you call 'the marketplace'. You will be in London, you will give interviews. The controversy is inevitable, isn't it?*

Gene Robinson: *Well, I believe what is inevitable is the opportunity for people around the globe, and particularly bishops around the globe, to have a new experience, and that is to sit with a person who is unashamedly gay and unashamedly Christian to talk about my journey and what my life in Christ feels like from where I sit.*

Changing definitions of marriage

While the Anglican Church remained caught in the seemingly endless coils of this debate, society at large was moving briskly on. In March 2012, David Cameron's coalition government launched a consultation on same-sex marriage. This shifted the focus of public discussion to the nature and meaning of marriage, and it brought the Roman Catholic Church out fighting, as *Sunday* reported that same month.

Edward Stourton: *'Marriage is a sharing in the mystery of God's own life: the unending and perfect flow of love between Father, Son and Holy [Spirit].'*[13] *That, at least, is how marriage is described in the letter from the Roman Catholic archbishops of Westminster and Southwark, which has been read out in churches across England and Wales today. It's part*

13 'A Letter on Marriage from the President and Vice-President of the Bishops' Conference of England and Wales', Catholic Bishops' Conference: https://familyofsites.bishopsconference.org.uk/wp-content/uploads/sites/8/2019/07/abps-letter-marriage-march-2012.pdf (10–11 March 2012, accessed 16 June 2023).

of the Catholic Church's campaign to make the government think again about allowing gay couples to marry.

To provide context for the debate, the programme asked three experts from different disciplines to reflect on the way ideas about marriage had changed over the centuries. Maureen Waller, author of *The English Marriage*, argued that the institution owed as much to Mammon as it did to God.

Maureen Waller: *Back in the 1650s, during the Republic* [the Commonwealth period from 1649 to 1660], *the state had allowed civil marriage. So this had given people the notion that they could get married without a priest present, or indeed, not in a church. And, you know, thousands of people did that. In 1753 you get Hardwicke's Marriage Act and, like everything to do with the English marriage, it was really driven by the need to preserve property intact. The act says that everybody has to get married in church by a priest before witnesses. For those without property, legitimacy wasn't that important. And in fact, the English had a fairly, sort of, casual attitude. Maybe half the population went to the altar pregnant.*

The other two contributors, the legal commentator Joshua Rozenberg and Adrian Thatcher, a visiting professor at Exeter and author of *God, Sex and Gender*, both highlighted how the concept of marriage had evolved.

Adrian Thatcher: *In the Christian faith, there is only one reality that doesn't change, and that is God. Everything else is subject to mortality – to the passages and ravages of time – and marriage has changed hugely over time. Is it a sacrament? Well, yes, it is, but no, it isn't. But yes, it is again. Must wives obey their husbands? Right up to the 1960s, the answer to that was yes.*

Joshua Rozenberg: *I suppose the public's respect for marriage has changed over the years. The formalities for conducting a marriage have changed. But ultimately, the principle behind marriage – that it was a union between one man and one woman, and registered publicly – I think that has remained.*

Adrian Thatcher: Now, it's not remarked [on] often enough that covenant theology is able to deal with same-sex marriage extremely effectively. The question is whether you can make that kind of covenant if you are in a same-sex relationship, and of course you can. The idea that marriage would be changed fundamentally if same-sex couples were admitted to it – it's true, of course it would be changed fundamentally. But marriage is always being changed fundamentally.

Not so, argued the Roman Catholic archbishop of Westminster, Cardinal Vincent Nichols, who joined the programme live immediately after that analysis.

Edward Stourton: The pastoral letter being read out in parishes in England and Wales today comes a week after Cardinal Keith O'Brien, the leader of Scotland's Catholics, called the plans to allow gay marriage 'grotesque'. The archbishop of Westminster, Vincent Nichols, is on the line. Good morning.

Vincent Nichols: Good morning, Ed.

Edward Stourton: Do you think gay marriage is 'grotesque'?

Vincent Nichols: Well, actually, our letter, as it says, is wanting to put before the Catholic people our understanding of marriage and the light it cuts on the importance of marriage for society. We don't actually talk about same-sex partnerships in this document – and that is quite deliberate, because this debate, as those very interesting clips have just shown, is essentially about what is the nature of marriage. And the main point that we want to make in this letter, or the first point, is that our understanding of marriage is based on our nature. It's not based on the way it's reflected in society, nor even simply in legislation, but it is written, as it were, into the broad patterns of human nature.

Edward Stourton: That is your view. And we heard in those clips all sorts of different views of what marriage is. We also have the dean of St Paul's saying marriage doesn't belong to the Church, and yet you seem to believe that it does belong to the Church, and that your view should prevail.

Vincent Nichols: No, I think precisely the point of this letter is to say that it doesn't belong to the Church; that it is a question of our understanding of human nature. And that's why, for example, the proposals by the government that we could split marriage into a civil reality and a religious reality fails to address the fundamental understanding that marriage is single. There is one marriage. There is a way into it through a civil partnership, a civil route, which is again quite recent. And there is a way into it through a religious route. But it's one reality.

Edward Stourton: Well, well, hold on here. I read out that very religious definition of marriage that you quote in your letter, and many Catholics will find that inspiring. For many atheist couples who are married, that will be completely meaningless. And we already have circumstances in which many married people don't share the Church's understanding of what marriage is. Why do you feel threatened by the addition of another form of marriage?

Vincent Nichols: Because I think what is being proposed is not another form of marriage; it's another form of relationship.

The sparring continued for several minutes, and towards the end of the interview the presenter returned to his original question.

Edward Stourton: Since you mentioned the perception that the Church is being anti-gay, let's return to the question of rhetoric. I asked you at the beginning of the interview whether you would associate yourself with the comments made by Cardinal O'Brien – his description of the plans as 'grotesque'. The equalities minister, Lynne Featherstone, has talked about the Church being stuck in the Dark Ages as a result of that sort of rhetoric. Do you think that those comments were regrettable?

Vincent Nichols: I don't think her comments are helpful.

Edward Stourton: No, I mean his.

Vincent Nichols: And I wouldn't use the same language as Cardinal O'Brien, as you can see from this letter. I think what we really need is a focus on what this debate is actually about. As we've heard in those clips, the reality of marriage is complex and sensitive, and it shouldn't be approached in this shortcut manner by the government.

The following year, in 2013, Cardinal Keith O'Brien was forced to resign as the leader of the Roman Catholic Church in Scotland when he was accused of predatory behaviour towards young priests and seminarians.

The same year saw the passing of the Marriage (Same Sex Couples) Act 2013, which introduced equal marriage in England and Wales. Scotland followed shortly afterwards and, while change was slower in Northern Ireland, the region eventually fell into line with the rest of the United Kingdom.

As British society went through this momentous revolution, the Church of England was focused on yet another report. The 2013 Pilling Report (chaired by the retired civil servant Sir Joseph Pilling) recommended several years of so-called 'facilitated conversations' – small groups meeting in hotels and conference centres to discuss sexuality with the guidance of a professional moderator. This had the effect of kicking the issue yet further down the road.

Vicky Beeching comes out

Sunday's coverage during this somewhat sterile period was enhanced by real-life testimony from some of those who suffered during the Church's long anguish of indecision. In July 2014, Vicky Beeching, a hugely popular and successful Christian singer–songwriter, came out as a lesbian.

William Crawley: *Vicky Beeching may be known to many of our listeners as a Christian singer and songwriter whose songs are often sung in churches and at worship festivals, but she's better known to many more this week after she revealed, at the age of thirty-five, that she's a lesbian, and that she's no longer prepared to hide that fact about herself. Vicky Beeching joins me now. Vicky, good morning to you. You've had an interesting week, haven't you? How are you doing?*

Vicky Beeching: *I'm doing OK. It's certainly been the strangest week of my entire life. So it's been many, many things rolled into one – highs and lows – and [I] still feel a bit dazed by it all, really.*

William Crawley: *I bet you do. What finally prompted you to come out?*

Vicky Beeching: *It was a real mixture of things. One of them was drawing a line in the sand for myself, saying that I wouldn't go past the age of thirty-five without really reconciling myself to this and speaking out. And the other thing is actually prompted by the Church of England saying yes* *to women bishops almost a month ago today* [see chapter 6], *and feeling like, now that topic is kind of done and dusted – gender equality in the Church – I think now the focus of the Church will be on sexuality, and I just feel like my voice is more useful in that conversation as an out gay person.*

William Crawley: *You trained in Theology at Oxford, and I suspect there's a bit of a theological journey here for you as well, not just a personal one. How did your own understanding of the Bible change over the years?*

Vicky Beeching: *I grew up in a kind of conservative Christian home, so we would have a traditional understanding of what the Bible says on sexuality. And it really took me from the age of... thirteen, when I first began to experience these feelings for other girls, until the age of thirty to really reconcile myself with the theology of it. So a long, long process, because the Bible means a huge amount to me and so does my faith. So I wasn't willing to throw my faith away just to pursue my orientation.*

William Crawley: *What's been the reaction of Christian friends and people within the Church generally?*

Vicky Beeching: *It's been wonderfully positive on Twitter. I felt a real outpouring of love on social media in general. I have had quite a lot of emails as well from people contacting me through my website that are negative, saying they're disappointed. But I'm just choosing to focus on the positive ones, because I think that's the best thing I can do for myself mentally.*

When she described her childhood, Beeching touched on a subject that would later become a controversy of its own, both within the Churches and, indeed, in British politics: so-called 'conversion therapy' – the idea that a person's sexuality could be changed by psychological or spiritual intervention.

William Crawley: *Well, obviously, you lived with this truth about yourself, as you've been saying, Vicky, for a very long time. What was your experience of the Church over the years while you were coming to terms with your sexuality?*

Vicky Beeching: *It was difficult, because I was raised in a church setting where it was taught that this was wrong, and actually where it was* *also taught that it was influenced by demonic factors. So I think that, psychologically, can really split you in two, because you feel like you have to choose between your faith and your sexuality.*

William Crawley: *You were told you were demon-possessed.*

Vicky Beeching: *I was, actually, at the age of sixteen. Yes. And that was very creepy, as you can imagine. And it sounds maybe silly for somebody logically to believe in demons and things like that. But when you are really just a child and you're told that, it can have very lasting consequences...*

William Crawley: *And I understand you experienced exorcism at one point, or an attempted exorcism.*

Vicky Beeching: *Yeah, well, it was fairly common practice to pray – in those more sort of Pentecostal settings where I grew up – for the... sort of powers-that-be that are causing you to be doing things you shouldn't to let you go. And I think linking my sexuality with demonic factors did really scar me. It made me feel like this was a part of myself that was not within my control, and was coming from very negative, negative places.*

No change on sex or marriage

Personal testimony also played a significant role in Ireland's referendum on equal marriage the following year. On 19 April, *Sunday* broadcast a clip from an interview the former Irish president Mary McAleese had given to the Newstalk radio station. In support of her case, she cited the Proclamation of the Irish Republic, made during the 1916 Easter Rising:

It is a debate about children. People have been saying it's about children, and we believe it to be about Ireland's gay children and about their future, and about the kind of future we want for Ireland. We want – in the words of the proclamation – the children of the nation to be cherished equally: the adult children, the children yet unborn, the gay children yet unborn. We want them to be born into a world where, if they fall in love with someone, they can express that love fully.

One of the programme's guests that morning, Dr Richard O'Leary, the spokesperson for the campaigning organisation Faith in Marriage

Equality, explained that the issue was a very personal one for the former president:

I'd just like to say that Mary McAleese's intervention was also very significant as an Irish mother, because yesterday her son Justin explained how he was a gay man and how he'd felt, you know, treated as a second-class citizen. So here we have an example of an Irish mother coming out and saying that what she wants for her gay son is that he could reach his full potential, be treated equally with other people and be allowed to access a civil marriage.

Ireland's Catholic Church campaigned hard for a 'no' vote, but the referendum turned out to be a significant milestone in the decline of Church power. More than sixty per cent supported the constitutional amendment to allow equal marriage, with majorities in every constituency but one.

The Church of England's 'facilitated' or 'shared conversations' – as advocated in the Pilling Report – came to an end in 2016. In early 2017, the Church's bishops announced their response: there would be no change in the Church's doctrine on sex or marriage. Instead, the bishops proposed to draw up a new 'teaching document' to allow 'maximum freedom' within the existing rules. This provoked a deluge of frustrated protests from those hoping for change. One retired bishop, speaking on *Sunday,* described the reaction as 'screams… which I think are some of the most negative responses I can remember to a piece of work by the House of Bishops'.

Dr Peter Selby, formerly bishop of Worcester, was one of fourteen retired bishops who published an open letter warning the House of Bishops that they were 'managing rather than leading'. He told *Sunday*:

What we saw was a failure of the 'shared conversations' process to lead to people's voices being heard – the people who are most vulnerable. You wouldn't know from this report that we're talking about some of our most gifted priests. You wouldn't know from this report that you're talking about people who are anxious for their jobs, people who have been deprived of jobs, prevented from doing jobs. You wouldn't know that, as my wife wrote many years ago when she was teaching vulnerable young people, you wouldn't know that a report like this simply tells them that the Church has nothing to say to them.

Contentious compromises

The Religion Media Centre has produced a scrupulously impartial account of the way this debate has developed in the Church of England, but even the centre's admirably neutral language cannot conceal the slightly surreal character of the position the Church then adopted.

In 2019, the centre reports: 'It was announced that gay bishops would be invited to the next Lambeth Conference, to be held in the summer of 2020, but their spouses and partners would not be – unlike the spouses of straight bishops. This was due to fears their presence would cause a widespread boycott by conservatives.'

The conference was delayed until 2022 because of the Covid pandemic. When it finally met in July that year, three conservative provinces – Nigeria, Rwanda and Uganda – stayed away, and conservative bishops refused to take Communion alongside gay bishops at the opening service. Mary Glasspool, of the American Episcopal Church – the first avowedly lesbian bishop in the Anglican Communion – did bring her wife, Becky Sander, along, but as *Sunday*'s reporter Harry Farley found, Becky was treated as something of a non-person.

Harry Farley: *Becky, in the background we have the spouses of all the bishops apart from the spouses in same-sex relationships. They're all having their photo taken together, and you are not allowed to be part of that photo. Give me a sense of what that feels like to you.*

Becky Sander: *Thank you for asking. For me, it's such a missed opportunity. It's absolutely a missed time for healing and openness, and encounter with each other.*

The archbishop of Canterbury, Justin Welby, used the conference to reaffirm the motion which, right back in 1998, rejected gay sex as 'incompatible with Scripture', but he also declared that there would be no sanction against Anglican provinces that took a different view. The fact that this somewhat rickety compromise was regarded as a success is a mark of just how intractable this debate remained.

And there was another, highly significant, compromise when the General Synod returned to the issue of sexuality in February 2023. The body voted to allow priests to bless same-sex couples who had contracted a civil marriage (a big step away from the traditional position), but maintained the ban on same-sex marriage in churches.

The outcome alienated people on both sides of the debate. Archbishop Welby announced that although he supported blessings for same-sex unions, he would not himself carry them out because it would create further division with some parts of the Anglican Communion.

8

Bioethics

The *Sunday* archive for the years 2007 and 2008 includes a significant cluster of debates and reports on bioethics. The programme's focus on this area reflected a more general public debate – wide-ranging and often intense – prompted by the hugely significant Human Fertilisation and Embryology Act, which became law in November 2008.

The first act of that name, introduced in 1990, established the Human Fertilisation and Embryology Authority (HFEA), which was charged with the regulation of fertility treatment and human embryo research across the United Kingdom. Scientific advances and changes in social attitudes over the following two decades made an extensive revision unavoidable, and proposals for updating the law challenged a whole range of theological and moral principles.

In August 2007, for example, *Sunday* broadcast a discussion on what were known as 'saviour siblings': children conceived through in vitro fertilisation (IVF) with the express purpose of providing a tissue match for a seriously ill brother or sister.

Edward Stourton: A highly contentious ethical issue has come up in the debate about the government's draft Human Tissue and Embryos Bill over the past few days. A couple of years ago, the House of Lords ruled that the parents of a child with a life-threatening condition can have IVF treatment designed to produce what's known as a 'saviour sibling' – a new baby who will provide a tissue match suitable for treating their older brother or sister. Well, now a committee of peers and members of the House of Commons wants the new bill to extend that right to parents of children who have serious illnesses, as well as those suffering from life-threatening conditions.

The first of the programme's guests, Dr Simon Fishel, managing director of the CARE Fertility Group, insisted that the proposed change in the law was simply a pragmatic step; one that made medical sense and would iron out an anomaly that was denying some families critical treatment.

Simon Fishel: Well, I see it as a healthcare option that is a last resort for these families. In a sense, there's a bit of medical hypocrisy if they're not allowed to access this technology... because many are even advised to try to conceive naturally for that very reason. And it puts that family into horrendous positions when trying to do so, for obvious reasons. So I think it's a natural extension of another technology for healthcare issues.

Edward Stourton: Can we be clear what the extension means? Because under the House of Lords ruling – as I understand it – if you have a child with a life-threatening condition, you can already apply for this kind of treatment. What sort of illnesses would be covered under the provisions that people of your way of thinking would like to see in the bill? What sort of illnesses would be covered if you got your way?

Simon Fishel: It's many of the very serious anaemias, because what we're talking about at this stage in terms of a tissue-matched sibling, it's mainly for stem cell transplantation – bone marrow stem cells, for example, and so it could be a whole range of diseases. But I think we need just to focus probably on where we are today, [which] is the blood-type disorder, the various different types of anaemias, of which there are many. There are the thalassemia sickle cell anaemias, which, of course, are life-threatening. There's aplastic anaemia. So there's a whole range of them, which, if they [the sick children] had a stem cell transfusion, would be absolutely cured from that disorder.

However, Dr Donald Bruce, a former director of the Church of Scotland's Society, Religion and Technology Project, argued that this form of medical intervention would, in any circumstances, run counter to the most basic Christian understanding of what it means to be human.

Donald Bruce: It's a really sensitive issue when you're dealing with a very sick or particularly a dying child, because obviously the desire to save the life of that existing child is a very powerful moral good. But even in medicine, the end does not always justify the means. And the means has to be morally acceptable as well. And selecting embryos as a match raises two or three really quite serious ethical problems, which you have to weigh against that other moral good.

First of all, it involves choosing a particular type of child; not, as it were, because of the child's own value alone, but because of its potential value to save another life. And that's something that obviously can't be done with the consent of the new child. So there's a conflict there with the commonly understood Christian understanding of a child as a gift valuable in itself, regardless of anything else. And the concern [is about] a situation where a future child is to be selected for its usefulness rather than for itself. And I think there is a real moral dilemma when you go down that route.

Edward Stourton: Well, except that Christianity teaches us that we're on this earth for a purpose, doesn't it? And why shouldn't that purpose be to help a sibling?

Donald Bruce: Well, indeed. But then that raises the question, what will that sibling, what will the new child, feel about it when a few years down the line it comes to know what's actually happened? And it was put to me very eloquently once by the head of an IVF clinic, who said, 'Suppose it fails, as it will undoubtedly fail, sometimes? If the primary reason why that child came to be had failed, would they have the same sense through the rest of their life that they'd failed in the reason they were created?' I think no one knows how a child would feel about it.

Edward Stourton: That's a very interesting pragmatic point, isn't it, Dr Fisher? It is conceivable that if you were, as a child who'd been born in this way, confronted as an adult with the information that you had been born because your parents wanted to treat an elder brother or sister, and not for yourself, that might be rather a traumatic experience.

Simon Fishel: Absolutely. And I think Donald makes a very, very valid point. And that is why we're lucky in this country. If this technology is used, it's regulated. And part of that regulation is very, very considered medical consultation, but also counselling as well. We have to remember, families would resort to this as a last resort. They don't want to do this. And you know, children are not born into this world with hang-ups and problems. We adults give them the big issues.

The role of fathers

The proper conditions for human flourishing were also at the heart of a *Sunday* discussion, broadcast in May 2008, on the role of fathers. Although the United Kingdom had not yet legislated for equal marriage at this stage (see chapter 7), civil partnerships were already well established, and social attitudes regarding what constituted a family were much less rigid than they had been at the time of the first Human Fertilisation and Embryology Act in 1990.

Trevor Barnes: The Human Fertilisation and Embryology Bill currently before parliament is being closely scrutinised by religious groups, anxious to ensure that the morality of the issues is keeping pace with the science. One aspect of the bill that's causing concern is that, as things stand, fertility clinics have to consider a child's need for a father before approving patients for treatment. Now, although this doesn't automatically rule out treatment for single women and those in same-sex partnerships, the government still considers the arrangement discriminatory and is pressing for 'supportive parenting' to replace the present wording, including 'fatherhood'. This has caused concern in some religious circles that the role of the father in the procreation process is being undermined.

Well, Dr Evan Harris, Liberal Democrat MP and a supporter of changes to the bill, came into our studio last night, and Dr Justin Thacker, head of Theology at the Christian Evangelical Alliance, took him on.

Justin Thacker: In this debate about the role of the fathers, the welfare of the child is the most important priority. And Evan, I just want to ask you, do you agree that the welfare of the child is the most important thing for us to be considering in all of this?

Evan Harris: Well, the bill does provide that the clinics have to judge the welfare of the child. And what the research shows is that children born to lesbian couples and indeed to solo parents – that's women intending to be solo parents, not women who are abandoned by their husbands or subject to divorce or other marital breakdown; in other words, single mothers – that children born to these families do very well and certainly no worse. So there's no justification on the basis of welfare of the future child to discriminate against these family types. And all the provision that forces clinics to check the need for the father as part of that welfare for the child when dealing with those sorts of family units is pointlessly and needlessly discriminate.

Trevor Barnes: *Isn't the real issue the quality of the parenting, not the gender of the parent?*

Justin Thacker:[1] *Well, I noticed that Evan didn't answer my question about whether the welfare of the child is the most important concern for him. Because the evidence is, in fact, that children who are brought up without fathers do worse on a whole range of measures. Just to give you a quick (s)canter through, they're twice as likely to drop out of school. Twice as likely to have a baby before twenty. Twice as likely to have mental health problems. Fifty per cent more likely to have difficulties.*

Evan Harris: *But those are different families, aren't they? Those are not children of lesbian parents or solo mothers. And that's the key question. There have been studies done of this group of people who are seeking fertility treatment, and there is no difference in outcome. What we do know, however, is that there are bad outcomes for children from broken homes – but that's not a fertility clinic question. Actually, if we were going to use this 'welfare of the child' principle, and select out couples who shouldn't be given treatment on the basis of the likelihood of their child, on average, to do badly, we would say, 'Let's not give treatment to poor people, because children from poor families have worse outcomes.' That would be outrageous. I think everyone would agree.*

Towards the end of the interview, Trevor Barnes raised the matter of Jesus' conception and birth. According to orthodox Christian teaching, the founder of Christianity was, of course, born to a virgin.

Trevor Barnes: *When all is said and done, though, Dr Thacker, you're coming at this from a Christian perspective, but in the New Testament, I mean, Joseph's fatherhood is highly problematical and Jesus himself is offering a challenge to the so-called traditional family.*

---

1 Dr Thacker has asked us to state that his traditionalist view of same-sex marriage has changed since he gave this interview.

Justin Thacker: Well, actually, it's as a former paediatrician myself I'm coming at this, both from a scientific perspective and a Christian perspective. And you're right that, you know, Jesus' family was highly unusual. I mean, there's some suggestion that Joseph died at an early age. It certainly was an unusual birth. But I don't see how that changes the debate we're having, which is that the evidence we know is that fathers are important for children. And if we're seeking the welfare of our children, fathers need to be present.

Trevor Barnes: And aren't you in danger, Dr Harris, of just rubbing the father out of the picture?

Evan Harris: Absolutely not. I mean, I would have thought... that the Christian view is not to unnecessarily impose unjustified discriminatory dogma on other people. I mean, every person of faith has the right to accept assisted reproduction or not, but they shouldn't close it down to other people on the basis of their own theology. That's not the sort of society we should live in when it comes to the delivery of healthcare. That's what we're talking about: delivering healthcare to infertile people.

Fault lines between Christian apologists and committed secularists like Evan Harris were to be expected, but some of the issues raised by the fertilisation and embryology legislation also illuminated significant differences between denominations and faiths.

The nature of humanity

In 2006, the Labour government decided to ban the creation of embryos that combined human and animal material, 'chimeras' as they were sometimes called, in reference to a species-mixing monster of Greek mythology. But in May 2007, the government reversed that decision. As *Sunday* reported the story, 'the Human Tissue and Embryos (Draft) Bill [now] says such hybrids could be created for research, though these embryos would have to be destroyed after fourteen days and would not be allowed to be implanted into a woman's body'.

The programme's discussion pitted Dr Peter Saunders, general surgeon and chief executive of the Christian Medical Fellowship, 'the largest group of Christian doctors', in Roger Bolton's words, against Rabbi Julia Neuberger, who was a member of the House of Lords' scrutiny committee for the bill. Baroness Neuberger was at the time a Liberal Democrat spokesperson on health, and she later served as the Senior Rabbi of the West London Synagogue (a Movement for Reform Judaism synagogue).

Baroness Neuberger declared that she had been persuaded to support the creation of mixed embryos by the scientific evidence. Research into diseases such as Parkinson's and muscular dystrophy could, she argued, be done 'more quickly, less expensively' using such embryos. Dr Saunders countered that 'all the clinically relevant advances in stem cell treatments thus far have come from ethically non-controversial routes', by which he meant the use of 'adult or umbilical stems cells', as opposed to those taken from embryos. But the discussion very quickly moved beyond concrete scientific issues to deeper questions about the nature of humanity.

Roger Bolton: *Peter Saunders, your argument, I think, as I understand, does relate to how we regard the human embryo. How do you regard the human embryo?*

Peter Saunders: *Well, from a Christian perspective, human beings, we believe, are made in God's image. God became a human being in the person of Christ. Christ died to save human beings. And these things are what we believe give human beings real dignity. We're different from animals. Human beings are special; they're precious. They're worthy of the greatest protection and utmost respect. And furthermore, the way human beings are made, created, is extremely important.*

Roger Bolton: *So does that mean you would be opposed to any form of any use of an embryo other than in terms of creating human beings?*

Peter Saunders: *Yes. We're certainly opposed to the creation of human embryos, growing them to a certain size and cannibalising them for their stem cell line... Not only because we regard it as unethical, but, as I was saying before, because we regarded it as unnecessary.*

Roger Bolton: *But let me stick on the ethics and allow Rabbi Neuberger to come back at this point.*

Julia Neuberger: *Can I just say, first of all, I think it's really important* *that one accepts that some of this new scientific research has taught us something – that the human embryo is not as unique as we thought before. And Onora O'Neill, the former BBC Reith Lectures presenter* [then president of the British Academy], *actually said that in the stem cell debate. She made it very clear; if it no longer looks as if the human cell material is so unique, then we do have to think differently about the unique quality of human embryos... And I think that she's been convincing, and I think the scientists are convincing.*

If you can reprogramme human cells or you can reprogramme animal cells so that you can actually develop them in slightly different ways, and you eventually use them for this kind of research, doesn't that suggest we're not so unique, and that you don't actually accept that very, very unique status for those human cells? And isn't that a strong ethical argument for saying that you should be able to use those cells for the benefit of other human beings?

Roger Bolton: *Dr Saunders?*

Peter Saunders: *Well, I think that creating human–animal hybrids and chimeras will diminish human dignity. It will blur moral boundaries and* [move] *across the fundamental line that's always separated humans from animals that many people have very deep feelings and intuitions about, and the possible ends do not justify the means.*

'Frankenstein' research

Not all Christian leaders shared Dr Saunders's absolutist position. In March 2008, *Sunday* interviewed Richard Harries, then recently retired as bishop of Oxford, but still serving as chair of the Ethics and Law Committee of the Human Fertilisation and Embryology Authority. Jane Little asked him about an intervention from Cardinal O'Brien, then leader of the Catholic Church in Scotland, who described the embryology bill as a 'monstrous' piece of legislation, which would allow 'Frankenstein' research (as we saw in chapter 7, the cardinal had a penchant for colourful language).

Lord Harries of Pentregarth, as he became soon after his retirement, was a well-known voice on Radio 4, where he regularly presented *Thought for the Day*. He took a rather different view.

Richard Harries: *Well, if we're just thinking for a moment about human and mixed embryos, we already use animal parts in bodies. So there can't be an absolute barrier on having some animal material in the bodies. And also, we share, as we know, something like 99.4 per cent of our genes with chimpanzees, for example. I'm not saying that there aren't some serious issues to be discussed, but we can't rule out the possibility of shared animal and human mixture altogether.*

Jane Little: *Anglican bishops have also been concerned. Tom Wright, a former colleague and bishop of Durham, called it 'tyrannical'. The archbishop of Canterbury [Rowan Williams] said he had a moral concern over hybrid research that he described as part of a very instrumentalist view of the human embryo.*

Richard Harries: *Well, I think, first of all, we have to bear in mind that the central organs of the Church of England now, for more than three decades, have clearly distinguished their position from that of the Roman Catholics. Now, the logic of the Roman Catholic position is that every fertilised embryo is, in fact, a person. Well, what we now know is that something like two-thirds, more than two-thirds, of fertilised eggs, are lost anyway. When a woman goes in for treatment, you might have eight or ten eggs fertilised. Two healthy ones are implanted, perhaps two are frozen for future use, and the others are eventually discarded. Now, the question is, what are we going to use these potentially discarded embryos for? That's one issue.*

But I think also what is absolutely crucial is that nothing can happen beyond fourteen days. Before fourteen days we're talking about a tiny bundle of multiplying cells less than the size of a pinhead; an undifferentiated mass of cells. And this has to be destroyed. Everything has to be destroyed before fourteen days. And the other thing is that nothing that has been tampered with in any way can be implanted in a woman's womb. So we're only talking about research at a very, very early stage.

That interview followed a political row over whether all Labour MPs, in particular Catholic Labour MPs, should be forced to vote for the Fertilisation and Embryology Bill under a three-line whip. The Catholic Church had been especially vocal in its opposition to the bill, and Cardinal O'Brien argued publicly that government ministers should resign rather than walk through the lobby in support of the legislation (the Cabinet included three prominent Catholics: the defence secretary, Des Browne; the Welsh secretary, Paul Murphy; and the transport secretary, Ruth Kelly).

Politicians and conscience

On 24 March 2008, Downing Street announced that there would be a free vote on the bill – the traditional parliamentary approach to issues of conscience. That prompted a *Sunday* discussion on politicians and conscience. It was intended to be a broad-ranging conversation, but it soon came back to the embryology bill. One of the guests was the former Liberal Democrat leader David Steel who, as a young MP, introduced the 1967 Private Members' Bill that made abortion legal.

David Steel: When it comes to the Catholic Church, they've spoken out very, very strongly on this issue. But to be fair to them, they're against any embryo research. They regard the embryo from the moment of conception as the equivalent of human life. And the difficulty that I have with the Catholic Church on this, as I had during the Abortion Bill, is that this has not always been the Catholic Church position. You go back to the time of Thomas Aquinas. They believed then that the soul entered the foetus at the time of quickening, around the twelfth or thirteenth week of pregnancy. And that was a quite different position from the position of the Catholic Church now...

I've always recognised the right of the Catholic Church to speak out on these issues and to expect their adherents to follow the teaching of the Church. What they haven't got a right to do, and this is where they step over the line, is to say the rest of society should follow what we say. And I don't think that is reasonable.

The Human Fertilisation and Embryology Act was finally voted into law with an overwhelming majority: 355 to 129. The prime minister, Gordon Brown, whose son Fraser had been diagnosed with cystic fibrosis, was a passionate champion of the research that this change would allow, and appeared in the Commons to vote in person.

The act did indeed make provision for 'human-admixed' embryos for research purposes, although it also regulated the practice to ensure that the 'chimeras' so feared by Dr Saunders could never come to term. The act also replaced the existing IVF legislation's reference to 'the need for a father' with 'the need for supportive parenting', and it made provision for same-sex couples to be recognised as the legal parents of children conceived thanks to donated sperm, eggs or embryos. Sex-selection of children for non-medical reasons was banned (the HFEA had, in fact, been operating a policy against this anyway) but the sex-selection of children for medical reasons was to be allowed in order to prevent the birth of children with sex-related diseases such as hemophilia.

Dignitas Personae

By coincidence, the month after the Act was granted royal assent, the Vatican issued what was clearly intended to be a definitive statement covering many of the areas that had led to so much fraught debate. *Dignitas Personae* ('the Dignity of a Person'), was an instruction from the Congregation for the Doctrine of the Faith, the Church's theological watchdog.

Roger Bolton: *Two days ago, the Vatican issued what many consider its most authoritative declaration on bioethics for twenty years. I asked John Allen from the* National Catholic Reporter *how significant the instruction – to use its proper name – was, and whether it was mainly a restatement of previous positions.*

John Allen: *For the outside world, there is no surprise here at all. The Vatican has restated its resounding opposition to embryonic stem cell research, to human cloning, to the freezing of embryos, to genetic engineering – and none of that is new.*

Roger Bolton: *Does it equate with murder such practices as the destruction of defective embryos in the IVF process?*

John Allen: *Yes, it does. This document is very clear that the human embryo from the first moment of conception is a person and, therefore, to destroy an embryo is tantamount to abortion which, of course, in Catholic moral thinking is tantamount to murder.*

Roger Bolton: And does it resolve the position about what to do with frozen orphan embryos?

John Allen: Yes, that's right. Of course, in the United States alone, the estimate is that there are something like 400,000 frozen embryos stored in fertility clinics in various parts of the country. Now, of course, according to Catholic moral theology, those embryos should never have been created and then frozen in the first place. But the fact remains that they exist.

In recent years, a number of very conservative Catholic moral theologians actually have argued in favour of what's known as 'embryo adoption'. That is, allowing people who are not the biological parents of these embryos, nevertheless, to bring them to term. And that has been seen as a way of saving their lives. But this document actually comes out quite strongly against that practice. The conclusion one draws is that the Vatican regards the freezing of embryos as so morally reprehensible that, to be blunt, there's simply no possible solution.

Treating Hindu patients

Britain's health secretary during the debates on the embryology bill, Labour's Alan Johnson, also took steps to make the National Health Service more sensitive to the needs and cultures of the country's growing non-Christian religious communities. The number of Hindus in the United Kingdom stood at a tiny 30,000 or so at the beginning of the 1960s, but by the end of the first decade of the new millennium that figure had risen to almost 1 million.

In December 2008, Alan Johnson's Department of Health published what *Sunday* identified as 'the first ever guide for health professionals about how to treat Hindu patients'. One of the authors, Dr Diviash Thakrar, explained what it was designed to achieve.

Diviash Thakrar: One broad aspect would be diet. A lot of Hindus are vegetarians. Now, for a Hindu vegetarian, that means no meat, no fish, no eggs. There's a percentage of Hindus again who'll have no onions and garlic, some even avoid mushrooms. Now, when you go into the hospital environment to get halal or kosher food, it's quite straightforward. But

173

when you ask for a diet that's vegetarian and that caters towards the Asian diet, it's quite difficult.

Roger Bolton: *What do they give you? Just lettuce and a couple of tomatoes?*

Diviash Thakrar: *Yeah, well, it's happened even as a doctor at the Royal College of Physicians going to talks, and I've filled in the dietary requirements, ticked all the boxes. I go there, and when I ask them, 'Look, you know, where's my food?' they'll give me a blank look. Then come back with a slice of bread and a bit of salad.*

Roger Bolton: *And what about when death and dying is involved, and the treatment of the body at death? Does that raise particular concerns for Hindus?*

Diviash Thakrar: *Death and dying are always very important for everyone. I think we all want to have a good death. With the Hindu perspective, the point of death is very important because it relates to where we feel we're going in our next life. When a Hindu person is dying, there'll invariably be a lot of paraphernalia around them. They'll have pictures, deities, they'll have their beads to chant their prayers on, and they'll expect a lot of people to come and visit them in these days to pay their respects. You'll invariably get priests that come along.*

One very important thing at this point in time is the idea of trying to get peace and tranquillity. You'll have a lot of chanting of the names of God. You'll have a lot of silent prayers. When Hindu patients are dying, a lot of them would like to have some holy water, which we call Ganga Jal [sacred waters from River Ganges] to drink, and maybe a Tulsi Leaf [holy basil]. And this is usually done just about the time that you're about to die. Now, if you're in an environment where this can't be facilitated, it sometimes can be difficult for the patient to ask, you know, 'This is what we would like.'

Roger Bolton: *So do you think that twenty years ago, thirty years ago, we might have said there would be a lot of prejudice around, perhaps for groups like Hindus and others? Do you now think it's mainly a question of ignorance?*

Diviash Thakrar: *I think there was maybe a lot of misunderstanding, and sometimes it's about communication. I don't think there's any intentional prejudice, especially within the health service, but there's always this unintentional feeling that when we increase in understanding about any* *group or community, or any people, it improves our empathy and our ability to look after them sensitively.*

Organ donation

The need to take account of religious sensitivities in the provision of healthcare threw up some unexpected dilemmas. Around the time of that interview, the government conducted a consultation on moving from an 'opt-in' system for organ donation to an 'opt-out' system – so that everyone would be considered a potential organ donor unless they had explicitly chosen that their organs should not be used to help someone else (as things turned out, the change to an opt-out system did not take place in England until more than a decade later).

The government task force charged with exploring the idea looked at possible religious objections to an 'opt-out' system, and in November 2008 Dr Abdullah Shehu, chairman of the Health and Medical Committee of the Muslim Council of Britain (MCB), came on *Sunday* to explain why it would worry some Muslims:

In Islam, we believe that organ donation is something that is good and encouraged. And to save the life of one person is to save the life of humanity. And a lot of us sort of work on that principle. But when organ donation is going to be an opt-out issue, then what is going to happen is that a lot of our people who may not be very much conversant or educated, in terms of the process and the procedure, may see it as something that the government is imposing on them, and therefore taking away the rights of the family to the body of their deceased relative or spouse. And that is something that can create disharmony between the family and also the medical practitioners who are involved in the discussion.

And in addition to that, obviously we know as Muslims we would like to bury our dead as quickly as possible. So this kind of organ donation will then create a situation whereby delay is created. And if such is created, then the question from the family will be: 'Is this purely because you want to take organs from our deceased person rather than actually helping the deceased or making their life a bit longer, or whatever the case might be?'

So these are some of the issues, and my other concerns are that, when we are dealing with a dying patient… I don't want a situation whereby our people who are less educated about this end up not bringing their dying relatives to the hospital because of fear of this organ donation. And some people might even say, 'I don't want to be taken to hospital in case they remove my organs,' simply because they don't understand.

Some Jews, it later became clear, also had reservations about organ donation, as *Sunday* explained at the beginning of 2011.

Jane Little: *The chief rabbi provoked argument over the issue of organ transplantation this week when he clarified the Orthodox view of when it is permissible. There's an ongoing debate within Jewish circles over the definition of death. Jonathan Sacks stated that it is when the heart stops beating, and this puts him at odds with the medical establishment, which takes brain death as an acceptable definition – so allowing for the artificial pumping of the heart while major organs are taken. I'm joined now by Rabbi Alexandra Wright, senior rabbi of the Liberal Jewish Synagogue in St John's Wood, London, and by David Frei, registrar of the London Beth Din, the chief rabbi's rabbinical court. Morning. Good morning, David Frei. The chief rabbi, Jonathan Sacks, wrote: 'We may not take one person's life to save another.' In his view, and in that of the court, would it be taking life if a donor's heart had not stopped beating?*

David Frei: *The Jewish definition of death is one which has been a subject of great debate over a number of years, and there are different views on this. The majority view of the major Halachic decisors[2] is that brain stem death or neurological death is not definitive, and therefore it would be prematurely terminating a life to extract a heart in those circumstances.*

Jane Little: *So cardiorespiratory death is definitive.*

David Frei: *That's right.*

Jane Little: *Alexandra Wright, under Jewish law, you cannot kill. So in order to support major organ transplantation, you'd have to accept brain stem death as the definition. How do you do that under Jewish tradition?*

---

2   Rabbis who decide matters in Jewish religious law.

Alexandra Wright: *Well, first of all, I think it's very important to say that what Jews share as far as basic principles go on this matter is greater than where we differ. The three principles on which a Jewish approach would be based is, number one, the duty to heal; that humanity is in partnership with God and therefore has a duty to heal. The physician has a duty to heal.*

The second principle is the saving of human life; that human life is considered precious and that its duration should be prolonged, except for breaking three cardinal prohibitions. In other words, Jewish law says that we may not practise idolatry, incest or murder in order to save human life. But all other commandments may be overridden – including, for example, the observance of Shabbat, the Sabbath. And the third principle is that even if there is only a possibility that the therapy will work, no certainty about it that a person will be cured, one should still undertake the attempt to heal.

Now, the one area of difference is, as you've just said, in the definition of death. And some branches of Judaism, Liberal Judaism included, would accept the medical version of brain stem death that a person cannot breathe independently. In other words, they would see that the brain stem which governs the respiratory system has stopped working.

Jane Little: *Very briefly, you accept that, and you'd be happy carrying a donor card?*

Alexandra Wright: *Yes, I would be happy carrying a donor card. And yes, Liberal Judaism does accept brain stem death.*

When Jane Little put the same question to David Frei, he would only say that: 'It will become possible if we knew that all procedures were consonant with our halachic demands.' And at the end of the interview, he put this difference of opinion in the context of the overarching divisions between Jewish traditions:

There's a fundamental difference between Orthodox Judaism and Liberal Judaism. Orthodox Judaism is very much based on precedent and authority, and we look to the sources. We don't just look to an assessment of what we think is the move of the zeitgeist. But we look to the sources of what is the definition of death, in common with other religions, who also have to grapple with the ideas of 'when does life commence?'

Hence, the Catholics have problems with stem cell research, for example, because they believe that life starts at a very, very early stage. We also have issues with beginnings of life and ends of life. And our authorities, they're not necessarily consonant with what the medical authorities say. We have a view on death, which is not necessarily going to be exactly the same as what the doctors say.

The end of life

Most of the debate prompted by the Human Fertilisation and Embryology Act related to – broadly speaking – the beginning of life. End-of-life issues proved an equally fertile source of *Sunday* controversy.

The independent Commission on Assisted Dying was established in 2010. It was chaired by the Labour peer Charlie Falconer, a vocal champion of a change in the law to allow assisted dying, and most of its members were of a similar mind. So when the commission reported in favour of such a change in 2012, it was no great surprise. But, as *Sunday* discussed, there was more nuance in the commission's story than there first appeared. Samira Ahmed was in the chair for this discussion.

Samira Ahmed: *This week, a report from the Commission on Assisted Dying concluded that terminally ill people with less than a year to live should be allowed medical help if they want to end their lives. I discussed the ethics of the commission's findings with Revd Canon Dr James Woodward, the Anglican canon of St George's Chapel at Windsor Castle, who sat on the panel, and also with Rabbi Dr Jonathan Romain, minister of Maidenhead Synagogue. Both have changed their minds on the issue. I began by asking Canon James Woodward how a fact-finding mission to Switzerland turned him strongly against allowing assisted dying in this country.*

James Woodward: *It's hard to put it into words, but there was a kind of eerie, disconnected sense that this did not feel right, that we are not in a position to demand choice over everything and anything, and that what was lacking in many of the conversations there in Switzerland – and subsequent conversations in the commission – was any sense of wisdom in and around morality, anthropology, what kind of God we believe in,* *who we are, and what indeed the role of pain and loss and change and suffering might be in human flourishing.*

Samira Ahmed: *Dr Jonathan Romain, you were very much against the idea, and yet you changed your mind in the opposite direction.*

Jonathan Romain: *Yes, that's right. Initially I was against it, because I think I was worried about the abuses of the system. But I've now changed my mind – partly because of this report, because I think, on a practical level, they're now talking about safeguards that it can only be somebody terminal, somebody mentally competent, and assuring that it's their free will.*

But also on a moral and religious level... I'm a congregational rabbi in Maidenhead, and I've seen so many people die in pain or sedated into oblivion. And I think this can't be the way to end a life which is sacred, which is given to us by [a] loving God. And I think to me it's a religious response to say, 'Yes, if that's what you want to do, fine. Or if palliative care can help, great. But if there is a point beyond which we cannot help you, then you should be allowed to die in dignity, die well.' And I think that would be a loving and caring response.

Samira Ahmed: *Canon James Woodward, what do you make of that argument?*

James Woodward: *I have a lot of sympathy with the experience of journeying alongside people whose suffering simply becomes intolerable. But in the end, I came out with the very strong ethical and theological conviction that this just isn't the right time to make such an extraordinary shift and change, which would absolutely change the face of so many ways in which the health and social care system operates, and the values which underpin it.*

Samira Ahmed: *Dr Jonathan Romain, couldn't this be, as Canon Woodward is implying, a situation where there shouldn't always be a choice?*

Jonathan Romain: *Well, I think to say you've got to die in pain... who's saying that? And for whose benefit are we forcing people to die in pain? But, you know, there is a concern that people accuse those in favour of assisted dying of playing God. But actually, that's a compliment and not an accusation, because we are constantly using our God-given abilities to overturn nature. Now, it could be to save a premature baby or to have a heart transplant. So why not, where we can actually do something positive, alleviate pain and distress – assuming the person wants it, and* *assuming that palliative care cannot help them any more? So that is a response that would be appropriate within a religious framework.*

Lord Falconer introduced a bill to reform the law in 2014, and again in 2020. At the time of writing, it remains illegal in the United Kingdom to help someone die.

Part 3

THE CHANGING FACES OF RELIGION IN BRITAIN

9

Jonathan Sacks: anti-Semitism, New Atheism and remembering the Holocaust

In much of Europe, the office of chief rabbi was created by secular powers as a mechanism for exercising control over a religious minority. For example, chief rabbis in medieval Spain acted as intermediaries between the Jewish community and the government, facilitating administrative tasks such as tax collection.

The story in this country is different. As the website of the Office of the Chief Rabbi explains: 'The Chief Rabbinate of England is an institution that first arose in the 18th century' and gradually expanded to represent Jews all over Britain and, indeed, its empire. 'That it evolved independently of a secular power, rather than being instituted by civil authorities,' the website states, 'marks it out as unique within the European Rabbinates.'[1]

The position of chief rabbi of the United Hebrew Congregations of Great Britain and the Commonwealth – to give him his full title – did, however, develop in a way that reflected the religious life of a country with an Established Church. The title 'evolved from a communal desire for official representation, akin to the Archbishop of Canterbury's role in Church life.'[2]

'A towering figure of faith'

From 1991 until 2013, the position was held by a chief rabbi who was especially well suited to the role of national religious leader. Jonathan

---

1 'History of the Chief Rabbinate', Office of the Chief Rabbi: https://chiefrabbi.org/history-chief-rabbinate (accessed 26 April 2023).

2 'History of the Chief Rabbinate'.

Sacks certainly spoke up for Jews, but his voice carried well beyond the confines of the Jewish community.

His natural relationship with a wider British audience perhaps owed something to his background. He was born in Lambeth and went to school in Finchley, and he studied Philosophy at Cambridge, Oxford and King's College London before he became a rabbi. His measured tones often seemed to be those of a scholarly don rather than a religious leader.

He was also a prolific and highly skilled broadcaster, and frequently appeared on *Sunday*. His death – at a relatively young age, and very soon after a cancer diagnosis – came as a shock to his many admirers, and *Sunday* marked it with a special edition. It was broadcast on 8 November 2020, and it was introduced with the following encomium.

William Crawley: *The former chief rabbi, Jonathan Sacks, Lord Sacks, who died last night at the age of seventy-two, was widely regarded as an intellectual and spiritual giant by Jewish communities across the world. As a faith leader, a prolific author, philosopher and theologian, he was equipped with an astonishing range of talents. He reached out to others far beyond his own faith, and that's been reflected in the many tributes that have already been paid to him in the hours since his death was announced. Political leaders – leaders from across the spectrum of world faiths – and many who knew him and learned from him as a writer, a rabbi or a public intellectual, often joining us on this programme or on radio for* Thought for the Day, *addressing issues of the moment in his broadcasting.*

Lord Sacks was succeeded as chief rabbi by Ephraim Mirvis, who joins us now. Chief Rabbi, good morning to you.

Ephraim Mirvis: *Good morning, William.*

William Crawley: *Jonathan Sacks seems to have lived more than one life. So before I turn to some of his many contributions, Chief Rabbi, can I ask you how you will remember him personally?*

Ephraim Mirvis: *I would sum up my many feelings in one quotation from the Bible: 'The prince of God in our midst.'³ This is the compliment paid to Abraham, our patriarch, by the children of the original Canaanites. And indeed, just like Abraham, our patriarch, Rabbi Lord Sacks, has been a*

---

3   Genesis 23:6, from the original Hebrew.

prince of God in our midst, and I notice that the original compliment was paid by people outside of Abraham's faith. And similarly, Jonathan Sacks has made a most extraordinary contribution; not just to the Jewish world, but to the whole world.

William Crawley: *Within the Jewish world itself, how would you assess his defining contribution?*

Ephraim Mirvis: *He made our ancient, glorious heritage relevant within our modern and ever-changing world. And I believe that that is the most significant part of his legacy.*

Rabbi Mirvis's tribute was followed by one from Marie van der Zyl, president of the Board of Deputies of British Jews:

He was a towering figure of faith to people of all faiths and none. And you can see there's a huge outpouring of grief and honouring of his memory from not just the entire Jewish community, but leading religious leaders, politicians, world leaders. And that's the greatest testament to his impact and reach well beyond the community. And he was seen as a key voice of morality and ethical integrity. And his opinion was sought out by the entire British media. On the radio, he spoke on critical issues of the day. [He was a] regular columnist in The Times, *and known for his clarity of thought and skills as an orator. He was one of the finest communicators in the world. And he is going to be so very, very missed.*

Anti-Semitism

The dangers of anti-Semitism were a recurring theme of Chief Rabbi Sacks's public comments. This interview, broadcast in January 2006, is one of the earliest of his contributions in the *Sunday* archive. It marked the 350th anniversary of the resettlement of Jews in Britain during the Commonwealth period.

Jonathan Sacks: *It seems to me a real cause for celebration, because there's no doubt that Jews in Britain have found this country one of the most tolerant places on the face of the earth. And our community is just very* *thankful for the chance to have been allowed to practise our faith in peace and genuine acceptance.*

Edward Stourton: *You've also talked in the year that's just gone about anti-Semitism having reached, I think you described it as, 'uncomfortable' levels. What did you mean by that?*

Jonathan Sacks: *All the old definitions and expectations have disappeared in a global age. And what we're finding is the transfer of conflicts thousands of miles away into daily life. That's what Britain discovered on 7/7* [the terrorist attacks in London on 7 July 2005, discussed in chapter 11] *and, before then, Madrid* [nearly 200 people were killed in attacks on the Madrid train system in March 2004, for which the terrorist organisation al-Qaeda was blamed] *and before then the United States* [a reference to 9/11]. *So you don't talk about anti-Semitism or Islamophobia or what have you as features of a national culture, the way we used to do. Is Britain an anti-Semitic country? Obviously, the answer is no. But we do find that through the internet, through email, through satellite television, conflicts are becoming globalised, and they can claim victims thousands of miles away.*

Edward Stourton: *And when you talk about 'discomfort', that's quite a carefully chosen word. What does the experience feel like of contemporary anti-Semitism?*

Jonathan Sacks: *A number of my rabbinical colleagues throughout Europe have been assaulted and attacked on the streets. We've had synagogues desecrated. We've had Jewish schools burnt to the ground – not here, but in France. People are attempting to silence and even ban Jewish societies on campus, on the grounds that Jews must support the state of Israel; therefore they should be banned. Which is quite extraordinary because Jewish identity is a religious identity, and British Jews see themselves as British citizens. So it's that kind of feeling that you don't know what's going to happen next that is making at least some European Jewish communities feel uncomfortable.*

The previous month, the newly elected president of Iran, Mahmoud Ahmadinejad, had denied the death of 6 million Jews in the Holocaust and claimed it was a 'myth' that Jews had been killed. When he was asked about those remarks, Rabbi Sacks showed his flair for the phrase that was bound to make a headline.

A 'tsunami of anti-Semitism'

Jonathan Sacks: Sadly, I wasn't surprised, because Holocaust denial and other forms of anti-Semitism – from the blood libel[4] to The Protocols of the Elders of Zion *– have been circulating in bestselling books and prime-time television in certain parts of the world now for several years. And this is all a kind of tsunami of anti-Semitism, which is taking place a long way from this country, but of which Europe seems unaware.*

Edward Stourton: That's a very strong phrase, 'tsunami of anti-Semitism'.

Jonathan Sacks: I don't say it lightly. I am very scared by it. And I'm very scared that more protests have not been delivered against it. But this is part of the vocabulary of politics in certain parts of the world.

More than twelve years later, in September 2018, Jonathan Sacks spoke in similarly vivid terms about allegations of anti-Semitism in the Labour Party. At the time of this interview, a controversial speech by the then-Labour leader Jeremy Corbyn had resurfaced. Mr Corbyn, as *Sunday* reported the story, had said that some Zionists 'don't want to study history' and 'having lived in this country for a very long time, probably all their lives, they don't understand English irony either.'[5]

The comments provoked Lord Sacks (he was by then retired and had been ennobled) to compare Jeremy Corbyn to Enoch Powell, the Conservative politician notorious, in the late 1960s, for the violence of his views on immigration (see chapter 19). The former chief rabbi also accused the Labour leader of being an anti-Semite.

Jonathan Sacks: I think it was these last revelations of a speech he gave in which he said that British Zionists, by which he means really the majority

---

4   The 'blood libel' is a reference to the ancient slur used to suggest that Jews murder Christian children to obtain their blood for Passover. The Protocols of the Elders of Zion is a fabricated anti-Semitic text widely circulated during the early twentieth century. It purported to be a Jewish plan for world domination.

5   'Jeremy Corbyn's 2013 remarks on some Zionists not understanding English irony', YouTube: https://www.youtube.com/watch?v=nEB9PwKYmmA (accessed 16 June 2023).

of British Jews, don't really have a British sense of irony. In other words, he was saying they're not really British. Now that is classic pre-war European anti-Semitism, and it set off a red light in my mind and in the minds of a great number of people throughout our community.

Edward Stourton: *The Labour Party have called what you said absurd and offensive, particularly because you linked him with Enoch Powell, who was, in his legacy, a toxic figure, I think it's fair to say, because of the famous 'Rivers of Blood speech'* [Enoch Powell, in fact, used a quotation from Virgil's Aeneid to warn against the impact of immigration, declaring that, 'Like the Roman, I seem to see "the River Tiber foaming with much blood"']. *Was that really an apposite comparison?*

Jonathan Sacks: *I think it was because, just like the Powell speech, it identified a group of British citizens and said, in effect, they're not really part of us. They're an alien element, and that is classic anti-Semitism. Now, if there were nothing else going on to make us alert about anti-Semitism, I don't think we would have got that upset about it. But the fact is that anti-Semitism has returned to mainland Europe. Jews have been murdered in Paris, in Toulouse, in Marseilles, simply for being Jews. And when a public figure issues an utterance that has echoes of that anti-Semitism and is, in effect, opening the door, letting the demons out, then that becomes very, very dangerous.*

And of course, there's a big difference between Enoch Powell and Jeremy Corbyn. There was never the slightest possibility that Enoch Powell would ever become prime minister. But Jeremy Corbyn is leader of Her Majesty's Opposition, and might become prime minister. And let me tell you that vast numbers of British Jews are very disturbed and anxious about that.

Edward Stourton: *Let me just pick you up on your interpretation of his words, because actually the Labour Party point out he was talking about a group of Zionists. He wasn't talking about Jews. In other words, he was talking about a group who believed certain things rather than a group who are defined by their race or their religion.*

Jonathan Sacks: *Anyone who's tracked the new anti-Semitism knows that the word 'Zionist' is today used as a code word for Jews…*

Edward Stourton: *Given how strongly you feel about this issue, do you think Jeremy Corbyn should resign?*

Jonathan Sacks: That is a decision for him and the Labour Party, not for me.

Edward Stourton: What else do you think the Labour Party needs to do?

Jonathan Sacks: Ed, I think we've known each other a while. You know, I've been in public life for well over thirty years. I've resisted for thirty years making any party political statement. But anti-Semitism was one of the greatest evils of Western civilisation for a thousand years. It reached a kind of horrendous denouement in the twentieth century, and everyone has to have zero tolerance for it. Because of what I have consistently said: the hate that begins with Jews never ends with Jews.

'Never change direction'

Some commentators remarked that Jonathan Sacks was more successful in representing Jews to society at large than he was at managing the sometimes fractious relationships within the Jewish community itself.

In 2002 he ran foul of a group of traditional Orthodox believers over his book *The Dignity of Difference*. The book attracted widespread international acclaim, but a group of rabbis argued that it endorsed relativism between religions, and that his statement 'No one creed has a monopoly on spiritual truth' cast doubt on the uniqueness of Judaism. Some of them took out an advertisement in the *Jewish Chronicle* to denounce the book as 'a grave deviation from the pathways of traditional and authentic Judaism',[6] and demanded that the chief rabbi repudiate his views.

Jonathan Sacks revised the text for the second edition. This, in turn, brought him into conflict with some more liberal Jews, who argued he had allowed himself to be bullied by the Orthodox. Rabbi Jonathan Romain, a prominent rabbi in the Reform tradition (see chapter 8), described the new version as 'a victory for the dinosaurs'.[7]

Speaking to Roger Bolton on *Sunday* some years later, Jonathan Sacks revealed that the row had brought him close to resignation. 'And

---

6 S. Bates, 'Fresh attacks on chief rabbi's book', *The Guardian*: https://www.theguardian.com/uk/2002/oct/18/religion.politicsphilosophyandsociety (18 October 2002, accessed 16 June 2023).

7 R. A. Greene, 'British chief rabbi revises controversial book', Jewish Telegraphic Agency: https://www.jta.org/2003/03/16/lifestyle/british-chief-rabbi-revises-controversial-book (16 March 2003, accessed 16 June 2023).

then I decided no,' he went on, '[because] were I to do so, I would be letting down every single person who ever put their faith in me.' He conceded that he had learned an important lesson about leadership during the episode: 'Clearly, I've driven at ninety miles an hour, where the community want to go at thirty miles an hour, so I have to slow the pace. But never give up, never be intimidated, never change direction.'

At around the same time as *The Dignity of Difference* controversy, Jonathan Sacks became caught up in a row with another section of the Jewish community, this time over his views on Israel. In an interview with *The Guardian* – which he gave, as it happens, to promote *The Dignity of Difference* – he said that: 'There are things happening [in Israel] on a daily basis which make me feel very uncomfortable as a Jew,' and that Israel had been forced 'into postures that are incompatible in the long term with our deepest ideals'. This was at the height of the Second Intifada (Palestinian uprising), when Israel regularly used military force in the West Bank in response to a deadly wave of suicide bombings in Israeli towns and cities.

Usually, the chief rabbi was only too happy to give his views to *Sunday*. Not so in the midst of the swirling controversy his comments had ignited. 'The chief rabbi, Dr Jonathan Sacks, not only declined to talk to *Sunday* himself,' the audience was told on 2 September 2002, 'his office also declined the opportunity for a representative to talk on his behalf.' The programme turned instead to the BBC's religious affairs correspondent.

Edward Stourton: *Last night, he [Jonathan Sacks] was at a synagogue in Golders Green, giving his first public address since the row erupted. Our religious affairs correspondent Robert Pigott was there, and he joins us now. Robert, did he mention all this?*

Robert Pigott: *He didn't, and it was quite noticeable that he didn't. But many in the congregation felt that he had just hinted at the issue. He preached on forgiveness. And this is something of a theme at this time of year coming up to the Jewish Day of Atonement, which is dedicated to forgiveness. And he reminded the congregation of Jonah calling on God for forgiveness and then saying, 'Forgive us, but don't forgive them. They're Israel's enemies,' which the chief rabbi, Jonathan Sacks, obviously didn't feel was God's way. So in a sense, there was some sort of hint at* *there being too little forgiveness about. But no reference to this particular controversy.*

Edward Stourton: *It's a pretty oblique reference, by the sound of it. What did people in the congregation think of it all?*

Robert Pigott: *Well, they were still troubled by what he'd said, and that there has been a degree of unhappiness with the way he's spoken out; not because he's spoken out, but because he seemed to criticise Israel. And you have to remember that Jonathan Sacks represents not the entire Jewish community in Britain, but about some 130-odd thousand of the more Orthodox believers – once the largest section of Orthodox believers. They share the sense of alignment in Israel, and I think that was reflected in what some of them said. I think most people felt that coming across as criticising Israel was a bad thing. And support for Israel in this community is particularly strong among Orthodox Jews.*

Edward Stourton: *And give us a flavour of the kind of responses that people gave you.*

Robert Pigott: *Well, some said that he should have thought more carefully before he spoke out. Some said that, although he had a perfect right to speak out, they didn't agree with what he'd said. But most people really took the line that he shouldn't have said it. There was a degree of disbelief that he could have actually said the words attributed to him, and suspicion of where they had appeared and the way they've been put. You have to remember, of course, though, as I was saying, that support for Israel is particularly strong among Orthodox Jews.*

New Atheism

None of this detracted from Jonathan Sacks's moral standing in the wider audience he reached through his books, or through his radio and television broadcasts. In September 2007, the chief rabbi fronted a BBC One programme called *Keeping Faith*, speaking up not just for Judaism, but for religion more generally. Roger Bolton described the show on *Sunday* as 'a passionate defence of religion, delivered at a time when books attacking faith by atheists such as Richard Dawkins and Christopher Hitchens are enjoying remarkable success in the bestseller lists.'

The chief rabbi's programme included a relatively rare interview with Tony Blair about his faith. Mr Blair converted to Catholicism in December 2007, several months after leaving Downing Street, but seldom talked about his decision. In the extract broadcast on *Sunday*, he explained:

> *My view is that faith is a vital part of the future; that it is something that is modern, that it is part of progress; and that it should not be either just an interesting part of our tradition or history or the property of fanatics. And I think there is a danger that faith becomes like that. You know, when I look at the future and think of the world I want my children to grow up in, of course I want the good material things in life for them, but I never want them to forget their obligation to the other. And also the important thing, which is a sense that there is something more important than you, which is, I think, really almost the basis of the religious ethic.*

But the chief rabbi's main target in his authored programme was clear, and he explained to Roger Bolton why he had made it.

Jonathan Sacks: *Because I think faith has come under a lot of attack recently. There have been some very angry books against religion. There's also been a general feeling that the face of religion in public today is sometimes very extreme. And I just think faith has come under attack.*

Roger Bolton: *But hasn't it always been under attack? And doesn't it deserve to be at the moment? When we look around, we can see a Middle East in many people's views being destroyed by people who are supposed to be of the same faith. We have Islamic fundamentalism, obviously, and in Northern Ireland and elsewhere we've had years of conflicts, which many would say are the result, directly, of religion. So is it surprising that religion is being questioned?*

Jonathan Sacks: *I actually think that this has to do with the fact that the voices that are heard in the media are very often the confrontational voices rather than the voices of conciliation. And one of the things that made me want to do this film is to listen to some other voices; the voices which show faith to be indeed part of the solution, not part of the problem.*

Amanda Hancox

Sunday presenter Clive Jacobs,
religious affairs correspondent
Ted Harrison and Archbishop
Robin Eames at the 1988 Lambeth
Conference

Amanda Hancox

Producers David Coomes and Eley
McAnish at the 1988 Lambeth
Conference

Mike Ford

Producer Mike Ford and presenter
Colin Morris meeting Archbishop
Desmond Tutu for an interview in
London in the 1990s

Mike Ford

Trevor Barnes worked as a reporter
and presenter on *Sunday* for
many years

Christine Morgan

Christine Morgan

Christine Morgan, who later became *Sunday* editor, going through the script with Debbie Thrower, who occasionally presented the programme (1992)

Reporter Alison Hillard cutting an interview on quarter-inch tape with producer Christine Morgan in the London *Sunday* office (1992)

Mike Ford

Amanda Hancox

When on location, the team had to edit on the hoof. Producer Liz Leonard working in her room in Jerusalem for the Millennium edition of *Sunday* (1999)

Amanda Hancox, former *Sunday* editor, with presenter Roger Bolton and the programme's current editor, Helen Grady

Maggi Hambling's *Good Friday* oil painting (2004)

The Dalai Lama at a 2004 press conference in Edinburgh with *Sunday*'s reporter Mike Ford in attendance

When it was announced in 2005 that John Sentamu would be the next archbishop of York, *Sunday* was there to cover the story

Edward Stourton at Cofton Park for
the beatification of Cardinal Newman
(2005)

Cofton Park stage (2005)

In 2005, the Make Poverty History
rally was held in Edinburgh to
coincide with the G8 Summit in
Scotland. Presenter Roger Bolton
broadcast *Sunday* from Edinburgh to
explore some of the issues raised by
the march

Roger Bolton broadcasting live from
Edinburgh when the Make Poverty
History rally took place in the city
in 2005

Mike Ford

Timothy P. Schmalz

Sunday reporter Mike Ford interviewing Chief Rabbi Jonathan Sacks about his first visit to Auschwitz-Birkenau, the former German Nazi concentration and extermination camp in Poland (2008)

Canadian sculptor Timothy P. Schmalz's *Homeless Jesus* outside the entrance of the Office of Papal Charities in Vatican City

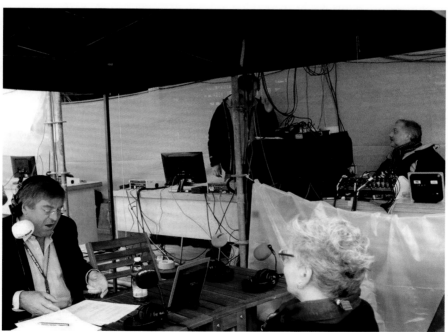

Carmel Lonergan

Presenter Edward Stourton broadcasting from St Peter's Square in Rome (2013)

Edward Stourton in the media area as the crowds awaited the arrival of the Pope in Philadelphia, USA (2015)

The Catholic Bishop of Northampton, Peter Doyle, looks ahead to the Synod on the Family in October 2015 with Edward Stourton for a special edition of *Sunday* from Philadelphia to mark the Pope's visit to America (2015)

Sister Sledge sisters Kim and Joni talked to Edward Stourton and producer David Cook before they sang for Pope Francis in Philadelphia, USA in 2015

Edward Stourton speaks to Dr Ed Kessler and Dr Muhammad Abdul Bari for a special edition of *Sunday* from the East London Mosque (2015)

In 2017, *Sunday* marked the 500th anniversary of the Reformation by taking listeners back to Hampton Court Palace in 1516 to explore the religious, political and social climate which generated the Reformation. Here, Fr Anthony Howe, chaplain to the Chapel Royal at the palace shows Edward Stourton and David Cook a prayer book from 1515

Emily Buchanan

Carmel Lonergan

Emily Buchanan talking to London vicar Marie-Elsa Bragg about her spiritual connection to Cumbria, and how it inspired her first novel. This formed part of a special edition of *Sunday* on religion in rural communities in 2017

Robi Damelin, an Israeli, and Ikhlas Shtayeh, a Palestinian, talk to Edward Stourton for *Sunday's* broadcast from Jerusalem to mark the seventieth anniversary of the establishment of the State of Israel (2018)

Carmel Lonergan

Catherine Murray

William Crawley presenting in *Sunday's* Salford studio with producer Carmel Lonergan and studio manager Sue Stonestreet

Outside broadcast in Rome with Phil Booth, Helen Grady and Ed Stourton to mark the tenth anniversary of Pope Francis's election (2023)

Roger Bolton: *What about the rise of secularism? Do you see it presenting a particular problem now to people of faith?*

Jonathan Sacks: *I think the rise of secularism was totally understandable and rather motivates me in what I do, because secularism began in the seventeenth century – and it did not begin because people lost faith in God. It began because people lost faith in people of God being able to live peaceably with one another. And I'm afraid I have to say to all of us – every single religious believer in this country – if we do not live peaceably together, there will be a rise of secularism and a loss of faith.*

Roger Bolton: *Do you see the popularity of the Richard Dawkins book* [the evolutionary biologist had published *The God Delusion* the previous year] *and other books like that as being an intellectual challenge to you? Did you feel threatened by the arguments, surprised by them?*

Jonathan Sacks: *No, no. I couldn't actually follow the arguments. They were not exactly at the deepest level of theological profundity. You know, I was reminded of what one Oxford academic said about another: 'On the surface he's profound, but deep down he's superficial.' Now, what bothered me in the Dawkins book was the anger, not the argument. There was too much anger in that book. I think religion deserves to be challenged in every generation. Any set of beliefs deserves to be challenged, but respectfully, civilly, without anger.*

Several years later, the chief rabbi and Britain's most famous atheist squared off directly during a Rethink Festival at the BBC's new home in Salford's Media City. Their meeting was chaired by Samira Ahmed, and *Sunday* broadcast part of it on 16 September 2012. Samira asked Richard Dawkins whether people needed God in order to be good.

Richard Dawkins: *I think it is really unrealistic to suggest that we need religion in order to come to moral decisions, or that actually we, as a matter of fact, do use religion. As I look historically at the way our moral values have changed, they have changed hugely over the centuries, over the decades, within any given century. My point is that the moral zeitgeist, which we all of us in a society share, labels us as being, shall we say, early twenty-first century citizens – much more than it labels us as* *being religious or non-religious. There's far more in common between a liberal, enlightened Jew and a liberal, enlightened atheist today, morally speaking, than there is between either of us and somebody of 200 years ago or even 100 years ago.*

Samira Ahmed: *Chief Rabbi?*

Jonathan Sacks: *First of all, I want to agree with Richard that you do not have to be religious to be moral. I would never be party to such a claim. We know the people who saved lives, often at risk to their own, during the Holocaust, some were religious, some were secular. I think the only thing they had in common was that they took for granted that they had to do what they had to do because that's what a human being does. And I think that moral sense is common to all of us. It's tremendously important not to let people say you have to be religious to be moral.*

Showing his flair as a debater, he then attacked from an unexpected angle, quoting research by the Harvard sociology professor Robert Pitman.

Jonathan Sacks: *Religious people are more likely to give to charity, more likely to do voluntary work, more likely to help a neighbour with housework, more likely to help somebody with a job, more likely to get involved in civic and voluntary associations and so on. And his finding was that religion is the predictor of all these things of altruism more than any other factor – age, income, educational level or ethnicity. But he said, and I think very wisely, that in his view this has got nothing to do with religious beliefs and everything to do with the power of religion to create communities. In other words, Richard is right in saying that we may not need religion to know what to do, but it's that constant rehearsal, in ritual, in prayer and in community, that encourages people to do what they know they ought to do.*

Professor Dawkins, usually so scathing about religion and so confident of the grounds for his atheistic case, was uncharacteristically conciliatory in his response. 'I want to pursue the very interesting point you were making,' he conceded. '...I certainly don't think we get our morals from religion. I certainly *hope* we don't. So do we get it from a sense of community? That's an interesting point. And I think it's arguable that in the post-religious age, which I look forward to, we're going to need to put in place some sort of substitute for the sense of community which religions over centuries of history have put in place.'

The Holocaust

In 2008, the chief rabbi visited Auschwitz in company with Rowan Williams, then archbishop of Canterbury. *Sunday*'s Trevor Barnes went with them.

Trevor Barnes: On this patch of grass in the centre of the Polish town of Oświęcim, known also by its German name, Auschwitz, there are only dead leaves, but as our guide has been explaining, this was once a focal point of Jewish life.

Guide: This was the site of the Great Synagogue. And when we talk about the Holocaust, it's sometimes difficult to know where we should actually be entering into this story. And I would suggest to all of you that we shouldn't be entering into the story at Auschwitz, when we walk through those gates. We should be entering into it right here, because this is the place that tells us about those individual people and who they actually were.

Trevor Barnes: And in 1939 there were 8,000 such individuals, over half the population who, together with a million-and-a-half of their fellow European Jews, were murdered in the two concentration camps just outside the town.

Guide: Most of the Jewish victims of the camp were killed, like this group, immediately after arrival into the camp. You can see the whole process took less than two hours... We're talking about groups of 1,000, 1,500 people. The door to the gas chamber was closed, and the gas called Cyclone V was used to kill them. Twenty minutes, everything was over. Everybody in the chamber dead. Corpses were then taken to the crematorium level. The last part of this building, all the women's hair had to be removed. Golden fillings and golden teeth were extracted. All the remaining jewellery.

Jonathan Sacks: Nothing was so worthless that the Nazis were willing to throw it away. They kept hold of everything: the artificial limbs, the glasses, everything. There was only one thing so worthless that they were willing to throw it away. And that was human life.

Trevor Barnes: *The chief rabbi, Jonathan Sacks, at Auschwitz for his second visit with the archbishop of Canterbury* [it was the first visit for the archbishop].

Rowan Williams: *It's very hard to describe the physical legacy of it all – seeing the crutches and the artificial limbs taken from the bodies of those murdered here. I think it's that physicality that strikes me, and the sight of children's clothes and children's dummies, that sort of thing. That's where the imagination gives up, because how anyone could think this was human behaviour defeats you.*

As we have learned, the office of chief rabbi was created in part as a counterpoint to that of archbishop of Canterbury. Rowan Williams had a great gift for words, and at moments like this, Jonathan Sacks was able to match him in choosing the right ones.

Jonathan Sacks: *I believe something will come out of this, because this is a life-changing experience for all of us, and I can see it in everyone. And at this age – when so much ethnic and religious conflict continues, when there is so much violence – a moment like this has brought all of us together in a sense of shared humanity that utterly transcends the particularities of our different faiths... So out of this valley of despair comes a journey of hope.*

10

Jewish identity

The medical advances discussed in chapter 8 threw up some unexpected questions about who can consider themselves Jewish. In March 2007, Sunday reported that:

> Jewish couples in New York who are seeking fertility treatment increasingly want more than a donated egg. They're demanding kosher eggs. In other words, they want their child to be Jewish right down to its DNA. The problem is that demand is outstripping supply, so specialist agencies are seeking suitable donors from Israel.

Matrilineal descent

The run on kosher eggs for IVF was, of course, connected to the traditional Jewish principle of matrilineal descent; the belief that Jewishness is passed down the generations through the maternal line. Though contested by some Jewish traditions today, the rule has its roots deep in history.

Immanuel Jakobovits, Jonathan Sacks's predecessor as chief rabbi, declared in *The Timely and the Timeless,* his 1977 collection of essays on Judaism, that: 'For over 3,000 years, whatever arguments and schisms may have divided some Jews from others, they were agreed on the definition of a Jew. *He was someone born of a Jewish mother or converted to Judaism according to Jewish law.*'[1]

Jakobovits quotes passages from Genesis and Deuteronomy to explain the biblical underpinning of the rule of matrilineal descent,

---

1 I. Jakobovits, *The Timely and the Timeless: Jews, Judaism and society in a storm-tossed decade* (Oxford: Routledge, 2004), p. 199.

and also cites the uncertainty involved in relying on the paternal line:

> *A child from a mixed marriage could not be 50% Jew, growing up with a half commitment or a double faith. A choice must be made, and once made, it must be consistently applied in all cases... Now, in making this choice, the certainty of maternity must be set against the doubt of paternity, however small this doubt may be. In such cases Jewish law invariably invokes the rule 'a doubt can never over-rule a certainty'.[2]*

IVF obviously complicates the picture, because it can create circumstances in which the genetic mother of a child and his or her birth mother are not the same person. That raises the question of whether Jewishness resides in the genes provided by a biological mother or the process of gestation and birth experienced by a surrogate mother.

For an answer, *Sunday* sought guidance from Dr Simon Fishel, a Jewish infertility expert at the Park Hospital in Nottingham (see chapter 8 for his contribution to another area of the ethics of fertility treatment). He dismissed the idea that 'there's any such thing as a Jewish gene or a Christian gene or... a Catholic gene or a Buddhist gene,' and delivered a clear verdict: 'If the birth mother is Jewish, the child is Jewish. And there's no argument about that, because it was set in train many, many, many centuries ago.'

To drive the point home, Dr Fishel cited the example of a Jewish couple who arranged for their surrogate mother to go through a kind of conversion process:

> *I know of a very Orthodox couple who used their own eggs, but they had to use a surrogate and the surrogate wasn't Jewish. And there was a slight conundrum here for the Jewish advisers – the rabbis that were dealing with them – as to what to do. And they decided that actually they would undertake a Jewish process, which is where a woman is bathed in... a holy bath, a ritual bath, and some blessings are made*

---

2 I. Jakobovits, *The Timely and the Timeless*, pp. 202–3.

on a monthly basis. They would do this with the child that was born of the surrogate, make some blessings, and the child was then Jewish.

Jewishness through conversion

The following year, the issue of Jewish identity was at the centre of a high-profile legal case heard in the High Court – and in this instance the main focus of the dispute was Jewishness acquired through conversion rather than birth. The children from two families who considered themselves Jewish were refused entry to the Jewish Free School (JFS) – the United Kingdom's largest Jewish school – because the beth din, the Orthodox rabbinical court (which operated under the authority of the chief rabbi), refused to recognise their mothers' conversions as legitimate.

The mother of one of the children – known as 'child M' – had been converted into a liberal stream of Judaism that the Orthodox court did not recognise. The other case was more complicated. Kate Lightman – who actually taught in a senior position at the JFS – had been converted at the Orthodox beth din in Israel, but her Jewish husband was, as the *Jerusalem Post* put it, 'a *kohen* – a member of the priestly class which brought animal sacrifices during Temple times'.[3] According to a strict interpretation of Halacha (the religious laws derived from the Torah), *kohens* are not supposed to marry converts, so the London beth din ruled that Kate Lightman's conversion had not been sincere.

The Lightmans lived an Orthodox life, and it fell to Kate's husband David to express his frustration to *Sunday*'s Trevor Barnes.

David Lightman: *It's clear to me I'm Jewish, my wife is Jewish by conversion twenty years ago by the chief rabbi of Israel. We have a Jewish house. We go to synagogue every week. We keep a kosher house. But she isn't Jewish enough for the chief rabbi, and therefore we can't get our daughter into JFS.*
Trevor Barnes: *But the school JFS itself is under the authority of the chief rabbi. In those circumstances, don't he and the authorities have the right to lay down the entrance criteria?*

---

3 'The JFS lesson', *The Jerusalem Post*: https://www.jpost.com/opinion/editorials/the-jfs-lesson (20 July 2009, accessed 15 May 2023).

David Lightman: It's a fair point, because our issue is not with the school. They're caught in this situation. But JFS was founded in 1732, and it was founded for Jews of all denominations. Now, as far as we're concerned, the chief rabbi and his office decided my wife isn't Jewish enough for him, despite her teaching at the school. As I say, despite her being a practising Jew for over twenty years, being leading members of our synagogue, etc., and so it's clearly unfair and discriminatory against people who are converted…

Our concern is that, if you are Jewish by conversion, you seem to get a different deal to if you are Jewish by birth. Now, the Jewish law, Halacha, passes Jewishness down through the mother; what they call the 'matrilineal line'. If your mother was halachically Jewish, as I say, by the Jewish line, you could be a child who's an atheist, your mother could be an atheist. You could exist solely on a diet of bacon sandwiches, and you could walk straight into JFS. I think it's incredibly unfair, which is why we are pursuing this case.

The Lightman family took their battle all the way to the Supreme Court, and eventually won. 'Schoolgirl at JFS after five-year fight', the *Jewish Chronicle* reported in September 2010.[4] Maya Lightman finally joined the school's sixth form.

Trevor Barnes's report on the episode stands out because it is one of the earliest in the surviving *Sunday* archive to tease out the differences between different Jewish traditions. It includes a defence of the Lightmans' position from Jonathan Romain, the Reform rabbi of Maidenhead Synagogue, and contributions from the Orthodox rabbi Alan Plancey, an adviser to the chief rabbi, who defended the treatment of the Lightman family like this:

Poor people. They may be the nicest people in the world, but if they fail one of the examinations, then what could we do about it? There's nothing I can change. I can't change the rules. These rules and codes are written down for thousands of years. It's not for me, Plancey,

---

4 'Schoolgirl at JFS after five-year fight', *The JC*: https://www.thejc.com/news/uk/schoolgirl-at-jfs-after-five-year-fight-1.17801 (3 September 2010, accessed 27 April 2023).

in the twenty-first century to come and say it's not fair. Lots of things are not fair.

More progressive Jewish movements

The report reflected a broad trend on *Sunday* towards reporting minority religions 'from the inside', explaining the nuances of different traditions within them. During his time as chief rabbi, Jonathan Sacks was such a dominant presence on the airwaves that his voice inevitably dominated in the coverage of most Jewish-related issues, but he did not speak for all Jews. Leaders of more progressive movements, such as Reform and Liberal Judaism, became increasingly insistent that their claims be heard alongside his.

In 2011, as Rabbi Sacks approached retirement, *Sunday* explored the different strands of Jewish tradition with the BBC's religious affairs correspondent Robert Pigott.

Samira Ahmed: *Now, the process has just begun to choose a new chief rabbi for Britain's Orthodox Jews. Lord Jonathan Sacks, who's in Rome… steps down in 2013 after twenty years. His replacement will be chosen amid increasingly bitter divisions among British Jews about the role and who he speaks for. I asked the BBC's religious affairs correspondent Robert Pigott to explain the significance of the job.*

Robert Pigott: *In simple terms, the chief rabbi is the leader of the United Synagogues. These are the Orthodox Jews in the country. It's a position with huge prestige; it's got great authority in that community. It's a position dreamed up in the Victorian era, and I think partly really to provide a representative for Judaism, which is very non-hierarchical otherwise. So there'd be a kind of archbishop of Canterbury for the Jewish community, and people say it was at least partly for the convenience of the non-Jewish population that it was invented. So you'll still hear the chief rabbi going to events like the Lambeth Conference a couple of years ago or speaking in the European Parliament or called in after a crisis to represent Jews as a sort of go-to Jewish leader.*

And the implication has always been that this role is to represent all Jews. But of course, now Liberal and Reform Jews are bitterly complaining that in 1840 the Jewish community in Britain was almost entirely Orthodox. But that's changed hugely, and they now represent a third of the population, with another twenty per cent of it being made up of the very rapidly growing ultra-Orthodox population, meaning that the chief rabbi now represents fewer than half of the total population.

Samira Ahmed: *So what does that mean for choosing a new rabbi?*

Robert Pigott: *I think the issue has become particularly fierce at this moment when the choice is made because of this issue of whom he represents. It goes right to the heart of a deep and rather widening rift in British Judaism between traditionalist Orthodox people and the Liberal and Reform movements over things like development and change in Judaism. So you've got issues like women rabbis. The Liberal and Reform movements have women rabbis. They're more sympathetic to homosexual relationships, to people who don't want to have their sons circumcised, to criticism of Israel, to mixed marriages, those sorts of things, than Orthodox rabbis would be. So these progressive Jews don't want to be associated with the kind of Judaism espoused by the chief rabbi, and they're increasingly frustrated about the status given to this one Jewish leader.*

The following year, *Sunday* broadcast a discussion that illustrated some of those differences. In July 2012, the Assembly of Reform Rabbis voted to lift the prohibition on rabbis taking part in marriages between a Jew and a non-Jew. To appreciate the extreme sensitivity of this issue, it is worth noting that in *The Timely and the Timeless*, the collection of reflections from Immanuel Jakobovits quoted above, 'marrying out' is compared with fraud and adultery.[5]

Marrying out

Sunday's casting for the debate was familiar. Rabbi Alan Plancey of the Borehamwood and Elstree Synagogue defended the Orthodox position, while Rabbi Jonathan Romain of Reform's Maidenhead Synagogue argued the case for change.

---

5 I. Jakobovits, *The Timely and the Timeless*, p. 209.

Jonathan Romain: *Well, we still maintain that same-faith marriages are the best option, and that way the couple are heading in the same direction. It's better for them, better for the children. But two things have now changed. Firstly, the numbers have shot up. Round about fifty per cent of Jews are marrying non-Jewish people. And we just simply can't ignore the new social reality. And secondly, in the past I think there was this attitude that if you marry out, then you were seen as opting out. Whereas the reality is now that many Jews, yes, they have fallen in love with somebody non-Jewish, but they are still attached to their Jewish roots and still want to be in touch with the community. And, therefore, by saying no to them we don't achieve anything. The marriage is still going ahead. But by saying yes, we're involved in what are the most important days of their life and, more importantly, we can continue for them to have that connection with Jewish life.*

Edward Stourton: *Sounds logical. Alan Plancey?*

Alan Plancey: *No, they're playing to the gallery. You know, I tried to give the analogy: if I like cricket, [but] then I don't like the hard balls they play with, I'll use a tennis ball instead, and I'll say, 'That's called cricket.' It's not called cricket. This is not called Judaism. We can't accept this intermarriage. It's all very well saying the numbers are going up. Perhaps we should be doing something with society, educating them. You see, we have rules, we have regulations, and we can't just change them to the whims and fancies of the community.*

Edward Stourton: *But just explain why you can't accept the idea that somebody might wish to remain within the Jewish community but marry somebody outside it?*

Alan Plancey: *Because there are rules and regulations. We're becoming emotional instead of being rational. Rational says these are the rules we have to play by, and if you want to opt out of them, you're opting out. You can't change them and say, 'I'm still Jewish.' Let me explain something to you; what the ground rules are. If a Jewish man marries a non-Jewish woman, the children are not Jewish. If, however, a non-Jewish man marries a Jewish woman, the children are Jewish, and I will do everything in my power to save those children – to keep them within the Jewish fold. They're making a statement by marrying out. They know they are doing wrong, and therefore we cannot come* *along and condone them by saying, 'Oh, we feel sorry – so many are doing it.'*

Rabbi Romain picked up on Rabbi Plancey's recognition that 'so many are doing it'.

Jonathan Romain: *Well, the point is that rabbis like Alan Plancey and many other great rabbis have actually protested against mixed-faith marriage for several decades, but it hasn't worked. You know, we've had all this objection to mixed-faith marriage, and yet the numbers are still rising. So in other words, it's not having any effect. What we can have an effect [on] is what happens after the mixed-faith marriage. Do they then leave the community or do they stay part of it?*

And what we've found over the last few years is that the crucial difference is how the community responds. And if the community rejects them, then obviously they're lost – and not just them, but their children and grandchildren. But if the community welcomes them and says, 'Look, you're still Jewish. You may not have done what we prefer as the best option, but you've still got these Jewish roots,' then they will continue to be part of the community.

Edward Stourton: *Alan Plancey, so, just to get something clear, if somebody in your synagogue marries out, they're out of the synagogue?*

Alan Plancey: *It depends. They're not out of the synagogue, but they're certainly considered to be lax in their observance of Judaism. They wouldn't want to stay within the synagogue because their children are not accepted if the woman is not Jewish. You know, by organising all these classes for mixed marriages, we are actually encouraging it. Perhaps the catalyst to the increase of mixed marriages is the fact that we are accepting them all and we have lowered our standards instead of being disciplined in our actions and saying, 'Look, we don't accept this. Perhaps you should think twice about what you are doing.' We will discourage people from doing this.*

Celebrating the Liberal movement

The conviction that Judaism has to move with the times is at the heart of the Reform tradition, and it is even more marked in Reform Judaism's progressive cousin, Liberal Judaism. In February 2011, the Liberal Jewish Synagogue (LJS) in St John's Wood, which is the oldest and largest Liberal synagogue in the country, celebrated its centenary. Trevor Barnes reported from the special Shabbat service that opened the centenary celebrations, and his despatch included some of the themes which have been recurrent in *Sunday*'s coverage of the Jewish community, including the laws governing Jewish identity. His guests included rabbi emeritus of LJS David Goldberg, senior rabbi at LJS Rabbi Alexandra Wright, then synagogue vice-chairman at LJS Michael Hart, and British historian Professor Geoffrey Alderman.

Trevor Barnes: *Just minutes to go before the centenary service, and there's palpable excitement in the air. All 900-plus seats are taken, including mine here in the gallery – giving me a ringside view of this landmark event.*

David Goldberg: *Liberal Judaism is the smallest of the groupings within Anglo-Jewry, but it's always been the cutting edge, and we've had an influence out of all proportion to our numerical size. I think so many of the innovations in Anglo-Jewry – for example, women's equality, women rabbis – you'll find the vast majority of them started with the Liberal movement.*

Trevor Barnes: *Rabbi emeritus David Goldberg, who was succeeded in 2004 by senior rabbi Alexandra Wright. Earlier this week... I came here to meet her.*

Alexandra Wright: *It's very much a contemporary community; very diverse, very, very inclusive, welcoming people from a very, very wide spectrum of backgrounds – people exploring their Jewish identity.*

Trevor Barnes: *From the entrance I moved into the sanctuary, dominated by what looks like a miniature Western Wall made of Jerusalem stone, in which the ark is set, housing the scrolls of the law – ornately wrapped and topped with decorative silver bells, just as you'd see in any other synagogue. So what sets this apart from Orthodox Jewish worship? Synagogue vice-chairman Michael Hart.*

Michael Hart: *Come and sit in one of our services and you'll see men and women sitting together. You'll see a proportion of the service read in English. You'll see great participation by those who are here. More recently, we've recognised same-sex commitment ceremonies. So we recognise the important role that some gay members of our community* *make. And we are welcoming to those where only one parent may be Jewish. So whether it's the father or the mother, we would be welcoming them, providing they're brought up as Jews.*

Trevor Barnes: *And it's this, arguably more than anything, that sets the Liberal movement apart from the Orthodox and even Reform wings, which assert that Jewishness is passed on through the mother, not the father.*

The report also touched on the still-raw debate over who has the right to speak in the name of the country's Jews.

Trevor Barnes: *Confirmation this week of the appointment of Baroness Julia Neuberger [for her contributions on bioethics, see chapter 8] as senior rabbi to the West London Reform Synagogue has introduced another dimension to the mix. With such a high-profile public figure and, like the pioneering Lily Montagu [one of the founders of the LJS], a woman leading a potential alliance of Judaism's progressive wing, could Julia Neuberger be a parallel chief rabbi in everything but name? Challenging the actual chief rabbi Jonathan Sacks's claim to speak for British Jews? Rabbi Alexandra Wright says not.*

Alexandra Wright: *It's not part of what progressive Judaism is. Because one of the principles which I think Liberal Judaism, progressive Judaism, generally is committed to is pluralism. It accepts a diversity of different voices and different points of view.*

Trevor Barnes: *But Geoffrey Alderman [author of a study on modern British Jewry] puts the appointment in a historical context, and he's intrigued.*

Geoffrey Alderman: *Very interesting. Julia Neuberger is already in the House of Lords. She is a very seasoned speaker in the House of Lords, a very charismatic figure. Of course, she won't be called 'chief rabbi', and I'm sure she herself would recoil from the idea. But I think we are seeing the emergence of a parallel Jewish religious establishment in this country, very well represented in the Upper House.*

'A colourful, solid quilt of Judaism'

The role of women is one of the principle dividing lines between different strands of Judaism. In Orthodox synagogues, men and women sit in separate areas. Women are expected to dress modestly, often covering their heads. The slightly more progressive tradition, known as Modern Orthodox, believes women should be given more opportunity, and communities in the United States have ordained women rabbis, but they remain a rarity. In the United Kingdom, Ephraim Mirvis, Jonathan Sacks's successor as chief rabbi, introduced a new role in 2016 that allowed women to teach in Orthodox synagogues, but in general the Orthodox tradition restricts the leadership positions women can hold.

Reform Judaism, by contrast, believes in the equality of men and women, and allows women to perform many of the roles traditionally undertaken by men, including that of rabbi. And in the summer of 2011, the Reform movement in the United Kingdom appointed a woman to the newly created role of senior rabbi to Reform Judaism. The job initially had a different title, as the rabbi in question, Laura Janner-Klausner, told *Sunday*.

Jane Little: There's some confusion actually over your title: 'Movement rabbi' or elsewhere you've been described as 'rabbinical spokesperson'. Can you clarify?

Laura Janner-Klausner: Well, I'm the rabbi of the Movement for Reform Judaism.

Jane Little: The rabbi of the Movement.

Laura Janner-Klausner: Yes, that's right. Internally, we call it 'Movement rabbi'.

Jane Little: But certainly not 'chief rabbi'.

Laura Janner-Klausner: Definitely not chief rabbi, because the tone of chief rabbi is a tone we don't want. It's a very hierarchical tone, and I represent other rabbis. Together we build policy, we build values. So this idea of a very, very more distant voice is not my voice. My voice is an equal voice with the other rabbis... I'm here as their spokesperson, and of our communities.

Jane Little: Still, some will see it as a challenge to the role of Dr Jonathan Sacks, who is the chief rabbi of Orthodox Judaism.

Laura Janner-Klausner: They may, that's right. Because it's an alternative voice; a voice that represents a Judaism that is lived by most Jews, which is unlike a very more Orthodox Judaism, because we are progressive and modern and outward-looking.

Jane Little: *As opposed to Orthodox Judaism. You sound quite critical.*

Laura Janner-Klausner: *No, no. Actually, one lovely thing is that I work really well with my Orthodox colleagues. I came from an Orthodox background as a child, and so it's just a different kind of Judaism, progressive Judaism. And I'm not critical of Orthodox Judaism. I come in saying this is* our *Judaism. It's a positive, modern, self-confident Judaism, which is equal for men and women, rather than* traditional *Judaism. But it's based on tradition. So we're a different voice and we work together.*

Towards the end of interview, Jane Little turned to the question of Rabbi Janner-Klausner's gender.

Jane Little: *Well, the obvious fact is, you're a woman, and a woman could never lead Orthodox Judaism. Are you trying to bring something different here?*

Laura Janner-Klausner: *Not because I'm a woman, but because I represent a very equal Judaism. So the woman's voice that you hear, I could easily be a man – because we have lots of wonderful male rabbis who could have represented our community who would be saying the same thing, but just in a male voice. So my gender is coincidental, but the voice that says we are equal is not coincidental.*

Jane Little: *What's your vision for Judaism here?*

Laura Janner-Klausner: *My vision is of a joyful Judaism. I think of it as – I'm a quilter talking about being a woman (most men don't quilt and I do quilt) – it's of a colourful, solid quilt of Judaism based on tradition where people come together and learn and enjoy being parts of the Jewish community. It's an outward-facing Judaism that's open to change, but is grounded in knowing capability and tradition.*

The evidence from the *Sunday* archive suggests Laura Janner-Klausner's 'quilt' is indeed an apposite metaphor for British Jewry.

10

Terror and Islam in Britain

'In the three years since the 11th of September 2001, many more acts of terror have been committed by Islamist militants,' Roger Bolton told the Sunday audience on 12 September 2004. He cited as examples two especially bloody atrocities that had been perpetrated in the days leading up to that morning's broadcast: the Beslan massacre,[1] in which 333 people, most of them children, were killed after a Chechen group seized control of a Russian school; and the bombing of the Australian embassy in Indonesia, which claimed nine lives.

'Islam is now increasingly associated with violence, in spite of the denunciation of terrorism by most Muslim leaders,' Bolton continued. 'This week, the Islamic Human Rights Commission [established in London in 1997] called on the government to address what it calls a "backlash" against Muslims in the UK following 9/11.'

The early years of the twenty-first century were an important period in the growth of Islam as a force in the life of the United Kingdom. The number of Muslims passed the million mark in the 1990s, and by 2001 (in the year of the 9/11 attacks) it stood at 1.6 million in England and Wales alone. At the time of writing, it is estimated that more than five per cent of the British population is Muslim, making this the second-largest religious group in the United Kingdom. As we shall see in chapter 12, this rapid expansion was accompanied by social tensions, but also some significant progress in community relations.

The enormity of the 9/11 attacks in New York, however, defined the politics of the era, both internationally and domestically. And the relationship between Islam and terrorism (or, in the view of many

---

1 Although the siege seems to have been inspired by Chechen separatism, it was widely reported as an act of Islamist terrorism at the time.

Muslims, the unfounded slur of such a relationship) cast a shadow over much of the news coverage of Islam's place in British society. *Sunday*, with its distinctive agenda, was especially well placed to reflect the Muslim perspective on the violence of the period.

In the aftermath of the Beslan massacre and the Australian embassy bombing, the task fell to Christopher Landau, a BBC religious affairs correspondent who later left the corporation to train for ordination. It is worth quoting his report at some length, because it reflects the complexity of the issues at play. It begins with two clips taken from BBC news bulletins.

News clip: *A ten-year-old boy presumed dead after being filmed in the Beslan siege video was found alive…*

News clip: *In a terrorist attack at the Australian embassy in Jakarta, six people are killed in a car bomb attack.*

Christopher Landau: *Listen to the news, and you could be forgiven for thinking that Islam and violence are somehow intrinsically linked. But Muslims are becoming increasingly frustrated that, all too often, news coverage across the media fails to distinguish between mainstream orthodox Muslims and those on the margins, inclined to violence. Abdal Hakim Murad lectures in Islamic Studies at Cambridge University, where he's also the Muslim chaplain.*

Abdal Hakim Murad: *British Islam is a broad church. Unfortunately, we do have a 'skinhead fringe', and some of the people attracted to groups like Al-Muhajiroun* [a radical group subsequently threatened with a ban from Britain] *really have the same relationship to Islam as the BNP or the National Front seem to have to the Union Flag. We apologise for the extremists, but really there's only a few dozen of them, and every side has extremists.*

Christopher Landau: *The problem is that Muslim extremism has been given wide media coverage, with little apparently done to dissuade the public from associating Muslim extremes with the mainstream. Dr Murad suggests that it's the media's responsibility to recognise the role it has played in fostering misinformation.*

Abdal Hakim Murad: *Islam as a political force is still fairly new, and the journalistic culture hasn't quite figured out who to turn to for an authentic voice. Everybody, when a bomb went off in Northern Ireland,* *knew that you went to the Catholic bishop or the Protestant pastor who would condemn the act. When something happens in Islamic places, the journalists aren't quite so clear about who they should go to or, if they are clear, sometimes they don't bother.*

Christopher Landau: *Dr Murad acknowledges that Islam has much to learn about how to get its moderate message across. But even if Muslims did develop a successful public relations strategy, that wouldn't solve the problem of the journalistic shorthand that describes terrorist acts and frustrates Muslim columnist Yasmin Alibhai-Brown.*

Yasmin Alibhai-Brown: *'Nine killed by Australian embassy bomb', headline. First line: 'Suspected Islamic terrorists detonated a huge car bomb outside the Australian embassy'. My own newspaper, The Independent, again looking at the same story, I think they call them 'Islamic terrorists', 'Islamic militants', 'Islamic fanatics', 'Islamic fundamentalists'.*

Christopher Landau: *What do you think this use of language actually says about the way Islam and terror are associated together in people's minds?*

Yasmin Alibhai-Brown: *Well, that's what it does. It is now almost impossible to extricate from the mind of an ordinary person watching the news or listening to the news or reading the newspapers that Islam is not a terrorist religion.*

Christopher Landau: *At the offices of the Vectone Entertainment Network in London's Docklands, satellite broadcasts are made in Bengali, Urdu, Hindi and Tamil across the Muslim world. Mufti Barkatulla is a senior imam who presents an hour's talk show each weekday afternoon. He believes part of his role is to convince Muslims that they must respond effectively to the post-9/11 climate.*

Mufti Barkatulla: *Usually everybody is innocent until proven guilty, but in this case, by the de facto, Muslims have been thought to be guilty until proven innocent. So what I promote is that every member of the Muslim community has to work hard to outreach, to go out and about, and introduce and interact in a manner to prove his innocence beyond any doubt. So there has to be some extra hard work, extraordinary efforts and interaction with every single community in all other religions in the neighbourhoods.*

Christopher Landau: *The call for outreach is made because there's an increasing realisation that the strong ties within Britain's Muslim* *communities can result in little interaction with wider society – with sometimes violent consequences in places like Burnley or Oldham [the scenes of serious rioting in 2001]. For Professor Salman Sayyid, a research fellow in the Sociology of Islam at the University of Leeds, it's essential to appreciate the background to situations where terrorism is carried out in the name of Islam.*

Salman Sayyid: *All of these issues require a certain kind of detailed knowledge, whatever position you take into them. In the absence of that knowledge, you end up interpreting everything in a kind of tabloid way of simply, 'This is terrorism, it is completely pathological, these are mad people, there is nothing behind all of this.' And I think that is something that perhaps needs to be put into check. But it also explains why the Muslim community finds itself out of sync quite often, because it doesn't start with that assumption that these people have got no grievances, these people have got no causes.*

Christopher Landau: *But acknowledging the legitimacy of a grievance, while condemning the violent act that's been prompted by such a grievance, is no easy task. Bringing terrorists and governments to the negotiating table can seem impossible, but perhaps it shouldn't. Dilwar Hussain is a research fellow at the Islamic Foundation in Leicester.*

Dilwar Hussain: *In many ways, what's happening with the Muslim community today is very similar to the way that the Irish community was associated with terrorism once upon a time.*

Christopher Landau: *And he [Dilwar] says that if terror carried out in the name of Islam is also going to be tackled, that requires an unprecedented dialogue between the West and the Islamic world, where discussion can proceed without either side claiming the rhetorical upper hand.*

Dilwar Hussain: *The very language that's used – the 'you are with us or against us' language, 'the axis of evil' language [President Bush used this phrase to identify America's enemies in his 2002 State of the Union address and frequently thereafter], is not helpful at all. If we are saying to people that violence will not resolve these conflicts, that violence will not bring peace to the world, then we have to act according to that message. We cannot then perpetrate violence upon a group of people and expect that to bring peace.*

212

That final sentence was a reference to the American-led (and British-backed) invasion of Iraq, which had taken place the previous spring. The violence that engulfed the country in the aftermath of Saddam Hussein's overthrow continued for several years, and two months after the broadcast of Christopher Landau's report, in November 2004, American forces launched Operation Phantom Fury, an effort to retake the city of Fallujah, which had been identified as a centre of the insurgency against the American occupation. It proved to be the bloodiest battle of the war, and afterwards it was said to have involved American troops in the most intense fighting they had faced since the Vietnam War. By the time the operation was officially concluded, nearly 100 American personnel had been killed and more than 500 wounded.

Fighting in Fallujah

War reporting is rare on the *Sunday* programme, but on 14 November the BBC correspondent Alastair Leithead was on the line live from Baghdad.

Alistair Leithead: *Well, there are pockets of violence, as the Americans call it, still going on. It does seem as if they're moving towards ending the battle for Fallujah, at least in the main assault sense. A couple of the officers on the ground have been saying the city is occupied but not yet subdued. And another man said that the insurgents were attacking, now they're running. And there is a growing sense of confidence from the Americans that they are moving towards an end here. But there are pockets of these insurgents left in other parts of the city that [the Americans] are supposed to already have control of. Fighting is still going on.*

Roger Bolton: *Aid is reported as reaching the city, but it can't get into it or isn't being allowed into it. Why is that?*

Alistair Leithead: *That's right. The aid trucks from the Iraqi Red Crescent have reached the main hospital in Fallujah. Now, that's on the other side of the river. It's on the outskirts of the city... Where the need is most, of course, is the centre and the south of the city. The American forces say it's just too dangerous for the aid workers to go through. And we really don't have an idea as to how many civilians were in the city when the assault began, how* *many are still inside the city, what kind of conditions they're in and what kind of a crisis we're facing. The Iraqi Red Crescent suggests that there is a humanitarian crisis there, because of course there's been no water or no power for the whole week, and there are very few food supplies as well.*

British troops acted in support of the Americans in Fallujah, and also suffered casualties (including four dead). However, they remained on the outskirts of the city and did not take part in the deadly fighting in the centre.

But even that level of involvement was extremely controversial for British Muslims. As Roger Bolton put it on *Sunday*: 'Opposition to the assault on Fallujah is, of course, widespread, not least among British Muslims. The MCB said it was utterly appalled by the US army's barbaric assault on the besieged and long-suffering Iraqi city.'

To underline the point, the programme broadcast vox pop interviews with worshippers at London's Regent's Park Mosque.

Vox pop: *I'm not very happy about what's happening in Fallujah at the moment. I think they should leave Iraq to the Iraqis. And the Americans are not invited into Fallujah. And I think everybody should just get out, basically.*

Vox pop: *It makes me really angry, to be honest. I'm really upset about how innocent civilians are losing their lives because of this battle. And they need somehow to take a different approach, because it's not working. That's really clear.*

As the Cambridge academic Abdal Hakim Murad observed, media organisations sometimes found it difficult to judge who could speak on behalf of British Islam. Sunni Islam (the majority tradition in the United Kingdom) does not have a figure akin to the pope or the archbishop of Canterbury, or even a version of Orthodox Judaism's chief rabbi. The MCB, which had delivered the damning verdict on the Fallujah operation quoted by Roger Bolton, was by this stage the best-known of several organisations claiming to represent Muslims. Bolton interviewed the organisation's deputy secretary general, Dr Muhammad Abdul Bari, who proved difficult to pin down.

Roger Bolton: Do you think... that armed resistance of the sort we're seeing in Fallujah is legitimate? Would you support the fighters who are ranged against American and British troops?

Muhammad Abdul Bari: Well, the people of Iraq have to decide, because the war has been imposed on them.

Roger Bolton: Sorry, sir, I was asking you, not the people in Iraq. Do you therefore think it's legitimate for people to fight against the American and British troops in Iraq?

Muhammad Abdul Bari: Well, it is for the people of Iraq to decide.

Roger Bolton: But it certainly could be legitimate? You're not telling them it's wrong?

Muhammad Abdul Bari: Well, what are you saying? That the occupation of Iraq itself was wrong?

London bombings

Britain's foreign policy, especially in the Middle East, appears to have been a significant motivating factor for the four suicide bombers who, the following year, were behind what came to be known as the 7/7 attacks. On 7 July 2005, the four men detonated bombs on London's rush-hour public transport system: three on Underground trains and one on a double-decker bus. Fifty-two people were killed in addition to the four bombers, and more than 700 injured, some of them very seriously.

Three of the four men – Mohammad Sidique Khan, a thirty-year-old father; eighteen-year-old Hasib Hussain; and Shehzad Tanweer, who worked in a chip shop – were identified as British-born children of Pakistani immigrants, all based in Leeds. The fourth killer, Germaine Lindsay (also known as Abdullah Shaheed Jamal), was a Jamaica-born convert who lived in Aylesbury, Buckinghamshire, with his son and pregnant wife. The 7/7 attack was, inescapably, a home-grown act of terrorism.

In a videotape broadcast later on the Al-Jazeera network, Mohammad Sidique Khan describe his motivation as follows:

Our religion is Islam – obedience to the one true God, and following the footsteps of the final prophet messenger. Your democratically elected governments continuously perpetuate atrocities against my people all over the world. And your support of them makes you directly responsible, just as I am directly responsible for protecting and avenging my Muslim brothers and sisters. Until we feel security, you will be our targets, and until you stop the bombing, gassing, imprisonment and torture of my people, we will not stop this fight. We are at war, and I am a soldier. Now you, too, will taste the reality of this situation.

Shehzad Tanweer's videoed statement, also broadcast on Al-Jazeera, included the warning:

What you have witnessed now is only the beginning of a string of attacks that will continue and become stronger until you pull your forces out of Afghanistan and Iraq. And until you stop your financial and military support to America and Israel.

Sunday's coverage of the immediate aftermath of 7/7 did not survive in the archive, but on the tenth anniversary of the attacks, the programme broadcast the testimony of Revd Debbie Hodge, a United Reformed Church minister. The double-decker bus bomb went off in Tavistock Square, near the offices of the British Medical Association (BMA), and she was among the first of those with medical experience to reach the scene.

Debbie Hodge: *It was a normal office day, and suddenly there was this explosion. And I knew from my previous life as a nurse in London that it was probably a bomb. I went to the front door and there was lots of noise, car horns. But the striking thing was metal confetti falling down in the square and people screaming.*
William Crawley: *How were you involved in the response?*
Debbie Hodge: *I spent the first half an hour or so helping [the] walking wounded move away from the scene of the bus and just making sure that they were in places that they felt safe in, and reassuring them that their deafness would probably be temporary. Because that was what many of them had found – that they suddenly couldn't hear. The explosion had been so loud that it had affected their hearing. Then I spent most of the*

day at the BMA helping with a guy who subsequently died, who was complaining that it's so cold in London and he'd come from Melbourne, Australia. So we could understand why he felt cold, although he was in a very bad way. And then there was another lady... and she'd broken her clavicle. But her concern was, 'I need to talk to my daughter because I had an argument with her this morning.'

William Crawley: Oh dear.

Debbie Hodge: And [she asked], 'What would have happened if I hadn't survived?' Those are the kind of poignant reminders both to that particular woman and to everybody that life is fragile, and we shouldn't squander the opportunities to be kind and to create peace.

William Crawley: Do you think you've been changed by that day, Debbie?

Debbie Hodge: Yes. I mean, there are some things now I do with more conviction, and there are some things that I don't do quite as easily now. One of the things that changed significantly at the time was my ability to be a chaplain. I say 'ability'. The skills were still there, but the attitude had taken a severe knock. In that, having sat with people who had half a shoulder blown off, legs severely damaged, in those kinds of conditions, lying on tabletops at the BMA when I was in the hospital working as a chaplain – and this is going to sound quite harsh – and the patient said, 'Well, they couldn't find me an extra pillow,' I'm thinking, 'Actually, you have a bed, you have three pillows already, you are pain-free.'

I found it quite frustrating to deal with what appeared to be trivial. And it took me a little while to come back to the recognition that for some people 7/7 happened in a major disaster way. But for every patient, they're having their own version of 7/7 in their crisis, whatever that crisis is. And if it is that I can't get comfortable because I haven't got an extra pillow, that's their crisis. And it took me a little while to come back to recognise that, and not feel frustrated that they weren't more thankful, I think.

Engaging young people

The 7/7 attacks had an enduring impact on the debate about Islam's place in British society, as well as on those caught up in the events of that day. On the second anniversary of the attacks, the MCB organised a conference to debate measures to prevent terrorism. The meeting was given an additional sense of urgency by various attacks in the days before it opened. On 29 June 2007, police identified and neutralised two car bombs in London, and the following day a jeep filled with propane gas cannisters was driven into the terminal entrance at Glasgow airport.

The MCB's London meeting was organised by Dr Muhammad Abdul Bari, the official who had been so reluctant to condemn resistance to British and American forces in Fallujah on *Sunday* three years earlier, who was now the council's secretary general. Shazia Khan's report on 8 July 2007 reflected the soul-searching about terrorism taking place for many Muslims, but also the divisions within the Muslim community.

Shazia Khan: Well, there were over 150 people that were actually invited to the meeting at the Islamic Cultural Centre, and they were made up mainly of imams, community activists, scholars. And I noticed that there were people from the Al-Khoei Foundation, for example, which is a Shia organisation. And I also noticed that there was somebody from the Hizb ut-Tahrir organisation. So clearly the MCB wanted to ensure that there was a broader group of people engaging in this dialogue. Essentially what happened is that opening comments were made by Dr Muhammad Abdul Bari, the secretary general of the MCB. After his opening comments I managed to catch up with him, and he told me why he thought it was important to have this meeting.

Muhammad Abdul Bari: So we have to improve our engagement with the young people or the women [and] with the masjid {with mosques].

Shazia Khan: There weren't many young people here today.

Muhammad Abdul Bari: Well, there are some. There were some. And so this is a big issue for all of us. But while they are Muslims, they are British citizens as well. So it's a collective responsibility to engage with young people, young Muslims, from all communities.

Shazia Khan: After Dr Bari's opening address, the press were asked to leave the meeting. It was then a closed meeting. But activity certainly didn't stop there. There was a large number of young Muslim men outside the conference who are kicking up a real fuss because they wanted access into the meeting. They felt that their views should have been heard.

Roger Bolton: And I gather that some of them were chanting that the organisers were lackeys and bootlickers of the Blair–Brown regime. So did they oppose the very idea of any discussion or rapprochement, if you like?

Shazia Khan: I don't think they opposed the idea of any discussion. They said they wanted to be part of those discussions... On the one hand they claimed not to be any sort of organised group, yet on the other hand they were handing out typed literature. The heading of this leaflet that they were handing out was: 'Allah exposes the hypocrites in our midst.' They didn't say that they were members of any particular organisation. All they said was that they were from east London and that they were just a group of people wanting to be heard.

Roger Bolton: But if they use phrases like 'a crusade for fellow Muslims', that's pretty insulting, isn't it?

Shazia Khan: It was pretty intense stuff. I think a lot of the delegates were very insulted by the literature that was being distributed and the rhetoric that was being used by these young men.

Roger Bolton: But it does seem to illustrate that there still seems to be a significant gap between those older Muslims who were perhaps inside the building and the younger Muslims who seem largely to have been outside.

Shazia Khan: Well, this is the point that one of the delegates I spoke to made. The person I'm talking about is Mohammed Shafiq. He's from the Ramadhan Foundation.

Mohammed Shafiq: The most important thing which I noticed, was that sixty or seventy per cent of the people who have turned up today were not from the young people. And if we want to deal with the issues that young people have expressed – their views that were expressed outside today – we have to engage with these people. We might not agree with them – I totally disagree with everything they said – but I think they should have a right to share their piece. So some of them should have been allowed in there to have their say.

Roger Bolton: I understand there is going to be a statement issued later today. What form will it take?

Shazia Khan: I think there's going to be a written declaration. It will consist of five main points. Firstly, an acceptance that there is a problem of extremism within the Muslim community, which doesn't sound very *groundbreaking. But when I spoke to Inayat Bunglawala, who is a representative of the Muslim Council of Britain, he said it's important because there has been a sense of denial within some quarters of the Muslim community. The second point will be that the community needs to work and cooperate with the police.*

The third point is commending the government for their measured response to what happened last week in Glasgow and in London. And the fourth point will be a declaration that those who carry out terrorist acts are enemies of Islam and of the wider community. And the fifth and final point is a statement that we need to acknowledge that foreign policy does have an impact on the way that young people feel.

To assess the significance of the MCB meeting, Roger Bolton turned to the Muslim academic and *Thought for the Day* contributor Professor Mona Siddiqui.

Mona Siddiqui: *Well, I think that any Muslim organisation who wants to organise something a week after the attack in Glasgow and then on the anniversary of the July 7th bombings is obviously making headlines, but is obviously also acknowledging that there is a problem – and it's not going to go away, and we have to face up to it. The real problem is, though, that apart from headlines... as you pointed out earlier, we don't see any action plan. We haven't really seen any great significant change in the way people perceive terrorism and extremism.*

Roger Bolton: *Well, is that a bit harsh? Because, I mean, I haven't heard the Muslim Council of Britain say as clearly, ever before, that Muslims have an Islamic duty to cooperate with the police to ensure Britain's safety. And when you also hear people like Inayat Bunglawala saying after the meeting that those who are killing civilians for what they believe is an interpretation of Islam are making a lethal misinterpretation, that's pretty significant, isn't it?*

Mona Siddiqui: *But that's their mental lethargy that they haven't acknowledged this before; not a significant leap in their engagement. I mean, people have been saying this for some time. And just because the Muslim Council [of] Britain hasn't acknowledged it, it doesn't mean that it's not been a reality. And so the real test will be that, once they've* *made this public announcement, what can they do? But I think the more significant point is that, for a start, as the report said, there weren't that many young people there. And so if it's the young people that you're trying to engage, how do you engage them when they don't give you credibility in the first place?*

Roger Bolton: *Well, getting credibility with young people is a problem for every faith. But let me put to you something that someone like Hassan Butt* [a former spokesman for the radical group al-Muhajiroun, now calling on Muslims to renounce terrorism] *said yesterday. According to him, many imams who preach at mosques in Britain refused to broach the difficult and often complex truth that Islam can be interpreted as condoning violence against the unbeliever. And instead, it repeated the mantra that Islam is peace and hope that all of this debate will go away. This has left the territory open for radicals. Do you think that sort of fundamental debate has to be undertaken?*

Mona Siddiqui: *Oh, absolutely. And… I've been saying for some time, Roger, that when people talk about, 'Oh, it's theology that's being misunderstood or abused,' well, actually, some of the people who are radicalising young people know their theology inside out. They just choose to project a certain type of theology. And of course, any faith can be used to project all sorts of issues, and Islam is no exception in that. So to keep saying that it is a religion of peace and that we condemn all violence may be true for some people, but on the other hand it can't be denied that Islam, like most monotheistic faiths, has enough resources in it for people to exploit to project violence.*

A public call for peace

Sunday covered another effort to change perceptions of Islam in September 2011. The UK branch of the Pakistan-based Minhaj-ul-Quran International organisation, founded by the prominent Muslim scholar Shaykh Muhammad Tahir-ul-Qadri, organised a mass rally with the explicit support of the British government and other faith leaders.

'A leading Islamic scholar received a standing ovation yesterday from thousands of Muslims at Wembley Arena,' William Crawley told the audience. 'Dr Muhammad ul-Qadri had just denounced terrorism and called for peace at the 12,000-strong rally, where video messages were also relayed from the archbishop of Canterbury and the community secretary, Eric Pickles.' The programme's reporter, Trevor Barnes, painted a picture of the scene.

Trevor Barnes: *Here in the main hall it's evidently a sell-out, with over 10,000 tickets sold at £10 a time, £35 for the VIP boxes. There are a few men in traditional dress, but most are in Western suits, ties or casual clothes. For the women, hijabs of all colours, styles and fabrics are universal, with only a sprinkling of full-face veils. The highlight of the programme has been an address by the founder of Minhaj-ul-Quran International, Shaykh Tahir-ul-Qadri.*

Muhammad Tahir-ul-Qadri (giving a speech): *In spite of statements and memorandums and condemnation of the terror in the voices of the ninety-nine per cent, true, peace-loving Muslims have not been heard, but have been drowned out by the clamour and noise of the extremists and terrorists, causing the rest of mankind to wonder, 'How could the Muslims have been so silent?'*

Trevor Barnes: *Dr Qadri was unavailable for interview, but I spoke to his representative, Shahid Mursaleen, and put it to him that the conference and the declaration emerging from it are idealistic rather than practical.*

Shahid Mursaleen: *No, we aim to promote this, and aim to get 1 million signatories and promote the message of true Islam. We believe that terrorism and terrorist suicide bombers do not represent Islam.*

Trevor Barnes: *You should be talking to the very extremists who Dr Qadri is condemning, and they are not here.*

Shahid Mursaleen: *They are listening. They are listening very carefully on the internet, through the media, through various channels as well as through the publications. We are not targeting the people who have been brainwashed to become terrorists. We are targeting the people who are confused; people who are looking for answers; people and young Muslims who are in the process of being radicalised at British campuses. We are trying to target those young, vulnerable people.*

May 2013 provided the most brutal evidence imaginable that messages of this sort were not reaching all Muslims. Fusilier Lee Rigby, a member of the Royal Regiment of Fusiliers, was attacked in the street near his base at the Royal Artillery Barracks in Woolwich. His attackers, two Muslim converts, ran him down in a car before using knives and a cleaver to hack him to death, and remained with his body until the police arrived, declaring to passers-by that they were avenging the killing of Muslims by British soldiers.

Trevor Barnes reported from the scene for *Sunday* and, among worshippers emerging from Friday prayers at the Greenwich Islamic Centre, he found 'universal condemnation' of what had been done.

But the programme's subsequent discussion of the causes of radicalisation revealed significant differences. William Crawley chaired the debate between Dr Alexander Meleagrou-Hitchens, head of research at the International Centre for the Study of Radicalisation at King's College London; Dr Qadir Baksh, chair of the Luton Islamic Centre; and Asghar Bukhari of the Muslim Public Affairs Committee, a lobbying and civil liberties group established to give Muslims a more effective voice in British politics.

Alexander Meleagrou-Hitchens: I suppose 'radicalisation' essentially refers to the process by which someone adopts what we would consider to be radical ideas. In this case, it would be the beginning of an adoption of the idea that Islam is not a spiritual religion, but is a political ideology. The idea that Islam and Muslims are under threat by the West ideologically and physically, as a war on Islam, and the belief that violence is the best way to respond to this – that would be it in sort of a nutshell.

William Crawley: So, politicisation and militarisation... Qadir, I know you've been working to combat this since even before 9/11. What, in your experience, leads some on that path?

Qadir Baksh: Well, first and foremost, you know, I would disagree with the gentleman who, as he said in 'a nutshell', defined radicalisation, on the point that he made [that] there's no spiritualisation in those that become radicalised, whereas you'll find them very, very spiritual. You'll find them in the mosque reciting Qur'an and learning Arabic, and so on and so forth. That's something characteristic of them. The second thing is that, yeah, I mean, we have to make a very, very clear distinction between radicalisation and violent radicalisation, because radicalisation, as understood by the wider society and government and policies at this stage, it's really when somebody becomes politically aware and wishes to make a political change. Now that, for me, is not a dangerous point, because there are a lot of non-Muslims and also moderate Muslims who would like to see a political change in the world, in their country and locality. The problem comes when that radicalisation or that political awareness, which I prefer to call it, turns to violent radicalisation. That's where the problem is, and that's what we should be discussing.

William Crawley: *So, Asghar, we've added a third dimension to this: the spiritualisation. Some will see that as an abduction of the spiritual for political or military purposes. But nevertheless, three strands so far laid out. There's clearly a failure to reverse this process of radicalisation. Who do you think is responsible for that?*

Asghar Bukhari: *Both the government and the Muslim organisations – the government who refuse to accept that this is all about policy. It's politics, politics, politics that radicalises Muslims, who see, you know, millions of people suffering around the world, and then… grow angry about it. Now, on the flip side of it, you have Muslim organisations who completely refuse to tackle the anger of young Muslims by teaching them a peaceful, political way forward. And that's why I reject your so-called security expert's opinion that says that, you know, anyone that's Muslim who becomes political is kind of somehow following a dangerous road. No, politics is a human way of tackling change. The problem here is violence; a violent pathway instead of taking a peaceful, political pathway.*

British foreign policy emerged as a raw issue once again.

Alexander Meleagrou-Hitchens: *Mr Bukhari has been on the airwaves since this happened, pushing this foreign policy line – the idea that this is only happening because of foreign policy. Now, I don't disagree that people are being recruited on the basis that they believe that there's a war on Islam and they look at what's happening in Afghanistan, they look at what's happening in Iraq, and that's a fairly easy way to convince someone. But I should say, if we look at the number of incidents that have happened in this country and in Europe, such as, for example, the killing of Theo van Gogh [a Dutch filmmaker murdered in 2004 after*

224

making a film that criticised the treatment of women in some Islamic societies]; *such as the constant threats of murder on people who draw cartoons of Muhammad; such as the attempt to burn down the house of the [wo]man who published a book called* The Jewel of Medina, *which was deemed to have been insulting to Muhammad... These are people who are not reacting to foreign policy. They're reacting to the idea that you can't offend Islam, and you can kill people on the basis of that.*

Asghar Bukhari: Yes, but you're conflating issues. Don't pick random extremist actions... and then try to tie them in with a terrorist attack that is clearly to do with foreign policy. That the attackers themselves say, 'An eye for an eye, a tooth for a tooth. You will never live in peace until we live in peace.' The head of the Bin Laden unit [the Bin Laden Issue Station – a standalone unit of the Central Intelligence Agency dedicated to tracking Osama bin Laden and his associates], *MI5 and MI6, all of these agencies and Chatham House* [the leading foreign policy think tank], *are all saying it's a foreign policy issue. And here, so-called security experts like yourself are trying to conflate issues and trying to make it as if it's anything, everything.*

Alexander Meleagrou-Hitchens protested energetically against the charge of 'conflating issues', and the testy exchanges continued for some time.

Anti-Muslim backlash

The *Daily Telegraph* reported that the killing of Lee Rigby had provoked an 'anti-Muslim backlash across [the] UK', including 'the attacking of mosques, racial abuse and comments of social media'.[2] The government-backed Tell MAMA organisation reported more than 200 anti-Muslim incidents – mostly online, but also including eleven physical attacks on mosques.

There was another spike in anti-Muslim feeling ('Islamophobia', as it was by then generally known) two years later in the wake of the series of attacks in Paris that left 130 dead. *Sunday* reported that: 'The

---

2 T. Whitehead, 'Woolwich attack provokes anti-Muslim backlash across UK', *The Telegraph*: https://www.telegraph.co.uk/news/uknews/terrorism-in-the-uk/10080300/Woolwich-attack-provokes-anti-Muslim-backlash-across-UK.html (25 May 2013, accessed 28 March 2023).

Metropolitan Police say the number of attacks on Muslims in London more than tripled in the aftermath of the terrorist killings in Paris, and that hate crimes against Muslims more generally have increased dramatically, too.'

One of the victims of such attacks, a Mrs Begum, told *Sunday* how she was accosted as she prepared to drive her children to her local mosque:

> *This man, a white male, he wasn't looking scruffy or anything, he was clean and everything, and he stopped me. He goes, 'You stupid ***.' He said about three times, 'You stupid ***.' I just looked at him. 'Are you talking to me?' Because I was in shock. I didn't know who he was talking to. Was he actually talking to me?*
>
> *He goes, 'Who you got in the car?' And he's leaning against my car to see who's in the back seat. My five-month-old was sleeping at the back and my three-year-old was sleeping at the front. He was looking at the back. 'Who you got in there? Who you got in there? You want to brainwash them and bomb us?' And that's when I got a bit scared, when he was leaning to see who's in the back seat. So I just jumped in the car straightaway and called the police.*

This was December 2015, more than a decade after the Christopher Landau report quoted at the beginning of this chapter, but many of the themes remained the same. Peter Oborne, a former chief political commentator for the *Daily Telegraph,* accepted that press coverage was partly responsible for negative images of Muslims. 'If you read the papers,' he said, 'you're suddenly presented with this enemy within. And it's ill-founded. It's not based on fact. Virtually every Muslim I've ever talked to in Britain is very proud to be a British citizen. But I think there is a tendency for people to start feeling "got at".'

The government strategy for combatting the radicalisation of Muslims, known as Prevent, involved identifying individuals and groups judged to be vulnerable, and countering radical ideology in public institutions, including schools, hospitals and prisons. As *Sunday* reported in July 2015, it was widely criticised – both on the grounds that it risked violating civil liberties and that it was ineffective.

William Crawley introduced a new initiative as follows.

In the wake of the 7/7 attacks ten years ago, there were renewed efforts by the government to engage with Muslim communities in an attempt to prevent violent extremism. But those Prevent strategies, as they've become known, have proven very controversial. Some critics say, far from challenging radicalisation, they have merely stigmatised Britain's Muslims.

The charity Citizens UK appears to be adopting a different approach. Tomorrow it will begin a new initiative aimed at working out how Muslim communities can participate more fully in civic society. And they'll be launching a Commission on Islam, Participation and Public Life, chaired by the Conservative MP and former attorney general [for England and Wales] *Dominic Grieve, who joins us now.*

Dominic Grieve accepted that the much of the criticism aimed at Prevent was justified.

William Crawley: *As you approach this work, how do you deal with the claims some people have made recently, that Muslim leaders in Britain, members of the Muslim community more generally, have been retreating from public life?*

Dominic Grieve: *I think that statement may well be correct. And if one finds oneself in a position where one feels stigmatised or there's a fear that if you say anything it's going to be misinterpreted, then I think it follows almost automatically that one becomes more and more reluctant to do it. One of the problems with the rise of forms of religious extremism is that the moderate voices tend to get extinguished. We've seen this on many occasions, and indeed we can see it with other faiths as well. And I think that is a potential problem.*

There are demands placed on Muslims… to conform in particular ways, which I think can sometimes militate against their ability to participate or their desire to participate. But as I say, this is an inquiry. We're not going out on a mission around the country to promote a particular line. Actually, we're going on a learning experience. The whole idea behind it is to improve our knowledge, so that we can come up with some recommendations.

William Crawley: And do you agree with those critics of the government's Prevent strategies that I mentioned earlier, who say that that the alienation you have just noted, that sense of stigmatisation that some Muslims feel, can be explained by those strategies getting it wrong?

Dominic Grieve: It may be. The Prevent strategy has undoubtedly been, in its origin... a perfectly worthy aim, but as I think is well known, it's always had a degree of tension within it. Is it trying to target a very small number of people who are thought to be on the fringes of radicalisation and might turn into violent terrorists? Or is it designed to try to further [the] integration [of Muslims] more generally?

And of course, the problem with these sorts of programmes is that they tend to put people under the microscope. And human beings, I think, do need their space. If somebody is constantly looking at them under a microscope and observing their every move and trying to conclude whether... they're on the way to becoming terrorists, I would have thought a certain amount of paranoia may start to be induced in human beings who come under that level of scrutiny.

So the key to this, I think, is engagement. We need to engage and encourage Muslims – most of whom, in my experience, see their future in the United Kingdom; in a country which is democratic and pluralist and multifaith – and say to them, 'How can we facilitate your engagement in wider society?'

The Manchester Arena bombing

Sunday is broadcast from the BBC's studios in Salford, so the Manchester Arena bombing on 22 May 2017 was very much on the programme's home turf. Salman Ramadan Abedi, a local man of Libyan heritage, detonated a nail bomb as people were leaving the arena after an Ariana Grande concert. Twenty-three people were killed, including the attacker, and many more were injured. The death toll included ten people under twenty, and the youngest to be killed was an eight-year-old girl.

The attack took place on a Monday night, and *Sunday*'s focus the following weekend was 'how people of faith are responding to the horrific attack in Manchester and how best to harness the goodwill that emerged in the aftermath of tragedy'. The bishop of Manchester, David Walker, set the tone:

> It's been probably the most incredibly moving week of my life. The enormous tragedy to which we all woke up on Tuesday morning, yet within hours of that, to see Manchester, at the same time as deeply grieving, coming together – the huge rally that we held in Albert Square. The messages that were given there, the way that people were hugging each other, lighting candles, laying flowers. You know, these last couple of days, having the Manchester symbol, the bee, tattooed onto themselves. So many ways in which people are saying, 'You won't defeat us.'
>
> ...There is anger, but anger can be a force for good if we use it not to divide us, but use it to turn against the perpetrators. Give them the one thing they don't want. The one thing they do not want is our unity. And if we can give them our unity, then that hurts them more than anything else.

The presenter that weekend was Martin Bashir, then the BBC's religion editor.[3] The Great Manchester Run went ahead on Sunday 28 May, despite the tragedy the previous Monday, and Bashir interviewed some of those taking part.

One of them, Muhammed Hussain, was running in aid of a charity helping Iraqi orphans. These were his reflections on that week's attack, and the long list of atrocities that had gone before:

> I think if we, as individuals, do study our history, history tends to repeat itself. And it's about the perspective and the message that is being thrown around. And media does have a big part to play in it. And if we do fall into this trap where we are allowing this message to be funnelled through – that Islam is the reason and Islam is at war with the West, and there's a clash of ideologies and we can't come together – then, you know, unfortunately, the reality is these

---

3 Martin Bashir subsequently resigned from the BBC, citing health reasons, after an inquiry was set up to investigate the way he secured his celebrated *Panorama* interview with Diana, Princess of Wales.

individuals have succeeded in their aims. We have to take control of the narrative.

At the end of the day, we are British Muslims within this society. You know, I don't have any plans to go back to live in the Middle East or in Pakistan. This is my country. I've been born here. I want, you know, my future generation to grow up in here. So the reality is, I do feel part of this society, and part and parcel of the fabric. And the point is, we have to work together to break this narrative that Islam is at a course against the Western values. There are a lot of values that we agree on and that we can work towards.

12

Islam and British society

What we have here from the outside is a fairly rundown, ordinary-looking terrace, and in many respects very plain. And certainly there's nothing here to suggest that this, in fact, was the first mosque in England set up in 1889, and hosting a Muslim congregation led by an Englishman.

Zia Chaudhry, a trustee of the Abdullah Quilliam Society, was interviewed on *Sunday* in August 2007 about his organisation's campaign to restore this quirky piece of British and Islamic heritage.

As you can see, this is a very dingy corridor. You can even smell the damp. Clearly, a lot of work needs to be done here. And if we go through this door towards the back of the building, and once you go down these steps, this is actually the entrance really to the prayer hall. Now, at the moment there's a wall there, but that wall was something that was added later. This used to be an open area where the congregation would gather for their services.

And here, this doorway that's now very rectangular and bland, in the past had a domed design that was very reminiscent of mosques that you'd see in the East. And bizarrely enough, at the side here there was an organ, and they used to have Muslim hymns. And so, again, there are features there that you wouldn't ordinarily expect of a Muslim community, but it shows that Muslim communities can adapt to their surroundings.

William Henry Quilliam, a Liverpudlian solicitor born into a Methodist family, converted to Islam after visiting Tangiers in 1887. He immediately set about converting others – including his immediate family – with enthusiasm, publishing a weekly magazine, *The Crescent*, as a record of

Muslim life in Britain. For a fuller picture of his influence, *Sunday* turned to Mohammed Seddon, a Muslim convert and academic specialising in the history of British Islam. Mr Seddon cited the grand title, 'Shaykh al-Islam', that Abdullah (the new name William took after his conversion) Quilliam was granted by none other than the Sultan of the Ottoman Empire, then widely accepted as Islam's caliph:

> *The fact that the title of 'Shaykh al-Islam' came from the Ottoman Sultan directly proves that Quilliam was seen as a very, very important and central figure from the Muslim heartlands. At the same time, I think what Quilliam provides for British Muslims today is a kind of cultural anchorage, if you like.*
>
> *He is a historical figure – he's very much a man of his own time and space – but in a way, he's kind of a man before his time. He's a kind of cultural signpost of what Islam might look like if it becomes an indigenous religion that's taken up by the majority of people here in the UK.*

Mr Seddon also outlined Quilliam's views on British foreign policy, which foreshadowed those held by many of his co-religionists more than a century later, during the years of Britain's involvement in Afghanistan and Iraq:

> *Quilliam wasn't afraid to speak his mind, and he was very anti-British Empire. In fact, he wrote a number of articles against the British involvement in the Sudan. And this, of course, created a lot of controversy surrounding Quilliam. Quilliam, his community and his other co-religionists were seen as a kind of fifth column, if you like. And as the country moved… towards the First World War, Quilliam was forced actually to go underground, and his community began to evaporate very, very quickly.*

'A British version of Islam'

The imperial policy pursued in Quilliam's day ensured that Britain and Islam were no strangers. By the 1920s, the British Empire included more than half the Muslim population of the world, and Britain had a profound impact on the way Muslim societies and political systems developed in Africa and Asia, and, of course, right across the Middle East.

But dealing with Islam abroad and from a position of power was one thing; accommodating Islam at home, in a society based on the principle of equality, was quite another. And the events described in chapter 11 had a profound impact on the way many Britons saw Islam, and the way many British Muslims saw Britain.

In the spring of 2007, the Blair government launched a range of measures to – as a *New Statesman* headline put it – 'develop a British version of Islam'. These included training for imams working in public institutions – for example, as prison chaplains – and encouraging mosques to register with the Charity Commission in return for public money. On 20 May, *Sunday* reported that 'the radical Muslim group Hizb ut-Tahrir' had rejected the initiative because 'the measures to regulate mosques, imams and madrasas are the latest evidence of creeping authoritarianism by a government that now insists on controlling Muslim religious institutions'. That accusation was, the programme also reported, robustly denied by the communities secretary, Ruth Kelly.

That morning's interview with a spokesman for Hizb ut-Tahrir very quickly became focused on the question of what a 'British version of Islam' might look like and, beyond that, what it means to be British. Dr Imran Waheed dismissed the government's proposals as 'another gimmick'.

Imran Waheed: I think there's a recognition on the part of our community that there is a need to engage with the wider society, and that we are open to improving our institutions – whether they be mosques or madrasas. But the premise here that the government is setting out is flawed. There is no evidence that mosques in Bradford, madrasas in Bradford or even the school at which this was launched have been involved in the so-called radicalisation of the Muslim community.

Roger Bolton: Well, let's just accept that for a moment, but also then say, if that is true, there's still a desire, is there not, to build a sense of Britishness about everybody here so that every person, whenever they've come to this country, [or] whether they've been born here, do feel part of this country. That is what the government is trying to do. You don't oppose that, do you?

Imran Waheed: Well, what I would say is, where is the evidence that mosques and madrasas have been building another mentality or engendering extremism within the people who attend them? That's what the government needs to set out. And what I would also say is that Ruth Kelly herself has called for a 'British version of Islam', and we hear this oft-repeated mantra of Britishness and British values.

But cabinet minister after cabinet minister has failed to explain to the Muslim community exactly what this means. We've seen attempts by Gordon Brown [at that stage prime minister-in-waiting, Tony Blair having announced his intention to resign earlier in the month] to define Britishness. Jack Straw [then leader of the House of Commons] most recently. But again, they have not been able to very clearly define what any of these things are. And it seems to me like the politics of assimilation.

Roger Bolton: Well, if you don't want to assimilate, do you want to live apart?

Imran Waheed: No, not at all. And that's why I said at the beginning that there is an agreement on the part of our community. And Hizb ut-Tahrir is urging the Muslim community to engage with the wider society more.

Roger Bolton: What do you mean by that? Could I ask you... what do you mean by being British? What is it to be British in your view?

Imran Waheed: Well, I think the issue has not been sufficiently defined by government.

Roger Bolton: But how would you define it?

Imran Waheed: Well, from my perspective, the Muslim who lives, whether in Britain or in Pakistan or in any particular country, has a duty towards his neighbours – to other citizens from an Islamic perspective, primarily. That duty is a duty of care towards them. And we believe that, in fact, for centuries madrasas have been teaching a curriculum which produces people who, by and large, are law-abiding citizens; people who have morals, people who look after their neighbours, people who have good spiritual values.

234

Rowan Williams on sharia law

Raw public feeling about the relationship between being Muslim and being British was vividly exposed by a 2008 speech given by the then archbishop of Canterbury on the subject of 'Islam and English Law'. Rowan Williams suggested that Islamic courts might in some instances legitimately be used to settle disputes between Muslims, and as a model he cited the example of the beth din courts, which are often used by Orthodox Jews.

Williams also gave an exclusive interview to the BBC correspondent Christopher Landau, which was broadcast earlier in the day on Radio 4's *World at One*. This ensured that his views attracted much wider attention, and his statement that the adoption of certain aspects of sharia law 'seems unavoidable' immediately became headline news. 'Certain provision[s] of sharia are already recognised in our society and under our law,' the archbishop declared, adding: 'We already have in this country a number of situations in which the internal law of religious communities is recognised by the law of the land.'

Williams's biographer, Rupert Shortt, argues that the archbishop was, in part, simply performing his traditional role of sticking up for religion in general. He was, Shortt writes, reacting 'against the aggressive promotion of a *laique* view of the state [secularism in the sense of a constitutional principle, based on the French model], where religion is seen as a private matter rather than a form of communal affiliation across national borders'. As an alternative, Williams proposed 'a scheme in which individuals retain the right to choose the jurisdiction under which they will seek to resolve *certain carefully specified* matters' – so that, for example, a Muslim couple seeking a divorce would be allowed to do so in a sharia court if they agreed on that.[1]

Neither Rowan Williams's carefully caveating, nor his habit of wrapping his ideas in abstract and often opaque language, could protect him from the eruption of rage – and that really does seem the right word – that followed. *Sunday* devoted more than half the programme to the episode on 10 February 2008, and Roger Bolton kicked off the show with:

---

1 All quotes in this paragraph from R. Shortt, *Rowan's Rule: the biography of the archbishop* (London: Hodder & Stoughton, 2008), p. 394.

It would be an understatement to say that there's been much heated debate since the archbishop of Canterbury's comments regarding sharia law and the extent to which the adoption of some aspects of it in the UK seem, in his words, to be 'unavoidable'. The media coverage has focused on what the archbishop himself called the darker side of sharia, such as beheadings, amputations and the secondary role of women.

Bolton went through a digest of the week's news coverage:

I've never known an archbishop of Canterbury, or indeed any British religious leader, be subject to such criticism and abuse as Rowan Williams has received following his lecture on Muslim law this week. Every newspaper from The Sun *– 'What a Burka' and 'Bash the Bishop' – to* The Times, The Independent, The Guardian [and] *the* Daily Telegraph *have been outspoken in their criticism.*

Today's Sunday papers make equally dismal reading for the archbishop. In the unlikely event that he opens the News of the World, *he can read an article by his predecessor, Lord Carey, which criticises him for overstating the case for accommodating Islamic legal codes. Also writing in the* Sunday Telegraph, *Lord Carey says that Dr Williams's acceptance of some Muslim laws within British law would be disastrous for the nation.*

And the programme's reporter, Kevin Bouquet, added that: 'The archbishop is said to be overwhelmed by the hostility of the reaction to his remarks.' For his report, Bouquet visited a sharia court in London, 'one of several already operating in the UK'. He noted that: 'Many of the decisions they make are to do with marriage and divorce. Critics of sharia law, many of them Muslims themselves, say it's their attitude towards women which would be most likely to bring them into conflict with the civil courts.'

He interviewed Humera Khan, the director of a Muslim women's organisation called the An-Nisa Society, who took the view that: 'The Muslim community needs to do a lot of work in improving the way we apply our sharia rulings, and definitely we need to encourage far more women to be qualified in Islam, generally speaking, and sharia law.'

Bouquet concluded his report with:

For many people who heard the archbishop of Canterbury's remarks, the very notion that some aspects of sharia law might be adopted as part of the British system was outrageous. But, in fact, it happens already. If the archbishop was trying to stimulate a debate, it could be that's what will happen – much as some of his critics might wish the whole issue would disappear.

In the discussion that followed, the guests turned much of their fire on the press. Leading the charge, Revd Giles Fraser said:

I think the big issue here is the way the press has treated the archbishop of Canterbury for raising a legitimate issue for him to raise. I think that's the big moral picture here. They've been a pack of dogs having a go at him without even trying to understand what he's said. And there's something sinister about a culture that judges first and tries to understand later.

Fraser, a Radio 4 regular on *Thought for the Day* and *Moral Maze*, claimed the archbishop's speech had been grotesquely misrepresented, and he warmed to his theme:

If you actually look at what the papers have been saying, what The Sun *was saying when they had two Page Three girls* [at the time *The Sun* still carried a daily picture of a topless woman on the inside page] *outside Lambeth Palace, dishing out cards for people to say 'Sack the archbishop of Canterbury' – and people have been saying he's almost an al-Qaeda sleeper – it's absolutely outrageous the way that the press has treated the archbishop of Canterbury. It's a form of cruelty and bullying. And this is a wise and gentle man trying to raise legitimate issues.*

Paul Vallely, a Catholic commentator, and then associate editor of *The Independent*, took a similar view, but pointed out that Rowan Williams's *World at One* interview had prompted 17,000 emails to the BBC website in the course of an afternoon. Clearly the public reaction had not been entirely confected by the press. Vallely felt the archbishop's advisers should carry some of the blame for the way the episode had unfolded: 'What Lambeth Palace should have done in that situation... was say, 'Look, this is going nuclear. We've got to do something about it. The speech isn't until tonight. We've got time to rewrite bits of the speech.'

The Muslim holy day

Rowan Williams survived the storm, but it was one of the rockiest moments of his time in office. That autumn provided an example of the kind of sensitivities that drove many of those 17,000 emails.

The Muslim holy day of Ashura commemorates the death of Husayn ibn Ali, a grandson of the Islamic prophet Muhammad, at the Battle of Karbala [now in southern Iraq] in 680 AD. Shia Muslims mark the occasion with demonstrations of mourning which, to many outside the faith, can seem extravagant. And perhaps the most controversial practice associated with Ashura is *Tatbir*, the ritual shedding of blood in remembrance of Husayn. Some Shia men flog themselves with what is known as a *zanjeer zani*, a flail made of chains and curved metal blades. Many Muslim authorities condemn the practice as an offence against the Islamic prohibition of self-harm.

In August 2008, a Shia man was convicted of child cruelty after, as *Sunday* reported, 'he encouraged two teenage boys to beat themselves during a ceremony in Manchester'. The programme despatched Kevin Bouquet to investigate the practice, and he spoke to a Shia youth worker.

Mohammed Imran Ahmed: *Nobody can be forced to do* zanjeer zani. *And it's not a thing where you have to do it if you're a Shia. So it's a completely optional thing.*
Kevin Bouquet: *You do it yourself?*
Mohammed Imran Ahmed: *Yes, I do it myself. Yeah.*
Kevin Bouquet: *Is it painful?*
Mohammed Imran Ahmed: *It's not painful, no. At the time you're in such a mind state, you're in such a state of grief, you have so much adrenaline pumping through your body that it's like you're transported to another*

zone. You can see, you're aware of your surroundings, but your mind is in a different place altogether. Your mind is 1,400 years back. You're picturing what's happened, the atrocities that went on.

Kevin Bouquet: *There will be people who will say this is a barbaric custom.*

Mohammed Imran Ahmed: *Yeah, there will be people, but they don't understand. It all comes down to understanding. If you gave somebody a pair of zanjeers, a pair of the blades, an hour after the ceremony had taken place and told him to do it, he would not be able to do it because that sense of emotion is gone.*

Kevin Bouquet's report also included evidence from a prominent member of Manchester's Shia community.

Aftab Ahmed: *I've developed a role where I apply first aid to people when they have done zanjeer zani. And I can categorically say, and honestly say, that there has never been a case which cannot be dealt with on the spot through the first-aid box.*

Kevin Bouquet: *So what kind of injuries do people tend to end up with?*

Aftab Ahmed: *The kind of injuries they get are usually scratches or pinpoints where the actual points of the blades are piercing the skin. When you look at the person, at their back, it looks quite horrific because there's lots of blood there. But when you wipe the blood away, all you see are pinpricks and maybe very, very slight grazes or cuts. It's not to kill yourself. It's not to harm yourself. It's not to harm yourself permanently. It's just an act to show your grief, and especially to associate yourself with Imam Husayn and his followers, and to oppose the people who murdered them.*

A spokeswoman for the Children's Legal Centre told Kevin Bouquet, unsurprisingly, that children should not take part in the ceremony. Julia Thomas insisted that: 'Our society's made a decision that we will protect children and young adults... from being subjected to violence and from being influenced to be violent to themselves. We've made that decision. We've created laws to protect them, and we have to enforce those laws.'

The leader of a Muslim youth group also welcomed the recent child cruelty conviction related to the ceremony. But the prominent Manchester Shia Aftab Ahmed (interviewed above) told Kevin Bouquet that the episode had left members of his community 'open to abuse and maybe attacks – physical, personal attacks – on people by… bigots, right-wingers and other people'.

Female leaders and mixed-gender socialising and homosexuality

Several weeks later, on 19 October 2008, *Sunday* reported on what was hailed as a milestone for British Islam. Roger Bolton told the audience:

> *Earlier this week, a conference in Oxford on Islam and feminism kicked off with a woman leading Friday prayers and delivering the* Khutbah *or sermon. Organisers have called it a historic event, comparing Dr amina wadud, the woman who led the prayers, with Emily Pankhurst, the suffragette. But many Muslims have criticised the event, saying it is un-Islamic.*

Dr wadud told *Sunday*'s reporter, Shazia Khan, why she believed women should be allowed to lead prayers:

> *My perspective on it is really three things. One is that there's nothing in the Qur'an or in the Hadith* [the collection of words and actions that Muslims attribute to the prophet] *that prohibits it. Two: the Prophet did it himself. He assigned someone as a female leader of prayer. And then my own theological research into the essence of Islam indicates a necessity for us to be able to move away from the tradition that restricted women from the practice of leading prayer.*

But when Khan visited a college in London where women could train to be Islamic scholars alongside men, she found little support for that view among the students. One female student told her: 'I really don't feel that I'm going to be any more empowered by leading prayer. I don't… because by doing that, I'm going to be belittling the laws of my religion. I actually feel silly about it.'

Another insisted that: 'Islamic law has been defined according to the nature of men and women. And I think that we need to follow the guidance of our Prophet and the tradition.' None of the female students she spoke to expressed any ambition to become an imam. They declared they were aiming higher; to become, for example, muftis – jurists able to issue opinions or fatwas on points of sharia law.

The position of women in Islam was a recurring theme of *Sunday* broadcasts in the years that followed. In May 2011, Edward Stourton reported the following:

> *This country's mosque and imams advisory board – MINAB, as it's known – is trying to promote the role of women in mosques. But the initiative has run into opposition from some traditional Muslim communities. There's been a vivid illustration of what a sensitive issue this is here in Manchester. A group of Muslims have broken away from their local mosque, claiming they were barred from running a project dealing with, among other things, women's issues.*

One of the trustees of the Manchester Islamic Centre and the Didsbury Mosque told the programme: 'We cannot have socialising of mixed sexes. We cannot have this here. There are so many venues they can meet. But here we have certain rules and regulations which we have to respect… It is against Islamic teachings, against Islamic values, to have unnecessary mixing.'

The breakaway group insisted they always segregated the sexes at their meetings, and one of their leaders, Tracey, put the dispute down to a clash of cultures:

> *When you come from a different country, you see as they see. So if [they are] from Saudi, they're going to be thinking women… have to stay at home, or maybe not be as loud and outspoken. But because I'm a British English girl, I like to feel that I can bring people in to speak to us on a level – not just [being] shut away and letting the men deal with it.*

In June 2013, the programme returned to similar territory.

Edward Stourton: *Muslim women and men should be allowed to pray together, and gay Muslims should be made welcome in mosques – so* *says a group called the Inclusive Mosque Initiative. Tamsila Tauqir is a member of its management committee. And we're also joined by Khola Hasan, a consultant on Islamic law and a member of a sharia council. Tamsila Tauqir, tell us a little bit about how this initiative came about.*

Tamsila Tauqir: *Morning. The initiative came about because a number of us felt... that current mosques don't really provide a welcoming space for a lot of people. They disenfranchise a lot of people, and especially women. And so what we're trying to do is, rather than try and change existing mosque spaces, we decided to set up another space that is more something that we feel comfortable attending for ourselves, and for other people who feel that they don't really want to go to current mosque spaces. And that's how it came about.*

Khola Hasan insisted on the traditional view of mixed congregations, but her response to the position of gay people in mosques was more nuanced.

Khola Hasan: *The issues that are really important in this campaign are men and women praying in a mixed group, which Islam has traditionally never permitted. It's always been said gender segregation [is necessary]... And the second issue, obviously, is of homosexuality; that they should be openly accepted in the community and allowed into the mosques. Generally, mosques don't stand at the door asking people what their sexual affiliation is or what their political inclinations are. Anybody is welcome to go into a mosque and pray because you are connecting with God in there.*

Polygamy

Exchanges like that underlined the tensions between Islamic culture and belief, and the social norms of the country in which British Islam was developing. Three months after that debate, *Sunday*, presented by William Crawley, reflected on polygamy because, 'according to some Islamic organisations, there is a rise in the number of Muslim women in Britain today choosing to become second wives'. He added that: 'Polygamy is, of course, illegal in the United Kingdom, but the *nikah* religious ceremony, which is governed by sharia law, permits Muslim men to marry as many as four wives, prompting critics to ask if some women are being pressurised into informal polygamous marriages.'

The Islamic legal scholar Khola Hasan was back on the programme, speaking once again in defence of Muslim tradition. She denied that women who accepted second marriages were under any kind of pressure.

Khola Hasan: *I certainly don't think that they're being pushed. They're choosing themselves. There is absolutely no element of coercion here. Often women are choosing to become second wives... because they left it a bit late, perhaps, to get married. And now in their forties, they're desperate to get married because under Islamic law you cannot have any kind of extramarital affairs. And the only choice really is to stay a spinster or to get married. And so they're thinking, 'Well, to become a second wife is better than not being married at all.'*

We also have this situation where sometimes a couple are very unhappy together, but they don't want to divorce because they've got young children. So the wife says to the husband, 'Well, instead of leaving me or instead of getting divorced, why don't you just take a second wife?' It's quite a pragmatic approach to the situation.

Tahmina Saleem, co-founder of Inspire, a Muslim women's organisation, argued that in many instances men took a second wife without consulting the first one, and pointed out that because these second marriages took place outside the United Kingdom's legal system, women who agreed to them were vulnerable if things went wrong:

Obviously, nikah *second marriages can't be registered, because... they would be bigamist marriages. It's against British law. What we're finding is that those women are not protected. They're seen as cohabitees, and any rights that they want to secure in terms of inheritance, maintenance for the children, property rights, etc. are very, very expensive and difficult to secure.*

The anxiety that drove the reaction to Rowan Williams's proposals in 2008 surfaced again six years later, when Caroline Cox, a cross-bench peer (she originally sat as a Conservative, having been appointed by Margaret Thatcher back in 1982) and a committed Anglican, set up an organisation called Sharia Watch.

Baroness Cox appeared on *Sunday* in April 2014, in debate with Aina Khan, head of the Islamic and Sharia Law Department at Duncan Lewis Solicitors.

Caroline Cox: *I think there are developments going on in our country today which are cause for concern. And unless we know about them, we can't think appropriately how to respond to them. I may emphasise that I believe in freedom of religion, of course, and I believe passionately that we all have a right to practise our religion freely – or non-religion. But what is happening in the name of sharia, I think, is cause for concern in many ways.*

Edward Stourton: *Can [you] be a bit more precise? What is it about the way these [sharia] councils work that worries you?*

Caroline Cox: *Well, sharia law inherently enshrines very discriminatory principles towards women. For example, a man can get a divorce very easily. Someone starts by saying, 'I divorce you.' The woman often has to pay, has to meet all sorts of conditions, there's inequality there. There's inequality in inheritance. A woman typically gets half that of a man or a boy. There's inequality in terms of childcare, and there is condoning of domestic abuse in many respects. This is fundamentally against the principles of our country and the commitment to eradicate gender discrimination.*

Edward Stourton: *Aina Khan, is that fair? Is there a basic problem with the councils in the sense that they have discrimination and inequality built into them?*

Aina Khan: *I don't think that's an inherent problem with sharia law. It's certainly the way sharia law is practised in certain cultures. And if we are going to introduce that wholesale into the UK, yes, perhaps there is real cause for concern. But I'm here to say to you, I'm a practising lawyer working under English law. I would not be applying sharia solutions for Muslim clients if they were not in those clients' benefit, and if they did not work under English law. Where the sharia councils are working together to introduce best practice and want to listen to criticisms from practitioners like me, who apply solutions every day, I would like to work* *with those sharia councils, and I'm pleased to report that is working very well, that partnership. I do find it frustrating with others, however.*

Edward Stourton: *All right. Baroness Cox, does that reassure you? And using that as a starting point, is your position that you would be happy to see these councils work if the sorts of conversations that Aina Khan has just talked about took place and councils did work in the way that she says they can? Or is your objection to the principle of them existing at all?*

Caroline Cox: *My objection is the principle of a quasi-legal system operating in ways that are fundamentally discriminatory against women at a time when we are meant to be getting away from gender discrimination. Many women are really suffering in this country at the present time. And while Aina may be doing good practice, and I'm delighted that she is, too many women are suffering right now. One woman said to me, a Muslim woman, 'I came to this country to get away from sharia law. It's worse than it was in my country of origin.' This is unacceptable in Britain today.*

Edward Stourton: *Just before I get Aina Khan to respond to that – staying with you, Baroness Cox – it is, of course, absolutely true, isn't it, that any woman in this country can go to English law if they're in England rather than going to a sharia council, and English law will always trump sharia law?*

Caroline Cox: *Well, technically, yes. But the reality is in many very closed communities there's huge pressure from families and from communities. It's not so easy for these women to get out and go to an English court. And very often they don't even know. Sometimes brides are brought into this country, married at the age of fifteen in a remote village somewhere abroad. They come in, they have no idea what their rights are. Technically, yes, they may have access to the law of this land. In reality, in closed communities, the reality is often no.*

The *Sunday* archive also reflects persistent pressure for change from within British Islam. At around the time of Baroness Cox's intervention, the programme reported that: 'Maslaha, a social enterprise set up to improve social conditions in Muslim and minority communities, says it had a huge response to a project to persuade more Muslim British women to engage with issues around gender equality.'

The BBC religious affairs correspondent Mike Wooldridge posed the question: 'How should British Muslim women operate within the Western ideals of feminism, which might be seen as requiring religion to be kept at arm's length?' Shelina Janmohamed, a commentator on British Islam and Muslim women, responded with an answer that echoed some of the arguments Rowan Williams made about the place of religion in society in his notorious sharia speech.

Mike Wooldridge: I suppose that Islam has presented itself, hasn't it, as being very much about the family and the family unit?

Shelina Janmohamed: Well, there's a balance within Islamic thinking between the rights of the individual, but also the rights of the family and ensuring that there is a very strong family dynamic. And I mean, this is obviously a wider question around: do we want a society which is based on individuals, or is it a society that we think about in units of society?

And a lot of Muslim women would say that they are attempting to find this balance from within an Islamic framework. And I think that's what distinguishes Islamic feminism from other strains of it, which is that Muslim women are going back to the core origins of the Qur'an and the traditions of Islam to say: 'How we can find a blueprint for the kind of society that we want to achieve?'

In the spring of 2016, continuing concern about the operation of sharia councils prompted the then home secretary, Theresa May, to appoint an independent review of their operation. Professor Mona Siddiqui, a professor of Islamic and Interreligious Studies at the University of Edinburgh (for her views on radicalisation, see chapter 11), was invited to chair the commission that would conduct the review, and on 16 May 2016 Professor Siddiqui explained her ambitions to *Sunday*.

Mona Siddiqui: First of all, to determine how many councils there are, how are they set up, who actually works in these councils. Who are the people who are processing complaints or appeals by individuals? And I suppose the most important thing is: to what extent is the application of what they say compatible or incompatible with the law in England and Wales?

Edward Stourton: One of the areas the home secretary clearly wants you to look at is *difficulties faced by women sometimes with these courts. What do you think those are?*

Mona Siddiqui: *Well, many of these courts are really used for marital disputes, especially in the areas of divorce. And for many women, Muslim women, just like for many Jewish women, if they're going to get a divorce, they want a religious divorce as well as a civil divorce. And sometimes they're trapped between two legal systems. They may go to these sharia councils in the hope of getting a divorce from a husband who is unwilling to divorce them, but actually be trapped in limbo for a long time because no one can actually make that happen. So women end up doubly disadvantaged, you know, because they're caught in two legal systems.*

Edward Stourton: *Technically, of course, sharia law can never trump civil law. And if you want to get divorced in a civil court, you can do that. But do you think there is a certain amount of social pressure, which means that in some cases women go to one of these councils, even though they're likely to come out worse from doing so, simply because that's what people do; that's what the community expects?*

Mona Siddiqui: *That's another aspect which I find quite intriguing. Why are people turning to these councils, first of all, when they know that whatever is said in the council cannot trump and should not trump civil law? But also, what solace, what comfort, are they getting from these councils when there is another legal system that would work just as well for them, if not better?*

Edward Stourton: *It's a really important question, that, isn't it? What's your instinct of what the answer might be? What is the value of a sharia court? Why would someone choose to go there rather than to a civil court?*

Mona Siddiqui: *My assumption is, and from the little evidence I have around these issues, that many of the people who work in these councils want to act as mediators and arbitrators, and get families to reconcile. And some of them are respected, and some of them are seen as people who can offer wise advice – not all of them. But is it really wise advice they're giving, or is it some kind of cultural cohesion that they're trying to preserve at the expense of a woman's right?*

And I have a feeling that it's this kind of forced cultural cohesion that they're trying to really contrive a sense of what that is. And one of the problems I think I'm going to probably discover is that many of the practices may be against Islamic law itself. It may simply be that in order to preserve a certain element of what they term as 'Islamic', they are going into practices or saying things or advocating things that might be very much against the ethical spirit of Islamic law itself.

Professor Siddiqui delivered her commission's conclusions nearly two years later. She was back on *Sunday* at the beginning of February 2018. Her inquiry had, she told the programme, revealed 'levels of bad practice', and instances of women being put under pressure and badly advised. But her commission also concluded that sharia councils met a real need, because: 'Even women who have had civil marriages have said that they still want that religious divorce. And that's why they go to these councils; in order for the councils to enable that piece of paper that tells them they are religiously divorced.' And she rejected the idea of closing the councils down.

Mona Siddiqui: *They're voluntary organisations. They have no legitimacy under civil law. They are voluntary organisations set up as a religious body to give religious advice. So you don't have to go to them. They can't override civil law, they're not courts. The people who adjudicate are not judges. And so, therefore, how can you shut down something that is a voluntary association? They could be set up in somebody's living room. How would you kind of monitor that?*

The more important thing is that they are a need in the community. And as I say, women who, even if they've had a civil divorce, many of them still expressed a desire to have a religious divorce. And you can't really deny that under so many regulations; not least of all the European Convention on Human Rights.

Edward Stourton: *Let's pick up on that last point because, as I understand it, your main solution for the problem of women going to these councils and being discriminated against or suffering in the rulings that the councils make is that all women who marry in Islamic ceremonies should also have a civil wedding so that they're protected by the law.*
Mona Siddiqui: *That's our first recommendation, and that's what we found*

a lot of people were advising women. I suppose one of the unusual things for me personally was to find that there were a lot of younger women and educated women who hadn't considered having their marriages civilly registered... And if you have an amendment to the Marriage Act, this will bring Islamic marriages in line with Christian and Jewish marriages. The celebrant of a marriage will have to civilly register their marriage either at the same time or before, but they are both Islamically and civilly registered.

Edward Stourton: *Quite difficult to enforce that, though, isn't it? I mean, presumably just the way that a couple can get together and live together, a couple could be married in the eyes of Islam, but not in the eyes of the law.*

Mona Siddiqui: *And that's exactly what happens if you have an Islamic marriage or a nikah at the moment. You may consider yourself married, but you're not married under the eyes of the law – so you have no civil protection if anything goes wrong. And that's really our number-one recommendation: that you really have to be protected under civil law and you're denying yourself so many other rights as well if you don't have a civil marriage.*

It is difficult to enforce it... So many people were simply not aware of this; that their marriage didn't count for anything unless it was registered civilly. Hopefully, if there is a cultural awareness, yes, we can't force it, but we're also hoping that celebrants would have the moral capacity and the moral diligence to enact that, knowing that there's a legal deterrent now.

The government (Theresa May was by then prime minister) welcomed Professor Siddiqui's proposals, but at the time of writing a change in the law on Islamic marriage is, according the government's website, still 'under consideration'.

Islamophobia persists

In 2021, the MCB, the organisation that emerged as such a significant voice for British Muslims during the early years of the century, elected its first female leader. Zara Mohammed was also the MCB's youngest secretary general, and in January 2022 she gave *Sunday* her assessment of the state of British Islam.

Zara Mohammed: This year... actually marked twenty years since the war on terror and 9/11. And I think, looking back, although I was very young at the time... we're looking at the landscape of what we've come through and really what we want to go forward doing. Unfortunately, according to the government's own statistics, forty-five per cent of all hate crime targets Muslims in Britain. And fifty per cent of the demographic that I represent – fifty per cent of all Muslims in the UK – are under the age of twenty-five. So... we've still got a long way to go. And particularly visibly Muslim women like myself are usually on the other side of verbal and physical abuse or institutional barriers. So I think that rampant Islamophobia is very much there.

But I'm very hopeful. I think my own election, in some ways, you know, helped shatter a lot of perceptions in a week. But also, I think more importantly, it's about giving the recognition of what British Muslims are doing and their role in society, which is so important as we move forward.

Zara Mohammed acknowledged that one thing in particular had not changed. The government broke off relations with the MCB in 2009 after its then deputy secretary general, Daud Abdullah, was accused of inciting violence against Jews and British service personnel. The relationship has never recovered, although Zara Mohammed insisted on *Sunday* that 'my door remains open, and I really welcome any conversation'.

13

Eastern spirituality

The 2021 census underlined the extent of change in the United Kingdom's religious, cultural and ethnic landscape during *Sunday*'s years on the air. For the first time, less than half the population identified themselves as Christian: 27.5 million (5.5 million fewer than in the previous census in 2011). Thirty-seven per cent ticked the 'no religion' box, raising the possibility that 'no religion' will overtake Christianity as the most popular choice by the time the next census takes place in 2031.

And in two of England's biggest cities, Birmingham and Leicester, members of ethnic minority groups had become the majority. Both those cities are home to large communities with roots in the Indian subcontinent and, overall, the 2021 census recorded 'Asian British' as the largest minority group, at just under ten per cent of the total population.

Immigration from the subcontinent, like immigration from the Caribbean, took off in the 1950s, as Britain looked for workers to help rebuild after the Second World War. The flow was largely choked off by the Immigration Act of 1971 (as the United Kingdom prepared to enter the European Economic Community), but Indians continued to arrive from East Africa in significant numbers in the 1970s after being driven from Uganda, Kenya and Zanzibar.

Britain's Sikh population

Sunday's coverage of the dharmic religions – those that began in the Indian subcontinent – provides a rich body of evidence regarding the way these British Asian communities have fared. The story begins in the programme's early years. One of the oldest surviving items in the archive is a rare report on a non-Christian subject from the 1970s.

In in November 1978, Michael Meech, a BBC reporter and presenter, visited a Sikh temple in Southall, West London – probably the gurdwara run by the Sri Guru Singh Sabha group, although this is not clear from the archive – in the company of a Sikh academic. The tone of his report was respectful, but today seems slightly patronising; reminiscent of an anthropologist visiting some exotic and newly discovered tribe.

Michael Meech: *I had to take off my shoes and deposit them in return for a ticket at the cloakroom, and was provided with a square of linen to cover my head and a safety pin, which turned it into a sort of nurse's cap. Then, with Professor Singh, I joined the queue to go into the temple itself. There was a line of people standing the length of the centre aisle, waiting to bow and pray in front of the holy book of the Sikh faith, which was displayed under a canopy at the front. As each bowed, he put his monetary contribution into a padlocked offertory box and then took his place in the vast congregation, all sitting cross-legged on the floor. And my seat on the floor was very close to the musical group who were singing a song to celebrate the guru's birth. I asked Professor Singh what was distinctive about the beliefs of a Sikh.*

Professor Singh: *If you look at the Sikh religion at the time Guru Nanak was born, there were two religions: Islam and Hinduism. Islam believed in one God and Hindus believed in one God, as well as in various gods. But Sikhism is committed to one God only.*

Michael Meech: *How would you sum up the Sikh way of life, then?*

Professor Singh: *He must earn his own livelihood through honest means. He must devote some time for prayers, meditation. And the third is, all these he must share with his compatriots.*

Michael Meech: *Part of that sharing is always having food available for anyone who comes to the temple. On Tuesday evening, I noticed that there were about twenty bottles of milk standing beside the canopy over the holy book – ready, I was told, for the meal that would follow the birthday celebrations. Hospitality, generosity and concern for human rights are characteristic of Sikhs, but they also have a distinctive appearance.*

Professor Singh: *You see, if you look at the Sikhs, the only thing which differs from others is their beard, their long hair and their turban.*

Michael Meech: *Why do you have beards and why do you wear turbans?*

Professor Singh: *Can I put a question to you here? What was the reason for Samson's strength? His strength lay in his long hair. If God has given us long hair, then why the man wants to cut it? The Indian social customs are that we must cover our heads. So we have to cover our head, and turban is considered to be the right headgear for that purpose.*

Sikhs in Slough

The 2021 census identified Slough, in Berkshire, as the borough with the highest proportion of non-white residents outside London. A decade-and-a-half earlier, *Sunday* had spotted Slough's significant role in the story of the Sikh community.

Slough gained national attention in the 1920s with the opening of the Slough Trading Estate, one of the country's first business parks, which inspired John Betjeman's famous attack on its unloveliness in his poem, 'Slough' (1937). The town's reputation has never really recovered, but the item broadcast on *Sunday* in April 2007 suggested that the Slough Trading Estate was also an important attraction for Sikh immigrants.

Roger Bolton: *Slough in the Thames Valley used to be known as the place John Betjeman would like to have bombed. More recently, Ricky Gervais ran an office there with the help of his colleague Stephen Merchant [a reference to the BBC television sitcom The Office]. Considerably less well known – well, I hadn't the faintest idea – is the fact that the largest community of Sikhs in Britain is to be found in the town.*

And this weekend, most Slough Sikhs have been out on the streets celebrating the festival of Vaisakhi, sometimes known as the Sikh New Year. At the same time, an exhibition has just opened, marking the development of Sikh life here since the first major wave of immigration from the Punjab in the 1950s. Trevor Barnes has been along to see it and to find out how life in Slough has mirrored the changing fortunes of the wider Sikh community in Britain.

Trevor Barnes: *Slough Museum in the high street, opposite the furniture store and the local estate agent, is the distinctly un-exotic location for* *this fascinating exhibition on Sikh life and culture. It's been organised by Ranjit Kaur Bhilku to coincide with Vaisakhi, if you like, the Sikh New Year. Why was the timing so important?*

Ranjit Kaur Bhilku: *Vaisakhi is very important to us, as it's the birth of the Sikh nation in 1699. And the... exhibition, 'Punjab to Slough', is actually celebrating Sikhs that live in Slough.*

Trevor Barnes: *Now, the title, 'Punjab to Slough', begs the question: why Slough? Why was it this particular town that attracted what is the largest concentration of Sikhs in the country?*

Ranjit Kaur Bhilku: *There were a lot of reasons. One of the reasons is the fact that we've got the largest trading estate here in Slough. So there's a lot of work available. And the ethos of working is very important with Sikhs – or working honestly with their hands.*

Trevor Barnes: *But tell me about some of the exhibits. Perhaps this model here, this mannequin here.*

Ranjit Kaur Bhilku: *Yes, this wonderful mannequin. She's dressed in a traditional Punjabi bridal outfit. This is very rare now, because a lot of the girls are choosing to wear the elaborate long skirts. It's actually been hand-embroidered. And she's wearing red bangles, which signified the fact that she's actually just got married. And that's how Sikhs have become. It's an amalgamation of the Western influence of cultures and the Sikh traditional Punjabi culture as well.*

Trevor Barnes: *Now, one of the photographs at the exhibition which is of particular interest to Dabinderjit Singh, head of the Sikh Secretariat, is this one here. Taken in the 1970s, the laying of the foundation stone of the first gurdwara. And your dad's in there somewhere, isn't he?*

Dabinderjit Singh: *That's right. My father's in there somewhere. This was very important to the Sikhs, because back in 1976 they needed a permanent place of worship. And we now have two gurdwaras in Slough. They're a vital part of the community, because that's where people tend to gather; not just for religious reasons, but for social reasons.*

Trevor Barnes: *OK. Well, in the photograph there's nothing but the foundation stone. Let's take a walk across town and find the gurdwara, as it stands now.*

Dabinderjit Singh: *And here it is. We've just come into the 'langar hall', the free food kitchen, where you can see there are literally dozens of people* *sharing in the free food kitchen. And this is something that's actually open to all; not just Sikhs, but non-Sikhs.*

Trevor Barnes: Now, how has life for this large population of Sikhs in Slough changed over the years? In the old days, when people came over – largely men – they were two, three to a house, to a room sometimes. That's all behind them with their smart cars outside the houses.

Dabinderjit Singh: That's right. I remember my father came in the 1950s. It didn't matter whether you were of a Sikh background, Hindu background or Muslim background. Often there were men living in the same house or mainly here for work. Then you get events like 9/11, which can be a setback. People question their identity, but it's very short-term. They come back and say, 'Actually, we need to reinforce why our identity is so important, why we're so different.'

I think what we're now seeing with the second and third generation is, 'Let's take the message of the Sikhs out to the wider community, [to] the non-Sikhs, because we've got so much to share and so much to offer.'

Dabinderjit Singh rounded off Trevor Barnes's report with the view that: 'We are no longer seen as a minority community. We are now very much part of the mainstream community and mainstream life in Slough and in the UK.'

Fighting in the First World War

Shared history can often be a powerful force for social cohesion, and early in the twentieth century Sikhs played a big part in events that still have a powerful hold on the United Kingdom's collective memory. Tens of thousands of Sikhs fought for Britain during the First World War, many of them serving in the trenches of the Western Front.

In the summer of 2014, *Sunday* ran a series of reports to mark the centenary of the July Crisis that led to the outbreak of that war. Each episode was dedicated to 'the way different faiths responded to the challenge'. Rahul Tandon, a BBC correspondent based in India and a frequent contributor to *Sunday,* began his report on the Sikh reaction to war with the shouts and stamps of a military drill.

Rahul Tandon: Here in the world's largest democracy, most people have no idea that more than a million Indians took part in drills like that during the First World War. Many volunteered to fight for what they said was their king. More than a quarter were Sikhs. I have come to Delhi to meet Rana Chhina, whose family served the British in the war, and who is trying to document the heroic contribution some Indians made.

Rana Chhina: For instance, the Sikhs, the 14th Sikhs – a very fine battalion – lost almost eighty per cent of its strength... on one particular day alone, on the 4th of June 1915, [during] the Battle of Krithia and the Gallipoli Peninsula [the Third Battle of Krithia was one of a series of assaults on a strategically important village, which led to heavy casualties on both sides]. *And when news of this battle came back to India, it actually saw a boost in Sikh recruitment because people were lining up now to fill the gaps of people who had fallen. It was odd, but it was true.*

Rahul Tandon: Why do you think that was? Was it to maintain the honour of that Sikh division?

Rana Chhina: Yes, I do think that it was primarily a matter of honour. And for the Sikh ethos in particular, which places a lot of emphasis on sacrifice and a soldier's death. So I think that actually gave a... boost to recruitment.

Adil Rana Chhina (Rana Chhina's son): The number of photographs that we've collected, and I can run through some of them: the first one that we see here is Subadar-Major Lal Singh of the 14th KGO Sikhs – one of the regiments that I just spoke about – and he was one of those who was killed.

Rahul Tandon: Going through some pictures of Indians who fought in the First World War is Rana's son, Adil. Like many from a younger generation, he sometimes finds it hard to understand why so many Indians volunteered to go and fight for their masters, the British. He's not just been looking at pictures; he's been going through letters sent back by soldiers. He says they were driven by a sense of duty to their families and their faith. One of the letters that Adil has seen was written by the Sikh soldier Bhagwan Singh to his family just before he died.

Adil Rana Chhina: He had written that his regiment had moved to Aden and that he was waiting to be sent to the front in France because he had heard of the fighting there. He expressed his eagerness, and he said that there's no greater glory than dying on the battlefield. He was from Gurdaspur, and he wanted the name of Gurdaspur to be written in glory. He wrote to his son advising him to join the army and said that: 'I would be able to live with the fact that you died in battle rather than hearing that you ran away as a coward.'

In his report, Rahul Tandon noted that this slice of history has very little resonance in modern India itself:

If you pick up your newspaper or turn on the television here in India, you'll hardly see any mention of the contribution that people from this country made to the First World War. The Indian finance minister has announced plans to build a national memorial to all Indian soldiers who have lost their lives while serving the country. Most people here don't even know that that includes Indians in World War One.

But the *Sunday* archive suggests that British Sikhs like to stress the past they share with the United Kingdom as a whole. 'Britain's half-a-million-strong Sikh community is one of the country's best-integrated religious minorities with a long history of public service, not least in two world wars,' William Crawley told listeners in February 2012. 'A new photographic history of British Sikhs has just been published. Trevor Barnes met up with the author.'

Peter Bance told Trevor Barnes that: 'The first Sikh in Britain was Maharaja Duleep Singh, who came as early as the 1850s. And [from] then on we had nobility, various other ruling princes, and also we had soldiers, Sikh soldiers, visiting the United Kingdom, fancy processions, Golden Jubilees and the Diamond Jubilee of Queen Victoria.'

Their conversation – which took place in a gurdwara – soon turned to the First World War.

Trevor Barnes: *Now, we're here in the main prayer hall, and it's worth remembering, alongside these devotional objects that we can see all around us, that the Sikh religion also is a martial religion, insofar as it doesn't turn the other cheek and it will, in self-defence, bear arms. And*

257

that meant, of course, that many Sikhs served alongside British soldiers in the First and Second World Wars.

Peter Bance: *That's right. The [Khalsa] Sikhs are a martial race, and it was partly formed because of the oppression in India during the seventeenth century. And the Sikhs were part of the largest voluntary force to serve in the First World War on the Western Front.*

Trevor Barnes: *And in fact, in front of us, from your book, we have one of the pictures of a proud Sikh soldier alongside an English captain… [with a written] recommendation from Asquith, the then prime minister.*

Peter Bance: *This was really a recruitment postcard, but at the same time it was also propaganda, because it was showing the Germans that we have the Sikhs on our side.*

A decade later, that past was again evoked in an item to mark Remembrance Sunday. Major Daljinder Singh Virdee MBE, a serving officer in the British Army and part of the Defence Sikh Network, launched an edition of the Sikh daily prayers, the Nitnem Gutka Sahib, which he said was 'designed and made for operations, what we call in the army, "the field environment"'.

Major Virdee explained that the book was:

Made to fit inside the chest pocket. And it comes in an outer case as well. It's thread-bound for ultimate strength of the pages. And the paper is made of something called polyart, which is a waterproof paper, which is wipeable, and it can be used in low light conditions as well. So it's very, very robust. And it's something that tomorrow, whether it's desert conditions or winter conditions, it will be able to survive and support the individual reading.

The major explained the inspiration behind the new design as follows:

It was actually an image of a Sikh who was fighting during World War One in the trenches in France. And what was really special about this image was that he had a Sikh prayer book with him. And that was really the light bulb moment for me to try and reintroduce this into the modern-day UK armed forces.

The Hare Krishna movement

The way *Sunday* has covered British Hindu history owes more to rockstar glamour than to a shared martial past.

George Harrison's 'My Sweet Lord' was a musical phenomenon. Released in late 1970, just after the break-up of the Beatles, it was partly inspired by a visit to India the group made at the height of their fame in 1967. It was the first number-one single by an ex-Beatle, and by the end of the year it was topping the charts all over the world. 'My Sweet Lord' remained an international hit throughout the early months of 1971, and it became the biggest-selling single by any of the former Beatles.

Its success reflected a growing Western interest in Eastern spirituality, generally, and the Hare Krishna movement, in particular. George Harrison – who was attracted to Hinduism and, indeed, Indian music – formed a close association with the International Society for Krishna Consciousness (ISKCON), as the Hare Krishna movement was formally known. In 1972, two years after the song came out, he made a substantial gift to ISKCON for the purchase of a mock-Tudor manor house near Watford. *Sunday* reported on the history of Bhaktivedanta Manor in September 2013.

William Crawley: *It's forty years since George Harrison of the Beatles donated the manor to the devotees, and in that time they have weathered planning rows, local objections and even allegations of child cruelty in India. But they're still here; if anything, flourishing more than ever. Trevor Barnes has been charting the movement's evolution from hippie outsiders to part of the Hindu mainstream.*

Trevor Barnes: *[Sri] Krishna Janmashtami at the Bhaktivedanta Manor; both a religious festival and a grand day out.*

Vox pop: *All sorts of people come. It's like a social as well as a religious programme. Young and old, there is so much harmony and cohesion.*

Vox pop: *When we went to see the cows and fed them, we had this buggy ride. I like that.*

Vox pop: *I like the place. They give us an in-depth knowledge of the religion.*

Trevor Barnes: *But if the Hare Krishna devotees are mixing effortlessly with ordinary Hindu worshippers here today, it wasn't always so. In* *the sixties, when the International Society for Krishna Consciousness, or ISKCON, was founded by Swami Prabhupada, it was viewed by many as a weird and wonderful sect, apart from the mainstream. Dr John Zavos, senior lecturer in South Asian Studies at the University of Manchester...*

John Zavos: *It's very much an outward-looking movement. One might even call it a proselytising movement, in the sense that it's always wanted to be bigger than Hinduism. In fact, there's always been a degree of tension between ISKCON and the idea of Hinduism. Swami Prabhupada didn't want to be confined by the notion of Hinduism. He saw ISKCON as a universalist movement.*

Swami Chandramauli: *At that time, people were looking for alternative ways of life, and Indian spirituality was one of the alternatives that was very much prominently on the scene at that time.*

Trevor Barnes: *Swami Chandramauli – an early devotee, now a travelling monk and teacher.*

Swami Chandramauli: *But we had some good fortune in coming in contact with the Beatles, and they liked us. And then one devotee named Shyamasundara made good friends with George Harrison, and then things just took off from there.*

Trevor Barnes: *It's a measure of how integrated the Hare Krishna movement has become, that among the guests here today are the great and the good of the British establishment. There are local councillors, vicars, mayors and mayoresses. And with me now, the deputy lord-lieutenant for Harrow, John Purnell. Things weren't always so harmonious, though, were they?*

John Purnell: *You're perfectly correct. We remember this place when it opened with George Harrison, and everyone thought, 'Oh God, George Harrison. It must be... hippies and bell-ringing and all that sort of stuff.' And I guess really the population as a whole tended to avoid it. But now it's very, very much part of the landscape.*

Srutidharma Das: *I really do believe there is no substitute for maturity, and I've seen that over the years.*

Trevor Barnes: *Srutidharma Das, a young devotee in the seventies and now the president of Bhaktivedanta Manor.*

Srutidharma Das: *We were young, and perhaps we were a bit boisterous.*

In our maturity we've realised that actually, you know, you have to learn to live with all the locality, all the other individuals, which really is our philosophy.

Shambo

In the first decade of the century, *Sunday* explored a number of conflicts between Hindu practice and belief, and British regulations on animal husbandry and environmental standards.

The story of Shambo, a Friesian bull adopted as a sacred animal by a Hindu community in Wales, offered all the ingredients for a long-running tabloid saga. In April 2007, a skin test for bovine tuberculosis returned a positive result, and the Welsh government demanded that the bull be slaughtered. The Skanda Vale temple objected on the grounds that sanctity of life is central to the Hindu religion. On 7 July, *Sunday* reported what seemed to be the final chapter in the ensuing drama.

Jane Little: The campaign to save Shambo, the sacred bull that tested positive for exposure to bovine tuberculosis, appears to have failed, with its slaughter likely to be carried out this week. Shambo is part of a herd at the Skanda temple in Carmarthen, Wales. Hindus there and around Britain have been praying over him and lobbying the Welsh Assembly to spare him on the grounds that killing him is against their religious rights and would desecrate the temple. But Jane Davidson, the assembly's rural affairs minister, said that, after considering long and hard their argument that Shambo should be isolated and treated with antibiotics, 'It is necessary that I take appropriate steps to protect animal and human health in this case.' Well, I'm joined by Brother Alex from the Skanda Vale temple. Good morning.

Brother Alex: Good morning.

Jane Little: You must be very disappointed, but do you accept that it's now over?

Brother Alex: Not at all, no. We've actually received notification from the Welsh Assembly that they haven't actually made a final decision. Having said that they were definitely going to on Friday, we've now heard that they won't be taking any decision until next Tuesday. So they're obviously realising that there's a lot more to consider than they first thought.

Jane Little: *But it doesn't look good, does it? And the Hindu Council UK [the* council, founded in 1994, is one of several umbrella organisations], *which did support you, has weighed in and said the Hindu community should now be objective and think about the greater good of society. It quotes the* Bhagavad Gita [one of Hinduism's holy scriptures], *and says it might be time to let Shambo go. Don't you recognise there is a higher principle at stake here: protecting human and wider animal health?*

Brother Alex: *Yes. I'm afraid it's unfortunate that the gentleman who made that statement didn't contact the temple here first. Because anybody purporting to represent the Hindu religion should take the sanctity of life extremely seriously, because it's a fundamental principle of our religious values. And there are very practical, very realistic alternatives to slaughter. Until those alternatives have been pursued and examined, then we shouldn't even be talking about slaughter as a possibility.*

Jane Little: *Now, we can hear the bells behind there and I'm looking on the webcam. You have this live webcam of Shambo, and in one he seems to be possibly eating right now. And in one of the pictures you've also got a bindi, a red dot on his forehead, and he's wearing a garland of flowers. Clearly a very special animal and sacred. But there is still the principle of health at stake here. He did test positive in this skin test for the exposure to the bacterium. And it is a risk, isn't it? This test is 99.9 per cent accurate.*

Brother Alex: *I think we have to put this in perspective. First of all, this claim of being 99.9 per cent accurate is something that's not substantiated. We've asked the Welsh Assembly for their statistics to back this up and they haven't given any statistics, and I question whether that figure is accurate.*

Jane Little: *Well, the minister, Jane Davidson, insists she has considered extremely carefully 'whether the rights of the community to manifest their religion should override the duty on me to protect animal and human health'. And she says that: 'Veterinary medical and legal assessments suggest this shouldn't be the case.' Will you resist them if officials turn up to put Shambo down?*

Brother Alex: *If it does come to that – of course, we very much hope and pray that it won't – what we'll be doing is having a special religious service to celebrate the sanctity of life. And it won't form a protest with, you know, placards and banners. That's not our style.*

Jane Little: *And you won't actively ring Shambo to prevent him being put down?*

Brother Alex: *Not as such. What we will do is have an act of worship which may take the form of a twenty-four-hour vigil or more. And we would deeply resent anybody interfering with our freedom of right to worship.*

In fact, the drama had another couple of turns to run. The following week a senior judge ruled that slaughtering Shambo would be unlawful, because the slaughter orders failed to give due weight to the Skanda Vale monks' rights to freedom of religion. But the judgement was overturned on appeal, and Shambo was duly put down. The Welsh government announced that a post-mortem revealed lesions typical of tuberculosis.

Open-air cremation

The following November, *Sunday* ran a report on the clash between the Hindu tradition of open-air cremation and government environmental regulations.

Roger Bolton: *Now, tomorrow, a judicial review is being held in the High Court to determine whether it is legal for Hindus to hold open-air cremations in the UK. The hearing follows a case in 2006 where the body of a young Indian man was burnt on a pyre in a field in Northumbria with the support of the Anglo Asian Friendship Society. Newcastle Council said at the time that it was illegal, and the society wants clarification of the law. It says it's a matter of human rights and religious freedom. Shazia Khan takes a look at what Hinduism says about open-air cremations and whether there is a demand for [them] in this country.*

Shazia Khan: *Worshippers chant at the home of Davender Kumar Ghai, a Hindu spiritual healer. The back room of his home in Gosforth,*

Newcastle, has been transformed into a colourful perfumed temple. It's from here that Davender, who is also head of the Anglo Asian Friendship Society, has been leading a campaign for the right to have open-air cremations, culminating in a High Court judicial review next week.

Davender Kumar Ghai: *We are committed on the open funeral pyre because the smoke should go in the sky... No disrespect to any religion, [but] Muslims and Jews, they have been allotted their own burial grounds. Why can't we have our own cremation ground? This is the god of death, you know, and that's what he says: that it should be open funeral pyre. Otherwise, the soul doesn't get the rest.*

Shazia Khan: *Many Hindus believe that open air-cremations are the most appropriate way for the soul to be released from the body after death. Restless, lingering souls are considered to be harmful to the living. Davender says crematoria are inadequate because there's a risk that a person's ashes could be mixed up with somebody else's, preventing the soul from escaping.*

Davender Kumar Ghai: *When we do the open funeral pyre [in India], somebody stays there because the pyre goes on for four or five hours. They stay there. When the ashes are cooled down, they collect the ashes and come home. Here [in the UK] we have to go [back to the crematorium] after four or five days. We don't know whose ashes we are getting. The ashes we are getting, we don't know whether the box was cleaned before the other body was put in. So there are so many things, you know, we cannot [accept] according to the religion.*

Shazia Khan's report recognised that while 'open-air cremations have been at the heart of Hinduism for 4,000 years' there were, within the Hindu community in Britain, 'mixed views about the importance of outdoor cremations'. The range of views was apparent when *Sunday* returned to this issue in February 2010. The item began with some evocative news from the archive.

News archive: *And now the Mahatma's son sets alight the sandalwood logs, the first leaping flames – and for the crowds, an unforgettable climax. A pillar of flame and smoke. And a last farewell to Mahatma Gandhi,* the man who symbolised, above all else, the hopes and aspirations of the India he loved.

William Crawley: *Footage there from the funeral of Mahatma Gandhi in 1948, who was cremated on an open pyre, according to Hindu tradition. Last week, a British Hindu won the right to follow in Gandhi's footsteps. The Court of Appeal ruled that Newcastle City Council was wrong to prevent Davender Ghai from being cremated on a pyre. I'm joined now by Shaunaka Rishi Das, director of the Oxford Centre for Hindu Studies. Good morning to you, Shaunaka.*

Shaunaka Rishi Das: *Good morning.*

William Crawley: *How significant is this decision for British Hindus?*

Shaunaka Rishi Das: *Well, it's significant for Mr Ghai. It's not as significant for British Hindus, because there isn't a clamour among most British Hindus for open-air burning of their body after death.*

William Crawley: *The decision here limited the permission to an enclosed pyre. Is that significant from a religious point of view?*

Shaunaka Rishi Das: *Well, I think the decision actually limited [the practice] to the 1902 Crematorium Act, which says you have to have it within a building. And the kind of compromise of this case was that there would be a hole at the top of the building. The case that still has to be argued is: can Mr Ghai, when he passes away, be cremated on a pyre or by electric or gas, as they do now? So the case isn't really over for Mr Ghai, he hasn't won that. He's won one part of the case, really.*

William Crawley: *What religious role is played by open pyres within Hinduism?*

Shaunaka Rishi Das: *Well, it's mainly culture. It's mainly custom. There's nothing in scripture that says it has to be in the open or anywhere else. So most Hindus in this country haven't had a problem using the crematoria that are dotted around the country. And in most of them – especially in north-west London or east London or in Leicestershire, where there are big Hindu communities – when you go to certain crematoria, they're decked out in a way that will satisfy every Hindu need. So most Hindus don't have a problem with the crematoria that exist already in the country. This is Mr Ghai's. He has a personal desire in this regard, and most Hindus would support his personal desire, but they wouldn't clamour themselves either way.*

Caste-based discrimination

The caste system is also often said to be 'cultural' and 'custom' rather than religious, but it has been closely associated with Hinduism and, to a lesser extent, the other dharmic religions. In September 2004, *Sunday* reported that the Labour Party Conference was being lobbied by British Asians demanding legislation to prevent caste-based discrimination in Britain.

'The newly formed Caste Watch UK organisation claims "casteism", as they call it, is ruining the lives of many in this country,' the programme told listeners. 'They say the abuse goes largely unreported and unrecognised, and may even be on the rise.' Martin Stott was sent to investigate the claims.

Martin Stott: It's a quiet evening in this small music and video shop in Coventry. As she waits for customers, twenty-four-year-old Reena writes up her master's degree dissertation on caste discrimination. Reena is from the 'Chamar' leather worker's caste, historically an untouchable. Here in Britain, that should mean nothing. But she only managed to buy this shop because the previous owner thought she was from his own, higher, Jat caste of traditional landowners. This isn't an isolated experience. Reena still has one elderly customer who'll only put money on the counter.

Reena: Every time she comes in, she refuses to put money in my hand like I'm an untouchable. And once I owed her about 50p change, and she just walked out. She does [it] on every occasion.

Martin Stott: Reena says younger generations are perpetuating the caste system, too; even celebrating it in popular modern British Asian music sold in the shop. She sent some of the worst examples back to the suppliers.

Reena: I think it's been reinforced with, like, Bhangra music [a musical style originating in Southall and associated with the Punjabi diaspora] being really popular now, and references being made to... caste. And higher caste number plates with 'Jat' written on them. T-shirts. I've seen a football T-shirt the other day with 'Son of a Jat' written on it, and that was in the middle of town.

266

Martin Stott's report also included a view from a representative of the Hindu Council, Jay Lakhani:

> *The hereditary caste that is practised in India, when it came to the United Kingdom turned into a very benevolent clan system. So these people mix in their own groups, they celebrate festivals in their own way. They might build temples as well. They would like to marry, perhaps, people within the same group. But this is because it is convenient socially to marry somebody with [a] similar background, with [a] similar diet, with [a] similar dress code, with similar linguistic abilities, with the same dialect. So it has nothing to do with hereditary caste system.*

But when *Sunday* returned to this subject nearly a decade later, very little seemed to have changed. William Crawley introduced his guest as follows: '[Let's hear from] a member of Britain's Dalit communities. She wishes to remain anonymous, but she's in her thirties and she works as an art director in Coventry.' This testimony was broadcast in August 2013.

Anonymous speaker: *I was absolutely oblivious to what caste was until I went to secondary school, where my identity stood out like a sore thumb. Because there were people in my class that were Sikhs and Hindus, and they had a very strong religious identity – whereas because I'm from quite a secular spiritual background – it aroused a lot of curiosity as to what I was, and I didn't ever quite fit in at school.*

But the kids at school kind of knew that I was from a different background, and I wasn't [one of] them. They would call me names that I didn't understand – what I now believe to be derogatory terms for an untouchable. So I took these words home to my parents, and that's when they kind of broke the bombshell that we're from an untouchable background. And we are low.

William Crawley: *And I know you've had an experience, also, with a shopkeeper. Can you describe that for us?*

Anonymous speaker: *Yes, myself and my husband run shops and businesses, and we have a local customer who... asked what caste I was and had a suspicion that I was an untouchable, and said, 'Are you one of them?*

Why are you an untouchable?' And I just didn't answer. So from that day onward, she'd never take money from my hand or any change. If she was buying an item, she'd just leave the money on the till and not take the change, or not want her goods being put into a bag by my hands.

Marrying out

Sunday's archive includes a number of items that reflect the way the process of integration can cause divisions within minority communities.

Among Sikhs, the issue of 'marrying out' became a source of contention. In 2017, BBC2 broadcast a televised adaptation of *The Boy with a Topknot: A memoir of love, secrets and lies* – a successful book about growing up as a Sikh in Wolverhampton during the 1980s. The author, Sathnam Sanghera, was a guest on *Sunday* on 17 November that year.

Edward Stourton: *Sathnam Sanghera had to handle some intimate family secrets, including mental illness, when he wrote his book. I asked him whether he was apprehensive about his story appearing on the small screen.*

Sathnam Sanghera: *It's very flattering, obviously, to have your life story turned into a TV film, but also it deals with the most painful things I've ever been through. So it's a rollercoaster, to say the least.*

Edward Stourton: *How much of a taboo is it among traditional Sikhs to go public about quite intimate things, as you say, in the way that you've done?*

Sathnam Sanghera: *I think Indians, in general, don't tend to talk about their family problems. When I was writing the book, I was trying to find some Indian family memoirs to copy or lightly plagiarise. And you know what? There's hardly any. It's very much a Western form to delve into your family's problems.*

Edward Stourton: *What about the issue of dating girls outside the Sikh community? How difficult was that, and what's the attitude towards it today?*

Sathnam Sanghera: *It was rare when I went through the experience. The book is partly about me telling my parents I wasn't going to marry a Sikh girl, like they wanted me to.*

Sunday then played a clip of the author's on-screen conversation with a girlfriend, explaining that: 'I have fifty-four first cousins so far. All of them have married a Sikh girl or boy. I know this. And I'm the one who's going to break ranks. I'll be the first... I mean, it's possible and probable I'll be disowned.'

Sanghera explained his inspiration for the book in the following way:

> *When I wrote the book, lots of my friends said: 'It felt like you were writing to me, trying to explain why you were the way you were.' And I think I wrote the book partly also to explain to my ex-girlfriends why I was so strange in that respect... Sikhs are highly integrated, and it's a very open, liberal religion, in theory. But at the same time, you know, there's a radical wing. There have been stories in recent years about fundamentalist Sikhs actually disrupting interfaith marriages because they don't want them to happen.*

That last sentence was a reference to an ugly episode reported on *Sunday* in September the previous year.

Edward Stourton: *You may have heard about the incident earlier this week when armed police were called to a Sikh temple in Leamington Spa because of a protest against a mixed-faith wedding there. Some of the protesters carried ceremonial daggers, which, although they're legal, made it all sound rather alarming. And as Trevor Barnes reports, the incident reflects a serious dispute among Sikhs.*

Trevor Barnes: *Fifty masked protesters and a SWAT team of Warwickshire's finest descending on the Leamington gurdwara behind me aren't what a bride and groom would expect on their big day. Ruby and Sunni certainly didn't when a similar protest at a different temple in Birmingham two years ago put paid to their plans.*

Ruby: *At seven in the morning, we had a phone call from the priest at the temple saying the wedding's going to be cancelled. We had protesters outside the temple. My relatives were there getting the refreshments ready for the morning for the congregation, and they described the scenes to me as very rude, very threatening, thuggish behaviour by people who had stormed the gurdwara in the morning and said, 'Get out of here!'*

Sunni: In fact, the police were also at my wife's parents' house as well, because some of these terrorists, which is exactly what they are, had turned up to my wife's parents' house as well to ensure that the Anand Karaj [Sikh marriage] ceremony wouldn't take place at her place.

Trevor Barnes: Activists from the group Sikh Youth UK, however, are committed to continuing what they claim are entirely peaceful protests against temples like the one in Leamington, which sanctioned the use of the so-called Anand Karaj for mixed-faith couples. Ruby's a Sikh, and Sunni is from a Hindu background. The Anand Karaj is the Sikh ceremony of holy matrimony that can be used, say protesters, only when both parties are themselves of the Sikh faith – an interpretation the Leamington temple committee clearly disputes. They've apologised for the disruption caused by the police action they requested, but so far have said little else publicly.

Could Sunday persuade them to say more? Well, the informal conversations I've had with men and women here have been extremely cordial. The reception has been extremely friendly. Despite that, however, no one – either on or off the committee – is willing to talk. But at the Guru Nanak Gurdwara in Birmingham, others are. Gurmel Singh is the secretary general of the Sikh Council UK.

Gurmel Singh: We're not against interfaith, interracial marriages. And indeed, I can say to you that if people want you to come to gurdwara to have blessings, that is possible. But we have this very clear ruling, part of our code of conduct, that the Sikh marriage ceremony is reserved for two Sikhs.

Sikh identity

Barnes's report then moved on to the issue of Sikh identity.

Gurmel Singh: We are British Sikhs, and we don't want to come across as fundamentalist or people who are absolutely rigid in some dogma. But this is what we're talking about here. It represents the core of what we actually believe in.

Trevor Barnes: Gurmel Singh of the Sikh Council UK... challenges the notion that the protests are driven only by ideological young hotheads within Sikhism's many youth movements. There is, he says, a universal issue at stake: preserving Sikh identity and spirituality from dilution.

Gurmel Singh: *Our experience has been that the weddings have essentially become costume events. So, for example, you would have a, let's say for the sake of argument, a white person marrying a Sikh girl. The person will come here, they'll wear the turban for the day and so on. And then later on they will go to a church. And the Sikh girl is now wearing a white dress and it's very much a Christian affair then. So... the religious value, the spiritual side of this, has been taken out, and they almost become costume events. The real essence of what a wedding represents is lost.*

The publication of the census data quoted at the beginning of this chapter coincided with two events that painted very different pictures of the place of British Asians in the United Kingdom.

In September 2022, there was an outbreak of communal violence between Muslims and Hindus in Leicester, a city with a reputation for harmonious community relations. As *The Guardian* reported on 23 September:

There have been reports of violent assaults, religious symbols being attacked and antisocial behaviour directed at both mosques and temples in recent weeks, with growing anger fuelled by social media speculation. Tensions boiled over last weekend, with violent unrest erupting on to the streets. People armed with sticks and bats carried out assaults, missiles and fireworks were thrown, police were injured, cars were smashed and 15 people were arrested – taking the total since the start of the unrest to 47.[1]

Some media reports also drew a link between the violence here and at the India versus Pakistan cricket match the previous month. On 25 September *Sunday* debated the roots of the trouble.

---

1 J. Murray, A. J. Khan and R. Syal, '"It feels like people want to fight": how communal unrest flared in Leicester', *The Guardian*: https://www.theguardian.com/uk-news/2022/sep/23/how-communal-unrest-flared-leicester-muslim-hindu-tensions (23 September 2022, accessed 2 May 2023).

Emily Buchanan: Communities in Leicester have been coming together to denounce the large-scale disorder over the past few weeks involving mainly young men from sections of the Muslim and Hindu faiths. Only yesterday a local group of Asian women from different traditions released a statement calling for unity, saying that neighbourhoods and families were living in fear, and recent unrest had torn apart our community.

...Dilwar Hussain is chair of the charity New Horizons in British Islam and also assistant professor at the Centre for Trust, Peace and Social Relations at the University of Coventry. And Sanjiv Patel is a spokesperson for Hindu and Jain Temples across Leicester. I asked Dilwar Hussain first whether he could throw any light on what is at the root of the disturbances.

Dilwar Hussain: I think the first thing I want to emphasise is that this is not a Hindu versus Muslim problem. And we've seen that because the vast majority of people, both on the ground as well as in the leadership, are resisting this and are saying that this is not the Leicester that we know. So I think it's really important that we frame this in its correct pattern and don't describe this as a huge-scale Hindu versus Muslim problem. In terms of why, I think there are three things for me. One is an issue around policing. I think the police were caught off guard, although now, over the last few days, they've become much more vigilant. I think there's something around elected leadership and the fact that the council and others in positions of power haven't seen this brewing and haven't seen this coming. And on a community level, I think there's some spillover of Indian subcontinent politics. There are newer communities that have settled into the city, and are facing poverty and finding their way... There's something around young men who are testosterone-filled, seeking violence and thrill, and there are extremist groups on both sides who are trying to manipulate the situation.

Emily Buchanan: Well, that's quite a few factors. Now, Sanjiv Patel, do you agree that there is this mixture, then, of different factors... maybe there not being enough preparation on the ground – although in fact, the local council says there's always been good engagement with different communities?

Sanjiv Patel: Well, firstly, I'd like to thank Dilwar for clearing it right up front. This is not any Hindu–Muslim event or series of events. It is much more about social cohesion. It's about all of the things that we've talked about. Yes, it takes us by surprise. And in terms of representation, I think wherever you get communities where they don't feel represented or don't feel heard, you get pent-up frustration. And we've seen that in various communities up and down the country over the years.

While Leicester's community leaders wrestled with the causes of this eruption of violence, the United Kingdom acquired its first Hindu prime minister. Rishi Sunak took office the following month.

'Some prime ministers famously "don't do God", Emily Buchanan told the *Sunday* audience on 22 October. 'Others wear their faith on their sleeves. Well, that's exactly what Rishi Sunak does. He sports a bracelet of bright-red thread on his right wrist. He swore on the Bhagavad Gita when he became a member of parliament, and he speaks proudly of his Hindu heritage.'

Buchanan then interviewed Anushka Sharma, a practising Hindu and former member of the Conservative Central Office (now the Conservative Campaign Headquarters), who currently works for the London Space Network. Part of the new prime minister's appeal, it became apparent, was that his own story echoed those of many of the families who were part of that 'British Asian' group identified in the census. Buchanan also asked her guest about that red thread on his wrist.

Anushka Sharma: *For many people it's something that we do before we kick off our pujas [a ritual means of paying homage, for example with a gift of flowers] and prayers. And so it's part of the protocol... It was just wonderful because, as Rishi has come to office, everything about his family history has really mirrored my family history in a really wonderful way: from pre-partition India, where his family have roots in modern-day Pakistan, similar to my father's side of the family; to his family's lineage in East Africa, and my mum and my grandmother being born in Kenya in East Africa; right now to... modern-day UK, where my grandparents, some forty-five years ago in south-west London, around Clapham, started.*

Emily Buchanan: *This Hindu background and faith, how do you see it showing so far? He's only been prime minister for a very short time, but how do you see that showing itself?*

Anushka Sharma: It's been wonderful seeing the images of him lighting diyas [clay oil lamps] outside Number 10, and then previously during the pandemic, when he was the chancellor, outside Number 11. It was a very... visual sign of his faith. And even just him standing outside Number 10 and waving with his hand up proudly with the kautuka, the red thread, around his wrist was such a visual for me, and something that really jumped off the cameras.

Part 4

MAKING WAVES IN THE WORLD

14

Religion and politics in the United States

Over the past quarter of a century, *Sunday*'s agenda has become increasingly international. This change in focus in part reflected the twenty-first century news agenda. Events such as 9/11 underlined that an understanding of religion is essential to any intelligent interpretation of world current affairs, and more and more often they pushed the programme to extend its reach beyond narrowly Christian subjects and domestic issues.

As we recalled in the Introduction, Colin Semper, *Sunday*'s first producer, was determined to escape what he saw as the 'ghetto' of religious broadcasting and to 'engage... in current affairs as of a right'. In the programme's early years, that often meant covering religious stories in Africa and Britain's former colonies (as we explored in chapter 4). With the big news stories of the new millennium, Semper's original ambition for the programme really paid dividends, and since the turn of the century *Sunday* has painted on an altogether broader canvas.

Sunday's challenge has been to interpret a world where religion still runs deep for an audience that has become ever more secular. The British media generally has, for example, long faced a particular problem in reporting the religious character of society in the United States. Ironically, it is especially difficult because American culture is so familiar. The dominance of American films, music and books has persuaded us all that we know the USA as well as our own country, and our shared language fools us into thinking we are more similar than we are. In fact, when it comes to religion, the two societies could not be more different.

At the time of writing, both the Pew Research Center (an authoritative American think tank studying religious trends) and the General Social Survey (which has been tracking social change in America since the early 1970s) estimate that roughly two-thirds of the US population self-identifies as Christian. That is well down from the ninety per cent who did so around the time when *Sunday* first went on the air, but it is still some twenty per cent higher than the figure for self-identifying Christians recorded in the UK's 2021 census. The United States, like the United Kingdom, is becoming more secular, but it remains a religion-soaked society.

The character of religion in the two countries is also very different. In the United Kingdom, the Church of England still claims the lion's share among Christian denominations – 26 million members, as measured by baptism – although weekly attendance is down to around 1 million. As the Established Church, its teaching tends to be middle-of-the road, although, as we have seen in earlier chapters, the membership includes a significant number of evangelicals who rely closely on biblical authority. The UK also has a Roman Catholic minority of more than 5 million.

Many of those who brought Christianity to the United States, by contrast, were seeking to escape precisely the kind of Christianity the Church of England represents, and those more radical origins are still reflected in the character of many of the US churches. Some 140 million Americans are Protestant, and a significant proportion can be classed as evangelicals, although it is difficult to find agreement on a precise figure. In 2012, *The Economist* magazine estimated that 'over one-third of Americans, more than 100 million, can be considered evangelical',[1] and two years later the Pew Research Center put the figure at just over a quarter of the total population.

A little over twenty per cent of Americans – some 70 million people – are Catholic, and even the smaller minority churches can claim, by the standards of most countries, big numbers. There are approximately 13 million Jehovah's Witnesses in the United States and 6.5 million Mormons, or members of the Church of the Latter Day Saints.

Finally, the United Kingdom's head of state is also the head (supreme governor) of the Church of England, and bishops still play an active role in the legislature. But religion is almost entirely absent from political

---

1 'Lift Every Voice', *The Economist*: https://www.economist.com/united-states/2012/05/05/lift-every-voice (5 May 2012, accessed 2 May 2023).

debate, and most politicians regard it as a toxic subject. The position in the United States is exactly the reverse. The United States constitution enshrines the principle of a separation of Church and state, yet religion is a hugely important factor in both its day-to-day political debate and in deciding how people cast their votes at election time.

A sudden conversion

President George W. Bush ('Bush 43', as he is sometimes known to distinguish him from his father, who was the forty-first president of the United States) is a striking example of a political figure who proved difficult to interpret for a British audience.

George Bush junior began his career in the oil industry and settled in Texas, where he earned himself a reputation for heavy drinking. But in the mid-1980s, an old school friend suggested they start attending Bible study classes together. Partly as a result – by Bush's own account – the future president gave up the booze. As one friend put it, it was: 'Goodbye, Jack Daniels; hello, Jesus.' This change set him on the course that took him to the White House. In 2003 he told an audience in Nashville: 'I would not be president today if I had not stopped drinking seventeen years ago.'[2]

His fateful invasion of Iraq started in 2003. Just before the war began, *Sunday* despatched Jane Little to Texas to explore the president's religious roots. She began her report at a match played by the Dallas basketball team the Mavericks.

Jane Little: Well, President Bush is often caricatured as a Bible-bashing, gun-toting Texan. And while that might not be totally fair, and certainly doesn't represent every Texan, he does come out of a particular religious conservative tradition that's deeply embedded here. Dr Tony Evans is the chaplain to the Mavericks, and he's also very close to Mr Bush. He's prayed with him many times, especially when Mr Bush was governor of Texas, and he was one of several ministers who

---

2   Both quotes from E. Stourton, *In the Footsteps of St Paul* (London: Hodder & Stoughton: 2004), p. 57.

counselled him when he was wrestling with the decision of whether to run for president.

Tony Evans: *It was a major spiritual decision. He wanted to know that this was God's calling on his life, and not simply running for an office for purely political reasons, or even for personal reasons, but that there would be a spiritual dimension; a sense of divine call regarding this.*

Jane Little: *The story of how the once-rabble-rousing alcoholic young man from West Texas found God at the age of forty, cleaned up his life and went on to become president is a classic redemption tale, and one that goes down well in this devout nation. But evangelist and friend James Robison insists Mr Bush's professions of faith come from the heart, not the focus groups.*

James Robison: *He kept one president of another country waiting another twenty minutes outside while we continued to pray together. He told some ministers on one occasion, 'I know why I'm in the White House. It was an encounter with God. Had it not been for that encounter, I'd be sitting on a bar stool in Texas.' I think he really believes that. I think when he called me on the telephone that day and said, 'I've heard the call'... he really believed it, but he will not play the religious card to make gains, politically or otherwise.*

Jane Little: *And... the fact that President Bush has conflated the war on Saddam Hussein with his war on terror, and portrayed it as a battle between good and evil, gives the impression to some that he's on a crusade, confident that God is on his side. Certainly, that's the way some here positively view it.*

Little then spoke to a senior figure from the Texas Christian Coalition, one of the many organisations in America's so-called Bible Belt dedicated to bringing a Christian influence to bear on politics.

Jane Little: *Mike Hannesschlager is the executive director of the Texas Christian Coalition.*

Mike Hannesschlager: *President Bush would be derelict in his responsibility as president – not just before the American people, but before God – if he did not act to get rid of the people who are going to kill us.*

Jane Little: *Does Osama bin Laden not also believe he has God on his side?*

Mike Hannesschlager: Osama bin Laden is wrong. So that's the answer to that question.

Jane Little: He's convinced he's right, just as President Bush is, though.

Mike Hannesschlager: Sure. But being convinced you're right doesn't make you right – and some things are right and true, whether anyone believes in them or not.

Jane Little: How do you know they're right, then?

Mike Hannesschlager: Because it is. God is the ultimate reality, and the Bible is his inerrant word.

'We don't do God'

In Britain, a political figure who expressed views of a similar nature would have provoked ridicule. It was around this time that Alastair Campbell, Tony Blair's director of communications, famously interrupted an interview with the prime minister to inform a journalist that: 'We don't do God.' And suggestions that Mr Blair and President Bush prayed together in the run-up to the war in Iraq were a source of some embarrassment to the British prime minister.

George W. Bush, however, continued to enjoy high levels of support – partly *because of*, rather than *despite*, his overtly religious views. In 2004, he won a second term as president, carrying thirty-one of the fifty states, and securing an absolute majority over his Democratic opponent John Kerry, a liberal Catholic.

In her 2003 report, Jane Little managed to turn up some opposition to the way he mixed politics and religion, but it was modest.

Jane Little: There are many Americans who idolise their president. His cowboy, man-of-the-people image is only enhanced by his appeal to America's free, democratic traditions under the guidance of God. But an hour's drive away in the state capital, you get a different scene. Austin calls itself the live music capital of the world. There's a big student population, and the city is the intellectual liberal outpost of this state. George W. Bush served as governor here for six years before he became president in 2000. Lawyer Cris Feldman says there's a striking example of how Mr Bush blurs the line of separation between Church and state.

Cris Feldman: I guess it's best symbolised when he was governor of Texas, He declared a certain day 'Jesus Day', as I recall. And while I'm not a practising Jew, I am Jewish. And it seemed awfully exclusionary. And what he did in the state is mirrored by what he's doing on a national level. His language is so exclusionary at times that it really does pit us against them; not just West versus East, but almost like true believers and good-doers versus evildoers and those that do not follow his same moral code.

Jane Little: President Bush has said himself that no one can judge his heart, but he comes across as a man who feels that this is his hour. His pastors told me that he's not a man to suffer from doubts or crises of faith. What he will be doing, said one, is praying every day; praying for God's wisdom to guide him through the difficult decisions ahead.

Equal marriage

By the time of the 2004 election, the debate about equal marriage was beginning to take off in the United States, just as it had done in the United Kingdom. But while the British parliament passed Labour's Civil Partnership Act that year (see chapter 7), the presidential campaign underlined the visceral opposition to any such reform from sections of the American electorate.

The Defence of Marriage Act, which prevented the federal government from recognising same-sex marriages, was already on the statute book. It had been signed into law by President Clinton in 1996, an action that many liberal Clinton supporters regarded as a betrayal. The programme George W. Bush offered his voters at this point included a commitment to take things a stage further. Bush proposed a constitutional amendment to ensure that same-sex marriage could never be legalised. And, as *The New York Times* reported, he declared: 'A measure of this sort was the only way to protect the status of marriage between man and woman,' which he called 'the most fundamental institution of civilisation'.[3]

3 D. Stout, 'Bush Backs Ban in Constitution on Gay Marriage', *The New York Times*: https://www.nytimes.com/2004/02/24/politics/bush-backs-ban-in-constitution-on-gay-marriage.html (24 February 2004, accessed 2 May 2023).

It was a clear gesture towards his evangelical supporters, and it seems to have worked. In the November vote, the exit polls suggested religious conservatives turned out for Bush in large numbers, and Roberta Combs, president of the Christian Coalition of America, told the *Christian Post*: 'Christian evangelicals made the major difference once again this year.'[4]

With the election of Barack Obama four years later, however, the issue returned to the top of the national agenda. In May 2012 – during the last months of his first term in office – President Obama took a bold step.

Samira Ahmed: President Barack Obama made history this week by becoming the first US president to publicly express support for gay marriage, though he didn't advocate a change in the law to allow it. With religious values a strong issue in American politics, Mr Obama's statement is regarded by some of his supporters as a brave move, which could turn a number of voters to Mitt Romney, his Republican rival. Mr Romney yesterday restated his belief that marriage should only take place between a man and a woman.

By this stage a number of individual states had taken matters into their own hands, passing state laws either banning or legalising equal marriage. Reporting from the United States, Jane Little unpicked the electoral calculation and risk behind the president's move on same-sex unions.

Jane Little: So you've now got a situation where thirty-one states ban it, six states and the District of Columbia have legalised it. And in the light of all this going on, especially since his deputy [Vice President Biden] endorsed it, President Obama's evolving position, as he'd put it, had become untenable, essentially. And predictably, his announcement drew condemnation from many religious leaders, especially evangelicals – some of whom were particularly annoyed that the president couched his decision in terms of his Christian faith and cited the golden rule that he said requires us to treat people equally. Well, I spoke to Dr Robert Jeffress,

---

4 K. T. Phan, 'More States Expected to Vote on Marriage Amendments', *The Christian Post*: https://www.christianpost.com/news/more-states-expected-to-vote-on-marriage-amendments.html (4 November 2004, accessed 3 May 2023).

senior pastor of the [then] *11,000-member First Baptist Church in Dallas, Texas.*

Robert Jeffress: *Polls change and people change, but God's word never changes. The truth is, President Obama has been all over the map on this issue. When he was running for Congress in the United States and Illinois, he was for gay marriage, and then he was against it when he was running for president. And then he was evolving, and suddenly his evolution came to an end conveniently right before a big Hollywood fundraiser.*

Jane Little: *That comment about the fundraiser referred to a dinner at George Clooney's house, where guests paid $40,000 a plate, and it raised about $15 million, I think, for Obama.*

Samira Ahmed: *What's been the reaction from other religious constituencies in America, then?*

Jane Little: *Well, this did have some political risks, because Catholics are key swing voters, and Catholics – especially Hispanics – live disproportionately in swing states. Cardinal Timothy Dolan, president of the US Conference of Catholic Bishops, put out a strong statement saying President Obama's comments in support of the redefinition of marriage are deeply saddening: 'The people of this country, especially our children, deserve better.' He went on to criticise other actions by the administration that eroded or ignored the unique meaning of marriage, so a very strong statement there.*

And there is a sense that the president has picked another fight with the Catholic hierarchy, which is already fuming over healthcare reform [Catholic bishops opposed Obama's healthcare reforms over the issue of insurance protection for contraception].

Black Christian leaders are also not happy. African Americans are Mr Obama's most loyal constituency, but also probably the most resistant in terms of a change with gay marriage. In terms of whether it's actually going to hurt him in November [at election time], I suspect he and his team have already calculated that one. And recent opinion polls show a real shift in attitudes here, including among Catholics, Hispanics and blacks. In 1996, for instance, twenty-seven per cent of the population was for gay marriage, with an overwhelming majority against it. This year, fifty per cent support gay marriage, with just under that against. So there has been a real change, and it could cost him a little bit, but not enough to cost him the election. That's his calculation, anyway.

Samira Ahmed: *Well, the other side of that calculation is: what does Mitt Romney have, if anything, to gain from this situation? What has he said about it?*

Jane Little: *Well, Mitt Romney has said he's opposed to gay marriage. And with that, there is a clear line between them now on cultural grounds. And I think where he has the most to gain is with the Republican Party base – the conservative evangelicals who've been very wary of Mitt Romney. Dr Jeffress was very outspoken against Mitt Romney's Mormonism. But now, in the light of Obama's support for gay marriage, he appears to have changed his mind, and says he'd vote for Romney over Obama.*

Robert Jeffress: *I think what this has done is, it has shown the deep contrast, the stark contrast, between President Obama and Governor Romney. Quite frankly, there have been a number of evangelical Christians who have been apathetic about Governor Romney. But I think the president has succeeded in energising evangelical Christians and social conservatives to get out and vote.*

Jane Little: *So Mitt Romney could capitalise on this. And in fact, today he's giving the graduation address at Liberty University, which is the largest evangelical university in the country. He's clearly courting those core Republican evangelical supporters. But in truth, the focus is already back on the economy. And this issue of gay marriage isn't going to dislodge that. I think the country has shifted culturally, and gay marriage just isn't going to be the galvanising issue that it was in 2004 when George W. Bush was able to use it to get conservative Christians out to vote, and they helped win him the election.*

In the event, Barack Obama won re-election with 51.1 per cent of the popular vote, securing 332 votes in the electoral college against Mitt Romney's 206. The issue of equal marriage was eventually resolved during his second term, by two rulings from the United States Supreme Court: in June 2013 and June 2015. The first struck down the ban on recognising same-sex marriage at a federal level, the second overturned all state-level bans.

By this time, the opinion polls were recording a general and significant move in favour of same-sex marriage, but that did not prevent continued opposition among many religious conservatives. Here's one Christian activist, Pastor Scott Lively, talking to *Sunday* in March 2014 (between the two critical Supreme Court decisions).

Scott Lively: I believe the evidence of the last half-century is that the sexual revolution has been a disaster for the Western world. The family is in collapse. There have never been as many divorces, sexually transmitted diseases, every kind of negative social indicator. And it's a direct consequence of turning away from the biblical standard of sexuality and embracing this sort of gay ethic of 'anything goes'.

Shelagh Fogarty (**a Radio 5 Live host who occasionally presented** ***Sunday***)**:** *You mentioned at the beginning of our conversation therapies to tackle homosexuality. Are you aware that the Association of Christian Counsellors has told Christian therapists in this country to stop using this kind of reparative or aversion therapy that is used in some places?*

Scott Lively: Yeah. I know the gay bullies have really put the screws to everybody in your country. It's a real shame. But... I just make the point that every human being is born either male or female, and that everyone is really heterosexual by design. And it's absurd to suggest that people cannot reorient to the sexual orientation that comports with the actual design of their bodies. It's an absurd position. I know many ex-gays, and they're very happy and glad to be out of what they consider to be a sort of an addictive type of sexuality.

And here are two other Christian leaders discussing gay couples with *Sunday*'s Matt Wells a few months later.

Edward Furton: They can make a commitment without being married and they can have the legal fiction of saying they're married, but it doesn't really make much of a difference, I don't think.

Matt Wells: In a grand suburban house in a suburb of Philadelphia that's now the National Catholic Bioethics Center, Edward Furton has a very different take on what's been won or lost. There's no point debating the legalities of a sacred institution, he says. Even though around sixty per cent of American Catholics recently surveyed now support gay marriage, he's confident that won't stand the test of time.

Edward Furton: It is simply a natural impossibility. It doesn't really happen. I know it sounds strange, but a marriage is only between a man and a woman. It can't be in any other way. It doesn't exist that way.

Matt Wells: Only if you accept that marriage is a religiously ordained institution, and of course in these cases, it's not. It's a civil marriage.

Edward Furton: Yeah, well, we're talking not only religiously ordained, but just by nature.

Matt Wells: How should the Church respond?

Edward Furton: Well, I think it's kind of a wait-and-see period here. I mean, you know we live in one of these times in history when we think that homosexuality is just a fine thing and it's very normal, etc. But this has happened over and over again in the history of the world. Typically, after a certain period of time passes and people begin to see the consequences of this new arrangement, they have second thoughts.

Sam Rohrer: The bigger issue here is a consolidation of power, a move towards tyranny, of which marriage right now happens to be the symptom driving the current discussion.

Matt Wells: One of the activists leading the Protestant evangelical opposition is former Pennsylvania state politician Sam Rohrer. As president of the American Pastors' Network, he's also toiling in the leafy suburbs of historic Philadelphia – and he's not prepared to let history take its course. Leaders need to rise up and inspire the culture warriors across all fronts, he says.

Sam Rohrer: In any culture, at any time, moral value and culture will rise and fall with the activity of their pastors. And so we're saying 'yes' for the moment. 'Yes, wake up everybody in America, because things are changing faster than you can imagine. Now, if you like it, do nothing. If you don't like it, and if you want to hold to moral truths that have given us what we have in this country, including our constitution and our freedoms in the United States, then pastors and the pulpit must be the ones to lead the way.' And that's our emphasis.

Cruz versus Trump

The evangelical conviction that America was facing a culture war played a significant role in the next presidential campaign. Seventeen serious contenders declared themselves candidates for the Republican presidential nomination in 2016, but two men very quickly surfaced as leaders of the pack: the Texas senator Ted Cruz and Donald Trump.

Senator Cruz had the kind of political profile that, on the face of it, should have guaranteed him an enthusiastic reception from evangelical voters. He was determinedly anti-abortion (except where a mother's life was in danger) and a vocal opponent of equal marriage. When the Supreme Court came down in favour of same-sex unions in 2016, the senator described the decision as the 'very definition of tyranny'.[5]

By contrast, Donald Trump, with two divorces in his past and little sign of serious religious affiliation, seemed an unlikely hero for evangelicals. American presidential campaigns are, notoriously, marathons, and *Sunday* first reported on the religious dimension of this epic struggle in November 2015. The programme spoke to Jessica Taylor, a reporter on America's National Public Radio (NPR) network.

Edward Stourton: To what extent is Donald Trump's own life – his own view of religion – to what extent are those things a factor in the judgements that evangelicals make about him?

Jessica Taylor: I think that's still a very big question. He says he is a Christian and that he goes to church. He has said that he goes to this church in Manhattan. They have said that he is not an active member, you know. And even he's been asked earlier on the campaign trail about his beliefs. And he says, you know, he's never asked God for forgiveness. And when he talks about taking Communion, the way he talked about it sort of seemed to demean it, almost saying, you know, he takes his little cup and his little wine and things.

Edward Stourton: And his cracker.

Jessica Taylor: Yes. His cracker and his wine. So it's not ways that you

---

5 I. Bobic, 'Ted Cruz Calls Gay Marriage Ruling The "Very Definition Of Tyranny"', *HuffPost*: https://www.huffingtonpost.co.uk/entry/ted-cruz-gay-marriage_n_55b00157e4b07af29d5 7677c (22 July 2015, accessed 16 June 2023).

would typically see someone who is very devout talking about it. And of course, forgiveness and asking God for forgiveness is pretty much the central tenet of Christianity. So, you know, the way he's talked about these things sort of seemed to raise questions about maybe how serious he is.

Edward Stourton: *And to be clear, again, going over some of the ground we talked about a little while ago, evangelical voters are absolutely critical in the early tests in the battle for the Republican nomination.*

Jessica Taylor: *Absolutely. They make up a very large block of Iowa – which, of course, will go first with their caucus – and then less important in New Hampshire. But in South Carolina they're going to be incredibly crucial as well. I mean, this is a state which is... sort of the buckle on the Bible belt. And for instance, if Cruz wins Iowa, I think he could get enough momentum out of it that could maybe carry him over into South Carolina. But I mean, we've had polls that came out this week showing that Trump still is in the lead in South Carolina, but Cruz is gaining. The problem is that we haven't seen evangelicals sort of rally around one candidate yet. We might be starting to see that, certainly with Cruz, in a way.*

A change in the religious right

The two crucial opening rounds in the nomination process went different ways. Senator Cruz won the Iowa caucuses on 1 February – as Jessica Taylor had predicted he might – and Donald Trump came out top in the New Hampshire primary just over a week later. When it came to the South Carolina primary, Trump won with a ten per cent edge over his nearest rival, and Cruz was beaten into third place. So from really quite early on in the campaign, Mr Trump enjoyed Christian support. In April 2016, *Sunday* explored why.

Edward Stourton: *In our coverage of the American presidential campaign, we've asked why it is that Donald Trump appears to have secured so much support from the so-called religious right when his main rival, Ted Cruz, is a committed Southern Baptist, and actually launched his campaign at a university linked with the Revd Jerry Falwell, one of the* *religious right's founding fathers. Part of the answer, of course, lies in the way Mr Trump has tailored his positions to appeal to a group of voters who have, over the past three-and-a-half decades, loomed very large in Republican politics. But could part of it also lie in a change within the movement we've come to call the religious right? Joe Miller reports.*

Joe Miller: *It markets itself as the biggest Christian university in the world, and the campus of Liberty University is so vast that you can see it from almost any vantage point here in the southern town of Lynchburg, Virginia. Beside me on the other side of a large fountain is one of the most impressive buildings; an arena in which thousands of students gather for convocation every week. It was in here that Texas senator Ted Cruz launched his campaign in the spring of 2015 with a Christian cri de coeur.*

Senator Ted Cruz (recording of speech): *Roughly half of born-again Christians aren't voting. They're staying home. Imagine instead millions of people of faith all across America coming out to the polls and voting our values.*[6]

Joe Miller: *Mr Cruz, the son of a pastor, seemed a shoo-in for the evangelical vote. But in January this year, at another convocation, the university's president, Jerry Falwell Jr, endorsed another man.*

Jerry Falwell Jr (recording of speech): *Please welcome back to Liberty University, Mr Donald Trump.*

Joe Miller: *The university was quick to point out that Mr Falwell's endorsement was a personal one, but Mr Trump has attracted significant support in the evangelical community, even among young voters... I'm in a coffee shop in downtown Lynchburg with two students from Liberty University who achieved a certain level of fame after being pictured at Donald Trump's speech wearing T-shirts that spelled out 'Trump'.*

Austin Miller: *My name is Austin Miller, [I'm] twenty years old, and I'm from a small town called Gold Hill in North Carolina. I'm thinking about going to seminary and then working with a mission organisation after college.*

---

6 T. Cruz, 'Ted Cruz speaks at Liberty University', *Washington Post*: https://www.youtube.com/watch?v=sNzEo0GDsUY (23 March 2015, accessed 13 July 2023).

Cody Hildebrand: *My name is Cody Hildebrand, and I'm twenty years old. I live in a small town right outside of Charleston, West Virginia.*

Joe Miller: *There are some things that Donald Trump has said that some people could construe as very anti-Christian. He said that he doesn't ask God for forgiveness. He supported abortion and Planned Parenthood in the past. Does any of that put you off?*

Cody Hildebrand: *I'm very aware of his divisive language. I mean, he's kind of a jerk sometimes, I'm not denying that. But one thing that is very attractive about Donald Trump is he has no filter. Even when he was at Liberty University and he mis-recited Second Corinthians* [a reference to Paul's second letter to the Corinthians] *– he said 'Two Corinthians', you know – the audience laughed, but that's him. But he says, one thing is for certain, that: 'I vow to protect the Christian faith if I'm elected president.' And that is just so refreshing to me.*

Austin Miller: *I mean, the only thing that bothers me is about his personal spirituality, because honestly I care about everybody's salvation. But when it comes to the presidential position, I want somebody who has good policy and good leadership. And that is stuff that Donald Trump has.*

Joe Miller: *Somewhere between a third and a quarter of all American voters identify as born-again Christians. And most of them support Republican candidates, which may explain some of Donald Trump's recent overtures to the evangelical base, like suggesting he would be in favour of penalties for those who perform abortions. But the faithful at Lynchburg's other great Christian institution, the megachurch Thomas Road Baptist Church, aren't necessarily convinced.*

Thomas Road Baptist Church (recording of announcement): *We're glad you're here to worship the Lord with us. Why don't you find about six or seven people, give them a high five, welcome them to Thomas Road today?*

Joe Miller: *The atmosphere inside the gigantic auditorium is electric. And even though there are thousands of worshippers, it's all incredibly friendly. So friendly, in fact, I've been invited to join four retired local congregants – Edward, Phil, Jan and Mark – for lunch in a restaurant across the road after the service.*

Speaker (saying grace before lunch): *Okay. Thank you, Father, for today.*

Thank you for this food. Make it of nourishment to our bodies. Thank you for the services today. And thank you for us running into Joe. We pray that you would bless him, give him safe travels and just open his eyes to what you are really all about...

Joe Miller: *Do any of you believe that Donald Trump is really a Christian?*

Speaker: *That's for God to judge. I mean, there are lots of things in his past that say, no, he can't be. But we're desperate for some change. And we see the hope of that coming from him.*

Speaker: *He's a populist, so he is speaking for the people; what he thinks the people want to hear. Do I think he would close the whole country off to Muslims? No, I don't think that. Would he not close it off because of his Christian values? I don't know. My concern is his moral compass. Where is that compass pointing at any one time? Is that compass subject to change? He said he supports Planned Parenthood. Well, Christians know that Planned Parenthood performs abortions. So a lot of his talk is not consistent with our Christian values. But [if] it's either he or Hillary [Clinton, the Democrat candidate and wife of former president Bill Clinton], I would hold my nose and vote for him.*

Joe Miller: *We're just about to finish our meal at Thomas Roads. Pastor Jerry Falwell's son, Jonathan, is walking past our table with his family. He's told his congregation to vote with their hearts, but would he ever encourage them not to vote for Donald Trump?*

Jonathan Falwell: *My job is to be a pastor that reaches out to all people... And I believe the people who are listening and hearing – and [are] part of our church and part of the larger Church, I think they're wise enough. I think they are intelligent enough to figure out who the people are that [are] more closely aligned with what we believe, according to God's word.*

Joe Miller: *Your father was the founder of the Moral Majority and the religious right. Are you a little bit dismayed that Christian voters, evangelical Christian voters, are being courted by a man – and let's say his name, Donald Trump – who says he's a Christian, but who some people would find very, very hard to reconcile his actions with Christianity?*

Jonathan Falwell: *I don't know Mr Trump, I've never met him, I've never had a conversation with him. There's no question if I had the opportunity to talk with him, I would try to give him some advice of, maybe he* *ought to say things differently and do things differently. And I would show him and point him to places in God's word that help us to see. But I'm certainly not going to judge his faith. You know, if he says he's a Christian, I'll take his word for it. But again, like all of us, we have to not just label ourselves. We have to live the life that points us to Christ.*

Trump's running mate

When the moment came for candidate Trump to select his vice-presidential running mate, he made his choice – not for the first time – with an eye to Christian evangelical voters.

Edward Stourton: *In the course of this American presidential campaign, we've tried to trace the evolution of the intriguing relationship between Donald Trump and the Christian voters of the religious right. That relationship took a further twist with Mr Trump's choice of running mate. The Indiana governor, Mike Pence, is a vocal champion of evangelical values. Here he is at the Republican Convention earlier this week.*

Mike Pence (from recording of speech): *I'm a Christian, a conservative and a Republican, in that order... I believe we have come to another rendezvous with destiny. And I have faith, faith in the boundless capacity of the American people and faith that God can still heal our land.[7]*

Edward Stourton: *Sarah Posner is a Washington-based writer on religion and politics. She contributes to, among others, the* Washington Post *and the* New York Times. *And I asked her about Mr Pence's background.*

Sarah Posner: *Mike Pence is currently the governor of Indiana, and he was known during his time in Congress as one of the most conservative members: very adamantly opposed to LGBT rights, very adamantly opposed to abortion, very much in favour of the infusion of conservative Christian values into American government.*

Edward Stourton: *His very public Christianity is intriguing, partly because, as I understand it, he was a convert to evangelical Christianity from Catholicism.*

---

7   R. T. Beckwith, 'Watch Mike Pence Speak at the Republican Convention', *Time*: https://time.com/4416456/republican-convention-mike-pence-video-speech-transcript (21 July 2016, accessed 16 June 2023).

Sarah Posner: Yes. And that's not terribly unusual in the United States. Many religious people have a fluidity between denominations. You do see quite a bit of Catholics becoming evangelical, and also sometimes the other way around. The religious right spent many decades building a relationship between conservative evangelicals and conservative Catholics. So while Catholics in general in the United States are more split in their politics, among evangelicals they tend to be a little bit more homogeneously conservative. My familiarity with him was from covering the religious right for over a decade, and the Mike Pence that I am familiar with is the Mike Pence who would go to conservative Christian conferences and give speeches that were very much like the speech that he gave at the RNC [Republican National Convention] last week – very much infused with the idea of an America that was founded on and continues to be guided by what he calls Judeo-Christian values.

Edward Stourton: Does that make it at all surprising that he's accepted the position on the ticket with Donald Trump, whose own personal life has been questioned by some evangelicals and who doesn't, in the way he conducts himself, really seem to express the sorts of values that you're talking about?

Sarah Posner: Well, I would place Pence's acceptance of the VP position as another piece in Donald Trump forcing the religious right to capitulate to him. Traditionally, how the religious right has engaged with the Republican Party has been to demand of the candidates – both presidential and congressional candidates – that the candidate adhere to and pledge allegiance to the religious right's religious and political principles. Finding itself unable to do that with Trump, finding itself unable to force Trump to fluently or literally talk about the Bible, or [to] talk about what they call biblical principles or a biblical world view – finding themselves unable to get Trump to talk about issues like same-sex marriage or abortion in the language that they use – they have found themselves in a position of having to capitulate to him. Because if they don't and he becomes the president, then they will have lost their place at the table in Washington. So I would consider Pence signing on to this ticket part of that process.

Edward Stourton: Do you think it will make a difference with evangelical voters?

Sarah Posner: I think evangelical voters were already resigned to Trump *being the nominee. There is a minority in the Never Trump camp who continue to say 'Never Trump', even after Mike Pence. But I think that the majority were already either enthusiastically on board with Trump or had resigned themselves to Trump being the nominee, and their opposition to Hillary Clinton [was] so strong that they would acquiesce to him being the nominee.*

Edward Stourton: *There have been incidents in the past, I believe, in Mike Pence's career when he has refused to endorse or get involved with nasty attack politics because he felt that they ran contrary to his Christian principles. Do you see any sign at all that any of that, or of his influence, may change the pretty brutal tone of the campaign so far?*

Sarah Posner: *There is absolutely nothing, in my view, that would change the brutal tone of the campaign. This is Trump's campaign, and this train is very clearly going to take a path of 'Hillary must be imprisoned'. Indeed, one of Trump's surrogates this week in Cleveland said that [Hillary] should be shot for treason, and there was no pull back from the campaign except to say that they did not agree with that assessment. So Pence, in this scenario, is the capitulation to Trump. He's not the moderator of Trump's extremism.*

Trump's attempts to capture the religious right in 2016 were triumphantly successful. In its first analysis of the vote, published within a week of the election, the Pew Research Center observed that:

While earlier in the campaign some pundits and others questioned whether the thrice-married Trump would earn the bulk of white evangelical support, fully eight-in-ten self-identified white, born-again/ evangelical Christians say they voted for Trump, while just 16% voted for [Hillary] Clinton. Trump's 65-percentage-point margin of victory among voters in this group – which includes self-described Protestants, as well as Catholics, Mormons and others – matched or exceeded the victory margins [in this group] of George W. Bush in 2004, John McCain in 2008 and Mitt Romney in 2012.[8]

8   J. Martínez and G. A. Smith, 'How the faithful voted: A preliminary 2016 analysis', Pew Research Center: https://www.pewresearch.org/short-reads/2016/11/09/how-the-faithful-voted-a-preliminary-2016-analysis (9 November 2016, accessed 3 May 2023).

Appointing Paula White

It is small wonder that President Trump tried to court the same group of voters again in the run-up to the election of 2020. In November 2019, he appointed the Pentecostal televangelist Paula White as adviser to the White House's Faith and Opportunity Initiative. It was, as *Sunday* reported, 'seen as a sign that President Trump is keen to keep the support of conservative evangelical voters'.

William Crawley: So who is Paula White, and how has she forged this preacher–president relationship? I asked the BBC's White House reporter Tara McKelvey.

Tara McKelvey: She's originally from Mississippi, and she went to a Bible college in Fort Washington, Maryland. She's definitely had a hard life. She talks openly about the way she's been physically and sexually abused, but she says she's not a victim. She says she's come out of these experiences and is a really strong leader. And this allows her to talk to people who have also been through these types of horrific things and put them at ease, and shows her real talent in terms of her leadership abilities.

William Crawley: And she's known Donald Trump, of course, for quite some time, hasn't she?

Tara McKelvey: That's right. Donald Trump, like a lot of people in this country, watches a lot of television. He saw her on TV when she was preaching in Florida. He got in touch with her, and she told me she couldn't believe that it was Donald Trump on the line at first. She thought it was a joke, but it was him. And she said that she realised at a certain point that he had not only been watching her on TV, but he'd memorised three of her sermons. So they got along really well. She joined his campaign, and she was a real force on the campaign. She told evangelicals why he was a candidate for them, and she got these evangelical voters to the polls. I interviewed Paula White last year. We were not far from the White House, and she told me about her relationship with Donald Trump.

Paula White (recording): I've had the fortunate ability to be in his life eighteen years… So relationship equity takes us a long way in life, period. I believe that we are to value our friends, so I'm grateful for the relationship and the ability to serve our nation, serve people around the world, and do it in the lane that I believe God's called me to. And that is, I am a Christian, I'm a believer and I'm a person of faith. And they're very strong convictions. I have to help all of humanity.

William Crawley: *What do we know about Paula White's particular approach to theology, the kind of doctrines that she holds dearly to?*

Tara McKelvey: *She's part of what's known as the 'prosperity gospel'. This is the idea that when you do good works and you believe in God and you're a good person, that good things will come to you. And that means a richer spiritual life. And it also means money – that your personal wealth will be enhanced because of who you are spiritually. It seems strange, and when you see it on TV it all looks a little bit odd, with dollar bills and so on. But if you keep in mind who this appeals to, these are people who are really living hand-to-mouth. They're thinking about money pretty much all of the time. And the idea that if you're good here on earth, then you'll be richer for it, that's very appealing.*

William Crawley: *Tara, Paula White has been Donald Trump's personal pastor, if we can put it that way, for quite some time. She delivered an invocation at his inauguration. Do we know what this new appointment as adviser to the White House Faith and Opportunity Initiative actually means? What does it entail?*

Tara McKelvey: *She will be the spokeswoman for the evangelical movement. She will be the eyes and ears of evangelicals within the White House. And certainly, she'll be talking to people within the White House about the issues that matter to evangelicals. And she will also be a physical, visible presence for evangelicals across the country. And presumably the hope is that she'll convince them once again to support Mr Trump in the election.*

William Crawley: *Evangelicals, of course, [are] obviously a very significant part of Donald Trump's base. But Paula White is controversial even within evangelical circles. What reaction has there been to that appointment?*

Tara McKelvey: *Some people say that she's not particularly qualified for this position, that a faith-based position within the White House means people of more diverse backgrounds. They think that she represents the ultra-conservative wing of the Christian movement, and they're worried* *about the kinds of policies that she'll be recommending within the West Wing.*

William Crawley: *And it has been reported, Tara, that this appointment could be seen as a tactical move... by President Trump as he tries to embolden his Christian evangelical voting bloc ahead of the next election.*

Tara McKelvey: *That's right. I was with Mr Trump a few days ago. We went to a big rally in Louisiana and the auditorium was filled with thousands of people, a lot of them evangelicals. Now, when I spoke to Paula White about this group of people in the United States, she says, 'Promises made, promises kept.' Mr Trump promised these evangelicals that he would appoint conservative judges. He did that. And that he would fight against what they see as these encroaching liberals and Democrats who are threatening to expand abortion rights and other things that are really important to evangelicals. She will make it clear that Mr Trump is on their side and that once again they should be backing him.*

Wafer wars

It was, of course, not enough to save Donald Trump from defeat at Joe Biden's hands in November 2020. But America's religious culture wars certainly did not end with Donald Trump's departure from the White House. Six months after taking office, the new president, a practising Catholic, came under fire over his position on the hottest of hot-button issues.

Emily Buchanan: *On Friday, tremors could be felt throughout the political fault lines of America's Catholic Church. A majority of members of the United States Conference of Catholic Bishops voted to go ahead with a process that could deny Holy Communion to those public officials who are at odds with the Church's teachings on issues like abortion. That could include President Biden, the nation's second Roman Catholic president. The decision even defied advice from the Vatican. Archbishop Joseph Naumann leads the Catholic Bishops' Committee on Pro-Life Activities and is one of President Biden's most vocal critics.*

Joseph Naumann: *It's a sad day for the nation, but it's a sad day, particularly for us as Catholics, to see a president who professes to be*

Catholic doing these things that are so contrary to our moral teaching. I think it's very contrary to what he campaigned on as being a unifying president. I mean, he's obviously in debt to pro-abortion forces within his party, and he's just conforming to them.

Emily Buchanan: *Well, I asked the religion journalist and author Sarah Posner to talk us through exactly what the Catholic bishops voted on and their arguments for it.*

Sarah Posner: *So they voted by a 168 to 55 vote in favour of just drafting what they call a formal document on the meaning of the Eucharist. And they've been talking about this for a while. The meaning of the Eucharist is that when somebody takes Communion, they're taking the literal body and blood of Christ, and they've been talking about doing such a document.*

But the way that they did it on Friday was making it clear that they were targeting politicians, particularly like US President Joe Biden who support abortion rights, and that politicians like that could be denied Communion by their bishop if the bishops pass it formally in their fall meeting in November, and if the Vatican approves it. And even still a local bishop could override it and let a politician or another person take Communion, even if they support abortion rights. So this is really about the traditionalists, the right wing, flexing their muscle here. It doesn't necessarily mean that Joe Biden will be denied Communion if he goes to Mass in Washington, D.C., where the bishop is opposed to this measure.

That extract is from a *Sunday* broadcast in June 2021, and the so-called 'wafer wars' have rumbled on ever since, most notably with the attempt to deny Communion to the House speaker, Nancy Pelosi, in May 2022.

Roe v. Wade

The following month, Christian evangelicals were delivered a dividend on their past support for Donald Trump. Unusually for a one-term president, Mr Trump had been able to appoint no fewer than three judges to the Supreme Court of the United States, fundamentally shifting the balance of the nine-member court. And in June 2022, the new, conservative-leaning court overturned the outcome of the case known as *Roe v. Wade*, the 1973 decision that guaranteed the right to abortion. *Sunday* reported the following on 26 June.

Emily Buchanan: Protests continue to rock America and abortion clinics are closing after Friday's Supreme Court ruling, which overturned the landmark Roe v. Wade *decision [of] fifty years ago. The change means individual states can now choose whether to allow terminations or not, and it means millions of women across the US have lost the legal right to abortion. President Biden has called the ruling painful and devastating for many Americans, and it's thrown up big questions about the role of religion in determining policy.*

The subsequent debate on the programme reflected some of the bitterness the issue of abortion has generated in the United States for so long. *Sunday* brought together Shawn Carney, the CEO and founder of 40 Days for Life, a pro-life campaigning group, and Rachel Laser, the president and CEO of Americans United for Separation of Church and State. Rachel Laser gave her reaction to the Supreme Court decision.

Rachel Laser: It is a complete insult to me as a woman. I'm also a mother. I have three children and two of them are girls. And I'm very concerned about the future and what it holds for women in this country, especially low-income women, women of colour, and women who are not capable of affording to work around whatever [abortion] bans might take place in this country.

But I'm also concerned, just as an American citizen and as a leader in the Church–state separation movement in this country, because Church–state separation is the guarantee of religious freedom. And religious freedom applies to all of us, not just some of us; not just far-right Christian extremists in this country. It applies to Jews whose religion tells them that they have to get an abortion if their lives are at risk. It applies to many Christians who also support abortion rights, and what we believe is what religious freedom in the First Amendment of our constitution promises all of us is the right to live and believe as we

300

choose, so long as you don't harm others. Because when you are harming others, you are imposing your religious beliefs on them through the government, and that takes away their religious freedom.

Emily Buchanan: *OK. Shawn Carney, how do you respond to that; that basically this new law is taking away the right to life and belief for those who don't necessarily share your beliefs?*

Shawn Carney: *This was expected. [The late] Ruth Bader Ginsburg* [a former Supreme Court judge known for her liberal views] *said that Roe was bad law. It was very bad law. They didn't just overturn Roe v. Wade. They beat it up with a baseball bat. We're dragging ourselves out of 1973 science and into 2022. This is a great day for women, for men, for all Americans.*

When you recognise the basic biological reality of another human being, when you recognise the dignity of another human being, you're not restricting their rights. You're actually making your country more free. There are 64 million abortions in America since we legalised it – 3,000 a day currently – and abortion advocates won't tell us if that's a good thing or a bad thing. Does the unborn child have a right to life? Why can't we abort a baby on the day of their birth? At thirty-nine weeks? At thirty-two weeks? Why do we regulate it? Why do we care about viability? We have lived in schizophrenia for nearly fifty years and the Supreme Court is getting us out of it.

Rachel Laser: *And I would just ask why you don't care about a ten-year-old who is raped by her father and who now will be forced to go forward [with] forced birth with her pregnancy. Why you don't care about a woman who was raped and who is in serious danger of having to go forward with psychological and physical trauma, really, with having the baby of her rapist. Why are those not concerns?*

Shawn Carney: *We work with a lot of rape victims, and we work with rape victims who buy the lie that somehow abortion is going to solve their problems. So you solve a tragedy with another tragedy. We work with rape victims who give their baby up for adoption. We work with rape victims who have had an abortion. And an abortion is not designed to heal these victims when they're vulnerable. So I don't like when people just throw that out there for shock value. It's not appropriate. And we work with rape victims. Y'all don't.*

301

Emily Buchanan: But what about the fundamental issue that the woman has the right to control what happens to her own body, and whether or not she decides to give birth or not?

Shawn Carney: Yeah, 'my body, my choice'. It's the oldest. It's the most washed-up argument. And the fact that there is somebody else is the problem. That's why they're seeking an abortion, because it's not their body. It's another body. It's their baby's body. That's why they want to end the life of that body.

So 'my body, my choice' is so lame, but it's also not how we operate. We've got to wear seatbelts. You know, we can't go streaking in the middle of the street. We don't act like this except when it comes to abortion. Abortion's been the most controversial issue of our time since it was legalised. We never got over it. We were never able to sleep at night. We kept moving the goal line of when you get your dignity, like you're a mutual fund [a professionally managed investment scheme] and you have more dignity over time. And we're getting out of the dehumanisation business. And it's the second time in our history we're doing it. It's a great day for America.

Rachel Laser: Friday's decision is an insult to women all across this country, and it's worse than that still. It is a huge danger sign about the state of our American experiment and American democracy... What religious freedom does is, it allows all of us to make our own decisions about our bodies according to our own belief systems. And as a Jewish woman, I am required to have an abortion if my life is at risk. This decision is a major blow to freedom and equality.

Shawn Carney: Alan Guttmacher [a prominent obstetrician and gynaecologist, and president of Planned Parenthood – now the largest provider of reproductive health services and abortions in the United States], *in 1962, said there's simply no medical condition where an abortion is going to save your life. All of this has nothing to do with religion. This is basic human decency.*

We don't act like this in our country, and we don't act like this in our day-to-day life. We don't let pregnant women get on a roller coaster. We just can't live in a fantasy world any more. We can't be schizophrenic and say, 'Hey, we're excited about your baby being born and we're going to throw a baby shower. And we know that you're having a boy or a

302

girl,' and over here say, 'Your baby has no rights whatsoever, and we can discard them in a brutal and barbaric fashion,' so we can act like, you know, life isn't there and there's no baby.

But this isn't, like, Shawn Carney or Catholics or Jews or Muslims saying life begins at conception. This is what medical textbooks tell us. Many of the few pro-abortion advocates who speak up at the local level are very ill-prepared for this moment because they haven't recognised a basic and beautiful human reality that is biological, not religious.

Emily Buchanan: OK. So, Rachel Laser, this beautiful human reality that Shawn is talking about, do you see that? How do you translate, I suppose, this ideal that all life will be saved into any kind of reality?

Rachel Laser: What I would say is, this is a win for far-right religious extremists in this country, and it's part of their agenda to undermine Church–state separation, which is foundational to our democracy. And it's hypocritical. It's gaslighting, because when you talk about lives at risk, the lives that are at risk are the lives of real women who are living and breathing and born in this country, and who have medical conditions that indicate against going forward with childbirth, which is more dangerous than abortion. And there are plenty of counterindications for pregnancy in this country. And it's also an insult to women's dignity and ability to participate as full citizens in our society.

The Capitol riot

The legacy of Donald Trump's close relationship with conservative evangelicals lingered on in other ways, too. When *Sunday* marked the anniversary of the storming of the Capitol by Trump supporters, William Crawley noted that: 'Live TV pictures of an unprecedented insurrection at the heart of the US legislative power system shocked the world. Some showed rioters carrying banners proclaiming "Jesus Saves" and "In God We Trust". Crosses were even erected by some in the crowd.'

The programme's guest on 22 January 2022 was Andrew Whitehead, co-author of *Taking America Back to God: Christian nationalism in the United States.*

Andrew Whitehead: Like many Americans, I watched the insurrection on TV. And while it was shocking to see the violence and the Christian symbols there, and then people kneeling in prayer, it wasn't surprising. Because as we tracked Christian nationalism here in the US, we knew and saw that their commitment to Trump and... [their belief] that he represented what they felt God desired for the country [meant] that they would be willing to do anything, even attack the Capitol, to ensure that he stayed in power.

Whitehead made a distinction between evangelicals and those he described as Christian nationalists. The latter group, he said, included 'white Catholics and white liberal Protestants and even Americans outside of religious traditions'. Christian nationalism was, he argued, a 'cultural framework' rather than an orthodox set of religious beliefs, and had its roots in the religious exceptionalism of the early American settlers – their belief that they had been sent by God with a mission for this new (to them) land.

So the conviction that, as Whitehead put it, this country is made for white Christians and that Christianity should be at the forefront could be traced back to the earliest colonial days. 'And Trump,' he concluded, 'is just part of that history.'

15

The Arab world after bin Laden

'For better or for worse – and most people in this country would certainly say for worse – Osama bin Laden was one of the most influential figures in his impact on religion to emerge this century,' *Sunday* declared on 8 May 2011. 'He changed the way Islam is seen and understood for millions of Muslims and non-Muslims, and the train of events set in motion by the bombings of September 11, 2001 has led to many thousands of deaths.'

The al-Qaeda leader had been shot and killed three days earlier by US Navy Seals at his compound in the city of Abbottabad, some thirty miles outside the Pakistani capital, Islamabad. The American raiding party flew his corpse back to Afghanistan – where US forces were then based – for identification. After Muslim burial rites were performed on the American aircraft carrier USS *Carl Vinson*, he was buried at sea – because according to American sources, no country would take his body – within twenty-four hours of his death.

Many Muslims were pleased by his removal from the scene. One of *Sunday*'s guests the following weekend, Dr Taj Hargey, the imam who chaired the Muslim Educational Centre in Oxford, gave him this damning obituary.

Taj Hargey: Well, he represents the Wahhabi and Salafi school of thought in Islam, which is a very rigid and narrow and ultra-conservative distortion of Islam. And as such, I think he has really contaminated and totally misunderstood the real ethos of a pluralistic and progressive Islam. So for me, al-Qaedaism and Osama bin Laden represent the Neanderthal aspect of Islam. And as such, I welcome his demise... it's highly significant that he's gone, because it shatters the illusions and the false dawn of al-Qaedaism... And he and his ilk... meaning the fellow travellers like the Wahhabis, the Salafis, the Deobandis [all fundamentalist schools of Islam, although many of their adherents would dispute this direct association with al-Qaeda] *and all the other groups that are aligned to this type of reaction in Islam, all of that now has been shown to be without divine invincibility. Because for decades now, the followers of al-Qaeda said that... 'God is protecting Osama bin Laden.' Where's that protection gone?*

Dr Hargey also suggested that bin Laden's death represented a 'golden opportunity for moderates and thinking Muslims', declaring: 'We need to set the agenda. They've been setting the agenda for the last ten to twenty years, and it's the moderate Islam, moderate Muslims, that need to set the agenda.'

President Obama, who ordered the raid on the compound in Abbottabad, had particular reason to celebrate its success. Osama bin Laden was killed just a few months before America marked the tenth anniversary of the 9/11 attacks. And in retrospect, that year (2011) appears to have been a turning point in developments right across the Middle East. All of them reflected, to varying degrees, the enduring regional impacts of that terrible day in New York a decade earlier.

Islamic State

In Iraq, 2011 saw the emergence of the Islamic State (IS) group as a real force. In February that year, Egypt's long-time leader, Hosni Mubarak, was driven from office, an event that led to what proved to be a bruising encounter between Islam and democracy. And protests in Syria the following month sent the country spiralling into its long civil war.

Islamic State – also known, at various stages in its development, as Islamic State of Iraq and the Levant; Islamic State of Iraq and Syria; and, by its Arabic abbreviation, Da'esh – emerged from the violence and chaos that followed the American and British invasion of Iraq in 2003. The group was noted for its brutality from its earliest days, and also for its sectarian character – directing its violence as much against Shia Iraqis as against the foreign invaders.

As the Middle East scholar Fawaz Gerges told *Sunday* in a later (2013) interview, the spread of sectarianism – mostly between Sunni and Shia

Muslims, but also extending to other, minority, religious groups in the region – was one of the many unintended consequences of the invasion of Iraq. Professor Gerges, a senior academic at the London School of Economics, argued on the programme that:

The Iraq War was pivotal. The Iraq War turned into sectarian strife. It poured gasoline on a raging fire. In fact, after 2003 it [sectarianism] spread to Bahrain, it spread to the Gulf, it spread to Lebanon, it spread to Syria. So foreign intervention unwittingly, indirectly, played a key role in... creating insecurities and fears in many Muslim countries.

In his 2017 book *ISIS: A history,* Professor Gerges argues that the authoritarian behaviour of the Iraqi prime minister Nouri al-Maliki, a member of the country's majority Shia community, played a significant role in Islamic State's rise. In the early months of 2011, Baghdad saw huge anti-government protests – similar to those in other Arab capitals – and dissatisfaction with the al-Maliki regime was especially strong among Iraq's minority Sunni population. Professor Gerges argues that Islamic State built its support on the back of this discontent, in part by 'reconnect[ing] with the Sunni rural community by allying, for a time, with local groups and militias.'[1]

In 2014, IS claimed international attention when it took a swathe of territory in the north of Iraq from the Iraqi army. It pushed forward in Syria, too, and at the height of its success it controlled an area that Gerges describes as 'as large as the United Kingdom, with a population estimated at between 6 million and 9 million people'. It could also call on 'a sectarian army numbering more than thirty thousand combatants.'[2]

Mosul

One of the biggest prizes taken by the group was the Iraqi city of Mosul – better known to Bible readers as Nineveh – famed for its association with the prophet Jonah and his three days in the belly of a great fish. There had

---

1 F. Gerges, *ISIS: A history* (Princeton, NJ: Princeton University Press, 2017), p. 1.
2 All quotes in this paragraph are from F. Gerges, *ISIS*, p. 1.

been a large and very ancient Christian community based in Mosul and the surrounding area, and in July 2011 *Sunday* reported on its fate. The testimony came courtesy of an extremely courageous piece of journalistic enterprise on the part of BBC reporter Jiyar Gol.

Edward Stourton: *The old Ottoman Empire used to have a system known as* dhimma *for managing minorities like Christians. The Christians had to pay a special religious levy, and there were restrictions on their rights. A return to that system is, it seems, one of the options being offered to Christians in the Iraqi city of Mosul, which is now under the control of the militant Sunni Muslim group ISIS. The other two options are conversion to Islam and death. The BBC's Jiyar Gol has just been to the area around Mosul, and he joins us now from Istanbul. Jiyar, it's a very dangerous area. How close to the city did you manage to get, and what did you manage to see?*

Jiyar Gol: *Well, we went to the region called Qaraqosh and al-Hamdaniya. Of course, we were escorted with the Kurdish security forces, Peshmerga. We managed to get close, somewhere around ten kilometres to the city of Mosul... We were in Mosul District, but the region where we were is predominantly Christians. The city of al-Hamdaniya was 200 to 300 metres away from the frontline. Almost ninety-five per cent, according to security forces, were Christians – pretty much Assyrian, Chaldean and Armenian. Many different sects were living in this city, and I managed to go to the front line.*

And the Kurdish Peshmerga, they showed me the position of ISIS – some buildings just a few hundred metres away from the front line behind Kurdish security forces bunkers. I could see their black flags flying overhead, and from a distance, on some roads, some people were walking on foot toward the Kurdish position.

Edward Stourton: *And what sort of things did Christians that you could talk to tell you about what was happening?*

Jiyar Gol: *Well, they said when ISIS on the 10th of June initially captured the city, it seems... they were kind to them. They seemed to be... after police, security forces and those government officials. And they said... 'You can stay in your home.' And even those people who left the city at the beginning, many of them returned to their homes. But... suddenly this issue came up.*

And on Friday, just a week ago, they issued a fatwa: convert, leave the city or face death. So many people said they were forced out.

Jiyar Gol explained that the IS fighters had demanded the payment of *jizya*, the tax levied on non-Muslims under the old *dhimma* system, from Christians. Some Christian houses, he said, were looted by the militants, while others were marked with the word *Naṣrānī*, the Arabic for 'Christian', after being inspected:

So they were going neighbourhood by neighbourhood, warning them, 'If you don't leave, you will face death, or if you don't convert to Islam, you face death or you have to leave the city.' So that's why many people left. And of course, at some of the monasteries, like [Mar] Behnam Monastery – from the fourth century, a very old one... the monks were forced to leave. They just could take their clothes. In many places... churches have been converted to mosques, or they have replaced the statues of Virgin Mary and the crosses with ISIS flags.

The persecution of Christians by Islamic State was soon picked up by Christian leaders outside Iraq. On 17 July, *Sunday* reported outraged reaction from senior leaders in the Church of England.

William Crawley: *The bishop of Leeds, Nick Baines, has launched a scathing attack on David Cameron's handling of the Iraq crisis. He questions whether there's a coherent strategy by the British government in response to the dire situation facing Iraqi Christians being targeted by the Islamic State terror group.*

In a letter to the prime minister published in today's Observer, *and written with the support of the archbishop of Canterbury, Justin Welby, Nick Baines condemns what he calls the silence of the UK government and its failure to offer sanctuary to Iraqi Christians fleeing from their homes. Addressing the prime minister directly, he writes, 'Does your government have a coherent response to the plight of these huge numbers of Christians whose plight appears to be less regarded than that of others?'*

Another senior cleric, David Walker, bishop of Manchester, came into the studio to voice his concerns. 'We see no coherent response to the ISIS movements in northern Iraq,' he said. 'We see communities being forcibly evicted from their homelands, where they've lived for many centuries. We see them struggling to find other places in the vicinity to settle.'

On the same programme, Caroline Wyatt – later a BBC religious affairs correspondent and *Sunday* presenter – gave an update from near Erbil, the northern city closest to the front line with Islamic State:

So first it was the Christians from Qaraqosh who fled, who came mainly to Erbil, but also to other smaller towns and villages beyond Mosul as the fighters took that town. That was a place where people had coexisted for centuries, quite happily together. We've been told by refugees who've come from there that now churches in Mosul are being destroyed. The wrong kind of mosques, as the Islamic State sees it, are being destroyed. And it is no longer a place where people can live together in peace.

Wyatt also recorded that many of the Christian refugees she spoke to felt they had been abandoned by the outside world:

We talked to many of those refugees; a lot of families living out in gardens, parks, dilapidated buildings, schools – which works until the school term comes back again – and pretty much everyone we spoke to of the Christian community here said they wanted asylum, but they no longer felt safe within Iraq. They no longer thought they had a safe haven; not least because while they had fled to safety in Erbil, just forty kilometres down the road are Islamic State fighters. And the Peshmerga, the Kurdish fighters, had not been able to hold them back...

I thought one of the interesting things was that talking to... any of these refugees here, they feel that, despite the fact that the West feels that it has done quite a lot so far, they feel that's not nearly enough. This is just the beginning, and they worry that this will be a long-term problem. And you are talking about something like 130,000 Christians who've been displaced – some 70,000 of them living in Erbil, some 60,000 beyond Mosul. These are a huge number of families with very young children who cannot live in those sorts of conditions for that much longer.

More persecution

Christians were not the only minority to suffer with the arrival of IS. The area around Mosul is also home to members of the Yazidi religion, an ancient monotheistic faith with its roots in pre-Zoroastrian Iran. Many Muslims regard Yazidis as devil worshippers, so they were treated especially harshly by the IS fighters. On 14 August, *Sunday* broadcast the testimony of a Yazidi living abroad, who described what had happened to his family:

Four of my uncles and their families, they are fleeing to Turkey now, and they're trying to cross the border. From every village of the Yazidis they are fleeing. It's like what happened 400 years ago in Turkey [the Yazidis faced an onslaught by Ottoman troops in the mid-seventeenth century]. Our history in Iraq and Kurdistan is going to be vanished. Everyone has fled. And those who cannot, they are dying in the mountains... It's a complete genocide. It's like Holocaust.

The reference to people 'dying in the mountains' related to what became known as the Sinjar massacre. After IS took the town of Sinjar at the beginning of August, some 50,000 Yazidis fled into the mountains, where they were trapped without food or water. Overall, it is estimated that some 5,000 Yazidi civilians were killed, and hundreds of women were abducted and taken as slaves.

In November that year, *Sunday* broadcast a first-hand and especially vivid account of the way IS treated Christians. Fr Jacques Mourad, a Catholic priest, was kidnapped by IS militants from his monastery in the area of Syria controlled by the group. He was held for several months before escaping and fleeing the country. His monastery, some 1,500 years old and an important pilgrimage site, was destroyed by IS.

As the BBC reporter Sima Kotecha explained when she introduced his interview, he was being looked after by a British academic on his visit to the United Kingdom: 'He's been friends with Exeter University professor Emma Loosley for twenty years. They met when she volunteered in his monastery. He doesn't speak English, so she's translated our interview with him.'

Emma Loosley (translation of Fr Jacques Mourad's words in first person):
I lived in a monastery called Mar Elian, or St Julien, in al-Qaryatayn, in the Syrian desert. And on the 21st of May last year, a group of jihadists from ISIS came, and they took me away, along with a man from Aleppo who was living and working with me as a volunteer in the monastery. They put us in the monastery car, and for four days we travelled across the desert. After four days we arrived in Raqqa [which IS declared its capital], where they held us for the next three months. We were tied up. We had blindfolds over our eyes, and they were trying to frighten us all the time with their words, threatening us. And we really thought during these four days – a lot of the time they just kept us locked alone in the car – that our lives had come to an end.

Sima Kotecha: When you got to Raqqa, can you describe what happened then?

Emma Loosley (translation, switching from the first to the third person):
By the time they reached Raqqa, having not eaten, having not drunk, having been in this situation for these four days, locked in the car, he kind of felt calm – that they'd finally arrived, that they finally got somewhere. And he just thought, 'This is it. They're going to cut my head off here.'

Sima Kotecha: How were you treated by the captors when you were detained?

Emma Loosley (third-person translation): When they arrived, they were... locked in this small bathroom with an iron door. They spent the first two days cleaning it because it was disgusting. It was so dirty. Someone would come and be horrible... and make threats. And then another person would arrive who'd be much less harsh, who'd be more friendly towards them. And this was a kind of routine after they were put in the bathroom.

Emma Loosley (first-person translation): *In this dreadful period, the one thing that really helped me was prayer. And out of this prayer, the thing that was most important, that helped me the most, was a strong feeling of being close to the Virgin Mary.*

Sima Kotecha: *Did ISIS ever put any pressure on you to convert to Islam?*

Emma Loosley (first-person translation): *Yes, they were constantly forcing [us], trying to make [us] convert, and they always returned to the same refrain, which was: 'If you don't convert to Islam, we're going to cut your heads off.' Obviously, to begin with, it was really frightening... imagining the moment they put the knife against your neck. But by about the eighth day, something changed in my soul.*

Sima Kotecha: *You must have experienced some incredibly dark moments. Are you able to convey how you were feeling during those times?*

Emma Loosley (first-person translation): *On the 11th of August, they took us to Palmyra* [the famous archaeological site in the Syrian desert, many parts of which were destroyed by IS during their occupation], *and what we didn't know was [that], several days before, they had taken 250 Christians from the parish of al-Qaryatayn hostage, and they were there in Palmyra as well.*

They opened the door to this prison, this big iron door. And I was really shocked because I saw everybody from my parish there. They'd taken every person from the elderly to the new babies, young children, men, women. And that was the worst moment of my life.

Sima Kotecha: *Then something extraordinary happened, didn't it? Because, well, I'll leave it to you to explain.*

Emma Loosley (first-person translation): *After three weeks in the prison, on the 1st of September, they took us back to al-Qaryatayn because they had received an order from [Abu Bakr] al-Baghdadi, the emir of ISIS, saying that the Christians were to be released and sent back to their homes – but on the understanding that they remain within the territory of the so-called caliphate. They were not to leave ISIS's territory.*

Emma Loosley (third-person translation): *Jacques asked, 'Why are we being set free?' And the envoy from Baghdadi took him to a small room and he said the official reason they were given was that the Christians of al-Qaryatayn had not taken up weapons against the Islamic State. And so for this reason, they were being allowed to return to their homes.*

Sima Kotecha: *So how did you eventually escape that hold of ISIS?*

Emma Loosley (first-person translation): *On the fortieth day, I felt I had to do something. I had to get out. So I spoke with a Muslim friend of mine who had been helping me, and he and many other Muslim friends had been trying to help their Christian friends and neighbours in any way they could, quietly. So I spoke to him and said I needed to get out. He took me on the back of his motorbike.*

Emma Loosley (third-person translation): *And they made it across the desert to a government checkpoint. And he left Jacques there, and from there Jacques was able to get to* [the Syrian city of] *Homs.*

Egypt

Events in Egypt during these early years of the century's second decade moved just as swiftly as they did in Iraq. Some 50,000 demonstrators gathered in Cairo's Tahrir Square on 25 January 2011, and the numbers steadily increased, despite the best efforts of pro-President Hosni Mubarak forces to disrupt the demonstrations. By early February, the protestors could be counted in the hundreds of thousands (there is some doubt as to whether the number ever reached 1 million, as reported at the time), and on 11 February President Mubarak stood down, handing over power to a military council. He had ruled the country for just short of thirty years, and the way he was driven from office was widely interpreted as evidence of the power of the democratic drive behind what became known as the Arab Spring.

The following month, a special edition of *Sunday* dedicated to the bigger questions raised by the country's revolution was broadcast live from the Egyptian capital; 'For centuries,' Edward Stourton declared in the headlines, 'this country was a great power in the Middle East. It's playing a decisive role in the Muslim world again today. Will Arabs finally control their own destiny? ...Or will the Arab revolutions be marred by fundamentalism and sectarian conflict?'

The programme began at the heart of the revolution.

Edward Stourton: *If you sit in the sunshine in Tahrir Square today, there's very little to evoke the extraordinary drama that unfolded here last* month. *President Mubarak's old party headquarters are still a burnt-out shell on one side of the square, but the traffic's moving freely and it's business as usual. But of course, what happened here was momentous, and people are still trying to digest the implications. I'm with two people who were in the square during the protest: Sally Zohney from the organisation Egyptian Women for Change; and Ethar El-Katatney, who's doing a course in journalism at the moment. I'd like to ask you both about the significance of what happened here, and particularly about the role of women. Sally, beginning with you.*

Sally Zohney: *People lived here for eighteen days with their families, with everything they needed. There were hospitals, there were people taking care of children, there was an art section, there was everything. It was like an independent republic.*

Edward Stourton: *Ethar, what did you feel about the way women were involved in this process?*

Ethar El-Katatney: *I think one of the most unique photos perhaps to come out of it was women praying right next to men... [because usually] there's so much sexual harassment. You know, a study by the Egyptian Centre for Women's Rights a couple of years ago found out that at least eighty per cent of Egyptian women are harassed, while seventy per cent of them are veiled. So to see that in Tahrir and none of that was in place, this was very inspirational.*

Edward Stourton: *Sally, I saw you nodding there. Did you find that you were treated differently as a woman here from the way that you generally were in society before it all happened?*

Sally Zohney: *I can say I was treated as Sally. Everyone here was on [an] equal foot[ing]. That was huge. That was a milestone.*

Edward Stourton: *Nevertheless, you took part in what was billed as a million-woman march in the square a couple of weeks ago. After it was all over you were harassed, you were shouted at. I think you were attacked. What does that tell us?*

Sally Zohney: *What happened was, on March 8th, a lot of women decided to celebrate the International Women's Day together, with no demands. Yes, it was brutal, it was a bit violent, but it shows what we need to work on. If we are calling for women's rights, you can't just be utopian and say 'We changed, we're fine, it's over.'*

Edward Stourton: I suppose, Ethar, the other question it raises is: how much really did change?

Ethar El-Katatney: I was disappointed. I thought there would be more change. But again, it's also important to point out that there were a lot of men there who were supporting women. They were just drowned out in all the voices. Change isn't going to come overnight. We have to be patient.

Despite her recognition that Egypt was a long way from a 'utopian' future, Sally Zohney's optimism was infectious. She declared: 'We have revolution now. You can say whatever you want, and you can never say to anyone, "You can't say this" or "You should change the way you think" or "You should not touch that topic". She added: 'It's exciting. Of course, it's scary, but it's all for a good end.'

Coptic Christians

But *Sunday* also reported that some groups were more scared than hopeful. The Coptic Christian Church has been established in Egypt since antiquity – long before the arrival of Islam – and it is estimated that Copts make up around ten per cent of the population. In the period leading up to the country's revolution, the Coptic minority faced a number of brutal attacks.

On Christmas Eve 2010, a gunman fired on a Coptic church in Upper Egypt, killing seven people, and that incident was followed in short order by the deadliest act of violence against the Copts in a decade. On New Year's Day an explosive device was detonated – possibly by a suicide bomber – as worshippers left the Church of the Saints, St Mark and Pope Peter, in Alexandria, killing twenty-three. And just before *Sunday*'s Cairo broadcast there was an anti-Christian riot in one of the capital's poorest districts.

Edward Stourton: The trouble happened in a scruffy suburb of Cairo. And the Christians here support themselves almost entirely by managing the vast quantities of rubbish produced by Cairo's 15 million or so inhabitants. Garbage is to Manshiyat Naser what steel once was to

Sheffield or coal was to Newcastle. It's an extraordinary sight. There's a truck ahead of us which has got so much garbage stacked on top of it, wrapped in bags, that it's almost hitting the second-storey windows of the houses it's passing, and it's at a perilous angle. Looks as if it could fall over at any moment. And every shop you look into, every house you look into, seems to have garbage stacked high inside it.

A local Coptic journalist explained (in translation) what had happened.

Journalist: Two Tuesdays ago, the Copts of this area and some Muslims came out protesting in solidarity [with] a church that was burned. And they went out protesting against what happened. Although it was a peaceful demonstration at the beginning and they just blocked the road, tensions started to rise between the protesters and some of the drivers who were on the road.

Then one of the drivers went to a nearby, heavily populated, area and he started saying that the Copts have kidnapped three Muslim girls, and they are moving towards burning some mosques in neighbouring areas.

Ten people, nine of them Copts, were killed in the violence that followed.

The Copts were right to worry about an upsurge in sectarian violence in the wake of Egypt's revolution. There was an unusually high level of attacks against them, their churches and their property in 2011. The community's leaders were also concerned about the role Egypt's Muslim Brotherhood might play in a post-Mubarak Egypt. Youssef Sidhom, editor-in-chief of the Coptic newspaper *Watani*, told *Sunday*: 'There is a wide area of mistrust concerning the political agenda of the Islamic Brotherhood group. They swing between fundamentalist strategies and very good, kind-hearted, patriotic strategies. And there lies the area of mistrust. I don't accuse them, but I don't trust them.'

Political Islam

The Muslim Brotherhood can lay claim to being the granddaddy of political Islam. Founded in 1928 by Hassan al-Banna, a schoolteacher, it was dedicated to the proposition that private and public life should both be regulated by sharia, the traditional body of Islamic law. The movement was originally focused on educational and charitable work, but soon became involved in politics, and it grew quickly – partly as a reaction against the spread of Western influence under British rule.

Both the British and the nationalist government of Gamal Abdel Nasser tried – unsuccessfully – to contain it. In 1966, under Nasser, one of the Brotherhood's most important thinkers, Sayyid Qutb, was first imprisoned and then hanged, accused of trying to overthrow the state. His death gave him the status of a martyr, and his ideas – including his advocacy of violent jihad – became hugely influential throughout the Middle East. Qutb has been described as the 'father of Salafi jihadism', and his books provided a foundation for the ideology of groups such as al-Qaeda.

The Muslim Brotherhood did not play a central role in the demonstrations that drove Hosni Mubarak from power, but it was formally legalised after his departure, and very quickly established itself as the largest and most organised political force in the new Egypt. In the immediate aftermath of the revolution, the Brotherhood was coy about its plans. A representative who spoke to *Sunday* refused to be drawn, even on the question of Islam's place in the country's new constitution, stating only that: 'We do believe in a civil state, and we believe everybody should be equal. But [at] the same time, our community has to express about its identity – without putting anybody on the side or ignoring anybody.'

Many Egyptian secularists – including some of those behind the Tahrir Square demonstrations – feared that if the country went to early elections the Brotherhood would use its well-organised network to secure power, and then hijack the country's hard-won democracy to impose an Islamist agenda.

But Tarek Osman, the author of *Egypt on the Brink*, a history of modern Egypt, told *Sunday* the challenge faced by those aspiring to a secular future was much deeper: 'The problem... in Egypt,' he predicted, 'is that however many votes you have over the next few years, it will most likely yield a significant percentage – I'm not saying a majority, but a significant percentage – for political Islam in a freely elected parliament.'

When the first parliamentary elections took place in December that year, the Brotherhood – running under the name of the Freedom and

Justice Party – duly showed their strength. *Sunday* returned to the story as the votes were being counted.

Edward Stourton: *The results of Egypt's first post-revolutionary parliamentary elections have been slow in coming through, and there are more rounds of voting yet to be held. But it now seems clear that Islamist parties will dominate the new People's Assembly, or lower house, when it meets. Reports say the Freedom and Justice Party, which represents the veteran Muslim Brotherhood movement, may have picked up as much as forty per cent of the vote. And candidates inspired by Salafism – an especially austere and culturally conservative form of Islam – have done well, too.*

The make-up of the parliament is critical to Egypt's long-term political future, because it will appoint a committee to draft a new constitution. Dr Omar Ashour is the director of Middle East Studies at Exeter University, and he has been in Cairo for the elections. Good morning.

Omar Ashour: *Good morning.*

Edward Stourton: *Were you surprised by the strength of the showing for Islamist parties? Because I suspect that many people in the West were.*

Omar Ashour: *No, I wasn't surprised at all. For the Muslim Brothers, that was expected. They aimed for around forty per cent of the parliamentary seats, and I think they probably will get what they aim for. This is the most organised of the political parties. It is the most organised political organisation in the country, and has a history of more than eighty years. They have a very complex network of social services and charity works, and have been the largest opposition in the country in the last twenty or thirty years.*

For the Salafi parties, it's different... They have strongholds in various areas outside of Cairo, especially in the Delta area. But the only thing is that they lack organisation, they lack political experience. They haven't participated in electoral politics before in Egypt, and mostly they were apolitical and decentralised.

Edward Stourton: *I was going to ask about that. I mean, correct me if I'm wrong, but I understood that Salafism has been somewhat suspicious of democracy as a political system in the past.*

Omar Ashour: Yeah, that's correct. Their stance is quite pragmatic. Before the revolution, many of the Salafi groups, especially the al-Nour Party, which now has around twenty per cent [of the vote] in the first phase, they were against the revolution. They were more or less saying that Mubarak is a legitimate ruler, and they were against the idea of being politicised in general. But after the revolution they decided to enter electoral politics.

A voting dilemma

By the time a presidential election was held the following summer, Egyptian politics had become polarised. The second round of voting saw the Muslim Brotherhood candidate, Mohamed Morsi, face Ahmed Shafiq, who had been Mubarak's last prime minister and was close to the army council, which had been running the country. The choice left many of Egypt's liberal secularists – those who drove the revolution – feeling disenfranchised.

Speaking on *Sunday* on 17 June 2012, Mariz Tadros, an Egyptian and a fellow of the Institute of Development Studies at the University of Sussex, explained the dilemma facing many voters.

Mariz Tadros: Well, on the one hand this is a very exciting moment. [For] the first time in its 5,000-year history, Egyptians are choosing their leader. On the other hand, the conditions under which they are exercising this choice are not entirely free. There's been a monopolisation of political power since the ousting of Mubarak between the army and the Islamists, leading to a very, very extreme case of political polarisation. And on the other hand, also, it's happening under a situation of extreme political insecurity. People just don't know what to expect any more.

Edward Stourton: What about the position of minorities? You are a member, I think, of the Coptic Christian minority. How are they likely to vote today?

Mariz Tadros: Well, I think part of the Coptic Egyptian population were part of the revolutionary movements. They played a key role in contributing or taking part in the uprisings that led to the ousting of

President Mubarak. And so I think, like some of the other revolutionary coalitions, they are likely to refrain from voting.

The prize went to the Muslim Brotherhood's Mohamed Morsi. His victory – by a modest margin – made him the first Islamist in the Arab world to win a democratic election. But many voters stayed at home, as Mariz Tadros had predicted. The turnout was just fifty-two per cent.

If all those abstentions reflected widespread scepticism about putting the Brotherhood in power, Mohamed Morsi very soon turned that into outright opposition by the way he governed. The following report was broadcast in September 2012.

William Crawley: *Egypt's president, Mohamed Morsi, is in a constitutional standoff with the country's judges after issuing a decree granting himself extensive new powers and banning all challenges to his decisions and laws. And there are concerns that the crisis could lead to a battle between Islamists and other religious and secularist groups. Our correspondent in Cairo is Jon Leyne. He joins me now. Jon, good morning. Tell us more about these powers the president has taken [upon] himself.*

Jon Leyne: *Well, if you look on the face of it, he really granted himself absolute power, because he's said the courts cannot challenge anything he does... Specifically, he's also sacked the prosecutor general, who's supposed to be, the judges would say, appointed by them not by him, and replaced the prosecutor general. But also, he said that the courts can't dissolve the assembly that's writing a new constitution, as they have done once before.*

Now, why does that become a sectarian issue? Firstly, obviously, because he is from the Muslim Brotherhood, the largest Islamist group here in Egypt, and the move is supported by other Islamists, such as the Salafists. But secondly, particularly because they're right at the key point of writing the constitution, and already that's divided on sectarian lines, or Islamist versus secularist lines. The liberals and representatives of Christian churches here have pulled out of that assembly, and a lot of people think that the president is trying to push through a very Islamist agenda in the constitution and turn this into more of – not completely, but more of – an Islamic republic.

William Crawley: *Ten per cent of the Egyptian population are members of the Coptic Orthodox Church. How is it likely to affect them?*

Jon Leyne: *Well until now, despite the fact the Muslim Brotherhood are a big political force, politics hasn't been sectarian or cut down the line between Islamists and secularists. For example, in the presidential election, quite a few liberals voted for Mohamed Morsi because, of course, the only alternative was a former general from the old system. So they chose him as the revolutionary candidate, even if they weren't in favour of Islamism.*

Well, now I think that dividing line is becoming much clearer. It is becoming Islamists on one side versus liberals, secularists and particularly Christians as well, on the other side. And of course, that is a very dangerous split, potentially. A lot of the protesters I've seen in the last couple of days have been chanting against the Ikhwān, against the Muslim Brotherhood – not just against Mohamed Morsi, but against the Brotherhood in particular, saying, 'We don't want to be ruled by this group, a takeover by this ideology.'

William Crawley: *President Morsi says he's doing this to protect the revolution. Others will say he's looking more like a dictator by doing so. What's been the reaction to this decision amongst judges, political groups, human rights campaigners?*

Jon Leyne: *Absolute fury, particularly by the judges. I was in a mass meeting of them yesterday – a huge great hall in the law courts with thousands of judges and lawyers and court workers there. I guess [there is] worry for their jobs, apart from anything else, because they're being put out of a job if he says they can't do anything. But also, the human rights groups have been very vociferous, as have foreign governments, including the United States... So very, very strong reaction indeed.*

'Winning the country back'

The end of this experimental Islamist government was swift and brutal. After mass protests at the end of June, on 3 July 2013, just over a year after taking office, Mohamed Morsi was removed in a coup led by Abdel Fattah el-Sisi, a former deputy prime minister and retired army general (he soon promoted himself to the rank of field marshal). And as *Sunday* reported on 14 July, the new regime immediately went after the country's former rulers.

Edward Stourton: *The way the authorities in Egypt have been trying to hunt down prominent members of the Muslim Brotherhood is prompting widespread international concern. Both the United Nations and the United States have urged restraint. But the public prosecutor's office in Cairo said this weekend that it's investigating the ousted president Mohamed Morsi and other senior Brotherhood members over complaints of spying and incitement to kill protesters.*

Reporting from Cairo, the BBC's Andrew Hosken found that although this was unquestionably a coup, it was, among many people, a popular one.

Andrew Hosken: *For many Muslims who protested against the one-year rule of Morsi, the Brotherhood's type of Islamism has been insidious. Wearing her hijab, Asmir Zainam* [spelling uncertain], *who protested against President Mubarak two-and-a-half years ago, considered the Brotherhood almost an alien force in Islam.*

Asmir Zainam (translation): *It was Brotherhood-ising the nation and just taking over everything. So that's why the people were kind of occupied. We were occupied. And the people on the 30th of June took to the streets to win their country back.*

Andrew Hosken: *The Brotherhood experiment proves that religion and politics don't mix, according to Hisham Kassem, a leading publisher in Egypt and a secular Muslim.*

Hisham Kassem: *Well, the speculation is, do they stay out for another eight years or is this the end of the Brotherhood? But nobody sees a short-term comeback of them – in other words, something people like myself did bet on from the start. There's no such thing as political Islam, like there is no political Christianity or political Judaism or Buddhism. You know, politics is politics and religion is religion. And the Muslim Brotherhood have had their opportunity and failed miserably.*

The el-Sisi regime's crackdown on the Muslim Brotherhood was described as 'the worst for eight decades' by the BBC's Middle East editor Jeremy

Bowen, who reminded *Sunday* in August 2013 that the organisation has often proved resilient in the past:

> *The Brotherhood has a strong core of support. It has very deep roots in Egyptian society. It's been going since 1928. It is very well organised. It is accustomed to operating underground as well, and under great pressure from the government. Back in the fifties, Nasser was putting people from the Muslim Brotherhood in jail and executing them, too.*

Syria

Protests in Syria began in early March 2011, a month after the Tahrir Square demonstrations succeeded in toppling Hosni Mubarak. They started in the southern city of Daraa, sparked by the imprisonment of a group of young men who were arrested for anti-government graffiti.

The confrontations between demonstrators and the police very quickly escalated into serious violence. On 18 March, police fired live rounds into a crowd outside a mosque, killing four people. Two days later, protestors set fire to the local headquarters of the ruling Ba'ath Party, and in the battle that followed, seven police officers and fifteen protestors lost their lives. The unrest spread across the country, even touching the capital, Damascus.

The demonstrators' initial demands were for democratic reforms, but they soon began calling for the removal of the country's president, Bashar al-Assad. The Assad regime had been in place since Bashar's father, Hafez al-Assad, took power in 1971. In the course of the second half of 2011, opposition to Assad developed into an armed insurrection, and the regime responded with the full force of the military.

Sectarian strife

At the beginning of January 2012, *Sunday* explored the sectarian religious allegiances and sectarian divisions that had begun to emerge as significant factors in the conflict.

Edward Stourton: *The Turkish prime minister, Recep Erdoğan, warned this week that Syria is in danger of civil war if President Assad continues* *his crackdown on dissent. So where are the country's fault lines opening up? Dr Thomas Pierret lectures on Contemporary Islam at Edinburgh University. Dr Pierret, just take us through the way the population of Syria breaks down in terms of religion and ethnicity.*

Thomas Pierret: *So there is a very clear majority, around seventy-five per cent, of Sunni Muslim, and then quite [a] large number of different non-Sunni Muslim sects, like the Alawites – which is the community of President Bashar al-Assad... the largest non-Sunni Muslim community – with probably a bit less than ten per cent. And then a few per cent of Druze, Ismailis, Twelver Shiites. And then probably, we don't know, but eight per cent or ten per cent of Christians of various churches.*[3]

Edward Stourton: *So quite a complex picture. What is it about the way that President Assad is acting that makes people believe that it renders the possibility of civil war more likely?*

Thomas Pierret: *So officially, of course, the Syrian government pretends it represents the whole population, regardless of their religion. But the most loyal popular base of the regime is, of course, among the community of the president, the Alawites. And they've been mobilising. Of course, first they have been recruiting a very large number of Alawites in the security forces – well above their proportion of the population. They have also been recruiting civilian Alawites informally in kind of popular militias, which they call 'popular committees'. Giving them weapons in certain villages, spreading rumours and fears that Sunni insurgents are about to kill the Alawites in order to ensure the loyalty of this community. So it's a kind of dangerous policy.*

Edward Stourton: *Is there evidence that people are beginning to think of themselves more in terms of those separate identities, those religious identities, and less in terms of simply being Syrian?*

Thomas Pierret: *I would say this feeling of sectarian belonging, it has always been quite entrenched in Syria, but of course not in a militant fashion. Now in certain places – and especially in the city of Homs, in central Syria, which has sizable Sunni and Alawite populations – definitely there is something which is starting to look like sectarian strife in that region.*

---

3 Dr Pierret has acknowledged a mistake here. The proportion of Christians is, in fact, five per cent or less.

Edward Stourton: What about the position of Christians? We've just been discussing the future of Christians in the Middle East more generally, a moment or two ago, but what about specifically in Syria?

Thomas Pierret: I would say Christians are not involved in violence at the moment, neither as victims, nor are there very many Christians in the army, either. They are very afraid, of course, of the situation because of what they have seen in in Iraq during the last years. So I would say that there is probably a majority which is quite supportive of the regime among Christians.

On 25 May 2012, the opposition town of Houla was subjected to a three-hour artillery bombardment, which began at 1:15 p.m., immediately after Friday prayers. When the shelling stopped, Syrian government troops began to move into the town together with members of one of those 'popular committees' Dr Pierret referred to. Known as *Shabiha* (thugs), these Alawite-dominated militias were especially feared by opposition groups, and in Houla they lived up to their murderous reputation.

The Guardian published a story about a twenty-nine-year-old woman named Rasha al-Sayed Ali after the *Shabiha* broke into her home:

She displayed her father's military identity card and told the men that he was a retired soldier. She said one of the men then grabbed her by the scruff of the neck and pushed her and four other women who were in the house into the corner of a room while they beat her father.

'Then they brought my father into the room and shot him in front of us,' she said.

'I saw my father's brains spill from his head.' One of the security men fired his gun into the ceiling, she said, and shouted: 'We took revenge for you, Imam Ali' – a reference to the most revered imam of the Shia Islamic faith.

'They were security men and Shabiha,' she said. 'One of them then said to the other, what are we going to do with the children? The other replied shoot them before the elders.'

Sayed Ali was shot in the chest. 'I fell to the floor. After a while, I looked around to see that all my brothers and my mother were sinking in blood. I started to crawl and could hear the cry of my cousin who was only one month old. The baby's mother was dead. Four of my sisters and my pregnant sister-in-law were killed. So was our neighbour. My brother's baby was two months old and sleeping upstairs. They shot her too.'[4]

The United Nations reported that 108 people were killed, including thirty-four women and forty-nine children. On 3 June, in the aftermath of the massacre, *Sunday* spoke to the veteran BBC war correspondent Fergal Keane.

Samira Ahmed: *Yesterday saw further violence in Syria, and seven people were also killed in Lebanon in clashes linked to unrest across the border. Meanwhile, UN peace envoy Kofi Annan warned that the spectre of all-out civil war, with a worrying sectarian dimension, grows by the day. Earlier, I spoke to the BBC's correspondent Fergal Keane, and I asked him if the conflict is turning into a sectarian civil war.*

Fergal Keane: *I think from the point of view of the Assad regime, this is not about religion, it is about preserving its power. However, there are strong suggestions that elements of that regime have been provoking the sectarian element, and certainly the people of Houla – who suffered an attack from what are believed to have been Alawite militiamen during the week – they would certainly see themselves as victims, as targets of sectarianism.*

So, too, one must add, will be elements of the Alawite population and the Christian population, who have experienced attacks; nothing on the same scale as what's happened, of course, in Houla, but nonetheless a sense among some of the minorities in Syria that they are being marginalised because of their religion.

Samira Ahmed: *Is there a sense of who might be stoking the tensions here?*

Fergal Keane: *Certainly, earlier in this conflict one could talk about stoking tensions. I think it's now taken on its own momentum, and that's the tragic thing about sectarian warfare. I saw this myself while [I was] a*

---

4 M. Chulov and M. Mahmood, 'The Houla massacre: reconstructing the events of 25 May', *The Guardian*: https://www.theguardian.com/world/2012/jun/01/houla-massacre-reconstructing-25-may (1 June 2012, accessed 8 May 2023).

young reporter covering the situation in Northern Ireland. I've seen it myself in the Balkans and in other parts of the world, that once a conflict gains its own momentum, fear very often is what drives people out to kill; fear leading to hatred, leading to killing. The sense that, if you don't attack the opposing community, they're going to attack you; if you don't finish them off, they'll finish you off. Indeed, that was the language that was used in many of the sectarian and ethnic conflicts of the early 1990s.

At the time of writing, the number of deaths in the Syrian civil war stands in the hundreds of thousands. One organisation, the Syrian Observatory for Human Rights, puts the total at just over 600,000.[5]

A dangerous time for journalists

And reporting on the turmoil of these years in the Arab world has proved a deadly task for journalists. In 2022, the Reporters Without Borders organisation recorded that: 'The two countries with the highest death tolls [for journalists] are Iraq and Syria, with a combined total of 578 journalists killed in the past 20 years, or more than a third of the worldwide total.'[6]

In January 2019, *Sunday* broadcast a discussion on war reporting with the BBC's chief international correspondent Lyse Doucet, who has vast experience of covering conflict. She told the programme: 'The media watchdogs who put the numbers on this say it is the worst ever time to be a journalist.' The interview took place at St Bride's Church, just off Fleet Street, which is sometimes known as 'the journalists' church'.

Lyse Doucet: I have to comment, because a little part of me is quite overwhelmed because I'm standing right in front of this altar, and I can see the photographs next to the single flickering candle of the journalists who've been killed. And in the front row are people who were friends. Jamal Khashoggi from Saudi Arabia [murdered at the Saudi consulate

---

5 'Over 606,000 people killed across Syria since the beginning of the "Syrian Revolution", including 495,000 documented by SOHR', SOHR: https://www.syriahr.com/en/217360 (1 June 2021, accessed 16 June 2023).

6 '1,668 journalists killed in past 20 years (2003–2022), average of 80 per year', Reporters Without Borders: https://rsf.org/en/1668-journalists-killed-past-20-years-2003-2022-average-80-year (30 December 2022, accessed 8 May 2023).

in Istanbul in 2018]. *Rory Peck* [killed while filming the October Coup in Moscow in 1993]... *Marie Colvin* [killed while covering the siege of Homs in Syria in 2012]. *And then, to the side, John Cantlie, who's still taken hostage by Islamic State. And we hope against hope that he is still alive* [in 2022 Cantlie's family held a memorial service for him].

And I think this is one of the modern threats, being kidnapped. And when we've seen and spoken to friends who've gone through the months and months, sometimes years, in a dungeon, chained to each other, living in absolutely barbaric conditions, I think all of us go out hoping that, 'Oh, my God, may that not happen to me.' But it has happened to too many.

Edward Stourton: *We've talked about the impact on journalists, but what about the stories we try to cover? Is it fair to say, Lyse, that there are parts of the world which just aren't covered? I mean, you've worked a lot in Syria, but huge moments in that war just weren't covered.*

Lyse Doucet: *Huge swathes of Syria were not covered, or they weren't being covered by foreign journalists who came in. Syrian journalists... made the best of technology. They were covering their own story and they died. They were beheaded. They were executed. They were killed in that horrible word, 'crossfire', trying to tell the story of their family, their community and of their street.*

But there was a certain point at which journalists stopped going in from outside because the risk of kidnapping, of killing, was simply too high. And therefore, years went by where huge swathes of Syria, where huge issues of consequence for Syria – for the region, for the world – were happening, and we simply didn't have any eyes on them.

16

The struggle between Israel and the Palestinians

We have touched on the evidence that religion has disappeared from politics and the public conversation more generally in the United Kingdom. The conflict between Israel and the Palestinians is a striking example of a story that has developed in the opposite direction. What began as an essentially political struggle over land and sovereignty is increasingly coloured by religious passions on both sides.

Most early leaders of the Zionist Movement – including Theodor Herzl, regarded as the intellectual father of Zionism, and David Ben-Gurion, Israel's first prime minister – were secular Jews. But at the time of writing, Israel's Likud government, widely referred to as ultra-nationalist, is kept in power by religious parties – one of them explicitly called the Religious Zionist Party. And the settler movement now includes many Jews who lay claim to the lands of 'Judea and Samaria' (the West Bank) on the basis of the Hebrew Bible.

On the Palestinian side, Yasser Arafat's Fatah movement and the Palestinian Liberation Organization were originally secular and socialist, embracing Palestinian Christians as well as Muslims. Today, Fatah's authority is increasingly challenged by Hamas, which was founded as an offshoot of Egypt's Muslim Brotherhood (see chapter 15), and which is committed to establishing an Islamic state in what is now Israel. Palestinian Islamic Jihad, another organisation with historic links to the Brotherhood, has strongholds in both Gaza and the West Bank.

Jerusalem

The way politics and religion mix is especially apparent in Jerusalem. Both Israel and the Palestinians claim it as their capital, and the city of course has a special religious significance for both Jews and Muslims. In November 2011, *Sunday* tried to unravel the tangle of history and holy sites that makes the status of Jerusalem such an incendiary issue. The item was prompted by one of the regular eruptions of violence that disrupt the city's life.

Edward Stourton: *The status of Jerusalem has been one of the most sensitive issues in the Arab–Israeli conflict for nearly half a century, and the area of Jerusalem, which Muslims call the Haram al-Sharif and Jews call the Temple Mount, is central to the religious passions that have helped drive that conflict. The latest trouble over the site this past week came after Rabbi Yehudah Glick, who has campaigned for Jews to be allowed to pray there, was shot and wounded. The Palestinian man suspected of the shooting, Mutaz Hijazi, was later killed by Israeli police. Matthew Kalman is a commentator for the Israeli newspaper* Haaretz. *And just before we came on the air, he told me what's been happening in Jerusalem this week.*

Matthew Kalman: *Well, the Temple Mount over the last few days has been the focus of intense attention and violence following the shooting of a Jewish activist who was a campaigner for the rights of Jews to pray on the Temple Mount, which at the moment they're not allowed to do. Following that, the Israelis closed the Temple Mount, which is the first time it's been completely closed since 1967. It was only for a few hours, but it sparked a diplomatic protest and some violence here in Jerusalem. And then it was reopened. And Fatah, the main Palestinian group, called for a 'day of rage' on Friday, which didn't really happen, mainly because it was pouring with rain here. But there have been sporadic outbreaks of protest and violence around Jerusalem and around the Temple Mount... for the last few days.*

Edward Stourton: *The activist you mentioned, Rabbi Glick, has been campaigning for Jews, as you said, to be allowed to pray on the Temple Mount. Explain to us why that is such an incendiary suggestion.*

Matthew Kalman: *Well, the Temple Mount, originally, if you like, was a sacred place for Jews. It was the site of the temple of Solomon and then of Herod for several centuries. And then, in the sixth and seventh centuries, it was conquered by the Muslims. And they built the Al-Aqsa Mosque*

331

[the 'Noble Sanctuary'] *and the Dome of the Rock there. So since that period it's been holy to Muslims as the place where Muhammad ascended to heaven. Briefly, it was taken over by the Crusaders, who turned the Al-Aqsa Mosque into a church. It was then recaptured by the Muslims, and since then it's been under the control of the Waqf, which is the Islamic trust that controls the site.*

When the Israelis conquered the city of Jerusalem in 1967, there was a fierce debate as to whether or not they should destroy the Al-Aqsa Mosque or at least try and rebuild a temple... the third temple for Jews. But the decision was taken then not to do that, and to hand control internally back to the Islamic trust. But since then, various Jewish groups have said, 'Look, this is a Jewish holy site. We'd like to be allowed to pray there.' But Muslims have become increasingly angry at the idea that Jews should go and pray on this Islamic holy site. And it's become very mixed up with politics as well as religion.

Edward Stourton: *That campaign has been going on for a while now. Have things been heating up in recent months and years?*

Matthew Kalman: *Well, for the last few months – ever since July, and the murder of a Palestinian teenager, Mohammed Abu Khdeir* [a sixteen-year-old Palestinian who was abducted in East Jerusalem, beaten and set on fire, possibly while he was still alive] *– there have been increasing protests and violence in Jerusalem. More to do with politics than religion, but the Temple Mount or the 'Noble Sanctuary', as the Muslims call it, has been increasingly the focus of the political rivalry between Israel and the Palestinians over who controls Jerusalem and who controls these ancient holy sites. So whenever there's trouble here, it always focuses on the Al-Aqsa Mosque; on the Noble Sanctuary, the Temple Mount.*

Edward Stourton: *And history has plenty of warnings about how this sort of thing could develop, hasn't it? I mean, I'm thinking of Ariel Sharon's* [prime minister of Israel, 2001–06] *walk on the Temple Mount, the Haram al-Sharif, back in* [2000]*, which led to the Second Intifada* [Palestinian uprising].

Matthew Kalman: *Yes. Well, that walk in 2000... was one of the events that triggered the Second Intifada, which the Palestinians know as the 'Al-Aqsa Intifada'. And on top of that, there are always rumours from extremist Muslims that the Israelis are somehow tunnelling underneath* *the Temple Mount, trying to destroy the Al-Aqsa Mosque. They're not. But those rumours have enormous currency and enormous religious power.*

There is, of course, plenty of history to fight over in Jerusalem. Almost any big building project or archaeological excavation is likely to be fraught with political and religious passion. In July 2011, *Sunday* reported: 'After years of bitter legal wrangling, the Israeli government has approved a plan by an America-based Jewish group to erect a museum on the site of a Muslim cemetery in West Jerusalem.' The Simon Wiesenthal Center planned to erect a 'museum of tolerance' – an ironic name, as the programme's presenter Jane Little pointed out, because there was fierce Islamic opposition to the plans. Matthew Kalman explained why Muslims objected.

Matthew Kalman: They're angry because the site, which is known as the Mamilla Cemetery or the Ma'aman Allah Cemetery in West Jerusalem, is a disused cemetery. About fifty years ago, part of it was paved over for use as a municipal car park, and a road was paved through it at that time, to no opposition. But now the Simon Wiesenthal Center has decided to build what started out as a $200 million project (now a $100 million project because of the economic crisis) which has involved the removal of hundreds of ancient graves from underneath what had been paved over as a car park. So now certain Muslim groups are getting very, very annoyed, and went to Israel's Supreme Court in order to fight the plans for the museum, saying that this was a desecration of this ancient cemetery and that, of all places to build a 'museum of tolerance', this was the last place that they should build it.

Jane Little: But the Supreme Court ruled in favour of the museum on the basis of a Muslim judge's ruling a few years ago that the cemetery could be moved.

Matthew Kalman: They did. In 1964, a judge in the sharia court in Jaffa ruled that this cemetery was now disused and could be used for other purposes. There is a clause in Muslim law that allows that. And indeed, back in the 1930s, the Mufti of Jerusalem himself cut off part of the cemetery so that he could build The Palace Hotel. And then, later in the

1940s, the Mufti of Jerusalem himself again proposed that the cemetery should be used to build a university in Jerusalem. So there are precedents not just for Muslim cemeteries being used, but the Muslim authorities themselves using Muslim cemeteries after they've become disused for other purposes.

Christians in decline

Christianity's holy sites in Jerusalem do not rub up against their Muslim and Jewish neighbours in quite the same way. The Church of the Holy Sepulchre, where Jesus is said to have been crucified and buried, is the setting for numerous disputes, sometimes violent ones, but those usually occur between the various Christian denominations that share responsibility for the site. However, every square yard of land in Jerusalem is precious, and there are also plenty of tensions between Church leaders and Israeli authorities.

Jerusalem's nineteenth-century Anglican cathedral, St George's, would not look out of place in an English county town, but it stands on highly contested ground. St George's is in East Jerusalem, which was taken by Israel in the Six-Day War of 1967, and is still regarded as 'occupied land' by the international community. It is a short walk from the Damascus Gate entrance to the Old City, which has frequently been the focus for protests and sometimes violent confrontations between Palestinians and Israeli police and soldiers.

The Anglican Diocese of Jerusalem was founded by the English Church Missionary Society, but since 1976, St George's bishops have all been Palestinian. In March 2011, *Sunday* reported a story that illustrated how tense relations between the Church and the Israeli authorities could be.

Edward Stourton: *The Anglican bishop of Jerusalem is going to court over a decision by the Israeli authorities to refuse [the] renewal of his residency permit. The Right Revd Suheil Dawani was born in Nablus in the West Bank, but his cathedral, St George's, is in East Jerusalem, which was taken by Israel in the 1967 war. Bishop Dawani told me why he's pursuing the legal route.*

Suheil Dawani: *After the Israeli authorities revoked my temporary residency permit, we did our best to resolve it quietly for the last six months. But when we received no answer... we decided, after consultation with my legal adviser, that now I think it is about time to go to the Israeli court to resolve it.*

Edward Stourton: *The Israelis, when they wrote to you about your permit, said, and I'm quoting here, that you had 'acted with the Palestinian Authority in transferring lands owned by Jewish people to the Palestinians and also helped to register lands of Jewish people in the name of the Church', and a senior Israeli source has said to us that you are being investigated, and that's why they didn't give you a new permit. What's your response to that?*

Suheil Dawani: *Last August, when I received a letter from the Ministry of Interior, I wrote a letter to the minister of interior just denying all these false accusations against me. In no way I did forge any documents or transfer any Jewish land to the Palestinians. So this is, you know, not existing. That's why, you know, I sent a letter. I didn't receive any response.*

Edward Stourton: *They haven't questioned you or anything of that kind?*

Suheil Dawani: *No, no. Two or three people from the Ministry of Interior office, they came to the church office in Jerusalem and we talked for one hour. And I denied all these allegations against me, false allegations. And it seems that they've been convinced that what I've said, that it's true.*

Edward Stourton: *The Israelis also say they've been willing to give you a work permit, just not a residency permit. But you won't accept that.*

Suheil Dawani: *No, they offered me A/3. A/3 is a visa permit for foreigners. And I told them that I am not a foreigner. I am an indigenous Christian who lives in this land all the time. I think this is very insulting to me to give me A/3 as if I am, you know, coming from somewhere else.*

Edward Stourton: *So what is your position at the moment? You presumably are liable to be arrested and deported at any time, in theory at least?*

Suheil Dawani: *Well, I can say that, according to the Israelis, I am an illegal citizen of the city of Jerusalem because I have no legal status in Jerusalem after they revoked my residency. So at any time they can come and ask me to leave, or maybe they cannot let me get into the city any time they want. So I am in a situation of insecurity.*

In September 2011, Bishop Dawani was finally granted a residency permit.

In January the following year, *Sunday* explored the wider pressure on Christians. It was estimated that Christians accounted for around two per cent of the population of Israel, the West Bank and Gaza (some 200,000 people), and, as William Crawley put it: 'What's not in doubt is that the number of local Palestinian Christians is in sharp decline.' Trevor Barnes reported from Jerusalem, where he interviewed Israel's deputy foreign minister Danny Ayalon.

Danny Ayalon: *It is very deplorable. The rights of minorities, especially Christians, in this region [have] been abused and [have] been deteriorating since the so-called Arab Spring began [see chapter 15]. This is something that is a concern for all of us. There is here more than just morality... there is a strategic interest for Israel to really make sure that Christian rights in the region will not be jeopardised.*

Trevor Barnes: *I'm in Beit Jala, one of the three villages that make up the district of Bethlehem some five miles outside Jerusalem. On this side of the valley is a scene that's probably not changed much for generations. On the other side, new buildings making up part of a Jewish settlement and, to the right, the concrete security barrier that's shortly to be making its way to just a few feet in front of where I'm standing. In the process, it will obliterate whole terraces of olive groves, fig trees and grapevines, and divide this farmer's land in two.*

Farmer: *We have... more than fifty Christian families living here in Beit Jala, and we are very afraid of the wall. This land is our future. It's our life. And when we lose it, so we will lose our life and our settlement. I am planning to leave this land and to go to any place, because there's no chance for a future, for life or for establishment here, because I am worried for my children.*

Trevor Barnes: *I put such concerns to the deputy foreign minister, Danny Ayalon. Rather than citing the Arab Spring as one of the reasons for the Christian exodus, ought not the Israeli government to be examining its own policies, in particular in places like Beit Jala – that of building a security barrier on Palestinian land?*

Danny Ayalon: *Well, the security barrier is just a means of security. Since it was built, it saved the lives of thousands of people: Israelis, Jewish* and non-Jewish. I can tell you that, so long as Israel was in control and the Jewish and Israeli rule was in Bethlehem, Bethlehem was a lively Christian town. Since we left, according to the interim Oslo agreement in '95, unfortunately the Christians have been driven out by those Palestinians who, gladly, of course, accuse Israel.

Trevor Barnes: While the Israeli government defends its policies on the grounds of security, Palestinians claim this is a smokescreen for the illegal appropriation of their land. And on this, as on so many other issues, there is no meeting of minds. But given that nobody doubts the fact of Christian emigration, what are its implications? Fr David Neuhaus is a Jewish convert to Catholicism and a Jesuit priest responsible for Hebrew-speaking Catholics in Israel.

David Neuhaus: Well, ultimately, that Christians will be more and more marginalised. Our mission does not only depend on how many we are; our mission depends on the quality of the presence that we can provide in a society that desperately needs the voice of the Christian community as a voice not only of political moderation, but a voice that speaks of values that are often lacking in other discourses in society.

Trevor Barnes: Some Christians also feel intimidated by the extremist ideologies of some of their Muslim neighbours – especially in Gaza, where Christians number less than one per cent of the population, being increasingly radicalised.

The US embassy move

Because areas of Jerusalem were taken by force and remain under occupation, most countries do not recognise the city as Israel's capital, and keep their embassies in Tel Aviv. But in the 2016 presidential election, Donald Trump campaigned on a promise to move America's embassy from Tel Aviv to Jerusalem. On 6 December 2017 – within a year of taking office – President Trump formally recognised Jerusalem as Israel's capital, and, as *Sunday* reported, part of the logic lay with the president's determination to cultivate an evangelical base (see chapter 14).

Edward Stourton: The Arab League has urged the United States to reverse its decision to recognise Jerusalem as the capital of Israel. The league's secretary general called the decision a dangerous violation of international law after an emergency meeting in Cairo. But how much did President Trump's decision have to do with religion as much as politics – if indeed you can separate those two things in the Middle East? Allison Kaplan Sommer has been writing about that question in the Israeli newspaper Haaretz. She's based in Israel, but is originally from the United States. Good morning.

Allison Kaplan Sommer: *Good morning. How are you?*

Edward Stourton: *I'm very well, thank you. And as I understand it, your message is, essentially, you believe that this was done to placate evangelical fundamentalists.*

Allison Kaplan Sommer: *Yes, it's very odd in the Middle East. We're used to things happening because of religion, but we're not as used to events occurring in the Middle East as a result of the domestic political agenda in the United States. And this move happened for a variety of reasons, but... I don't think it would have happened if the evangelical Christian community in the United States hadn't felt so strongly about it.*

Edward Stourton: *And you indeed link it very directly to the special Senate election, which is due in Alabama this week.*

Allison Kaplan Sommer: *Right. Well, the evangelical Christians need to turn out for that election. They need to vote for Roy Moore, the Republican candidate who's under the shadow of a sexual abuse of minors scandal. They need to turn out and vote, and they need to turn out enthusiastically. And Donald Trump is very popular there; he won overwhelmingly there in 2016, and he's thrown his support behind Roy Moore. And this move, recognising Jerusalem as the capital, is a very clear signal to the evangelicals in Alabama and elsewhere that he's their man and he's on their side.*

Edward Stourton: *Can you take us through the theological ideas which explain why this project is so dear to conservative evangelical hearts?*

Allison Kaplan Sommer: *Well, I'm no Christian theologian, but I'll do my best to summarise what I've learned... So apparently this is something that dates back to the nineteenth century that evolved among evangelical Christians in the United States around 1840. It's a belief in 'end of times'. The progression of events goes – and they find biblical sources to back up this theory – that when the Jews make Jerusalem the capital, it's going* to set off a chain of events that will have some sort of event that will be like an Armageddon-like event. Because God loves the Jews, eventually the Jews will convert to Christianity and all of the Christians will be delivered by the rapture up to heaven. Their bodies will be transformed, and sinners will be wiped off the earth. And then... Jesus Christ will return to the earth. And then there will be, I don't know, a thousand years, many years of celestial-type paradise, to come. That is how I understand the progression of events. And it sounds absurd to many of us, but apparently millions of American evangelical Christians are brought up on this theology, which has been popularised by a set of novels in the United States called the Left Behind series.

Edward Stourton: Well, I was going to ask, how does that go down in Israel? I'm sure the decision for many people is welcome about Jerusalem. But how do those sorts of ideas go down?

Allison Kaplan Sommer: First of all, most Israelis are quite ignorant, I think, of this exact theology. They don't like to look a gift horse in the mouth, frankly. There is very strong support by the evangelical Christian community in the United States towards Israel. They donate millions and millions of dollars in charity. They show political support in the United States. So those Israelis who maybe are aware of this kind of theological belief that lies behind the support probably choose to look the other way. So I would say the attitude of the Israelis is maybe wilful ignorance, but in some cases actual ignorance – but not total ignorance. Because Israelis are very aware of when some of these evangelical Christians try to come to Israel [to] expand the Jews for Jesus or the Messianic Jewish movement, as they prefer to call it. They are very suspicious of them and regulate very closely their ability to come to Israel and to try to actively get Jews to convert.

If Donald Trump really did make this hugely significant change in American policy in the hope of influencing a Senate race in Alabama, it was a bad call. His candidate, Roy Moore, lost narrowly.

Celebrating Israel's 'birthday'

In February 2018, the United States announced that the embassy move would take place in May, coinciding with events to mark the seventieth anniversary of the establishment of the State of Israel. On 12 May, the anniversary acquired a little glitter when the Israeli singer Netta Barzilai won the Eurovision Song Contest with 'Toy', and the following day *Sunday* was broadcast live from Jerusalem. The programme began with some history.

Edward Stourton: *Israel was founded in war. Immediately after the independence declaration, four Arab states attacked Israeli forces. And events of recent days in Gaza and along the Syrian border have underlined that conflict is still very much alive. But President Trump has given the Israelis a popular birthday present by moving the American embassy here to Jerusalem. That ceremony will take place on Monday to coincide with Independence Day.*

I'm at Damascus Gate, perhaps the most impressive of the entrances to the old city of Jerusalem. And later on Sunday, thousands of people are expected here to mark the capture of this part of the city in the Six-Day War in 1967. In general, Israelis feel they have plenty to celebrate after seven decades. Micah Goodman is an Israeli historian.

Micah Goodman: *We're celebrating something that ended and something that began. We're celebrating 1,900 years of being stateless, of having no sovereignty, no independence. And those weren't great years. And Jews don't have great memories of those years. They were experiences of being lonely, many times persecuted, and Jews were wandering around the world. And after 1,900 years, Jews are not lonely any more. They have sovereignty and they're not wandering any more. So we're celebrating the end of not-such-great times and also the hope of the beginning of times that could be a lot better.*

Edward Stourton: *And it's important to remember in any conversation about what happened seventy years ago, that the context was the Holocaust.*

Micah Goodman: *Zionism, the movement whose goal was to create the State of Israel, started way before the Holocaust... The conditions of living in exile, of being stateless and having no sovereignty, Zionists understood from the very beginning that these are not sustainable conditions way before the Holocaust. The Holocaust proved Zionism was right, but the Holocaust started a lot after Zionism.*

Edward Stourton: *Let's talk a bit about early Zionism, because in the early days it wasn't automatic that Israel, Jerusalem, these places would be the home for the Jews, was it? I mean, people talked about Uganda and all sorts of places.*

Micah Goodman: *Well, there was a disagreement among the founding fathers of Zionism about the location of the Jewish state. And from the very beginning, everybody knew that the best location would be this land, would be the Holy Land, would be Israel. But Theodor Herzl thought that, 'What if we can't get this land? What if it's not achievable diplomatically? Then we should compromise on land somewhere else.' Like Argentina was one offer, like Uganda was another offer. But the thing is, he was a minority. Most of the Zionists said that we [would] rather not have a state in the wrong place… and wait to have a state if it's in the right place, if it's in the land of Israel.*

Edward Stourton: *Theodor Herzl was a very secular Jew, as indeed was David Ben-Gurion, who founded the state. Did it begin as a secular enterprise?*

Micah Goodman: *Yes. The founding fathers of Zionism were secular, and many people think Zionism couldn't have begun if it was religious, because the religious mentality at the time was a passive mentality: we don't have to own our history; we have to wait for God to redeem us. It's a passive mentality. It's a waiting mentality. And since Zionism said, 'We're not waiting any more and we're not passive any more', they had to have a secular mindset of a sense that we are our own, our life, and not controlled by someone bigger than life in order to start acting and moving. And that's why secularism triggered Zionism.*

Edward Stourton: *Nevertheless, I was looking at the wording of the Declaration of Independence, which was read out by Ben-Gurion seventy years ago, and it begins: 'The Land of Israel is the birthplace of the Jewish people. There their spiritual, religious and political identity was shaped.' And it goes on to say that here the Jews gave the world 'the Book of Books'. So the Bible and God were there right at the beginning, weren't they?*

Micah Goodman: *Well, according to Ben-Gurion it was the Bible, not God. He was proud of the Book, not about the God that is the hero of that book. And that is what's so weird and interesting about Ben-Gurion. Imagine* *maybe British people or English people are proud that Shakespeare's writing comes from England. That's part of the pride of England. The fact that the Bible was written in this land is a part of what makes us proud of this land. And that's an interesting point in the Declaration of Independence. We're not proud of the views – there's nice views here, there's a nice sea here – but we're proud of what was created here. Not the hills, not the valleys; the Book that was created here is a pride of the people that live here today.*

The Parents' Circle

But history in this troubled land is, of course, highly contested. The conflict Israelis celebrate as the War of Independence is known among Palestinians as the *Nakba*, 'the catastrophe'. Hundreds of thousands of Palestinians fled their homes, and many of them and their descendants remain in refugee camps here and in neighbouring Lebanon, Jordan and Syria.

Away from the celebrations, *Sunday* spoke to some of those who had suffered in the long years of violence since Israel's creation.

Edward Stourton: *This is a meeting of the Parents' Circle. It's an organisation dedicated to forging links between bereaved families from both sides of the conflict. And it's been holding events like this for more than twenty years. I'm here to meet two members of the circle: Robi Damelin, who's Israeli; and Ikhlas Shtayeh, a Palestinian.*

Robi Damelin: *I lost David, my son. He was killed by a Palestinian sniper. He was doing reserve duty. He was a student at Tel Aviv University, studying for his master's in the Philosophy of Education.*

Actually, when the army came to tell me that he'd been killed, apparently, I said, 'You may not kill anybody in the name of my child.' And that started everything that I wanted to do, to prevent other families from experiencing this pain.

Edward Stourton: *Ikhlas, what happened in your family?*

Ikhlas Shtayeh: *I lost my father when he was driving on the minor road near our village. A German settler living in Israel shot him a bullet, which penetrated his hand and then settled in his heart and [he] died* *instantly. It was a big shock for me. I felt when I heard this news that now I am blind, although I have been blind from birth, and his loss is the biggest loss for me in my life.*

Edward Stourton: *Robi, you said that right from the first you started to think of these sorts of conversations. Have you been surprised by anything you've learnt in the course of meeting people – from what I suppose some would say was the other side?*

Robi Damelin: *I almost certainly recognised right from the beginning that the pain is the same pain, and the minute that I met Palestinian mothers at a seminar, bereaved mothers, I recognised what a strong force we could be if we could stand together on the same stage and talk in the same voice. This is what would get me out of bed every day because I see that if we don't have a reconciliation process as an integral part of a future peace agreement, all we'll have is another ceasefire until the next time.*

Edward Stourton: *Ikhlas, what do your family and other Palestinians who are friends, and so forth, think about the way that you talk to Israelis?*

Ikhlas Shtayeh: *Actually, I've been offended by many people around me telling me, 'How do you go and talk to them and shake hands with them?' Because I'm a strong woman and I came from a very strong background, I used to say something. I believe in peace and I love peace. And I believe that our Israeli partners also want peace. Pain is pain, whether it is to the Israelis or to the Palestinians.*

Edward Stourton: *And Robi, have you found in the same way that some Israelis take you to task about talking to Palestinians?*

Robi Damelin: *Well, particularly after I started a conversation with the man who killed David. Many people thought this was crazy and could not understand it [at] all. And yes, I've had death threats, and yes, I get very ugly letters and mails. But that doesn't stop me because I think we need to talk to people who don't agree with us, because if we don't they become more radical. I'm disturbed by the fact that even a university in Tel Aviv did not allow me to come in and talk to the students. I find that a very frightening part of what is happening. And the fact is that the occupation is killing the moral fibre of my country. And I love Israel. Don't make any mistake; I didn't become a Palestinian. But I think that if we don't end this occupation, I hate to think about what's happening* to our nation. And I think that much of the violence is a consequence of the occupation.

Edward Stourton: We're here because Israel is celebrating its seventieth birthday. And of course, that's an event that your two communities have a completely different view of. I wonder, starting with you, Robi, what does the celebration – the birthday party, if you like – mean to you?

Robi Damelin: For me, this is not a celebration until we end the conflict. Of course, there are wonderful things that have happened in Israel over the past seventy years. I'm proud of much of what we do in Israel, but the bottom line is that we have to end the occupation. It is killing the moral fibre of Israel.

Edward Stourton: Ikhlas, what about you?

Ikhlas Shtayeh: For me, again, it's not a celebration. As long as we are living with violence and violence is growing, and there is conflict, I think there is no celebration. I think the big celebration is to make reconciliation reaching to a justice and peace agreement, and giving the Palestinians, our people, our basic rights.

Edward Stourton: A final question to you both. Religion very often likes to think of itself as a force for peace. And I wonder what you both think about the role that religion is playing in this conflict. I mean, you are a Muslim. What do you feel about the role of religion?

Ikhlas Shtayeh: In fact, I am a secular woman. I'm sorry to say that I became secular because religion, whether it is Islam or Judaism, had brought us to this big conflict, which every day makes us lose more and more people from both sides.

Edward Stourton: Robi, what about you?

Robi Damelin: Well, I'm certainly not religious in any way. And the thing that disturbs me so much – and I think if your listeners would really listen to this message and they would stop taking sides, being pro-Israel or pro-Palestine – is actually what they're doing is importing our conflict into your countries and creating hatred between Jews and Muslims. And I don't think that this is about religion, our conflict. I think it's about land. And if your religion teaches you to hate, then choose another religion.

17

Religion in China

The coded message required the preparation of twenty-one cups of tea and eighteen bowls of rice. At 9 p.m. on 18 June 1981, a tugboat duly approached the coast near Shantou in Guangdong, in south-east China.

The city had been one of the 'treaty ports' established to allow Western trade with China during the nineteenth century, which made the cargo of this smuggling operation oddly appropriate. The tugboat was carrying 'vast crates containing 1 million Bibles written in Chinese', according to Paul Estabrooks, one of those unloading on the beach that night. He told *Sunday* about his memories forty years later, in June 2021.

Paul Estabrooks: This is the miracle of it all… We were there for two hours, making incredible noise. I mean, that barge was not a quiet one. To get the gates down on the side, to be able to pull those blocks off into the water and then tow them with three little noisy outboard motor rubber boats to the shore, where the men pulled them up and then cut open the waterproof wrapping with shears, and passed the boxes of Bibles one to another, daisy-chain style. There was a lot of noise and it was a full moon night, so it wasn't that dark, actually. And the fact that we could do that and spend two hours making all that noise and not be stopped was almost unbelievable.

Hundreds of people were involved in distributing the haul. At the time, Estabrooks explained: '[Chinese Christians] weren't allowed to have what it was that they needed for their worship. They did not have Scriptures and they were crying for them. Everybody we met was always asking for them.' This was five years after the death of Chairman Mao, and Christianity had been ruthlessly suppressed during his Cultural Revolution.

Estabrooks and the rest of the twenty-strong crew who carried out 'Project Pearl' were engaged by the Open Doors charity, which still campaigns against the persecution of Christians today. He and the other Bible smugglers made good their escape, but the operation did not go entirely smoothly.

Paul Estabrooks: Four hours after we left, some of the fishermen who had been out there fishing and watching all of this, which was something we couldn't control, they went into town and said that they saw a bunch of Russians come and leave something on the beach. We had all let our beards grow, and they assumed by our black beards that we were Russians. And this is what they told the authorities.

So the authorities sent out a patrol, and by this time everything was off the beach. There was no garbage on the beach, there were no wrappings. There was absolutely nothing. It was like nothing had happened. But there were still boxes of Bibles. There are ninety Bibles in a box, forty-five pounds. And some of those boxes were still sitting up under the tree line, waiting to be taken. And they found them. They found some and they threw them in the water, including whole boxes... And those boxes went around the corner and down the river to the city of Shantou, which was very close by. And the fishermen there just fished these things out of the water and began to use them for wrapping their fish, you know, just extra paper. And the Christians in town began to recognise that their fish was wrapped with these pages of a Bible, and they were desperate for them.

The Dalai Lama

Almost all the China-related items in the *Sunday* archive are, like this one, about religious resistance to the country's communist authorities. In 1950, the communist government in Beijing ordered the invasion of Tibet, and took control of large areas of the country. The following year, the two sides agreed that Tibet would submit to Chinese authority while maintaining a degree of autonomy. But the arrangement never really worked, and in 1959 Chinese troops laid siege to Lhasa, Tibet's capital.

The Dalai Lama, who was regarded as both the spiritual leader of the country's Buddhist population and the political leader of the nation, escaped his palace disguised as a soldier and made his way across the Himalayas to India. He established an exiled community at Dharamsala, where he has been based ever since, and became an enduring focus for opposition to China's occupation of Tibet.

During his years in exile, the Dalai Lama also secured a worldwide reputation as a religious teacher and a symbol of spirituality. During his 2012 visit to Britain, the China expert Isabel Hilton told *Sunday*: 'As a spiritual leader, I can't think of anyone with a higher profile or a more general influence. He attracts enormous audiences of people, not all of whom would call themselves practising Buddhists, but simply because he has a very profound impact wherever he goes.'

But for the Chinese authorities, his political influence matters more than anything – even though he formally handed over political power to an elected leader in the Tibetan government-in-exile in 2011. In a *Sunday* discussion marking the sixtieth anniversary of his flight from Lhasa, the chief correspondent of the Reuters news agency in India, Krishna Das, stated flatly that:

China considers the Dalai Lama as a dangerous separatist. They actually released a white paper recently called 'Democratic Reform in Tibet: Sixty Years On'. The Chinese say that there was a grim and backward feudal system in Tibet when the Dalai Lama was there. They say they got rid of that. They have brought about economic reforms in Tibet.

The truth about Tibet

It is extremely difficult to get an accurate picture of what is happening in Tibet, but evidence from the *Sunday* archive suggests that many Tibetan Buddhists would challenge Beijing's rosy interpretation of the decades of Chinese rule. The spring of 2008 saw the most serious anti-Chinese protests in Lhasa since the 1980s, and on 8 March *Sunday* reported that: 'The word from the country's government-in-exile is that thirty people have been killed in the riots there.'

Patrick French, the author of a book on Tibet, and a sometime committee member of the group Free Tibet, predicted the episode would end badly for the protestors.

Patrick French: If you look back over the last fifty years, and particularly to the late 1980s… when similar riots took place, the kind of power of the Chinese communist state means that the demonstrators have really got no chance. You know, the only future that awaits them is being dragged off to prison.

Edward Stourton: How central are the [Buddhist] monks to what's happening?

Patrick French: I think they're very central. I mean, I spent three months in Tibet when I was researching my book, Tibet, Tibet, *and I interviewed quite a few monks and nuns. And I think they very much felt that part of their religious duty was to stand up and be counted, to risk protests… even though they knew that they were putting themselves in immense danger by doing that. I think it's something that's really, really grown ever since the Dalai Lama went into exile. The idea that the religious community has a kind of sort of moral or national duty to do something, and also the fact that they… don't have dependants because, you know, they're celibate monks and nuns. They don't have the same risk that somebody who was married, who had children, would have by protesting.*

Three years later, *Sunday* reported an outbreak of self-immolations by monks in western Sichuan, a heavily Tibetan area that borders Tibet itself. 'There have been seven such protests in the past four weeks,' the programme recorded on 11 November 2011, adding that: 'The Dalai Lama has been accused of terrorism in disguise by the Chinese, because he said prayers for those who've immolated themselves.'

Professor Peter Harvey, a recently retired specialist in Buddhist Studies from the University of Sunderland, gave his interpretation of the episode.

Peter Harvey: Well, it seems to be a result of particular Chinese pressure on some of the fringe areas of the Tibetan area within China overall. I think the first one of these was a couple of years ago, but it really seems to have taken off in the last maybe six months. It is something, as far as I know, that's completely new in Tibetan Buddhism, although not completely new within Buddhism overall.

Edward Stourton: *So there is some precedent for it elsewhere in Buddhism?*

Peter Harvey: *Yeah, well, the most famous, well-known precedents are in the Vietnam War. Well, actually just prior to Vietnam War, in 1963, when a very old Buddhist monk set fire to himself. This was at a time when the president of South Vietnam was Catholic. There was a lot of pressure against Buddhism and Buddhists, and he set himself on fire to try and bring the world's attention to this and change things. And then during the Vietnam War there was a spate, particularly 1970–71, when there were a number of such self-immolations.*

Edward Stourton: *And is there any indication of why it's been taken up by monks and nuns in China today?*

Peter Harvey: *The only thing I can really think of is it's a combination of the current pressure on them, and – this is just pure speculation on my part – the prevalence of suicide bombings in the world, where people are killing other people while killing themselves. Clearly, the Tibetan Buddhist monks and nuns couldn't do that because it would be a terrible way to go. And possibly they're thinking, 'Well, we need to draw attention to the plight that they're under,' but they don't want to be killing anybody else. And so they're doing this as a kind of altruistic act of self-giving, self-sacrifice, to try and bring benefit to their people. Although even within Tibetan Buddhism, it's a very controversial act. There are different attitudes towards it.*

Evangelism in China

Christianity's history in China is long and complex. The Italian Jesuit Matteo Ricci, perhaps the most famous early missionary, learned Chinese, wrote several versions of a Chinese–Portuguese dictionary and created the first world map marked in Chinese characters. In 1601, he became the first European to be invited into the Forbidden City, as his skill in predicting eclipses was much admired. Later, in recognition of his services to China, he was the first foreigner to be buried in Beijing.

But nineteenth-century Christian evangelism has left a more problematic legacy. Thousands of Protestant missionaries – many of them from Britain – poured into China when the country opened up following the end of the Second Opium War in 1860. Because they had arrived on the back of the British and French victory over China's imperial armies, they became associated with the 'Century of Humiliation', the period during which China was subjugated to Western powers, and the spread of Christianity was resented by many Chinese nationalists.

The Taiping Rebellion against the Qing dynasty, which devastated much of the country in the 1850s and 1860s, was led by a man who proclaimed himself the brother of Christ, and aimed to convert the country to his version of Christianity. It was one of the bloodiest civil wars of all time, and cost some 20 million lives, which did little to advance Christianity's reputation.

Protestant, Catholic and Orthodox missionaries all became targets in the anti-colonial Boxer Uprising at the end of the century. In the summer of 1900, it was reported that forty-four foreigners from missionary families – including children – had been executed in Shanxi. By the time the uprising ended the following year, 136 Protestant missionaries and fifty-three children had been killed, along with forty-seven Catholic priests and nuns. It is estimated that 30,000 Chinese Catholics, 2,000 Chinese Protestants and a smaller number of Orthodox converts were also killed.

That backdrop helps explain the difficult relationship between the Christian Churches and the Chinese government – which, as a communist regime, has of course been unsympathetic to religion of any kind. The Catholic Church was effectively suppressed in China in the early 1950s, and 1957 saw the establishment of a state-sponsored organisation called the Chinese Patriotic Catholic Association (CPCA), which answered to the government in Beijing and did not acknowledge the primacy of Rome. Some Catholics refused to join and went underground, worshipping in secret. The Vatican ran an underground hierarchy to minister to them, which operated in competition with the system of state-approved bishops belonging to the CPCA. In consequence, two separate Catholic Churches developed in China.

China versus Rome

The situation of Chinese Catholics has been a focus for Vatican diplomacy ever since. In July 2011, *Sunday* reported a serious deterioration in relations between Beijing and Rome.

Jane Little: For a few years it looked as though China and the Vatican had found a way of working together. Not any more. Certainly not since China went ahead and ordained another bishop without the Vatican's approval. That's three out of four so-called illicit ordinations this year. Edmond Tang is director of East Asian Christian Studies at the University of Birmingham.

Edmond Tang: I think basically we have seen a hardening of the Chinese position since last year. They have acted against the Protestant house churches, and also now we see them doing the same with the Catholic Church in China, particularly the underground Catholic Church. Since 2006, there was a tacit agreement between the Vatican and China over the choice of candidates, which meant that both sides would consult and agree on a candidate. It seems now that the Chinese side has decided to break the agreement and started to ordain a series of bishops without Vatican approval.

Jane Little: Well, let's point out there are two Churches. There's the official state-sanctioned one, and then the underground one that's loyal to Rome. And China has always insisted on control over religions. And as you say, there has been sort of a tacit support, a sort of 'managing to get along together' before. So what's changed?

Edmond Tang: I think most people would not use the idea of two Churches, but rather, you know, tension in two communities, because even in this state-sponsored Church, I would say that ninety per cent of the bishops have expressed their allegiance to Rome since the 1990s. So the hope was, in the early 2000s, to move towards reconciliation between the Vatican and China, but we have seen this is not the case any more.

Edmond Tang ascribed the change in mood partly to the completion of the Beijing Olympics in the summer of 2008. 'Particularly during the Olympics, the Chinese side did not want this to become an international issue,' he noted, 'but now that the Olympics are gone and China's economy is on the rise, I don't think China in that sense needs the Vatican, and therefore it is less open to Vatican negotiation.'

The following year brought a reminder of how tough the communist authorities could be in matters of religion. In July 2012, *Sunday* broadcast an item about the mysterious case of the disappearing bishop.

William Crawley: *A newly ordained Catholic bishop in China has gone missing after he resigned from the government body that controls the Church. That's the Chinese Patriotic Catholic Association. For more, we can talk to John Sudworth, the BBC's correspondent in Shanghai. John, let's talk first about the bishop himself, Bishop Thaddeus Ma Daqin. What do we know about him?*

John Sudworth: *Well, we know that he is a man who has so far enjoyed the patronage of the Chinese Patriotic Catholic Association. This is a body that was set up back in the fifties under Chairman Mao, essentially out of a fear of the alternative authority in Rome. And it's led to the current irony, where a nominally atheist state reserves for itself the right to appoint its own Catholic bishops. Ma Daqin was one of those ordained at a service last Saturday here in Shanghai. But what's remarkable is, at the end of that ordination he made this speech in which he said he was resigning his position in the Catholic Patriotic Association. And it appears, as a result of that, it has been seen as a serious challenge to the authority of the state and the Communist Party to meddle in Catholic affairs. And he has since disappeared.*

William Crawley: *What prompted his resignation at this point?*

John Sudworth: *We don't know. I've spoken to a friend of his, who has said that he was well aware that making this decision and speaking out in this way [was a risk] – although the speech itself simply said his new appointment as bishop would make him too busy to concentrate on anything other than Church affairs, which is why he was resigning from the state body, the authority that controls the Church here. There wasn't anything necessarily overtly provocative about the statement, but the resignation itself was enough. And the friend that I've spoken to has told me that Ma Daqin knew what the consequences would be. He told me that the bishop had chosen belief over freedom.*

William Crawley: *Do we know that he has gone into hiding, that he's missing, or is there something more sinister at work here? Has he been disappeared by [the] authorities?*

John Sudworth: *It's sinister in the sense that, clearly, he has deeply angered the Church authorities controlled by the Communist Party. But the friend I spoke to told me he knows that he is safe. He is not in any sort of personal danger. But what appears to be the situation is that he has been told to take a kind of period of enforced reflection. Ma Daqin sent a text message last week to Catholic priests in the diocese in which he said, 'I need a break. I'm tired and I'm making a personal retreat.'*

Now, that's a remarkable statement for a man who was ordained just two days previously and appeared full of energy and enthusiasm for his new role at the weekend. And it does seem that he has been leant on very heavily, and he's withdrawn from public life under duress, while... the authorities decide what to do with him next.

It later emerged that the bishop's 'period of enforced reflection' meant house arrest in a seminary. He was subjected to 'political lessons', and four years later he recanted his opposition to the CPCA. But at the time of writing, he is still in detention.

Things began to change with the election of Pope Francis. The new pope was determined to end the divisions among Chinese Catholics, and made relations with Beijing a priority.

The negotiations between the Vatican and the Chinese government were carried out in great secrecy, and they took five years to bear fruit. Even before an agreement was reached, Francis was criticised for giving away too much in his efforts to please the Chinese authorities. For example, in Shantou – the scene of the Bible-smuggling operation that began this chapter – the Vatican put pressure on its own bishop to stand aside in favour of a bishop appointed by Beijing.

But in September 2018, *Sunday* reported that: 'The Vatican and the Chinese government have announced an agreement to settle their long-running dispute over how the Catholic Church in China is run.' The heart of the deal was the appointment of bishops, which, it was agreed would now be a shared process. The programme's guest that morning was Benedict Rogers, the East Asia team leader for Christian Solidarity Worldwide.

Benedict Rogers: *Well, obviously, the full text has not yet been released, but my understanding is that there is an agreement that they will effectively share responsibility for the nomination of bishops between the Chinese regime and the Vatican… I believe the pope will have final authority on the approval of nomination of bishops, but the Chinese regime will have a hand in it as well.*

Edward Stourton: *But the pope will have some kind of veto, it would appear.*

Benedict Rogers: *That's what it would appear, yes.*

In theory, this gave Rome the prizes of a single, united hierarchy and a recognition of papal primacy by all of China's Catholics. But even as the deal was agreed, doubts began to surface – not least because the actual text of the agreement was never published, so an independent assessment of its implications was impossible. Benedict Rogers told *Sunday* that even some Chinese Catholics were sceptical.

Benedict Rogers: *I think opinion both in the Church in China and around the world is extremely divided on this. Some people would argue that this could be a step forward; it could result in some greater protection for Catholics in the country, but I think many people are very concerned, particularly about the timing of this. Because this comes really at a time when China is intensifying what some would say [is] the worst crackdown on Christianity, and indeed on religion as a whole, possibly since the Cultural Revolution.*

New regulations earlier this year really tightened restrictions on the state-controlled churches as well as the underground churches. Just very recently, new regulations on religious activity online have been issued. Churches have been closed, crosses destroyed. And of course, there's the crackdown on the Uyghur Muslims in Xinjiang, where nearly a million people have been put in 're-education camps'. So it couldn't come at a worse time, I think. And many people would be saying, 'How is this possibly going to help Catholics?'

Edward Stourton: It's been something that Pope Francis has been extremely keen to pursue, hasn't it?

Benedict Rogers: Yes indeed, and for very understandable reasons... China is such a huge and important country, with obviously a large Catholic Church... just because of the size of the country. And he's understandably wanted to normalise the situation. But I think the timing is the biggest concern at the moment.

Edward Stourton: And what's your view, as somebody who campaigns on the issue of religious freedom around the world? Do you think that, on balance, this was a wise thing to do, particularly given that, as we said, it's a problem that's been there for many decades?

Benedict Rogers: Well, I can understand the motivation for it, but I do think, on balance, that it's extremely risky. I think China has shown that it doesn't have a good record of honouring agreements. I mean, in a different context, you just have to look at its attitude to the Sino–British Joint Declaration relating to Hong Kong, which it's completely trampled on. So I'm not optimistic that the Chinese government will really honour this deal.

Trouble in Hong Kong

Benedict Rogers's reference to Hong Kong proved prescient. The following spring, the former British colony erupted in a series of demonstrations that continued for the rest of the year and into 2020. They were sparked by the introduction of a bill in the legislature, which would have made it easier for Beijing to extradite people from Hong Kong to the Chinese mainland.

In the summer of 2020, the Standing Committee of the National People's Congress, the main legislative body in Beijing, passed an amendment to Hong Kong's Basic Law covering 'secession, foreign interference, terrorism and subversion against the central government'. The National Security Law, as it became known, was introduced without debate in the Hong Kong Legislature, and had a chilling impact on dissent. This item was broadcast on *Sunday* on 12 September 2021.

William Crawley: China's sweeping crackdown on dissent in Hong Kong continues. This past week, several members of the pro-democracy Hong

Kong Alliance were arrested and charged with subversion. Their alleged crime: organising the city's annual vigil for victims of Tiananmen Square. Historically, many of Hong Kong's pro-democracy protests have been rooted in Christian faith. When protesters sang, they often sang hymns.

But intriguingly, many of the key players on the other side of those barricades also had their roots in Christianity. To explore those connections, we turn to the journalist and author Michael Sheridan, whose new book is The Gate to China: A new history of the People's Republic and Hong Kong.

Michael Sheridan: *For many years, Hong Kong was the only city in China where all religions could be practised with complete freedom. It actually gained an importance after the communist revolution of 1949, because so many religious and clergy were expelled from the mainland. They took refuge in Hong Kong and came to [have] an extraordinary, and indeed disproportionate, effect on the life of the city.*

William Crawley: *What kind of Christianity was there across the Christian traditions?*

Michael Sheridan: *All the Christian traditions were represented. The Roman Catholic Church, of course, had been present since the Renaissance. The Protestant churches, the nonconformist Churches, had all gone into China with the foreign powers, alas. And to the Chinese, a lot of modern Christianity is political. It's associated in their minds with the years when the Western powers, and Russia and Japan, all put pressure on China and took chunks of its territory. One of which, of course, was Hong Kong...*

William Crawley: *After the British departure, how would you characterise the relationship between the Christian denominations, the institutions in Hong Kong and the Communist Party?*

Michael Sheridan: *One of the remarkable and indeed admirable things about Hong Kong is the degree of tolerance and respect extended on all sides to believers and worshippers, and indeed militant atheists in the Communist Party. It's a tribute to the people of Hong Kong that, for many years, from the middle of the 1990s until the violent disturbances of 2019, the differences and the conflicts never boiled over into real trouble.*

William Crawley: *It's odd, isn't it – or it seems odd to outsiders like myself, watching from afar – that when we see the rise of pro-democracy activism in the period after this, we hear hymns being sung. And yet you* *also recognise that, on the other side of the barricades, as it were, the Christian faith is actively shaping some of the responses to them.*

Michael Sheridan: *The people who started the mass peaceful protests of 2015 did so from a platform almost explicitly Christian in its ethics and its outlook. On the other side, you have a cadre of administrators who very often grew up through the religious schools, particularly the Catholic schools, and they graduated into government. There was a strong tradition of public service inculcated by the Roman Catholic schools. So you have this paradoxical situation where the people on both sides of the barricades have come through the same educational system and absorbed... the same values as they grew up [with].*

Michael Sheridan's predictions for the future of religion in Hong Kong were dire:

Make no mistake; freedom is dying in Hong Kong. The question for people there is: how do you manage the requirements of your daily life of worship and belief, and reading and writing and interacting with others, within the constraints of a National Security Law that essentially imposes on Hong Kong the same grim regimen [as] in mainland China? So one needs to remember that the Communist Party is about control. It doesn't really mind what you believe in private, but you must not challenge the party in public. This is at the core of conflicts between Chinese communism and organised religions of all kinds. The party means to compel believers to observe their faith within the framework of a party-approved organisation. Believers, naturally, are not always inclined to accept that.

So far in Hong Kong, the delicate balance has been preserved. But make no mistake about it; religion is on the list in Hong Kong, and its time will come. All expression which poses a threat, as they see it, to the national security of China, is punishable.

Cardinal Zen arrested

The following spring brought powerful evidence to back up those predictions. In May 2022, police arrested Cardinal Zen, the ninety-year-old former bishop of Hong Kong. He and four others detained with him were all trustees of a humanitarian fund that had provided money and legal advice to more than 2,000 people who had been arrested during the 2019 protests.

Zen's arrest provoked a furious intervention from Chris Patten, the last British governor of Hong Kong. And Lord Patten was almost as tough on the Vatican as he was on the Chinese authorities. His interview was broadcast on *Sunday* on 15 May 2022.

Edward Stourton: The Catholic Church in Hong Kong has, for more than two decades, held services to mark the anniversary of the killings in Tiananmen Square in 1989. It won't happen this June the fourth. The Church recently cancelled the Masses because its leaders fear they'll be accused of violating Beijing's National Security Law. And they clearly have good reason to worry. This week, the authorities arrested the former bishop of Hong Kong, Cardinal Zen, claiming he'd been 'colluding with foreign forces'. The cardinal has been released on bail, but he is ninety years old. I asked Chris Patten, who knows him, how he was likely to cope with the experience. Lord Patten was the last British governor of Hong Kong, and is himself a Catholic.

Chris Patten: He's a wonderful, brave, courageous, tough pastor. I know him reasonably well. He is precisely the sort of person one wants as a leader of the Church in Asia and elsewhere. He's been an outspoken advocate for a sensible Catholic view of social policy, of human rights and civil liberties. He's one of the most important Catholic Christian leaders in Asia. He's a truly great and decent and honourable man, and it is outrageous that he's been the subject of so much criticism by the united front press in Hong Kong – that is the communist press – and that the government have buckled, as ever, and have locked him up.

Edward Stourton: Well, I was going to say, what's your interpretation of why they've done it now?

Chris Patten: Well, it's not the only example of pressure on the Catholic Church; it's happening across the board. And I think it's because the united front, the pro-Beijing press, have been attacking him for weeks or months because he was involved in raising money to help those who were threatened with imprisonment during the huge demonstrations from 2019 onwards, with up to 2 million people taking part. And the communist regime is now even targeting lawyers who have been defending people when they've been brought to trial. So he's been caught up in that, and they hate him because he is a great Chinese pastor who has the guts and the gumption to stand up to them.

Edward Stourton: *To what extent do you think his arrest is connected with John Lee's* [Beijing's approved candidate in Hong Kong's 2022 chief executive election, a post he still holds at the time of writing] *rise to the position of chief executive in Hong Kong?*

Chris Patten: *It might not be directly connected, but John Lee has got the job because he was the police or security chief responsible for the brutal crackdowns on the demonstrations in 2019 and beyond. He happens to be a Catholic, but then General Franco was a Catholic, and I wouldn't have found myself supporting him. He is there because Beijing thinks he's the tough guy who can simply rule Hong Kong like a police state, which they want it to become. They want Hong Kong without Hong Kongers.*

Edward Stourton: *You mentioned Cardinal Zen's sometimes difficult relationship with the Vatican, and he did disagree very much, didn't he, with the deal that the Vatican did with Beijing to regularise the position of the Catholic Church in China? What was his concern about that?*

Chris Patten: *Well, his concern about that was what everybody is concerned about: that doing a deal with this Communist Party leadership is completely barking, and it would have been questionable at the best of times. But we have a communist leadership now, which is being much tougher in its crackdown on religion – not just the Catholic Church, but also the other Christian Churches – with the taking down of crosses, with the closing of churches, with bishops and priests still being locked up. And what we hear from the Vatican is the worst sort of noises of realpolitik. And the Vatican is always at its worst – think of the thirties and forties – when it starts being dominated not by a concern for human rights, but by worries about realpolitik.*

Now, I don't doubt that there are some good intentions. It's been thought that we could build a bridge between the underground Church, which was the Church which has always been in communion with the Vatican, and the patriotic Church, which is the one which is allowed by the communists and dominated by the communists. But I just think that while that may have been the intention, it's a mad time for it to be done.

By this stage of the interview, the former Hong Kong governor was really getting into his stride.

Chris Patten: *Of course, we don't know the details of the agreement, so nobody can actually mark what's happening. What we hear from the Vatican is all sorts of strange noises. Admittedly, it was some time ago the chancellor of the Pontifical Academy of Social Sciences talked about the communist regime in Beijing being 'the best implementer of Catholic social doctrine'. I mean, what's he talking about? Forced abortions, forced sterilisations, the sale of body parts. What's happening in Xinjiang, and now what's happening in Hong Kong, where the arrest of Cardinal Zen and others with him isn't the only thing that we should be worried about?*

Last year, after the Masses, which take place in many Catholic churches to mark the vigil for the massacres at Tiananmen Square or the killings at Tiananmen Square on the 4th of June, there were police outside church, just taking pictures of people going in and out. And those Masses, alas, have been cancelled this year because people are… worried about the Masses being thought to be somehow seditious. It's a very tough situation. And I think Catholics in Hong Kong are starting to feel the squeeze.

Edward Stourton: *Well, we're approaching the twenty-fifth anniversary of the handover of Hong Kong, aren't we, which you, of course, were such a central part of. It's, by the sound of it, a pretty grim prospect for the future of the Church in Hong Kong.*

Chris Patten: *Yes, it is. And it's something which I think, frankly, the Vatican should be speaking out about more. I'm a great supporter of what Pope Francis has been trying to do, but I don't know who's advising him on China. It can't be the diplomatic service, which is extremely good and sophisticated and thoughtful. But I think he's getting some pretty rum advice.*

He obviously would like, at some stage, to go to China. I think he'd like to beatify Matteo Ricci, the great Jesuit missionary in China. And that's all understandable. But to do a deal with this lot! ...And if these deals are so good for the Church, why doesn't the Vatican make plain what is in them? Why isn't it transparent? I'll tell you why it isn't, because the communist regime – and it was the same with us before 1997 – they hate anything being transparent because it removes some of their ability to put pressure on those they're negotiating with.

So I just hope the Vatican will wake up now with this awful arrest, with the increasing pressures on the Church in Hong Kong; and I hope that they will speak up for a wonderful pastor who is exactly the sort of human reason why many of us, despite occasional doubts, remain Catholics.

The Muslim Uyghurs

Lord Patten was not alone in those views. In July 2020, Benedict Rogers, the Christian Solidarity Worldwide spokesman who told *Sunday* about his concerns over the Vatican deal with China when it was first announced, was back on the programme to discuss the other big religious story in China in recent years: the plight of the Muslim Uyghur minority.

'It's very striking that this current pope, in particular, Pope Francis, pretty much every Sunday at the Sunday Angelus speaks about one issue of injustice around the world or another. And noticeably absent from his speaking about injustice is China as a whole,' he complained, citing in particular the pope's reluctance to discuss the treatment of the Uyghurs, 'which has to amount to one of the most serious mass atrocities of our time.'

His assessment was endorsed by James Palmer, the deputy editor of *Foreign Policy* magazine. 'The pope has made the kind of calculation that a lot of people were making about China in the 1990s or 2000s, but it seems radically out of date and naive now,' he told the programme. '...I suspect that Francis may be lulled into this notion that he can accomplish something for Catholics... by not saying anything. But I think that's very dangerous, because of course there's a point at which your silence effectively becomes collaboration or even endorsement.'

Sunday first covered the Uyghurs in March 2014, and the news peg for the story was an act of terrorism, which of course is how Beijing believes all discussion of the Uyghurs should be framed.

Shelagh Fogarty: The Chinese authorities have placed responsibility for a mass stabbing at a railway station in the south-western city of Kunming with separatists from the far north-western region of Xinjiang, home to the largely Muslim Uyghur minority. I'm joined now by [the BBC's] Celia Hatton in Beijing to find out more. Celia, first of all, who are the Uyghurs? Tell us a bit more about them.

Celia Hatton: Well, the Uyghurs are an ethnic group living in the north-western region of Xinjiang, as you said. And at one point they were the dominant group living there. But Xinjiang is very rich in resources... so the Chinese government has been eager to move more Han Chinese into the region. And so that's upset a lot of Uyghur Muslims, who are linked to the Turkic Muslim groups.

Shelagh Fogarty: And is it as simple as feeling outnumbered, or do they feel that they themselves are being discriminated against in some way?

Celia Hatton: Well, it's a little bit of both. There's quite a vast spectrum. Many Uyghurs resent communist government rule. They say that it's not something that they chose. They do feel outnumbered. They're now a minority; Uyghurs number about forty per cent of people in Xinjiang now in comparison to sixty per cent of Han Chinese. So many dislike regulations and policies that they say suppress their religion.

So in many parts of Xinjiang they're actively dissuaded from wearing headscarves and beards and burqas. And on a wider note, they say that discrimination prevents them from getting jobs and government benefits in comparison to the Han Chinese.

Shelagh Fogarty: And how does this attack fit in? Have there been others? Is this the first?

Celia Hatton: No, there have been other attacks. However, this one was particularly well co-ordinated. It involved ten people: men and women. And witnesses have said that the attackers seemed particularly well trained. They got past security barriers quite easily. It was also [a] very large attack. Twenty-nine people were killed and 130 people wounded in just a few minutes before they were stopped by the Chinese police.

In the course of the second half of the decade, however, it became apparent that Uyghurs were suffering something much more serious than discrimination over jobs and benefits. Huge numbers were being detained in camps – possibly hundreds of thousands.

In 2017, the BBC's John Sudworth reported that the detention policy had been extended to children:

> *China is deliberately separating Muslim children from their families, faith and language in its far western region of Xinjiang, according to new research. At the same time as hundreds of thousands of adults are being detained in giant camps, a rapid, large-scale campaign to build boarding schools is under way.*[1]

It was, for obvious reasons, a very difficult story to report. The Chinese made it impossible for foreign reporters to reach the region, but in January 2020, *Sunday* broadcast testimony collected in neighbouring Kazakhstan.

Edward Stourton: *It's estimated that as many as a million Muslims have been held in detention camps in China. The Chinese say the camps are 're-education centres' designed to combat terrorism. But Human Rights Watch claims Uyghurs from the province of Xinjiang and other Muslims have been locked up and subjected to brainwashing to persuade them to abandon their faith. The BBC's Rustam Qobil travelled to the border between Kazakhstan and China to interview some of those who have escaped the camps.*

Rustam Qobil: *Xinjiang in western China has been the ancestral homeland for ethnic Uyghurs, Kazakhs and other Muslim minorities for thousands of years. But it's only Kazakh Muslims who are able to move and live freely back and forth over the border between East Kazakhstan and western China. Thousands of Kazakh Muslims who were used to living and working on both sides of the border have disappeared. People like Gulnur's husband. In her family home, about half an hour's drive from the city of Almaty [in Kazakhstan], forty-six-year-old Gulnur is making tea for her family. But there is one person missing around the table.*

---

1   J. Sudworth, 'China Muslims: Xinjiang schools used to separate children from families', BBC News: https://www.bbc.com/news/world-asia-china-48825090 (4 July 2019, accessed 9 May 2023).

Gulnur (translation): My husband was a trader, but as he crossed the border into China, his documents were taken away and he was arrested. He called me and said he was under the threat of being sent to a camp. They told him they were arresting him because he had WhatsApp on his phone.

Rustam Qobil: *Also sat around the dinner table is a sister-in-law who spent fifteen months in the camps in China.*

Sister-in-law (translation): I didn't know what camp it was. They told me that I'll go to school. They searched me at the entrance and sent me to one room. Women told me to take off my clothes. They gave me a uniform red top, black trousers. They took me to a classroom. The room was full of women. Someone said, 'A new student arrived.' They all applauded. Xi Jinping's [president of the People's Republic of China] *picture was hanging on the wall in the classroom. There were also cameras everywhere, and a picture warning that praying was forbidden.*

Rustam Qobil: *In the beginning, she was told she had to study new skills in a school for a couple of weeks only. The authorities told her it's because she married a foreigner, a Kazakh citizen, and lived abroad. The camp she was sent to was surrounded by high walls and guarded by armed officers. More than 800 people, she told me – Uyghur, Kazakh, Uzbek and other Muslim women – were also held there.*

All women had their hair cut short. We were not allowed to mention religion or the language differences. We couldn't say 'Allahu Akbar' or pray. The place wasn't like a school; it was a prison. They taught us to eat, live and work together with the Han Chinese people, and that everyone will be one united Chinese people, and there will be no Uyghurs or Kazakhs. They taught us this unity could only be reached if the religion and language differences were eliminated.

Rustam Qobil: *The Chinese insist the camps have been established to prevent terrorism. They say, since the 1990s, Xinjiang had become a battleground of terrorist incidents, killing thousands of innocent people. In the last violent protests by Uyghur Muslims in 2009, more than 140 people lost their lives.*

Back in Almaty, I'm going to meet Joanna Lillis. She's one of the few Western experts on Central Asia in China. I hope she can help me understand what is happening to Uyghur and Kazakh Muslims in Xinjiang.

Joanna Lillis: *...I think Islam is a threat because what the Chinese state wants its citizens to believe in is actually China itself, is actually the religion of Chinese as a great power, and so on. And really, Islam looks like a threat because it's something they can't control.*

The persecution of Uyghurs and of religion more generally in China was one rare area where the Trump administration and much of the international community were of like mind. In 2019, Donald Trump's ambassador at large for international religious freedom, the Kansas governor Sam Brownback, gave his views to the BBC's Harry Farley. The interview was broadcast on *Sunday* on 19 March, and Mr Brownback's judgement was unforgiving:

The observation is that what they're doing to the Muslims in the western part of China, what they're doing to the Protestant house church leadership, what they're doing to the Falun Gong [a new religion which originated in China in the 1990s, but later ran foul of the government], *what they've done to the Tibetan Buddhists, what they've done to virtually every religion, particularly in the last couple of years, it amounts to, effectively, a war on faith. What we hope to see take place is for China to respect people of faith and to allow them to practise freely, as is guaranteed in the Chinese constitution, as is guaranteed in the UN Declaration of Human Rights.*

Part 5

IN SEARCH OF THE GRANDEUR OF GOD

18

Sacred places, art and a portable organ

'The world,' according to the great Jesuit poet Gerard Manley Hopkins, 'is charged with the grandeur of God.'[1] Over the decades, *Sunday* has interviewed many guests who have gone in search of that grandeur. Some of them were trying to find it in conventional ways – through pilgrimage or art – while others were downright eccentric.

In 2003, *Sunday* launched a quest to find the nation's favourite spiritual place. Well-known people such as the author Susan Howatch; then poet laureate Andrew Motion; the film-maker Anthony Minghella; and the singer Toyah Willcox all nominated their favourite spiritual places, along with more than 2,000 listeners. The choices ranged from the island of Iona to St David's Cathedral in Pembrokeshire; the Avebury Stone Circles to Lindisfarne; St Peter's Chapel in Bradwell-on-Sea to Euston Station.

One of the most unlikely nominations was a place more often associated with punishment and violent death than spiritual peace and enlightenment. *Sunday's* reporter Mike Ford accompanied one of the programme's listeners to the Tower of London.

Tour guide: *Down this bloody road you will find the entrance to the bloody tower. Go there. But remember what happened inside. Two young boys would be murdered in their beds.*

Mike Ford: *William the Conqueror's great fortress here on the Thames mightn't seem an obvious location in our search for the nation's favourite spiritual place, but one of those whose nominations centred on the Tower of London is Sonia Jacks, a teacher from Hounslow. Now, Sonia, people*

---

1 G. M. Hopkins, 'God's Grandeur', The Poetry Foundation: https://www.poetryfoundation.org/poems/44395/gods-grandeur (accessed 16 May 2023).

usually associate the tower with torture and execution, but do you actually find that part of it uplifts your soul?

Sonia Jacks: *Yes. There's a very special place here that I've had some associations with over the years as a teacher and a visitor to the tower, and it is a very special place to me. Would you like to come and see it now?*

Mike Ford: *I'd love to see it. Lead me to the tower!*

Sonia Jacks: *OK.*

Mike Ford: *Well, we're now on the second floor of the White Tower, which was built in 1077. So your crown jewel is in here, is it, Sonia?*

Sonia Jacks: *Yes, it is indeed.*

Mike Ford: *Show me the way. My word, you'd never believe this was here.*

Sonia Jacks: *Yes, it's St John's Chapel in the middle of a fortress. And it really is a delightful little place. And as you can see, the colour of the lighting makes – I don't know whether it is actually sandstone, but it has that real golden light to it – very simple Norman architecture. So it has a real atmosphere, and people as they come in become quiet.*

Vox pop: *I would think this is a very good nomination. Your impression when you walk in is, it's very beautiful and very worshipful.*

Vox pop: *I'm an Anglican priest. I appreciate the peacefulness in so much noise and bustle, and I appreciate the simplicity of the architectural style.*

Vox pop: *It's beautiful. It's magnificent. The architecture, the windows, and it takes your breath away when you come in the door.*

The chapel did not, however, carry the day.

Roger Bolton: *The eventual winner was the Shrine [of Our Lady] at Walsingham in East Anglia. Earlier I spoke to Fr Philip North* [later a prominent opponent of the campaign for female ordination, which is described in chapter 6], *priest administrator of the Anglican shrine, and asked him whether he'd been surprised that Walsingham had won the 'Nation's Favourite Spiritual Place'.*

Philip North: *I was surprised, to be honest. I wasn't surprised that we'd been nominated, but I didn't think we'd actually win it. So it was a lovely surprise.*

Roger Bolton: *And what's been the consequence for Walsingham? Do more people inquire? Do more people come?*

Philip North: *We've certainly found that we've got a lot more people coming who are perhaps in the area, or tourists or visitors popping in to explore and see what Walsingham is about. But also, I've met a number of people who've come and stayed at Walsingham or who have come on a pilgrimage who've heard about Walsingham from the* Sunday *programme, and it's been extraordinary to see the impact that the place has made on them.*

Roger Bolton: *And when people say to you, 'What is the essence of the Walsingham experience?' what's your reply?*

Philip North: *It's a place that points people to encounter with Jesus Christ. I think that would be my reply. That's Mary's role in the Church, and it's a shrine very much associated with Mary. But the heart of the pilgrimage is the Holy House, which is a replica of the home in Nazareth where Mary received the angel's message. And that house is just simply a place of encounter. It's a place of intense quiet and extreme beauty, and it's a place where many, many people have met with God and heard his voice in all sorts of different ways.*

Roger Bolton: *The conflict in this country, the religious conflicts in this country, have meant that there aren't great architectural remains at Walsingham* [Walsingham was one of the great medieval places of pilgrimage, but the original shrine was destroyed during the Reformation]. *So what is the essence of Walsingham's connection with the past? Not in stones, perhaps, but in spirit and faith?*

Philip North: *The connection is, we see ourselves very much in continuity with pilgrims who have come to Walsingham for hundreds and hundreds of years since 1061 for the same thing. And Walsingham is the same now as it was then. The stones might be different, the faith is just the same.*

The other thing you mentioned are the divisions of the past. Those are very significant in Walsingham. We have two shrines – a Roman Catholic and an Anglican one in the same village – and we're absolutely committed to working together and praying together for that day when the Church will be one again, and those wounds of the past, which I think are very close to us at Walsingham, that those wounds are healed.

371

Religious art

It is sometimes said – in recognition of the power of descriptive writing – that radio 'has better pictures than television'. But art on radio presents obvious challenges. Some of the items about religious art in the *Sunday* archive really shine because of the stories they told.

In 2015, *Sunday* broadcast a special edition on religion and art, and turned – unusually – to a newspaper journalist, Cole Moreton, as a presenter. The story of Jesus' death and resurrection has, of course, inspired artists for centuries. Cole Moreton went to see the artist Maggi Hambling to find out why she creates a work of art every Good Friday. Hambling, famous for her land and seascapes as well as her portraits, is not a believer. She describes herself as 'an optimistic doubter'. And yet...

Maggi Hambling: Well, it all began with this little painting... [which] hangs in Hadleigh Church, dedicated to my parents. That was the first. And every Good Friday, I have a go at Jesus... And it can be a sculpture, it can be a drawing, it can be a painting. I deliberately don't think about it before the morning of Good Friday, just to see what [happens]. My mother was very churchy... She ran flower festivals, she ran the Mothers' Union, and Good Friday was always miserable...

Cole Moreton: It's supposed to be, I believe.

Maggi Hambling: Well, depends how you look at it. It's life and death at the same moment, which is the point of art, of course. But I remember from childhood it was always very miserable. And it has obviously gone very deeply into me, because I find it difficult to think about other things on Good Friday. I mean, the image of the crucifixion is what happens for me once a year.

Cole Moreton: Hang on a minute. Life and death at the same moment is what art's all about, you said?

Maggi Hambling: Yes.

Cole Moreton: What do you mean?

Maggi Hambling: Well, I think in a great painting you are in the territory where life and death meet. You can feel what it is to be alive and feel what it might be like to die at the same time. Mysterious territory.

That edition of the programme also included an item on the work of the Muslim artist Mohammed Ali. For twenty years, using his artistic name 'Aerosol Arabic', he travelled the world creating murals that combined street art with Islamic design and calligraphy. Trevor Barnes talked to him in his home city, Birmingham.

Trevor Barnes: Graffiti, classically defined as inscriptions scribbled, scratched or sprayed on walls, has a long history from the caves of Lascaux [in south-western France] 17,000 years ago to this studio wall here in Birmingham. Mohammed Ali is the artist in question, completing a canvas armed with spray cans, rollers and paintbrushes. Now, Mohammed, you're a Muslim, your faith informs all you do, so does that make this work and all the work you do religious art?

Mohammed Ali: Religious art? I have a bit of a problem with that, because I think it has all kinds of connotations in terms of preaching or proselytising, whereas my art doesn't do that, I don't think. I hope my art is about asking questions for us to ponder upon; values that are relevant to modern society. And often religion is perhaps put into a certain bracket, where it's not seen as relevant.

Trevor Barnes: So what are your themes, then?

Mohammed Ali: I started off exploring universal values: justice, freedom, peace, knowledge, seeking of knowledge or perseverance, a spiritual reliance on a divine creator.

Trevor Barnes: Why street art and why graffiti?

Mohammed Ali: Human beings want to tell their stories, and they also want to tell them in public spaces they want others to see. There's something quite liberating about having your story out in a public space. It's reclaiming space and questions about ownership of space, and people who perhaps who are powerless through this act of graffiti, achieving that status of power, actually, and saying, 'I exist, and this is my voice. This is my story.'

Trevor Barnes: Well, we're going outside in a moment to see some of your work in its element; outdoors, in situ. But it's worthwhile remembering, you know, having been commissioned from Dubai to Malaysia, Australia to Lancashire, you've also been commissioned by the Vatican, where you did a kind of live performance to sound. What was going on there?

Mohammed Ali: *Yeah, I was invited to speak as well as actually perform at the same time on stage in front of 1,000-odd Catholics and other faiths as well. There was an interfaith gathering. And I was able to paint live on stage, sequenced with a soundscape that I'd created, of kind of Gregorian chants fused with Islamic call for prayer, as well as vocals from a jazz vocalist friend of mine.*

Trevor Barnes: *The fact that you were using the call to prayer and Gregorian chant, did it give you, consciously, this feeling of an act of worship – that's sacred art rather than religious art?*

Mohammed Ali: *Well, I mean, my hair stands on end even thinking about it. There were people in the audience that were in tears. So clearly something special was happening in that room, you know. Bringing these different expressions together, I think it led to this kind of electric feeling of, 'Wow, this is something we need to explore more.'*

Trevor Barnes: *Well, we've come to one of your outdoor pieces here in the inner-city area of Sparkbrook in Birmingham – a mixture of Islamic decorative stuff on the left and I think a bit of a Celtic knot to the right. 'Who controls the past controls the future.' What's the point of this piece?*

Mohammed Ali: *This is the street I was born and raised on, so it was kind of close to my heart as well. And really, it's about kind of the narrative of the area. And in fact, for me growing up in the eighties here, it was kind of ethnically diverse. There was a strong Irish community. We were kind of in and out of each other's homes, which we don't see so much today, unfortunately.*

Trevor Barnes: *Do you think the danger is that, as this kind of art becomes more mainstream, it loses some of its subversive edge, if you like?*

Mohammed Ali: *I think if this was a piece of art that was commissioned in terms of its theme and its content, then I'd say there is that danger. But when walls are offered, and as the artist you're freely able to say what you want to say, even if it's as contentious as this very statement here, which can be interpreted in many different ways, I think there is no danger there because it really is kind of 'life reflects reality'…*

Trevor Barnes: *Do you think you're working in a tradition of Islamic art? I mean, the aerosol, the paint can, could be the modern-day equivalent of calligraphy and script.*

Mohammed Ali: *Well, absolutely. Calligraphic script, Islamic script and* *geometric patterns here; for them to be painted with the spray can is adapting and using modern tools and updating the traditional calligrapher's pen and ink. I think it speaks volumes. It says a lot about actually reclaiming your voice and actually projecting your faith and an expression of faith in a confident and bold way that I don't think can be achieved in any other way.*

Homeless Jesus

The Canadian sculptor Tim Schmalz is another artist who likes to site his work in public spaces. He is a Catholic and specialises in large-scale religious sculptures, and his most famous work is a life-sized bronze known as *Homeless Jesus* or *Jesus the Homeless*. It depicts Jesus as a homeless person, sleeping on a park bench.

Casts of the sculpture were installed in cities across North America and even in the Vatican. But in 2014 Schmalz found himself in a predicament that fitted the biblical verse: 'Foxes have holes, and birds of the air have nests, but the Son of Man has nowhere to lay his head' (Matthew 8:20, ESV). Having decided to install his sculpture in ten world cities, he began to look for a site in London where its message would have maximum impact.

Tim Schmalz: *I like to consider the sculpture a visual translation of Matthew 25, where Jesus basically directly states that whenever you see the marginalised, the broken in society, you are indeed seeing him. That's the hope; that it almost becomes a permanent visual representation, a three-dimensional ambassador of some of the most powerful ideas of Christianity.*

Edward Stourton: *It is a very striking image. Jesus is lying on a bench covered in a cloth or a blanket of some kind and you can't see his face. Why not?*

Tim Schmalz: *Well, two-fold, really. The more important one, I wanted to keep very close to the Scriptures where Jesus says that when you see the marginalised, you are seeing him. So it's not necessarily one specific face I want to put in that. When you look at the whole history – 2,000 years of representations of Jesus – it seems like it's usually just this one face.*

And I think if we want to be more authentic to the Gospels, we could loosen ourselves from those traditions, and have a more philosophical or theological representation of Jesus. Therefore, when I do not put the face of Jesus on the piece, it becomes everyone in a sense. It helps to make the piece more personal. One can imagine their own relationship with Jesus and fill in the blanks themselves.

Edward Stourton: *And you want people to... sit on the bench and interact with the sculpture in that way?*

Tim Schmalz: *Yes. Interestingly enough, as I was working on the piece, I decided that I would leave a little bit of space where some[one] can sit uncomfortably near or actually on the sculpture. I... consider this a position of meditation, [of] prayer, that you can get really close up to the piece. The sculpture is unique also, because it does not require a base or an ostentatious pedestal.*

The point is, it is supposed to emerge within the environment, and hopefully be misconstrued initially for a real homeless person. And then you walk up to it, you realise it's a sculpture, and then on closer inspection, perhaps you sit down on the bench, and then you realise that the feet have the wounds of being on the cross. And then that's the 'eureka moment' of the piece, where you realise it's Jesus.

Edward Stourton: *Now, as I understand it, you have now got a project underway to get casts of the sculpture in ten world cities. And you've got a patron who is mysterious but clearly rich, because he's willing to help you do that. One of those cities is London. Why London?*

Tim Schmalz: *The piece is meant to be seen. That's part of it. It's meant to be put in an urban environment. So my hope is to, in the UK, to find a home for the* Jesus the Homeless *that forever can promote and be a visual reminder of 'whenever we see the least of our brothers and sisters',[2] that we should understand the spiritual connection between them and our faith.*

Edward Stourton: *We put out the message about the statue before going on the air, and one of our listeners has suggested somewhere at the heart of power: Downing Street, Buckingham Palace, somewhere like that. Is that [the] sort of thing that you had in mind?*

---

2   A reference to Jesus' words in Matthew 25:40.

Tim Schmalz: Oh, that would be great... And my hope is that, in the UK, I can have it in a spot where people can really experience it. And it's interesting because one of my favourite essays is by Oscar Wilde. It's an essay on art. And he says, I'm paraphrasing, but he stated that the people in London did not see the fog till the painters started painting it. And I find this fascinating because it's true. Art has this mystical power about it. And hopefully when this piece gets to London, the invisible people out there will become more visible, and the awareness will grow then.

The statue sparked the imagination of *Sunday*'s listeners, and for the next few weeks, suggestions for a suitable site flooded in – ranging from outside parliament and the Royal Parks to George Square in Glasgow. Trevor Barnes was dispatched to look at some of the suggested sites in the capital.

Trevor Barnes: The parliamentary sketch writer and humourist for hire Quentin Letts thinks the pavement here outside the investment bankers Goldman Sachs would be a good idea. Funnily enough, they don't and declined our invitation to comment. Others, though, are less reticent.

Cathy Corcoran: I know exactly where I would like to see it placed.

Trevor Barnes: And Cathy Corcoran, as we'll soon hear, has a professional stake in the matter. More from her in a moment, when her preferred location will be revealed. For now, though, I'm off to meet London Blue Badge tour guide Diane Burstein near St Paul's Cathedral. She has a few suggestions of her own.

Diane Burstein: We're in the ruins of a church called Christ Church Greyfriars, and adjacent to it is the headquarters of Merrill Lynch, the American bankers. So I thought it would be a great idea, not only because it's a spiritual place. Originally there was a Franciscan friary here, and the Franciscan friars were the social workers of their day. But also, you've got the bankers who might be on very good salaries sitting here on the benches eating their sandwiches. And if they see a sculpture of Christ as a homeless man, well, maybe it'll give them a bit of food for thought...

Trevor Barnes: For maximum impact, the statue will have to be put in a public place. Well, sites don't come more public than Trafalgar Square here. And perhaps even the fourth plinth behind me could make way for it. It's currently home to a blue chicken. Anyway, let's see what passers-by and sightseers would make of any possible new additions to the street furniture.

Vox pop: *I like it. I like the idea of a comparison between Jesus and a homeless person.*

Vox pop: *I just wonder if it's a little bit patronising in some way.*

Vox pop: *I don't know. It isn't the view of Jesus that I would imagine.*

Trevor Barnes: *The church of St Martin-in-the-Fields overlooking the square has long been associated with care for the homeless, and has a long tradition of patronising the arts. An ideal spot, you would have thought, for siting the sculpture. But after much debate and consultation, the idea got the thumbs down. Richard Carter, you're the associate vicar for mission at St Martin's. Why?*

Richard Carter: *Well, I think the first people to ask about something like a statue of a homeless person is to ask homeless people themselves. So I took this to one of the homeless groups I work with and got their opinion. They said it would be good to have that statue outside the Houses of Parliament to make politicians think about their policies, which actually cause homelessness. But they said here around St Martin's, where there are so many people who are homeless, actually it's a bit of a stereotype of homelessness.*

Trevor Barnes: *Trafalgar Square, Buckingham Palace, the Houses of Parliament and Victoria Station – all suggested in emails by you – come under the jurisdiction of Westminster City Council, whose offices are just behind me. And like the City of London, they have broad guidelines for the siting of new sculpture. Their thirty-three-page document stipulates, among other things, that any public statue should a) be desirable in design terms, b) have a contextual link between the subject and its location, and c) be of sufficient quality to earn a place in a world city. Which does rather prompt the question: is the sculpture really good enough to justify all the fuss?*

Cathy Corcoran: *What it does is remind us of an unpalatable truth; the fact that there are thousands of homeless people who are going to be bedding down on our streets tonight, and we're the seventh-richest country in the world.*

Trevor Barnes: That was Cathy Corcoran, whom you heard earlier, chief executive of the Catholic homelessness charity, the Cardinal Hume Centre. But I wondered whether the sculpture in the end was merely a way of nodding at the problem rather than, as they and indeed St Martin's are doing, actually tackling it in practice...

Cathy Corcoran: I think it's a symbol, and we all need symbols. So I think there's room for both of us. If it was just a sculpture, yes – what would that do? But if it leads people to my organisation, leads them to see the truth and the facts about homelessness and poverty rather than the myths, I think it's a very good thing.

Trevor Barnes: So where would you like to see it placed?

Cathy Corcoran: I know exactly where I would like to see it placed. I'd love to see it in the piazza outside Westminster Cathedral, here in the heart of London. It's where we were founded. It's the reason we were founded.

In the end, Methodist Central Hall, just across Parliament Square from the Palace of Westminster, offered to install the statue outside their building. But their application and subsequent appeal were rejected by the City of Westminster Council because 'the proposed sculpture would fail to maintain or improve (preserve or enhance) the character or appearance of the Westminster Abbey and Parliament Square Conservation Area' owing to 'its location within the City Council's Monument Saturation Zone'.[3]

Finally, two years after Tim Schmalz started looking for a place for *Homeless Jesus* in the UK, Manchester City Council approved a plan to install it outside St Ann's Church in the city centre. At the church – in the heart of Christmas market territory – the bishop of Manchester, David Walker, gave *Sunday* his verdict on the statue.

David Walker: [It's] part of the great tradition in which Christian art has been used to depict the way that Jesus shares our suffering. From the Isenheim Altarpiece of the Renaissance [a sixteenth-century sculpted and painted altarpiece on display in Colmar, Alsace] *through to the*

---

3   M. Cornwell, 'Westminster Council rejects "homeless Jesus"', *The Tablet*: www.thetablet. co.uk/news/5324/westminster-council-rejects-homeless-jesus (23 March 2016, accessed 16 June 2023).

way that soldiers depicted Christ suffering in the First World War – [they] showed him on the barbed wire as one of them. And so we're entering into that tradition by having this sculpture of Jesus entering what's a major form of suffering today in a city like Manchester: being homeless.

Edward Stourton: Judging from this afternoon, there'll be plenty of people who'll see it. How would you hope they'd react?

David Walker: Well, I hope it will remind them of the compassion of Christ for us, and him entering into our state of affairs. That he is one of us. And of course, at this time, Advent, we remember how that first time he came to live as one of us; to live a fully human life and to enter into human experience in its entirety. And of course, we do say that he had no place to lay his head.

Edward Stourton: And do you think that people, as they go about their business – Christmas shopping and so forth – appreciate the scale of the homelessness problem here?

David Walker: They might not understand the scale, and it has been roughly doubling every eighteen months in the centre of Manchester since my time here... but they'll know something of seeing people by the sides of the streets. But what I'm touched by is how many people do stop and talk to someone who's homeless, how many offer them a cup of tea or a sandwich or something. There's some real human connection between the people who are shopping or working in the city centre and those who are sat by the side of the street, homeless.

Edward Stourton: The statue is of Jesus as a homeless person sleeping on a park bench. I wonder what you thought of the idea.

Vox pop: Yeah, I think that's quite a good idea, actually.

Vox pop: But maybe the money could be better spent on actual homeless people and changing the problem, rather than just a statue evidencing it.

Vox pop: I'd say it's a bit off-putting, to be honest.

An organ adventure

The *Homeless Jesus* saga – like the search for the nation's favourite spiritual place – was a good example of the way dialogue with listeners can bring a programme to life. The most eccentric experiment of this kind began in 2007, when a sharp-eyed member of the *Sunday* team spotted an unusual advertisement in the *Church Times*.

Roger Bolton: *'Wanted: one organist for concert in remote Bolivian jungle accessible only by raft. Must be prepared to face rapids, alligators, 86 F temperatures. Ability to swim a bonus.'[4] It's quite serious, and is connected to an expedition being led by the British explorer [Col] John Blashford-Snell. Not content with exploring a vast meteorite crater in the Amazon jungle, he and his team will be transporting a church harmonium upriver as a gift to the tribespeople helping them. Trevor Barnes reports.*

Trevor Barnes: *The sun rises over the Bolivian rainforest and dawn breaks in a second Eden. Well, not exactly. My own expedition started further north than that, and has brought me via Woking and Basingstoke to the Dorset home of one of the country's best-known explorers. Good morning. John Blashford-Snell, I presume.*

John Blashford-Snell: *Indeed. Thank you very much for coming. Well, why don't we go up to my den and take your coat off? Come up there and we can have some coffee.*

Trevor Barnes: *Now, what is the purpose of this latest Amazonian expedition?*

John Blashford-Snell: *The Scientific Exploration Society's been asked by the Bolivian Geological Institute to seek a meteorite that is thought to have crashed into the Amazon jungle between 5,000 and 30,000 years ago. It's created a hole about five miles across. To get into this area we need the assistance of the local people. It's a good 700 kilometres from the capital of Bolivia, and we've got to get there by boat and over land. And they wanted help, and we'd like to help them so they will help us, and the results help everybody.*

Trevor Barnes: *And so in return you're actually presenting them with a harmonium, which you'll be transporting up the Amazon. That's going to be a pretty hazardous undertaking, isn't it?*

John Blashford-Snell: *Yes, indeed. We're giving them not only the harmonium, but a well, a clinic and a school as well. But the harmonium*

---

4 J. Malvern, 'Church Organist Required for Jungle Meteorite Hunt', *The Times*: https://www. thetimes.co.uk/article/church-organist-required-for-jungle-meteorite-hunt-36fllnffxn8 (12 March 2007, accessed 16 June 2023).

is the way of bringing everyone together. They love music. They have no electricity or television or radio, and they built this little chapel especially to have a harmonium. Now we've got to get it a long way up some very difficult terrain to this village. And we're taking with us an organist. And the organist's task will be to instruct the local people how to play this when we go away and leave it behind.

Trevor Barnes: *Now, by any standards a church organist isn't normally an essential part of an Amazonian expedition. What qualities will he or she have to possess?*

John Blashford-Snell: *Well, as long as they're fit enough to run to catch a bus, that'll be all right. It's going to be quite uncomfortable. The temperature will be in the nineties, and it could be quite humid. And they've obviously got to be prepared to put up with living in a tent, bitten to death by mosquitoes, dodging a few snakes, and living on canned or dehydrated food or fish from the river for six weeks.*

Trevor Barnes: *And alligators as well, apparently.*

John Blashford-Snell: *Oh, there are plenty of alligators, but they are not particularly aggressive. They tend to shy away from mankind. The biggest problem are the rapids of the river and the logjams, which we've got to scoot over. We're using special mahogany boats, which will ride over these logjams. They race at them, cut the engine, skid over the top and jump in the other side. Be interesting to see how the organ is going to survive this sort of transportation.*

Trevor Barnes: *Well, so much for the expedition and the personnel. But what of the harmonium itself. In particular, will it withstand the rigors of the forest and the swamp? The next leg of my journey takes me along perilous terrain, upcountry to Sherborne and to the home of one of Britain's outstanding concert organists, Margaret Phillips. Well, Margaret, you're playing a harmonium very similar to the one that will be transported up the Amazon. Is the instrument up to it?*

Margaret Phillips: *Well, I think that depends... how carefully they pack it and what dangers they come across on the way, really. What will happen to it when it gets there is probably more to the point, because with the high heat and humidity there will be all sorts of problems with keys peeling and glue coming unstuck, and perhaps leather being eaten by termites and goodness knows what else.*

Trevor Barnes: *I mean, what's your opinion in general on the whole idea of a church instrument like this being exported to a remote South American tribe?*

Margaret Phillips: *Well, one's first impression is that it's barking mad, I think. But on the other hand, if it's going to be something they haven't had before and they're going to enjoy having it, well, why not?*

A month after this broadcast, no less than four organists joined the expedition, and the team acquired a doctor to boot. Susie Booth, a GP, and one of the organists, Peter Waine, came into the studio to explain why they had decided to rise to the challenge.

Susie Booth: *I heard on the programme that they wanted an organist, and I play a little bit at the local church when our proper organist is away. I thought, 'Oh, I fancy doing that, going up the Amazon and playing an organ'. So I rang up the colonel and said, 'I'd love to be your organist.' And he said, 'Oh well, I've got an organist now, but I still need a doctor.' So I said, 'Well, I'm forty-nine, not fit, don't know anything about expeditionary medicine, never been to South America.' And he said, 'Oh, you're a GP. You can cope with malaria, dengue fever, snakebites, can't you? That'll be OK.'*

Edward Stourton: *How are your tropical diseases?*

Susie Booth: *Well, I'm a lot better now than I was two weeks ago.*

Edward Stourton: *Peter Waine, what made you want to do this?*

Peter Waine: *Originally, a friend who runs a choir at our local church in Didsbury, Manchester, was hearing your programme and phoned me a couple of days later. I quickly went on the website to investigate the idea of going down the Amazon, because I've been to Bolivia five times before, working in an orphanage.*

Edward Stourton: *You're quite a veteran in this field, then.*

Peter Waine: *Not in the Amazon, no, but travelling to Bolivia, yes. And it was quite an exciting thought to join an expedition... I'm involved in sports, and to combine physical exercise and potential for music...*

There's a hidden gem church in Manchester that has a very famous, magnificent 'Stations of the Cross' by Norman Adams [a twentieth-century British artist], which inspires me, particularly at this time of year. And having been at that church for many, many years, it's intrigued me to find that out in the Amazon they would require somebody to play the organ. So thankfully, Col John Blashford-Snell accepted my application and mentioned that there are other organists going as well.

Edward Stourton: I was going to say – because there are four of you, you're going to be fighting over the thing, aren't you?

Peter Waine: I think we'll have to possibly fight to help maintain the instrument in a very, what you would call Amazon-type climate, which presumably is very humid.

Susie Booth: The Bolivian Indians have built a Catholic chapel at the top of their village, and the people in the next village have got a grand piano. So to have a harmonium is wonderful.

Edward Stourton: And organs are quite sensitive, presumably, to climactic conditions.

Peter Waine: I met a person last night at church who said he used to own one of these types of organs, which is a harmonium pedal organ. And there's leather in it, as he had for his bellows. It would be a concern to me that the leather would be able to withstand extremes of climate.

Edward Stourton: So I presume you're going to have to teach them not just how to play it, but how to manage it and maintain it.

Peter Waine: We might have to learn how to rebuild the thing before we even go, I've been advised, so it's becoming more of an adventure all the time.

Edward Stourton: Am I right in thinking that you two hadn't met until this morning.

Peter Waine: We'd never met until half an hour ago.

Edward Stourton: Are you worried about it?

Susie Booth: Yes. I lurch from sheer terror, on the one hand, to, 'This is the opportunity of a lifetime. And I can't faff it up.' Half my friends think I'm absolutely mad and the other half think, 'Oh, I wish I was going instead of you.'

Edward Stourton: Well, I mean, brilliant that you've come forward and, you know, best of luck.

Peter Waine: Thank you. Thank you for the programme and introducing us to the idea.

19

Celebrity

Sunday is most emphatically not a celebrity show, but its archive includes some notable interviews with famous people. They are a heterogenous bunch, linked only by the fact that they were well known for their prominence in fields that had nothing – at least not obviously – to do with religion. All of them, however, were invited on to the programme to discuss a subject with a religious dimension, often their personal faith (or in some cases, the lack of it). Here is a selection.

Enoch Powell (30 September 1973)

Enoch Powell showed an interest in religion from an early age. Intellectually precocious, as a child he would lecture his parents and lead evensong at the family home in King's Norton, Birmingham, every Sunday. He went through a period of atheism as a young man, but joined the Church of England after the war, and was a church warden at St Margaret's, Westminster.

No Easy Answers, his considered reflections on Christianity and the relationship between religion, politics and economics, was published at the height of his political fame. His views on all these topics were austere.

Powell is best remembered for his so-called 'Rivers of Blood' speech in 1968. Warning of the social consequences of large-scale immigration, he declared that: 'Like the Roman, I see the Tiber foaming with much blood.' Edward Heath, the Conservative leader at the time, immediately sacked him from his position as shadow defence secretary.

Less well-remembered is the fact that the speech made Powell hugely popular. He received some 120,000 letters of support, and polls showed huge majorities in support of his views. In 1969, a Gallup poll pronounced him the 'most admired person in British public life'.

He was interviewed about his book by *Sunday*'s Ted Harrison. For reasons that are not clear in the archive, we join the conversation halfway through – or, as Powell, a classicist, would probably have preferred, *in medias res*.

Enoch Powell: *I then suppose that the heart is separated from the intellect. And in using sometimes the description of myself as passionately logical, I suppose I have implied that. A heart totally detached from a brain would be a very strange apparition, wouldn't it?*

Ted Harrison: *What I searched for in this book was compassion. In fact, the word 'love' is so infrequently used that I didn't see it for the first time until page twenty.*

Enoch Powell: *I'm not surprised. I have a suspicion in my own profession of politics of this word 'compassion', and perhaps I run a mile to avoid it. You see, when politicians talk about compassion, they mean they're making other people pay in order to earn them votes. And then they say, 'Look at us. What a compassionate party we are, and compassionate people,' and I get so sick of this, that perhaps the word itself is slightly suspect to me.*

Ted Harrison: *You take [issue] with those who like to think of the gospel as a social gospel, and you set out...*

Enoch Powell: *You've said it well. They 'like to think of it'. There's precious little basis for their thinking.*

Ted Harrison: *You almost set out deliberately to debunk some of the well-known and conventional interpretations that they rely on...*

Enoch Powell: *Yes, because I regard them as false and impoverishing. We want to twist Scripture into fitting in with our notions and our desires, and what we want to find there. Of course, we want to find a general doctrine that we should be rewarded in the next life for giving a cup of cold water to the odd person. But that's not what we are told... We're told much harder things than that.*

Ted Harrison: *When it comes to salvation, you say very few are chosen.*

Enoch Powell: *That's what the Gospel says: 'Narrow is the gate that leads us to salvation and few there be that find it.'[1] But we don't want to believe that. We don't want to believe that in this democratic age, this welfare state. 'What use have we got,' people say, 'for a religion which says only*

---

1   A reference to Matthew 7:14.

a minority find the way to salvation. We must alter it.' And so they set about altering it. They set about forgetting what doesn't fit with what they don't want to hear.

Ted Harrison: *But you're almost saying that one has to be equipped with an IQ of about 150 to be able to be saved.*

Enoch Powell: *No, I didn't say that. But of course, there are propositions which are implicit in the gospel which demand from those who accept them the greatest intellectual effort of which they are capable; and you must remember that the first commandment – the first and great commandment – tells us to love the Lord our God with our mind as well as with other parts of ourselves.*

The following year, Enoch Powell left the Conservative Party and took his bracing religious views to Northern Ireland, serving as the Ulster Unionist MP for South Down from 1974 to 1987.

Justin Fashanu (8 May 1983)

Justin Fashanu's footballing career began with spectacular success. He won the BBC Goal of the Season award in 1980, and when he was transferred from Norwich City to Nottingham Forest the following year he became Britain's first £1 million black footballer. That same year he became a born-again Christian. He was gay, and struggled to reconcile his beliefs with his sexuality for the rest of his life.

It was said that his relationship with Brian Clough, the Forest manager, deteriorated after Clough discovered his homosexuality. He was loaned to Southampton and then, in December 1982, sold to Nottingham Forest's local rivals Notts County for the much smaller fee of £150,000. By the time he gave this short interview to *Sunday*'s long-standing presenter Clive Jacobs his career was on the wane, and there was talk of another transfer.

Justin Fashanu: *I was offered the chance to go to Manchester City, and I decided to pray about it before I actually made my mind [up] one way or the other. And I really felt that God was telling me to stay put.*

Clive Jacobs: *The possibility of relegation didn't cross your mind* [Manchester City were relegated from the First Division that season]?

Justin Fashanu: No, not at that time. All I try to do is... what he wants me to do... There's no guarantee that because you've got God on your side you're going to be a multi-millionaire and a very, very successful man. That's not necessarily what he says. A lot of the time it's true, but not necessarily. So, I could have gone to Manchester City, and we could still be in, or they could still be in the problems that they are at the moment.

Clive Jacobs: You read the Bible a lot?

Justin Fashanu: Yes, I do.

Clive Jacobs: You're quoted as being a millionaire. I won't embarrass you by asking you if that is actually the fact. But if you're not, you must be pretty close to it. What do you make of the phrase in the Bible that it's easier for a camel to pass through the eye of a needle than it is for a rich man to enter the kingdom of heaven?

Justin Fashanu: Yes. Well, that is what he's saying there, is that he doesn't mind you being rich, he doesn't mind you having materialistic things, but he does mind if they become your gods and they become a big, big part of you. They hold on to you. I'm prepared. If God said to me, and really spoke to me and said, 'Justin, I would like you to go to Africa, India, China and become a missionary, and to leave all your earthly possessions behind,' I will do it. The materialistic things have not got a hold on me. Yes, I like the nice car. Yes, I like the diamond ring and things. But if I have to let them go, I will let them go.

In 1990, Justin Fashanu became the first prominent British footballer to come out publicly as gay. His playing career ended in the middle of that decade, and he moved to coaching and managing roles in the United States. In 1989, he was accused of sexually assaulting a young man in the American state of Maryland. He left for Britain before the police could take him into custody, and in May that year he took his own life. In his suicide note he insisted that the sex had been consensual.

Jeffrey Archer (1 April 2007)

The former Tory MP and party chairman Jeffrey Archer – or Baron Archer of Weston-super-Mare, as he is formally known – is famous for making things up. His talent in this regard has earned him great wealth;

his novels have sold hundreds of millions of copies. It also landed him in jail. In 2001, he was found guilty of perjury and perverting the cause of justice, and was sentenced to four years imprisonment.

In 2007, his writing took an unexpected turn with a book called *The Gospel According to Judas*, an account of the events of the New Testament from the perspective of the apostle who is said to have betrayed Jesus. The story is attributed to Judas's son, Benjamin Iscariot, and the book is generally classed as a novella. But Archer had some scholarly help with the writing, as Roger Bolton explained on *Sunday*.

Roger Bolton: *Who, but the noble lord [Jeffrey Archer], would be able to persuade the Pontifical Biblical Institute in Rome to host the launch of his latest fiction? It's called* The Gospel According to Judas, *and purports to have been written by Judas's son, Benjamin Iscariot. Jeffrey Archer wrote the book with the assistance of a member of the International Theological Commission to the Holy See, Professor Francis J. Moloney. I put it to Jeffrey Archer that most people read his books in the hope of excitement and pleasure. Why should they read this one?*

Jeffrey Archer: *Well, I think they would find the story of Jesus of Nazareth told in a linear way, very much like a novel in the sense that it has a beginning, a middle and an end. And what I hope they would find is surprises and twists, because they will have been brought up to believe, as I was, that, for example, Jesus walked on water, Jesus turned water into wine. Judas himself betrayed our Lord, which he does in the book, but received thirty pieces of silver from the high priest to do so. All of those are removed because the professor said they never happened.*

Roger Bolton: *So, Professor, can I sort out whether this book does have or does not have the imprimatur of the Roman Catholic Church?*

Francis J. Moloney: *No, the imprimatur of the Roman Catholic Church is only given to a book that deals with faith and morals. At this stage, I would say the Catholic Church, at the highest level of this leadership, is aware of the book and has not commented. And if it hasn't commented, I would say that is tacit approval.*

Jeffrey Archer: *But I would add to that, on October 18th last year, the pope, addressing a group of pilgrims, talked about Judas for the first time in a major statement. And you won't find a great deal of difference between* *what the pope said to the pilgrims and what we have said in* The Gospel According to Judas.

Roger Bolton: *And it is the case that the professor was recommended to you, is it not, by the former archbishop of Milan, Cardinal Martini* [Cardinal Martini was widely judged to be a possible pope]?

Jeffrey Archer: *Correct. I flew over to Rome to see Cardinal Carlo Maria Martini. I said to him, 'Who is the finest person you've ever taught?' And he said, 'Professor Frank Moloney.' And I said, 'Do I have your...'*

Francis J. Moloney: *The only mistake he's ever made!*

Jeffrey Archer: *'Do I have your permission to go and see him with your blessing?' And he said, 'Yes, you can.'*

Roger Bolton: *Why did you want to write about Judas?*

Jeffrey Archer: *Now, my interest was quite simply, as a young man many years ago, it puzzled me why the eleven disciples were all saints and Judas was a sinner. After all, hadn't Peter denied our Lord? And Judas betrays him, and he still betrays him in this book and ends up the biggest sinner of the lot. I thought, 'This is a bit too black and white for me.'*

Roger Bolton: *And could I ask about the parameters – what you allowed, if you like, the novelist to write? Because, I mean, I believe you fell out about the ending a bit.*

Francis J. Moloney: *We sure did. The book nearly came to a conclusion over that issue. Right from the beginning, the very first time we met, I said to Jeffrey, 'Jeffrey, I will allow you to write things that may be improbable, but I will not allow you to write things that are impossible.'*

Roger Bolton: *Well, impossible? For example, in the book, does Judas tells us that the virgin birth didn't happen, and that Jesus is the son of Joseph?*

Francis J. Moloney: *That's correct.*

Roger Bolton: *Is that what you believe?*

Francis J. Moloney: *No, that's what* Judas *believes. The perspective of Judas, who is a committed Jew, can only understand Jesus in terms of Jewish tradition. The Messiah must be the son of a legitimate Jewish wedlock.*

Roger Bolton: *When you were writing the book, Jeffrey Archer, when you were taking out of the story what you didn't want to use, to what extent were you influenced by the argument that a great deal of what is...*

contained in the present Gospels is written afterwards to justify what's in the Old Testament?

Jeffrey Archer: *Yes, it's a very a fair point. And time and time again I would go back to the professor, and he said, 'Well, you'll have to read Zechariah, you will have to read Isaiah.' And I had to. I had to go back and read. And in particular, the professor pointed out that in Matthew he definitely was taking great chunks out of Zechariah, putting it into Matthew to make excuses for Judas, because you don't find Judas hanging himself in any other Gospel than Matthew. And the professor convinced me that, because of that, I could let him live and not have him die the way that had been suggested in Matthew 27.*

Roger Bolton: *You left some miracles in, but you've taken some out. On what basis did you decide, for example, that the turning water into wine and walking on the Lake of Galilee should be taken out?*

Francis J. Moloney: *Yes. This is based on categories that we New Testament scholars use for the understanding of miracles. And the category [of] those miracles that I am doubtful about would be what we call 'nature miracles'. I have no doubt that Jesus was a miracle worker. But once you get to nature miracles... you begin to find the repetition in the story of Jesus of the sorts of things that the God of Israel did in the Old Testament. So in the latter decades of the first century, when the early Church – now convinced that in Jesus the divine was among us – with great ease they transferred stories about the God of Israel and said, 'Not only is the God of Israel the Lord of the elements and all those sorts of characteristics, but so is Jesus.' And they did that with the greatest of ease.*

Roger Bolton: *So are you saying, in a way, as a leading Catholic scholar, [that] the Gospel of Judas is more accurate an account of Jesus' miracles than the Gospels of Matthew, Mark, Luke and John?*

Francis J. Moloney: *[The Gospels] are true because they proclaim the truth.*

Roger Bolton: *But that doesn't happen?*

Francis J. Moloney: *That is not measured by the facticity of the event.*

Roger Bolton: *Some people would think we're going in to casuistry here. On one hand you're saying it didn't happen, in fact; on the other hand, it's true.*

Francis J. Moloney: *Exactly. But that's because we all worked out of a twenty-first century rational mind that says the only thing that's true is what happened. That is [not the way we should determine truthfulness].*

Ian Paisley (9 January 2011)

In early 2011, *Sunday* broadcast a special programme to mark the 400th anniversary of the publication of the King James Bible. Guests included the prominent Labour MP Frank Field, the then archbishop of Canterbury, Rowan Williams, and the Revd Dr Ian Paisley.

There is some doubt about whether Paisley had earned his honorifics. He co-founded his own Church – the Reformed Fundamentalist Free Presbyterian Church of Ulster – in 1951, and was given an honorary doctorate by the Bob Jones University in South Carolina in 1966.

There was no doubt at all, however, about his commitment to the Bible, nor about the hugely important part he played in Northern Ireland's politics. He served as first minister in the devolved Northern Ireland Assembly from May 2007 until June 2008. His political style was combative, and he was famous for the way he denounced his enemies – especially the pope. This interview suggests he believed that his favourite version of the Bible was, like Unionism, beset with fierce foes.

Edward Stourton: Ian Paisley, for so many years the firebrand of Unionist politics in Northern Ireland, is another great champion of the King James Bible. He's written a book about it called My Plea for the Old Sword. *And it's the only translation permitted in his Free Presbyterian Church, which celebrates the sixtieth anniversary of its founding this year. He calls it 'the Book of Books'.*

Ian Paisley: There's a special book, and when one thinks of what has been achieved through it... I am amazed... it's a miracle that it's here, and I'm talking to you about it today.

Edward Stourton: Who do you mean when you talk about its 'enemies'?

Ian Paisley: Well, those that wanted to destroy it and those still in a campaign [who] want to destroy it. And I mean, it has been burned. It has been buried. It has been attacked. It has been torn up. It has been stood upon. But the people that did all those things, their names are forgotten. But the old Book still stands.

Edward Stourton: And to what extent is this book and this version of the Bible tied up with your particular approach to the Christian message?

Ian Paisley: Well, very, very much so, because I am a fundamentalist, as you know, and I believe the Bible is a fundamentalist book, and there is no other book. And that's the book we have to turn to. And when its commandments are kept and its privileges are enjoyed, that leads to happiness and peace.

Edward Stourton: *And is it fair to say that you see this as a very Protestant, as opposed to Catholic, version of the Bible?*

Ian Paisley: *I don't think that we can say that, because I think we have to say there is only one true religion. And if it's going to be truly presented, it has to be presented in the way it has been presented, and the word of God.*

Edward Stourton: *Can you give us an illustration of the language that you find particularly appealing; a passage that especially speaks to you?*

Ian Paisley: *Yes. [If] you're asking me that, I would say Psalm number 19:*
> *The heavens declare the glory of God; and the firmament sheweth his handywork.*
> *Day unto day uttereth speech, and night unto night sheweth knowledge.*
> *There is no speech nor language, where their voice is not heard...*
> *The law of the LORD is perfect, converting the soul: the testimony of the LORD is sure, making wise the simple.*
> *The statutes of the LORD are right, rejoicing the heart: the commandment of the LORD is pure, enlightening the eyes.*
> *The fear of the LORD is clean, enduring for ever: the judgments of the LORD are true and righteous altogether.*
> *More to be desired are they than gold, yea, than much fine gold: sweeter also than honey and the honeycomb...*
> *Keep back thy servant also from presumptuous sins; let them not have dominion over me: then shall I be upright, and I shall be innocent from the great transgression.*
> *Let the words of my mouth, and the meditation of my heart, be acceptable in thy sight, O LORD, my strength, and my redeemer.*

Philip Pullman (19 June 2011)

In the summer that followed *Sunday*'s celebration of the King James Bible, the author Philip Pullman was honoured by the British Humanist Association. Pullman, a republican and a vocal campaigner on issues ranging from library closures to Brexit, is, in political terms, about as far from Ian Paisley as it is possible to imagine. Yet their interviews for *Sunday* were, in a way, companion pieces. Pullman, like Paisley, was profoundly influenced by the Bible.

Edward Stourton: *Philip Pullman, author of the trilogy* His Dark Materials, *was honoured for services to humanism at a ceremony here in Manchester this weekend. It's the first time the British Humanist Association has bestowed what they plan to be an annual award. The choice of Philip Pullman is notable, not least because he's one of the archbishop of Canterbury's favourite modern writers. I talked to him just before last night's ceremony and asked him if he was happy to be described as a humanist.*

Philip Pullman: *It's a word that comes… close… [to an]other… word I like, which I've only come across in the last year or so: the word 'possibilian', which was invented by the neuroscientist David Eagleman in his clever little book* Sum, *which deals with forty different kinds of afterlife which might happen. But I am a humanist. I mean, as far as I can see, we are the only conscious beings there are: human beings.*

Edward Stourton: *And 'possibilian', you said. What does that mean?*

Philip Pullman: *Well, it's a fancy word for 'agnostic', perhaps. I call myself an atheist because I have no evidence that God is there. No feeling that God is there. I've never seen any evidence that God is there; nothing that convinces me that I ought to believe. So in a sense I'm an atheist, but in a bigger sense I'm an agnostic. I have to say that, because obviously I don't know everything. And one of the things I don't know might be that God is there somewhere, but I haven't come across him yet.*

Edward Stourton: *You also described yourself as a Church of England atheist. What did you mean by that?*

Philip Pullman: *Well, I was brought up in the Church of England – quite firmly in the Church of England. My grandfather was a clergyman, and I spent a lot of time in his household as a young child. I know the Bible pretty well. I know the prayer book even better. And, you know, these things go very deep when you come across them as a young child. They form your way of thinking. They form your way of forming sentences,* even... I can't get rid of that influence, and I wouldn't even if I could. It's part of me.

Edward Stourton: There are other atheists who have a similar experience. Richard Dawkins, for example, talks with great affection for the Church of England, and its rituals and its traditions. Do you feel that? Do you feel that the Church of England has been an enriching experience, if you like?

Philip Pullman: Undoubtedly, yes. And it is specifically the Church of England – I mean, the Christian Church in a wider sense, I suppose... because that's the tradition I come from. I couldn't write, for example, about being Jewish or about being Muslim. I don't have that in my bones, in the nerves of my brain. It's not there. But Christianity is.

Edward Stourton: And does it influence your writing?

Philip Pullman: Oh yes, undoubtedly. A number of the themes I find myself going back to again and again are those that the Christian Church has made its own, you could say. The difference between innocence and experience in William Blake's terms; the whole question of what happens when we die, which is one of the deepest questions human beings have ever asked themselves. These form themselves naturally for me in sort of Christian terms.

Edward Stourton: Would it be fair to say that you write as if we are religious creatures, even if you don't think that we're justified in having religious belief?

Philip Pullman: Yes. It's a little bit more nuanced than that... I wouldn't say that we're not justified in having a religious belief, because beliefs go a lot deeper than reason in many cases. The problem with religion, as far as I'm concerned, is not that it's there at all, but that it has political power. When religion acquires political – with a small 'p', power, the power to influence other people's lives, to tell them what to do, what to wear, what to eat, and so on – the moment it acquires that sort of power, it goes bad.

Edward Stourton: And you have some pretty trenchant views about what the Church of England is doing at the moment, I think, on areas like homosexuality?

Philip Pullman: Yes. There's a strain of zealous bigotry in the Church of England, as there is in any large organisation, and it's getting more and more noisy, and more and more aggressive at the moment. And I don't *like it at all. In one sense, this is none of my business because I'm not a believer. In another sense, it is my business; it's the Established Church. It has a say and a little bit of power in the way we run the country. It is the 'established' bit, so I do have a right to say about it, and that's what I don't like. I like a broad church.*

Edward Stourton: *You have, I think, also said that you've had transcendental experiences, if not religious ones. What did you mean by that?*

Philip Pullman: *If it means anything, it means transcending the material world and entering a sort of spiritual realm. I don't believe there is a spiritual realm, because I believe everything is material. I think we are made of matter. The whole world is matter, there's nothing but matter. Matter is a very interesting thing. So the experiences I've had are few in number, very few, when I seem to be caught up in a sort of excitement that must have been purely material in its origins, but it had a sort of universal feel about it, a sort of universality; a sense that I was everywhere and I knew everything and I was aware of things in a much deeper and richer way than I normally was. A very thrilling and very extraordinary sensation.*

Edward Stourton: *But as far as you're concerned, essentially a sort of tangle in the synapses or something of that kind, rather than an indication of anything any deeper, or more [of a] spiritual reality in the universe?*

Philip Pullman: *Yes, I think so. But we must be aware when we say 'essentially' this or 'only' that, or 'merely' this or 'simply' that, or 'no more than' that. These little adverbial phrases don't help very much because they seem to reduce it to that. Yes, it is a tangle in the synapses, among other things.*

Edward Stourton: *But absolutely not including the experience as an indication of a 'higher reality', as religious people would put it.*

Philip Pullman: *That was not my experience. But then that was only my experience.*

Postscript

Amanda Hancox, *Sunday*'s editor when many of the items included in this book were broadcast, reflects on the way the programme has changed. She joined the BBC's Religion and Ethics department in 1985, and was editor of *Sunday* from 2001 until 2020.

Delving into the archives while researching this book, I was both delighted and overwhelmed. Delighted because of the quality and range of stories covered over the last fifty years, and overwhelmed because of the sheer number of interviews, discussions and features that could have had a worthy place in this book. What to keep in and what to leave out? The agony of choice!

When I first joined *Sunday* in the 1980s, religion was very much in the news. The Churches were playing a crucial role in challenging apartheid in South Africa; the holiest Sikh site, the Golden Temple, was stormed by Indian armed forces; Terry Waite, the archbishop of Canterbury's envoy, had been taken hostage; Pope John Paul II was making a big impact on the world stage; and the Church of England clashed with the Thatcher government over its 'Faith in the City' report and the miners' strikes.

During this time, *Sunday* was a well-established programme. It was staffed by a committed team of journalists with religious expertise and a passion for bringing stories about the world of religion to a wider audience. The programme was broadcast every Sunday morning, 7:40am to 8:30am, from the *Today* studio. The team worked to tight deadlines, with reporters and producers only coming together each week on a Friday morning to decide and set up the stories – often working late on Saturday evenings to get everything cut and ready for transmission.

Broadcasting live gave *Sunday* the ability to react to breaking news stories, but this presented its own challenges. I remember once our main interviewee after the 8 a.m. news bulletin disappeared. After several attempts to contact him, I desperately phoned around to find someone to step in at the last moment. Finally, the wife of a vicar, hearing the desperation in my voice, got her husband out of the shower to take my call. 'Yes, I'm happy to do the interview in three minutes,' he said. 'Just let me get a towel!'

When Radio 4 changed its schedule in the 1990s and *Sunday* moved to its current time of 7:10 a.m., the programme received complaints from clerics saying the new time would clash with early-morning services. However, unlike the religious press, who serve the interests of particular Christian denominations or religious traditions, *Sunday*, with an audience of over 1 million, broadcasts to the general Radio 4 audience. Some are religious, but most are not.

Sunday has always endeavoured to avoid taking sides. Its ambition is to examine what is being said and to press interviewees to get to the nub of the issues at hand. While some religious leaders relished this approach, I have had several bishops and even archbishops annoyed that their answers were challenged. They assumed that because it is a religious programme, we would be sympathetic and endorse their point of view.

When a story broke, *Sunday* often encountered a wall of silence from religious institutions; an unwillingness to put anyone up to articulate their side of the story and to be questioned. The producers and reporters played a cat-and-mouse game with press officers. A press release would be issued, often on a Friday afternoon, with quotes from the religious person at the heart of the story, who mysteriously seemed to disappear for the weekend when *Sunday* requested an interview.

Reporters and producers then had no choice but to phone around, hoping to sign up an alternative voice before the press officers could intervene. Once, over lunch, a director of communications moaned: 'Why is the BBC obsessed with balance? Why can't you just have one person on their own instead of always wanting to balance it with other voices who disagree?'

Over the years, *Sunday* quite rightly moved away from being predominantly Christian to reflecting stories about other faith traditions, both in Britain and abroad, and included a variety of faith voices in national debates on issues of the day. Even though the programme was, in effect, reflecting a changing Britain back to itself, we received a steady trickle of complaints along the lines of: 'We are a Christian country, and you shouldn't be covering non-Christian stories.'

Sunday provided a window for the listeners into the rich tapestry of arts, culture and beliefs of different faiths. However, reporting news stories from religious minority communities had its own challenges. As mentioned in chapter 9, the office of chief rabbi was one answer to having a voice in the public square. For non-hierarchical religions such as Islam, Sikhism and Hinduism, the question of who speaks for whom continues, even today, to be a live issue.

In the early years of *Sunday*, we often encountered a lack of understanding as to how the media worked and how to engage with programmes such as *Sunday*, and little in the way of media training. An array of organisations would claim to be the voice of their faith, even though they often disagreed with each other as to what that message should be. It was largely left to individuals to educate the wider public about their faith and to speak to the media.

This could be problematic when a big news story broke. For instance, when the row over the publication of Salman Rushdie's *The Satanic Verses* erupted and a fatwa was issued against the novelist on charges of insulting Islam, the media descended on the Muslim communities. But it was difficult for the secular press to know who was really representing the views of the communities and who was seizing this opportunity to put their own views forward. It's at times like this that *Sunday* can offer a corrective, and provide informed voices on these stories. In 1992, *Sunday* was entered for the prestigious and fiercely competitive Sony Radio Awards. It won bronze in the 'Best breakfast show: speech based' category. This was a great achievement for Christine Morgan, editor at the time, and for the team, and it re-enforced *Sunday*'s reputation for quality journalism.

During much of the 1990s and into the 2000s, religious news was dominated by two big issues: the ordination of women to the priesthood and subsequently women bishops; and issues around sexuality in the Church of England and its implications for the Anglican Communion. These issues (covered, respectively, in chapters 6 and 7) reflected a collision of strongly held religious views about justice, discrimination and exclusion on one side, and religious authority and tradition on the other.

For *Sunday*, long-running stories present a particular challenge. As I mentioned earlier, *Sunday* broadcasts to a general audience, the majority of whom are not religious. This means *Sunday* has to make difficult choices every week about which stories to include and which to leave out, and how to tell each story in a way that engages both the secular listener and those with an informed interest in religion. With long-running issues such as women clergy and sexuality, decisions had to be made as to how often to return to the story – which arguments, twists and turns on the often tortuous road these issues took to cover – all the while trying to explain to an often-bemused secular audience the theology underpinning these issues and why coming to a consensus was so difficult for the Church.

There were moments of fatigue for the production team. Even though these issues were so important for the people involved, the arguments often came down to the same key theological issues, and for a broadcaster it was sometimes difficult to find something new to say, and different contributors to engage the listener.

When I returned to *Sunday* as editor in the 2000s, the religious landscape felt very different. There was less deference towards religious leaders, religious literacy was in steep decline and there was a growing marginalisation of religion, marked by a lack of interest in it among the general public. But two things happened that brought religion sharply back into focus.

I can remember standing with the production team around a television screen in the office watching the planes slam into the Twin Towers on 9/11 in shock and utter disbelief, trying to take in what had happened and what the consequences might be. As America grounded all planes, no one knew what the response might be or who would be targeted next. I had a reporter at that moment flying out to Jordan to record some features for the programme, and desperately needed to contact him to get the first flight back while he still could.

While the daily news programmes pore over every immediate aspect of the story, *Sunday*, like all weekly programmes, has to take stock and work out how to add something of value. It is clear to all that 9/11 was a defining moment and changed the way many saw Islam. *Sunday*'s reporting on Islam became more about covering subsequent wars, terrorist attacks, the reactions of UK Muslim communities and the unpacking of Islamic theology than about art and culture. The team reflected on this decade of uprising and unrest by taking *Sunday* to New York for the tenth anniversary of 9/11, to Cairo for the constitutional referendum after the downfall of President Mubarak, and to Jerusalem several times.

The second development is best illustrated by the response to Richard Dawkins's book *The God Delusion*. His controversial challenge to belief in the existence of God brought to the public attention a debate that had been growing for some time between atheism and religion. Atheism and secularism were in the ascendency, and there was a growing confidence when it came to questioning belief in God. Religion was seen as a private, not a public, matter.

So Christianity found itself having to justify its place in the public square. Bishops in the House of Lords were challenged, as was the existence of religious schools. Increasingly, people were turning their backs on institutional religion in favour of a more personalised spirituality. *Sunday* extended its coverage of humanism, atheism and the nones (those who identify has having no religion). The programme also launched a competition to find the nation's favourite spiritual place (see chapter 18), and the places nominated illustrated the changing landscape. They ranged from churches to stone circles, to Rabbi Lionel Blue's nomination of Euston Station.

When I left the BBC in 2020, the original ethos of impartial reporting and explaining religion to a wider audience was still at the heart of the programme. The religious landscape is very different now, and revelations of sex abuse and issues over sexuality and women have been very damaging. But religion and spirituality still play an important and powerful part in millions of people's lives around the world. Understanding religious beliefs and how they inspire and influence the way people live their lives is still as important as ever.

Contributors

The following is a complete list of the people who contributed to the episodes of *Sunday* containing the interviews and reports quoted in this book. The authors and publishers have made every effort to contact each person, and would like to thank all who have replied to their request for permission to include transcripts of comments that were broadcast in the original programmes. The names are given in their order of appearance within the book.

William Crawley, Emily Buchanan, Roger Bolton, Jane Little, Trevor Barnes, Ted Harrison, Kevin Bouquet, Luke Walton, Robert Pigott, David Willey, John Laurenson, Mike Wooldridge, Shazia Khan, Mary Harte, Robert Mickens, Samira Ahmed, Ruth Gledhill, Harry Farley, Rahul Tandon, Martin Stott, Shelagh Fogarty, Colin Semper, Gerald Priestland, Paul Barnes, David Winter, Joyce Bennett, Ann Cheetham, Alphaeus Zulu, Tony Black, Clive Jacobs, Desmond Tutu, Brian Herd, Syed Pasha, Donald Coggan, Dennis Potter, John Robinson, Graham Leonard, Donald Soper, Eric James, David Cooper, Clifford Williamson, Bob Heron, John Stephenson, Anthony Howard, David Jenkins, Peter Price, Francis Davis, Stephen Lowe, Hazel Blears, Justin Welby, Stephen Cottrell, Basil Hume, Cormac Murphy O'Connor, Pastor Jack Glass, David Samuel, Frank Skinner, John Cornwell, Sister Myra Poole, William Oddie, John Wilkins, Margaret Hebblewaite, Peter Smith, Paul Vallely, Clifford Longley, Thomas Reece, Jan Graffius, Helen Grady, John Hunter, Julian Filochowski, Juan Hernández Pico, Jack Sullivan, Peter Tatchell, Austen Ivereigh, Daniel Seward, Richard Duffield, Eamon Duffy, Frances Knight, Kieran Conry, Ann McNamara, William Swindells, Rubin Phillip, Ishmael Mukuwanda, Rowan Williams, Kate Hoey, Dan Damon, Shingi Munyeza, Shingai Nyoka, Mary Raftery, Alan Shatter, Joe Little, Marie, Garry O'Sullivan, Gina Menzies, Gerry O'Hanlon, Marie Collins, Noel Treanor, Colm O'Gorman, Diarmaid Ferriter, Donal McKeown, Mary Currington, Ruth

Contributors

McDonald, Ian Elliot, Brian D'Arcy, Sean Brady, Michael Kelly, Christina Rees, Geoffrey Kirk, David Banting, David Holding, Vincent Nichols, Helen Hamilton, Pete Broadbent, Judith Maltby, Sandra Millar, Quentin Letts, William Naphy, Gene Robinson, Gregory Venables, Stephen Bates, Martin Dudley, Colin Slee, Henry Orombi, Maureen Waller, Adrian Thatcher, Joshua Rosenberg, Vicky Beeching, Richard O'Leary, Peter Selby, Simon Fishel, Donald Bruce, Evan Harris, Justin Thacker, Peter Saunders, Julia Neuberger, Richard Harries, David Steel, John Allen, Diviash Thakrar, Abdullah Shehu, David Frei, Alexandra Wright, James Woodward, Jonathan Romain, Ephraim Mirvis, Marie van der Zyl, Tony Blair, Richard Dawkins, David Lightman, Alan Plancey, Michael Hart, Geoffrey Alderman, Laura Janner-Klausner, Christopher Landau, Abdal Hakim Murad, Yasmin Alibhai-Brown, Mufti Barkatulla, Salman Sayyid, Dilwar Hussain, Alistair Leithead, Muhammad Abdul Bari, Debbie Hodge, Mohammed Shafiq, Mona Siddiqui, Shahid Mursaleen, Alexander Meleagrou-Hitchens, Qadir Baksh, Asghar Bukhari, Mrs Begum, Dominic Grieve, David Walker, Zia Chaudhry, Mohammed Seddon, Imran Waheed, Giles Fraser, Mohammed Imran Ahmed, Aftab Ahmed, amina wadud, Tamsila Tauqir, Khola Hassan, Tahmina Saleem, Caroline Cox, Aina Khan, Shelina Janmohamed, Zara Mohammed, Michael Meech, Professor Singh, Ranjit Kaur Bhilku, Dabinderjit Singh, Rana Chhina, Adil Rana Chhina, Peter Bance, Daljinder Singh Virdee, John Zavos, Swami Chandramauli, John Purnell, Srutidharma Das, Brother Alex, Davender Kumar Ghai, Shaunaka Rishi Das, Jay Lakhani, Sathnam Sanghera, Gurmel Singh, Sanjiv Patel, Anushka Sharma, Tony Evans, James Robison, Mike Hannaschlager, Cris Feldman, Robert Jeffress, Scott Lively, Edward Furton, Sam Rohrer, Jessica Taylor, Joe Miller, Austin Miller, Cody Hildebrand, Jonathan Falwell, Sarah Posner, Tara McKelvey, Shawn Carney, Rachel Laser, Andrew Whitehead, Taj Hargey, Jiyar Gol, Caroline Wyatt, Jacques Mourad/Emma Loosley, Sima Kotecha, Saleh Zohney, Ethar El-Katatney, Omar Ashour, Mariz Tadros, Jon Leyne, Andrew Hosken, Hisham Kassem, Thomas Pierret, Fergal Keane, Lyce Doucet, Matthew Kalman, Suheil Dawani, Danny Ayalon, David Neuhaus, Allison Kaplan Sommer, Micah Goodman, Robi Damelin, Ikhlas Shtayeh, Paul Estabrooks, Patrick French, Peter Harvey, Edmond Tang, John Sudworth, Benedict Rogers, Michael Sheridan,

Contributors

Chris Patten, Celia Hatton, Rustam Qobil, Joanna Lillis, Sam Brownback, Mike Ford, Sonia Jacks, Philip North, Cole Moreton, Maggi Hambling, Mohammed Ali, Tim Schmalz, Cathy Corcoran, Diane Burstein, Richard Carter, John Blashford-Snell, Margaret Phillips, Susie Booth, Peter Waine, Enoch Powell, Justin Fashanu, Jeffrey Archer, Francis J. Moloney, Ian Paisley, Philip Pullman.